Reconciling Indonesia

Indonesia has been torn by massive internal conflicts over the last decade. The absence of functioning national tools of reconciliation and the often limited success of an internationally established 'reconciliation toolkit' of truth commissions and law enforcement, justice and human rights, forgiveness and amnesty, requires us to interrogate commonly held notions of reconciliation and transitional justice. *Reconciling Indonesia* fills two major gaps in the literature on Indonesia and peace and conflict studies more generally: the neglect of grassroots agency for peace and the often overlooked collective and cultural dimension of reconciliation.

Bringing together scholars from all over the world, this volume draws upon multi-disciplinary theoretical perspectives, extensive fieldwork and activists' experience, and explores the ways in which reconciliation connects with issues like civil society, gender, religion, tradition, culture, education, history, displacement and performance. It covers different areas of Indonesia, from Aceh in the West to the Moluccas in the East, and deals with a broad variety of conflicts and violence, such as communal violence, terrorist attacks, secessionist conflicts, localized small-scale conflicts, and the mass violence of 1965–66. *Reconciling Indonesia* offers new understandings of grassroots or bottom-up reconciliation approaches and thus goes beyond prevalent political and legal approaches to reconciliation.

Reconciling Indonesia is important reading for scholars, activists and anyone interested in current developments in Indonesia and the broader region and in new approaches to peace and conflict research.

Birgit Bräuchler is assistant professor of social and cultural anthropology at the University of Frankfurt.

Asia's transformations
Edited by Mark Selden
Cornell University, USA

The books in this series explore the political, social, economic and cultural consequences of Asia's transformations in the twentieth and twenty-first centuries. The series emphasizes the tumultuous interplay of local, national, regional and global forces as Asia bids to become the hub of the world economy. While focusing on the contemporary, it also looks back to analyse the antecedents of Asia's contested rise.

This series comprises several strands:

Asia's transformations
Asia's Transformations aims to address the needs of students and teachers. Titles include:

Debating human rights
Critical essays from the United States and Asia
Edited by Peter Van Ness

Hong Kong's history
State and society under colonial rule
Edited by Tak-Wing Ngo

Japan's comfort women
Sexual slavery and prostitution during World War II and the US occupation
Yuki Tanaka

Opium, empire and the global political economy
Carl A. Trocki

Chinese society
Change, conflict and resistance
Edited by Elizabeth J. Perry and Mark Selden

Mao's children in the new China
Voices from the Red Guard generation
Yarong Jiang and David Ashley

Remaking the chinese state
Strategies, society and security
Edited by Chien-min Chao and Bruce J. Dickson

Korean society
Civil society, democracy and the state
Edited by Charles K. Armstrong

The making of modern Korea
Adrian Buzo

The resurgence of East Asia
500, 150 and 50 year perspectives
Edited by Giovanni Arrighi, Takeshi Hamashita and Mark Selden

Chinese society, second edition
Change, conflict and resistance
Edited by Elizabeth J. Perry and Mark Selden

Ethnicity in Asia
Edited by Colin Mackerras

The battle for Asia
From decolonization to globalization
Mark T. Berger

State and society in 21st century China
Edited by Peter Hays Gries and Stanley Rosen

Japan's quiet transformation
Social change and civil society in the 21st century
Jeff Kingston

Confronting the Bush doctrine
Critical views from the Asia-Pacific
Edited by Mel Gurtov and Peter Van Ness

China in war and revolution, 1895–1949
Peter Zarrow

The future of US–Korean relations
The imbalance of power
Edited by John Feffer

Working in China
Ethnographies of labor and workplace transformations
Edited by Ching Kwan Lee

Korean society, second edition
Civil society, democracy and the state
Edited by Charles K. Armstrong

Singapore
The state and the culture of excess
Souchou Yao

Pan-Asianism in modern Japanese history
Colonialism, regionalism and borders
Edited by Sven Saaler and J. Victor Koschmann

The making of modern Korea, 2nd edition
Adrian Buzo

Re-writing culture in Taiwan
Edited by Fang-long Shih, Stuart Thompson, and Paul-François Tremlett

Asia's Great Cities
Each volume aims to capture the heartbeat of the contemporary city from multiple perspectives emblematic of the authors own deep familiarity with the distinctive faces of the city, its history, society, culture, politics and economics, and its evolving position in national, regional and global frameworks. While most volumes emphasize urban developments since the Second World War, some pay close attention to the legacy of the longue durée in shaping the contemporary. Thematic and comparative volumes address such themes as urbanization, economic and financial linkages, architecture and space, wealth and power, gendered relationships, planning and anarchy, and ethnographies in national and regional perspective. Titles include:

Bangkok
Place, practice and representation
Marc Askew

Hong Kong
Global city
Stephen Chiu and Tai-Lok Lui

Representing Calcutta
Modernity, nationalism and the colonial uncanny
Swati Chattopadhyay

Singapore
Wealth, power and the culture of control
Carl A. Trocki

The city in South Asia
James Heitzman

Global Shanghai, 1850–2010
A history in fragments
Jeffrey N. Wasserstrom

Hong Kong
Becoming a global city
Stephen Chiu and Tai-Lok Lui

Asia.com is a series which focuses on the ways in which new information and communication technologies are influencing politics, society and culture in Asia. Titles include:

Japanese cybercultures
Edited by Mark McLelland and Nanette Gottlieb

Asia.com
Asia encounters the internet
Edited by K.C. Ho, Randolph Kluver and Kenneth C.C. Yang

The internet in Indonesia's new democracy
David T. Hill and Krishna Sen

Chinese cyberspaces
Technological changes and political effects
Edited by Jens Damm and Simona Thomas

Mobile media in the Asia-pacific
Gender and the art of being mobile
Larissa Hjorth

Literature and Society
Literature and Society is a series that seeks to demonstrate the ways in which Asian Literature is influenced by the politics, society and culture in which it is produced. Titles include:

The body in postwar Japanese fiction
Edited by Douglas N. Slaymaker

Chinese Women Writers and the Feminist Imagination, 1905–1948
Haiping Yan

Routledge Studies in Asia's Transformations
Routledge Studies in Asia's Transformations is a forum for innovative new research intended for a high-level specialist readership, and the titles will be available in hardback only. Titles include:

The American occupation of Japan and Okinawa*
Literature and memory
Michael Molasky

Koreans in Japan*
Critical voices from the margin
Edited by Sonia Ryang

Internationalizing the pacific
The united states, Japan and the institute of pacific relations
in war and peace, 1919–1945
Tomoko Akami

Imperialism in Southeast Asia
'A fleeting, passing phase'
Nicholas Tarling

Chinese media, global contexts
Edited by Chin-Chuan Lee

Remaking citizenship in Hong Kong*
Community, nation and the global city
Edited by Agnes S. Ku and Ngai Pun

Japanese industrial governance
Protectionism and the licensing state
Edited by Yul Sohn

Developmental Dilemmas
Land reform and institutional change in China
Edited by Peter Ho

Genders, transgenders and sexualities in Japan*
Edited by Mark McLelland and Romit Dasgupta

Fertility, family planning and population policy in China
Edited by Dudley L. Poston, Che-Fu Lee, Chiung-Fang Chang, Sherry L. McKibben and Carol S. Walther

Japanese Diasporas
Unsung pasts, conflicting presents and uncertain futures
Edited by Nobuko Adachi

How China works
Perspectives on the twentieth-century industrial workplace
Edited by Jacob Eyferth

Remolding and resistance among writers of the Chinese prison camp
Disciplined and published
Edited by Philip F. Williams and Yenna Wu

Popular culture, globalization and Japan*
Edited by Matthew Allen and Rumi Sakamoto

medi@sia
Global media/tion in and out of context
Edited by Todd Joseph Miles Holden and Timothy J. Scrase

* Now available in paperback

Vientiane
Transformations of a Lao landscape
Marc Askew, William S. Logan and Colin Long

State formation and radical democracy in India
Manali Desai

Democracy in occupied Japan
The U.S. occupation and Japanese politics and society
Edited by Mark E. Caprio and Yoneyuki Sugita

Globalization, culture and society in Laos
Boike Rehbein

Transcultural Japan
At the borderlands of race, gender, and identity
Edited by David Blake Willis and Stephen Murphy-Shigematsu

Post-conflict heritage, postcolonial tourism
Culture, Politics and Development at Angkor
Tim Winter

Education and reform in China
Emily Hannum and Albert Park

Writing Okinawa: narrative acts of identity and resistance
Davinder L. Bhowmik

Maid in China
Media, mobility, and a new Semiotic of power
Wanning Sun

Northern territories, Asia-pacific regional conflicts and the Åland experience
Untying the Kurillian Knot
Edited by Kimie Hara and Geoffrey Jukes

Reconciling Indonesia
Grassroots agency for peace
Edited by Birgit Bräuchler

Critical Asian scholarship

Critical Asian Scholarship is a series intended to showcase the most important individual contributions to scholarship in Asian Studies. Each of the volumes presents a leading Asian scholar addressing themes that are central to his or her most significant and lasting contribution to Asian studies. The series is committed to the rich variety of research and writing on Asia, and is not restricted to any particular discipline, theoretical approach or geographical expertise.

Southeast Asia
A testament
George McT. Kahin

Women and the family in Chinese history
Patricia Buckley Ebrey

China unbound
Evolving perspectives on the Chinese past
Paul A. Cohen

China's past, China's future
Energy, food, environment
Vaclav Smil

The Chinese state in Ming society
Timothy Brook

China, East Asia and the global economy
Regional and historical perspectives
Takeshi Hamashita
Edited by Mark Selden and Linda Grove

The global and regional in China's nation-formation
Prasenjit Duara

Reconciling Indonesia
Grassroots agency for peace

Edited by Birgit Bräuchler

LONDON AND NEW YORK

First published 2009 by Routledge
2 Park Square, Milton Park, Abingdon, Oxon OX14 4RN

Simultaneously published in the USA and Canada
by Routledge
270 Madison Ave, New York, NY 10016

Routledge is an imprint of the Taylor & Francis Group, an informa business

© 2009 Editorial selection and matter, Birgit Bräuchler. Individual chapters, the contributor.

Typeset in Times New Roman by Swales & Willis Ltd, Exeter, Devon
Printed and bound in Great Britain by the MPG Books Group

All rights reserved. No part of this book may be reprinted or reproduced or utilized in any form or by any electronic, mechanical, or other means, now known or hereafter invented, including photocopying and recording, or in any information storage or retrieval system, without permission in writing from the publishers.

British Library Cataloguing in Publication Data
A catalogue record for this book is available from the British Library

Library of Congress Cataloging in Publication Data
A catalog record for this book has been requested

Library of Congress Cataloging-in-Publication Data
Bräuchler, Birgit.
  Reconciling Indonesia : grassroots agency for peace / Birgit Bräuchler.
  — 1st ed.
  p. cm. — (Asia's transformations)
  1. Conflict management—Indonesia. 2. Social conflict—Indonesia.
  3. Ethnic conflict—Indonesia. 4. Reconciliation. I. Title.
  HN710.Z9C611276 2009
  303.6'909598—dc22
  2008052337

ISBN10: 0–415–48704–8 (hbk)
ISBN10: 0–203–87619–9 (ebk)

ISBN13: 978–0–415–48704–7 (hbk)
ISBN13: 978–0–203–87619–0 (ebk)

To my Dad

Contents

List of illustrations xv
Notes on contributors xvi
Preface xix

PART I
Problematizing 'reconciliation' 1

1 **Introduction: reconciling Indonesia** 3
   BIRGIT BRÄUCHLER

2 **Global conflict in cosmocentric perspective: a Balinese approach to reconciliation** 34
   ANNETTE HORNBACHER

PART II
Restorative performances: 'traditional justice', rituals, and symbols 55

3 **Swearing innocence: performing justice and 'reconciliation' in post-New Order Lombok** 57
   KARI TELLE

4 **Social reconciliation and community integration through theater** 77
   BARBARA HATLEY

5 **Mobilizing culture and tradition for peace: reconciliation in the Moluccas** 97
   BIRGIT BRÄUCHLER

PART III
'Traditional justice' under scrutiny: human rights, power, and gender   119

6 Reconciliation and human rights in post-conflict Aceh   121
LEENA AVONIUS

7 The problem of going home: land management, displacement, and reconciliation in Ambon   138
JEROEN ADAM

8 Women's agencies for peace-building and reconciliation: voices from Poso, Sulawesi   155
Y. TRI SUBAGYA

PART IV
Victim–perpetrator conceptualizations: history education, civil society, and religion   173

9 Reconciliation through history education: reconstructing the social memory of the 1965–66 violence in Indonesia   175
GRACE LEKSANA

10 Civil society and grassroots reconciliation in Central Java   192
PRIYAMBUDI SULISTIYANTO AND RUMEKSO SETYADI

11 A bridge and a barrier: Islam, reconciliation, and the 1965 killings in Indonesia   214
KATHARINE E. MCGREGOR

Index   233

Illustrations

Figures

2.1	'Ground zero' in Kuta, Bali, a few weeks after the bombing in 2002: the small shrine and tree miraculously survived the explosion	45
3.1	The *garap* rite. The *klian* administers the potion consisting of water mixed with soil from the tomb of Wali Nyato, using a banyan leaf as a spoon. Desa Beber, Central Lombok, 1997	67
4.1	*Bang-bang Sumirat*: Haryo Tratap/Suharto in monster mask	86
4.2	*Jaran Sungsang*: Violent pounding of poles in a wooden trough, *lesung*, opens the performance	87
4.3	*Jaran Sungsang*: Sugeng, beaten to death by the group, lies across the *lesung*	88
7.1	Living conditions in the IDP camp in Karpan	140
7.2	Kayu Tiga before the Protestant community came to be resettled there in 2006	141
7.3	Rebuilding the Bethabara church in Kayu Tiga	143
9.1	The Sacred Pancasila Monument, with the seven army officers and the national symbol – Garuda	179
9.2	The diorama of torture located near the Sacred Pancasila Monument. One of the kidnapped generals was depicted as the victim of PKI's brutality	180
10.1	*Kado untuk Ibu*: 'The voices of former women political prisoners'	204
11.1	"Beware of the PKI": The cover image of the East Java NU publication, *AULA*, 5(XXIX), May 2007	225
11.2	An image accompanying one article in *AULA*, 5(XXIX), May 2007: 28	226

Maps

1.1	Case studies in *Reconciling Indonesia*	4
5.1	Moluccas (Province of Maluku and Maluku Utara)	99
5.2	West Seram, Ambon, Lease Islands	102
5.3	Lease Islands	103

Contributors

Jeroen Adam is a PhD student at the Conflict Research Group, Ghent University, Belgium where he is writing a dissertation on displacement, social transformation, and access to land in post-conflict Ambon. He is also a junior affiliate for the Households in Conflict Network, Institute of Development Studies, Brighton. Ongoing results of this research project have already been published in *Social Development Issues* and *Inside Indonesia*.

Leena Avonius is Director of the International Centre for Aceh and Indian Ocean Studies (ICAIOS) in Banda Aceh, Indonesia. She received her PhD in anthropology at Leiden University in the Netherlands in 2004. She is the co-editor of *Human Rights in Asia: A Reassessment of the Asian Values Debate* (Palgrave 2008). Her research interests include human rights, collective violence, and the processes of social change.

Birgit Bräuchler (PhD) is assistant professor (Wissenschaftliche Mitarbeiterin) of social and cultural anthropology at the University of Frankfurt. Her main research interests are media and cyberanthropology, conflict and peace studies, and the revival of tradition. She is author of the book *Cyberidentities at War* (transcript 2005) and has published widely in a variety of peer-reviewed journals and several edited volumes on the expansion of the Moluccan conflict (Eastern Indonesia) into cyberspace, the globalization of local conflicts, Islamic radicalism on the Internet, online identity politics, and the challenges of the revitalization of traditions. Currently, she is engaged in a research project on *adat* revivalism and the peace process in Eastern Indonesia.

Barbara Hatley is Professor Emeritus in the School of Asian Languages and Studies at the University of Tasmania. Her research interests include Indonesian performing arts, modern literature, and gender studies. Her book *Javanese Performances on an Indonesian Stage: Contesting Culture, Embracing Change* (NUS Press/Asian Studies Association of Australia, Singapore 2008) looks at theater as an expression of social and cultural transformation in Central Java from the 1970s onwards. Several other recent publications focus on gender representation and the work of women performers in Indonesian theater, such as 'Subverting the stereotypes: women performers contest gender images old and new', *Review of Indonesian and Malayan Affairs*, 41(2), 2007, and 'Hearing women's voices, contesting women's bodies in post New Order Indonesia', *Intersections*, 16 February 2008.

Annette Hornbacher (PD, PhD) received her doctoral degree in philosophy at Tübingen, and her Habilitation (German qualification for Professorship) in cultural anthropology at the University of München. Since then she has been a Professor at the Universities of München and Heidelberg. She conducted fieldwork in Indonesia and particularly in Bali where she worked on ritual dance drama as a representation form of kinesthetic knowledge. Presently she is member of a research network on 'Religious dynamics in Southeast Asia', founded by the DFG (German Research Foundation) and works on cross-cultural ethics.

Grace Leksana was active in Sekitarkita Community in 2003, as the program manager for human rights school discussions. Sekitarkita Community is a civil society organization which focuses on distribution of information on human rights, culture, and environmental issues. In 2004, she joined the Indonesian Institute of Social History (ISSI) which is a non-governmental organization that has been working for historical mainstreaming in analyzing social issues. With ISSI, she conducted an oral history project on the history of Chinese education in Indonesia. Both of these organizations have been working closely (along with other human rights organizations) on issues of past human rights violations and reconciliation in Indonesia. She finished her Master's degree in the Institute of Social Studies, The Hague, in December 2008.

Katharine E. McGregor (PhD) is a senior lecturer in Southeast Asian History at the University of Melbourne, Australia. Her research to date has centered on the themes of Indonesian historiography, history, memory, and violence. She published her first book, *History in Uniform: Military Ideology and the Construction of Indonesia's Past* in 2007 with Asian Studies Association of Australia in conjunction with National University of Singapore Press, KITLV, and University of Hawaii Press.

Rumekso Setyadi is a researcher and a documentary film-maker working with the non-governmental organization Syarikat, Yogyakarta, Indonesia. He was involved in the making of documentary films such as *Kado Untuk Ibu* (2005), *Diculke Ndhase, Digondheli Buntute* (2006), *Sinengker* (2006), and *Barbaring Lakon* (2007). Currently he is working with Priyambudi Sulistiyanto on a film documentary about reconciliation and performance in Yogyakarta.

Y. Tri Subagya is chairman of the research and fellowship program in PUSdEP (*Pusat Sejarah dan Etika Politik*, Center for History and Political Ethics), the University of Sanata Dharma, and a part-time lecturer in the Faculty of Political and Social Science, the University of Atmajaya, Yogyakarta. In 2001, he received his Masters degree on Anthropology from Ateneo de Manila University. His research focuses on issues related to ecology, cultural politics and religious study, inter-communal conflict, and transitional justice. His publications include *Perbincangan Umum tentang Rencana Pembangunan PLTN di Indonesia* (1995), *Menemui Ajal, Etnografi Jawa tentang Kematian* (2004), *Jerat Bantuan, Jerit Pengungsi: Kesehatan Reproduksi Masyarakat Poso Paska Konflik Bersenjata* (2005), and *Pergulatan Identitas Dayak dan Indonesia: Belajar dari Tjilik Riwut* (2006).

Priyambudi Sulistiyanto (PhD) teaches at the Flinders Asia Centre, School of Political and International Studies, Flinders University, Adelaide, Australia. His current research looks at the politics of reconciliation and local politics in post-Suharto Indonesia. His publications include *Thailand, Indonesia and Burma in Comparative Perspective* (Ashgate 2002), and, co-edited with Maribeth Erb and Carole Faucher, *Regionalism in Post-Suharto Indonesia* (RoutledgeCurzon 2005), and, with Maribeth Erb, *Deepening Democracy in Indonesia? Direct Elections for Local Leaders (Pilkada)* (ISEAS 2009). His articles have appeared in *Third World Quarterly*, *Sojourn*, *Journal of Contemporary Asia*, *Kasarinlan*, *Inside Indonesia*, *Dignitas*, and *Indonesia*.

Kari Telle received her PhD in Social Anthropology from the University of Bergen in 2003, and is currently a senior researcher at the Chr. Michelsen Institute (CMI) in Bergen, Norway. She has published on religion, ritual, sorcery, material culture, and kinship. Her current research project 'Searching for Security: Religious mobilization and the politics of "insecurity" in Indonesia' examines popular initiatives to provide security and combat crime emerging in Balinese and Sasak communities on Lombok in the post-Suharto period.

Preface

This volume is about the Indonesian people's search for reconciliation and peace. The chapters are written by international scholars from different disciplinary backgrounds such as anthropology, conflict and peace studies, political sciences and law, history, and Southeast Asian Studies, and are based on extensive fieldwork conducted in various locations in Indonesia. *Reconciling Indonesia* benefits immensely from its interdisciplinarity and the fact that some of its contributors are both academics and human rights activists. This enables us to illuminate the topic from various angles, which is essential considering the complexity of the issue at stake.

The present work stems from an international conference on *In Search of Reconciliation and Peace in Indonesia and East Timor*, which was held at the Asia Research Institute (ARI), National University of Singapore, from 18 to 20 July 2007. Several factors drove me to organize this conference during my postdoctoral fellowship at ARI (January 2006 until April 2008): my research experiences in the Moluccas, where grassroots initiatives for reconciliation play an important role in the peace process; the general imbalance between an oversupply of literature on conflict and a shortage of literature on grassroots agency aimed at solving those conflicts; and the lack of publications on reconciliation in Indonesia. My feeling was that the constant emphasis on conflicts and the neglect of people's initiatives to solve them can turn into a self-fulfilling prophecy in the long run and make it even harder to break the vicious circle of violence underlying so many communal conflicts. The conference at ARI offered a great opportunity to bring excellent scholars and activists together from all over the world, to reflect on these topics, to make existing work and research on peace and reconciliation in Indonesia visible, and to add a sound comparative perspective to my own experiences and findings in the Moluccas. All participants were out to uncover cases in Indonesia, where people themselves took the initiative – often in the face of an inactive state – when it comes to sustainably resolving conflicts, to cope with past violence, and to re-establish broken relationships. All of these initiatives are very much influenced by the specific local sociocultural context. Nevertheless, it was not our aim to produce an idealistic counter-image to an Indonesia that is often depicted as drowned in conflicts and violence. To the contrary, all participants critically examine those initiatives and the crucial problems and challenges that come along with it.

Many people helped to make this a successful project; unfortunately I cannot name all of them here. Special thanks go to Anthony Reid, director of ARI at the time, and Chua Beng Huat, head of my research cluster at ARI, for supporting my ideas, giving me plenty of leeway to organize the conference and helpful advice whenever I asked for it. This project would not have been possible without the generous financial support of ARI and the expertise and professionalism of the ARI administrative staff members Valerie Yeo, Alyson Adrianne Rozells, Rina Yap, and Henry Kwan. Many thanks to all of them!

Since I was not able to include all papers presented at the conference in this volume and since I also had to drop the East Timor section, I would like to use this opportunity to express my thanks to all speakers, chairpersons, and discussants for their share in making it such a fruitful, constructive, and successful event: Jeroen Adam, Aris Ananta, Leena Avonius, Muhammad Najib Azca, Jamie Davidson, Aimee Dawis, Maribeth Erb, Annette Field, Arianne Gaetano, Lian Gogali, Bob Sugeng Hadiwinata, Noorhaidi Hasan, Barbara Hatley, Vannessa Hearman, Annette Hornbacher, Stella Hutagalung, Irwanto, Douglas Kammen, Lia Kent, Grace Leksana, Kar Yen Leong, Katharine McGregor, Michelle Miller, Rita Padawangi, Agung Ayuh Ratih, Anthony Reid, John Roosa, Henriette Sachse, Rumekso Setyadi, Shin Yoon Hwan, Y. Tri Subagya, Priyambudi Sulistiyanto, I Ngurah Suryawan, Sachiko Suzuki, Neles Tebay, Kari Telle, Fadjar I. Thufail, Joy Tong, Sherly Turnip, and Justin L. Wejak. My thanks also go to the great international audience that actively engaged in our discussions.

A select number of contributors were invited to revise their papers according to the book's themes, thus linking them to a broader reconciliation debate beyond the specific case studies and beyond the Indonesian context. The chapters underwent several rounds of revisions. I would like to thank the authors for bearing with me during this intensive process, for their cooperation and for sharing my enthusiasm to make this a useful book of a high standard. I would also like to thank Sonja van Leeuwen, Stephanie Rogers and the editorial board of Routledge, Mark Selden, the Asia's Transformations Series editor, and the anonymous reviewers selected by Routledge for their trust in this project and their helpful comments.

I would like to thank Maribeth Erb, Priyambudi Sulistiyanto, and Tim Winter for their help in the planning phase of the conference. Tim's advice on how to set up such an event was very much appreciated. Maribeth sacrificed her valuable time to give me a hand in the selection process of the conference abstracts and in discussing the conference outline. I am very grateful for Budi's encouragement and affirmation in this early stage and his help in spreading the word about the conference among Indonesian colleagues and in the Indonesian activist circle. Several other people I would like to thank for discussions during the planning phase, the event itself, and the publication phase include Chua Beng Huat, Jamie Davidson, Arianne Gaetano, David Hill, Gerry van Klinken, Michelle Miller, Anthony Reid, Kari Telle, and YouYenn Teo, and, of course, the many people who helped to spread the word about the conference. I thank Shamala Sundaray for giving me a helping hand with the final copy-editing process.

More generally, I would like to thank my dear friends and colleagues at ARI who made my stay in Singapore such a pleasurable, fruitful and successful one. I thank my partner Jörg for jointly and successfully getting through this difficult phase of long-distance relationship. I dedicate this book to my dad, who always encouraged me in all my endeavors and who made the effort to come all the way to Singapore to visit me and explore this part of the world.

I hope that this book contributes to a more critical, but at the same time more constructive and also more positive outlook on the future of Indonesia and post-conflict situations more generally. The book shows that common people are not only passive victims of large-scale conflicts initiated and planned by people outside of their circles. It acknowledges their agency, especially when it comes to fostering grassroots reconciliation and getting back to normalcy after violent conflicts. It is the people that matter and that can make a difference, even when governments, states, and the international community remain silent or are incapable of solving violent conflicts. This, of course, must not blind us to the challenges and problems coming along with reconciliation from below and must not release national governments and the international community of their responsibility when it comes to the rehabilitation and reconstruction of society, the seeking of the truth, and the prosecution of perpetrators. The contributions to this volume will give the reader the possibility to assess grassroots reconciliation initiatives in one specific country, to explore cultural dimensions of reconciliation processes and thus to gain new perspectives and insights regarding the broader peace and reconciliation discourse.

Part I
Problematizing 'reconciliation'

1 Introduction
Reconciling Indonesia

Birgit Bräuchler

Reconciling Indonesia explores grassroots initiatives for reconciliation, thus going beyond established notions of reconciliation pivoting on state actions and political and legal approaches. Recent large-scale conflicts in various parts of the world have given rise to a 'reconciliation toolkit' of truth commissions and law enforcement, justice and human rights, forgiveness and amnesty. These mechanisms get more and more internationalized and are supposed to be the means not only to stop conflict and violence, but also to reconcile warring parties and create sustainable peace. But as studies on conflict and conflict resolution worldwide show, there is no such thing as a blueprint for reconciliation and some scholars warn against an unreflexive standardization of comparative models.[1] Reconciliation means different things to different people in different circumstances. *Reconciling Indonesia* is not about reconciling Indonesia as an entity. Reconciliation is a multidimensional process that takes place on different levels: interpersonal, between individuals and communities, among communities, between communities and the state, among states, and, what is so far hardly considered in the relevant literature, between the human and the non-human world that share a common cosmology. The often limited success of such standardized mechanisms requires the exploration of other means for reconciliation that take grassroots agencies – the agency of civil society groups, the common people and their immediate local representatives – and the sociocultural contextualization of conflict and reconciliation into account; in other words, reconciliation from below.

Avruch (1998) argued that no conflict can be understood and analyzed, let alone sustainably resolved, without taking its cultural context into account. All too often this important insight has been marginalized or even ignored by political scientists, by international relations and legal scholars who clearly dominate the debate in academia, and by national and international policy makers. Taking this into account would require much more time-consuming in-depth studies of the cultural and ethnographic settings of reconciliation processes and their historical backgrounds (see also Boege 2006: 3). Furthermore locally rooted mechanisms are often collective-oriented and thus in seeming conflict with Western norms of individual justice and accountability.[2] It is precisely this often neglected collective notion of reconciliation that the contributions to this volume address. Especially due to the absence of important national tools of reconciliation, it is essential in contemporary

Indonesia to work on community reconciliation, and, for researchers and activists, to look at the "micropolitics of reconciliation at the communal and intercommunal levels" (Theidon 2007: 97).

The volume thus also aims to fill a major gap in research on Indonesia. At first glance, Indonesia seems to be all about violence and conflict – be it traditional practices such as head-hunting, the age-long struggle against the colonial powers, the 1965–66 massacres, the invasion of East Timor in 1975, the suppression of Papuans, the long war in Aceh, and the many post-Suharto conflicts – and the flood of publications underlines this.[3] So there is an urgent need for reconciliation, but unfortunately almost nothing is written yet about the Indonesian people's search for peace and reconciliation. As Amirrachman (2007a: 16) recently stated, Indonesia "actually has a positive potential as well that needs to be dug up and revitalized in order to foster peace and development" (translation by the author). It is that kind of careful optimism and positive outlook that I would like to promote and that – together with my experiences in the conflict and post-conflict Moluccas – spurred me to organize the conference on which this book is based (see preface). To invest in the study of reconciliation processes in Indonesia and how diverse groups of Indonesians try to come to terms with their troubled past is of major importance to fostering ongoing reformation and democratization processes throughout the country; moreover, the success of these processes will profoundly affect the stability of the entire region.

Covering different areas of Indonesia, this volume analyzes grassroots reconciliation initiatives and explores the ways in which reconciliation connects with issues like civil society, gender, religion, 'tradition', culture, history, education, displacement and land, 'traditional justice' mechanisms, and performance.[4] The book argues that each particular case requires an individual approach to reconciliation that takes into account the kind of underlying conflict as well as the sociocultural setting. Yet the totality of the cases also suggests the range of parameters of

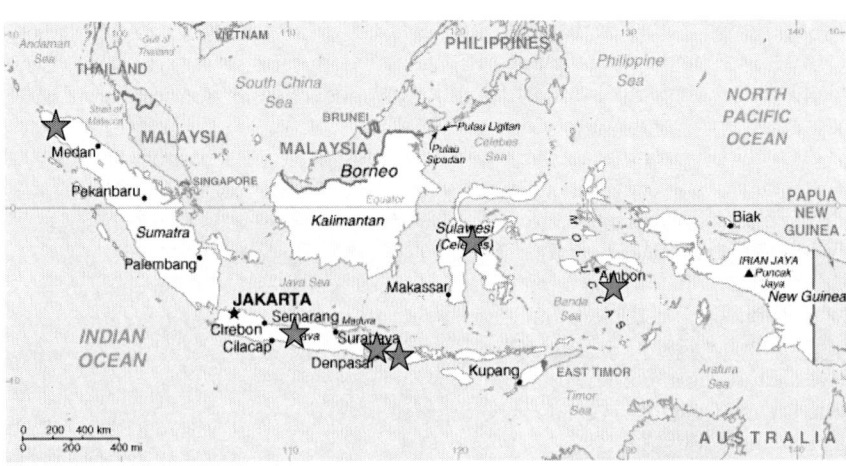

Map 1.1 Case studies in *Reconciling Indonesia*

grassroots reconciliation initiatives, and allows the reader to reflect on their prospects for success. To illustrate this, the contributors deal with different types and scales of conflict in different sociocultural and historical settings such as state-sponsored organized violence (Java), terrorist attacks (Bali), secessionist conflicts (Aceh), communal conflicts (Moluccas and Sulawesi) and localized small-scale conflicts (Lombok). This variety gives expression to the complexity of the conflict and reconciliation landscape in Indonesia and underlines the fact that the local, the national and, in some cases, the international level are always intertwined. All of them have to be taken into account as a prerequisite for a successful nation-wide reconciliation and reformation process.

The focus of this book is on contemporary reconciliation processes that are connected to recent developments and conflicts of the post-Suharto era, but also – due to the centrality of this conflict – with the failed 'coup' of 1965 and the following pogrom in Indonesia. The chapters analyze different dimensions of reconciliation and introduce diverse grassroots initiatives and actors of reconciliation – non-governmental organizations (NGOs), religious organizations, teachers, local religious communities and figures, local *adat* communities and figures, refugees, artists, women – thus contributing to a better understanding of local meanings of reconciliation and the various 'cultures of reconciliation'. The ownership and the cultural anchoring of reconciliation processes are considered essential for their success. Moreover, as some of the chapters show, local ideas of a world in balance stress the importance of cosmological dimensions of reconciliation. The book also reflects on the challenges of collective reconciliation and the emphasis on grassroots concepts of reconciliation. Problems such as the following can also inhibit reconciliation: the instrumentalization of traditions by 'traditional' leaders to get access to resources belonging to an *adat* community; an outsider's appeal to local communal approaches that give preference to collective reconciliation, thus enabling the individual to entrench impunity and profit from a sociocultural system of which s/he is not actually a part; questions of power and hierarchy; the difficulties in bringing victims and perpetrators together to initiate the reconciliation process and dissolve the barriers between them; or the neglect to involve the society at large.

The volume interrogates commonly held notions of reconciliation and highlights the importance of communal and grassroots reconciliation generally and in the Indonesian context in particular. The book is divided into four parts. The first part, consisting of this introduction and Annette Hornbacher's chapter, problematizes the notion of a global *ethos* and the reconciliation concept as such in conjunction with a re-evaluation of the human rights and culture debate. The second part comprises contributions by Kari Telle, Barbara Hatley, and Birgit Bräuchler, and explores the potential of 'restorative performances' as resources for reconciliation, including traditional justice mechanisms, rituals, symbols, and theater. The chapters by Leena Avonius, Jeroen Adam, and Tri Subagya form part three of this book that puts 'traditional justice' under scrutiny by analyzing shortcomings of traditional conflict resolution mechanisms, the (mis)use of power, and the (often neglected) role of gender. In the last part Grace Leksana, Priyambudi Sulistiyanto and Rumekso Setyadi, and Katharine McGregor deal with the struggle over memory involved in reconciliation processes. Examining NGOs, religious organizations and history education, they highlight civil society efforts to cope with a violent past and discuss victim-perpetrator conceptualizations. The chapters' distribution follows their main themes, but each chapter also contributes to topics introduced in other sections. Cross-references in this introduction will underline this. The multidisciplinarity of the volume is a first step in addressing the complexity of the issues at stake and the multidimensionality of reconciliation processes. The fact that some authors are scholars and activists at the same time makes it possible for them to contribute important insights into the case studies presented here.

Truth, justice, and reconciliation

The notion and popularity of reconciliation is a rather recent phenomenon. Huyse (2008b) briefly summarized the change in how nations and people worldwide tried to cope with the aftermath of civil war, genocide, or a brutal dictatorship and deal with those who committed grave human rights violations:[5] While the emphasis in the Nuremberg and Tokyo tribunals after World War II was on accountability, the tendency from the end of the 1940s to the mid-1980s was "to look away from such painful legacies" as in Cambodia, Spain, or Chile (Huyse 2008b: 2). From the mid-1980s onwards "the global growth of a human rights culture blossomed" and resulted, among others, in the creation of the ad hoc tribunals of The Hague (for the former Yugoslavia) and Arusha (for Rwanda) and of the International Criminal Court (ICC), and "in the gradual spread of the principle of universal jurisdiction" (Huyse 2008b: 2). However, questions about the general applicability of such trials were soon raised. Moreover, the limited reach of courts, their limited success or failure to convict the masterminds behind violence and atrocities, and the inability of retributive justice to provide relief or healing for people affected by mass atrocities, led to the search for alternative mechanisms to mere 'criminal justice'. Transitional authorities make increasing use of official truth seeking in an effort to come to terms with a violent past, be it in Latin America, South Africa, Germany, or East Timor.[6] These processes are often heavily influenced by international donors who consider truth and reconciliation commissions (TRC) an essential part of the 'transition package'. Some of these truth commissions were able to make remarkable contributions, as Hayner (2002) argued, by delving much further into conflict patterns and consequences than any trial of individual perpetrators could have done. The South African case is often cited as a successful model. Many others, however, have not lived up to the people's expectations or have failed. Peace and reconciliation practitioners became aware that one tool is not sufficient to assure sustainable peace and reconciliation and that multidimensional approaches were needed that suit the particularities of each society after a violent conflict.[7] 'Reconciliation' has become a key term in international conflict and peace discourse, yet one that remains insufficiently conceptualized and poorly understood.

Let's take a quick look at two concepts/tools commonly closely associated with reconciliation (at least by international experts) – truth and justice – and raise some questions. Most of the prominent means of so-called transitional justice such as truth commissions, amnesty, trials, reparations, or forgiveness were developed for nations that are undergoing the transition from authoritarian regimes or despotism to democracy, and often include how to cope with massive human rights violations in past and ongoing conflicts.[8] A common perception is that reconciliation is not possible without justice, but perceptions of what justice implies vary widely. The justice concept typically underlying international discourses on conflict resolution and reconciliation is a retributive one, justice that is meant to punish the offender. But in so-called 'weak states', proper justice mechanisms are often not in place or they are not able to cope with the scale of the atrocities. Moreover, outright punishment may not be appropriate in every context whether due to the political situation or the specific culture of a post-conflict society whose priority might be the restoration of community life (Huyse 2003b: 102). And revealing the truth or sanctioning perpetrators does not automatically imply reconciliation. Furthermore, very often, activities and negotiations of courts and truth commissions do not sufficiently, if at all, involve the communities affected, that is, the victims.[9]

Next to the problem of how and what kind of data to collect, and how to document and represent the truth, other, even more substantial questions arise such as whether, when, how, and what people actually want to remember (compare Hayner 2002), or what actually constitutes truth, what truth are we looking for and whose truth, individual or collective truth, or objective (factual), subjective (narrative), or intersubjective (shared) truth (Forsberg 2003: 73). Can there be such a thing as 'neutral' truth after a violent conflict or mass atrocities? Of course, the same question can be asked when it comes to justice: Whose justice would we want to apply, justice for whom, and what does justice imply? Any answer to these questions very much depends on the specific sociocultural and historical background and would therefore be highly contextual. The risk of truth seeking is to create 'facts', to create a normative single 'history' and 'truth', that many feel left out of because their 'truth' is not covered; their stories are not looked at. Mahmood Mamdani, one of the strongest critics of the South African TRC, calls this "compromised truth" (Hayner 2002: 74).[10] Another major shortcoming of truth commissions is that in most cases there are no mechanisms set up to take care of the people after they have told their truth; no long-term therapies are offered (Hayner 2002: 135, 141; Minow 1998: 73). And last but not least, although TRCs are much more victim-oriented than court trials and victims do get a say and can talk about their traumatic experiences, they are nevertheless still treated as 'objects', not as agents of reconciliation. They are, to put it bluntly, only part of a system set up and regulated by higher-level actors, thus denying the agency of the kind of people that are the main actors in this book.

Reconciliation in Indonesia

What is the situation in contemporary Indonesia with respect to justice, truth, and human rights? The step-down of Suharto and the politics of his successors had many positive follow-ups, such as the independence of East Timor in 1999, an

Aceh policy that led to a Memorandum of Understanding in 2005 and peace between the Indonesian military and the Acehnese Independence Movement GAM (*Gerakan Aceh Merdeka*), and the passing of a decentralization law in 1999 and 2004 that deals with both the devolution of political authority and fiscal decentralization.[11] This new decentralization policy was accompanied by a trend of revitalization of *adat* – tradition and customary law – in many parts of Indonesia, which on the one hand, enables communities to revive local cultures and re-install local structures that have been destroyed by the unification and centralization efforts of the Suharto regime. It also opened up new spaces for the democratization of history, the renegotiating of the past and remembrance of trauma and violence, as Zurbuchen and her contributors (2005a) argued, which is so important for reconciliation in Indonesia. On the other hand, decentralization also led to the rise of ethnic discrimination and exclusivity through the instrumentalization of ethnicity by local elites (the so-called *putra daerah* issue, literally 'sons of the region'), the decentralization of corruption, and the increased exploitation of local resources through reinstalled 'traditional' rulers.[12] Some of the chapters in this book focus exactly on these contradictions (see especially Adam's chapter) and on the newly emerging negotiation processes in post-Suharto Indonesia (see e.g. Leksana and Sulistiyanto & Setyadi).

Various factors helped the emergence of the many allegedly ethnic and religious conflicts that erupted all over in post-Suharto Indonesia: the weak governments of president Suharto's successors, B.J. Habibie, Abdurrahman Wahid, and Megawati, the slowness of the democratization process on the one hand and the radicalness of the decentralization policies on the other, the poor performance of the security forces, and the absence of an effective judicial system (see e.g. Crouch 2004). These factors also inhibit reconciliation. In Indonesia, debates on reconciliation typically focus on human rights issues, justice, and law enforcement and are very much influenced by national and international NGOs and agencies such as the UN. Human rights violations run like a thread through Indonesia's history, and even now, irrespective of the country's move towards democracy, the signing of important international human rights conventions over the last years including the UN Declaration on the Rights of Indigenous Peoples of 2007, and the passing of a Law on Human Rights in 1999, human rights still have a difficult standing in the country. Following South Africa's example, a draft bill establishing a TRC (*Komisi Kebenaran dan Rekonsiliasi*, KKR) was submitted to the Indonesian parliament in 2001 (van Zyl 2005: 332) and converted into law in 2004. It was intended to investigate political killings, disappearances, and massacres that occurred during the Suharto regime. Due to the current president's hesitance, this commission was never put into action and the law was nullified in December 2006 because of its many legal flaws by the Constitutional Court without providing any replacement.[13] But the Indonesian people are not only refused admission to a 'truer history', there are also only insufficient efforts taken to legally deal with the many human rights violations of the past, be it in Aceh, East Timor, or Papua or with other incidents, in which the Indonesian government and security forces have been involved, and of the more recent violent conflicts all over Indonesia.

Due to this lack of state initiatives, the lack of retributive justice and truth-seeking bodies, the Indonesian people have to get active themselves, if they want to overcome past and recent atrocities that led to deep divisions in Indonesian society. As this book clearly shows, this frustrating deadlock pushed the grassroots in Indonesia to take over the reigns and get themselves active in their search for peace and reconciliation (compare Ruth-Heffelbower 2002). Many of these initiatives draw on local cultural resources and concepts, which is in line with two recent phenomena: the revival-of-tradition trend all over Indonesia, and an internationally growing awareness among peace practitioners that reconciliation processes have to be locally contextualized, locally owned and driven, and have to adapt to local timing and tempo (Huyse 2003a: 163; Merwe 2003: 122).[14] But, as indicated earlier, these concepts and the underlying understanding of what justice is often differ from those promoted in international discourses. Annette Hornbacher makes this ideational divide the subject of her contribution to this volume. In 'Global conflict in cosmocentric perspective: a Balinese approach to reconciliation' she analyzes the Bali bombings of 2002 and 2005 and the opposing reactions towards these violent attacks: the Western project of the 'war on terror' on the one hand and Hindu-Balinese attempts to restore cosmic balance on the other. Contrasting the (Western) theory of a universal '*ethos*' common to all religions and cultures and seen as prerequisite for peaceful coexistence with the ambivalent role of religion in global conflicts, Hornbacher argues that these different approaches to conflict management are the outcome of religious-based differences concerning ethics, individual responsibility, humanity, and concepts of 'evil'. In line with this, Pouligny, Doray, and Martin (2007: 22) have argued that "an overarching, moralizing and binary view that involves merely the struggle between 'good' and 'evil'" is ignoring the complexity of most situations and dehumanizes the "perpetrator" which makes his/her reintegration and reconciliation impossible. In the Balinese context, it was not an allegedly global *ethos*, but rather local (religious) perceptions of conflict and peace that contributed to the re-establishment of harmony and thus fostered 'reconciliation'. Hornbacher's contribution is also a strong plea to broaden common conceptualizations of reconciliation to not only consider humans and the visible realm, but also locally prevalent cosmological and religious perceptions of the world that determine people's notions of what reconciliation means (see also Telle and McGregor this volume).

'Reconciliation' is usually not part of local vocabularies in Indonesia. Although the Indonesianized term *rekonsiliasi* has often already been adopted in local contexts due to outside influences and in order to bridge the terminology gap, this does not imply, however, that the underlying notions have been adapted as well.[15] In most local contexts in Indonesia there are cognate expressions for restoring relationships and reintegrating the community, such as *baku bae* which means restoring friendly relationships and being friends again in the Moluccas (Malik *et al.* 2003), *peusijuek* which is part of a traditional justice mechanism in Aceh that cools down the situation and finalizes a 'reconciliation' process (see Avonius this volume), *meka sareka* or *tapan holo*, which are *adat* institutions of peacemaking and restoring an atmosphere of brotherhood among the Lamaholot people on Flores

(Kopong Medan 2006), *motambu tana* a ritual to resolve resource conflicts and land disputes among kinship groups in Central Sulawesi by burying a buffalo's head (symbolizing the past) in the ground (see Subagya this volume), or the *garap* ritual that is used in Lombok to restore social relationships (see Telle this volume). A prominent example from East Timor is *nahe biti*, that is, rolling out the mat, sitting together, and restoring peace (Babo-Soares 2004). An Islamic concept also used in the Indonesian context is *islah*, which means making peace after the occurrence of injustices. Whereas the results of these processes on the surface might be similar to those of the more standardized reconciliation processes described earlier in this introduction (provided they are successful), the methods applied and the way to get there differ tremendously. This volume will provide sufficient proof for this, though not all the chapters deal with traditional justice and peace mechanisms, it also looks at the innovative means by which the grassroots try to cope with past violence and conflicts.

Underlying the internationalized concept of conflict, peace, and reconciliation is a notion that conflict is inherently bad, that needs explanation, while the opposite is seen as 'normal', and that there is an 'evil' that is opposed to the 'good' and an orderly life; very basic assumptions that simply don't exist in all societies.[16] Another issue that has been overlooked in international reconciliation discourses for too long is the orientation towards collectivities or communities, not individuals, of these locally anchored 'reconciliation' processes. Collective reconciliation is important in all of the Indonesian case studies; the emphasis is on restoring relationships not between individuals but between the communities they are part of (sometimes including their dead members and the cosmologically or religiously prescribed invisible), and to reintegrate the offenders into society: be it following small or larger-scale conflicts; conflicts in local groups or between local groups; or between other groups of society such as religious communities or communities that got into conflict because of a seeming ideological divide like in the anti-communist massacres in 1965–66, or after the world got out of balance due to outside influences as in the Bali case. Casting a glance at the human rights and culture debate is rather illuminating here.

Human rights and culture

The international human rights debate heavily influences reconciliation discourses and activities on all levels, including the national and the local. A lot has been written about the universalism-relativism debate, that is, whether human rights that were formulated in a specific Western context can be universally transferred to any other cultural setting. Not everybody agreed with the upcoming 'human rights imperialism', and culture was used as a reason to not conform as the 'Asian values' debate clearly showed (see e.g. Jacobsen & Bruun 2000). With the increasing emphasis on the cultural dimension of human rights, collective rights came into the foreground, in particular indigenous rights. After long discussions this finally led to the adoption of the aforementioned UN Declaration on the Rights of Indigenous Peoples by a majority of votes in favor – among them Indonesia – in 2007. Among others, the declaration emphasizes indigenous peoples' right "to determine the structures and to select the membership of their institutions in accordance with their own procedures" (UN 2007: Article 33.2), including juridical systems and customs, as long as they are in accordance with international human rights standards (UN 2007: Article 34). A simple statement, but a major dilemma: Who, in the end, is entitled to judge what is in line and what is not? As I have outlined elsewhere in more detail, the granting of collective rights helps local cultures to survive, but also bears dangers when, for instance, collective rights become exclusivist rights or blind us to essential internal differences of a seemingly homogeneous community (Bräuchler 2008).

In reaction to these debates, Woodiwiss (2004) stated that human rights should be de-sacralized, in the sense that they should not be mistaken for ends, but still be seen as an instrument that helps people to protect themselves against abuse. Communitarian values and traditional leadership do not necessarily have to be oppressive and/or contradict international human rights. Accordingly, I would like to argue that we have to de-sacralize the Western understanding of reconciliation and justice by allowing other understandings of what conflict, peace, and reconciliation imply, to enter the discourse. This includes other concepts of what it means to be human, what it means to live a dignified life and what personhood implies. We have to open our eyes to "the obviousness of the 'social'", to use Chua's (2004: 8) words. Whereas Western models assume that the community is healthy if the individual is, it is the other way around in many non-Western societies (Daly & Sarkin 2007: 68–9). These assumptions have tremendous impacts on how reconciliation is conceived and how it 'works'.

Part of the problem is the notion of culture underlying the debates about human rights and traditions, including their role in reconciliation. Both laws on cultural rights and policies addressing the inclusion of traditional mechanisms into peace-building processes often implicitly assume that culture is a fixed set of elements that never change. The new Indonesian autonomy law is a good example of that, since it only grants villages the right to return to their traditional structure, if they can *prove* their cultural authenticity and that they still live their traditional lifestyle. However, culture is not only politicized and essentialized by lawmakers, but also by the people themselves who want to use it as a means for resistance or by local elites as a means to obtain more power (see e.g. the *putra daerah* issue). In all cases 'culture' is reified and deprived of the flexibility that makes it survive and able to adapt to changing social, political, and economic circumstances (compare e.g. Harrison 1999). It is also important to discard the well-maintained, but in my eyes rather absurd, division of tradition and modernity. Both nationalist politicians in Indonesia and peace and development workers, more generally, have been using such invented oppositions for a long time to depict culture and tradition as pure romanticism and as hindrance to development, thus ignoring that all cultures and traditions are undergoing constant changes not only due to external influences such as colonialism, nationalism, and globalization, but also due to regional and internal dynamics. Traditions are not only constantly changing, but are also creatively revived and (re)invented at certain times. The reasons can be quite diverse, such as political upheavals, resistance towards the state, efforts to reclaim political, and economic rights, conflicts, or the search for conflict solutions (Bräuchler & Widlok 2007). And some of the chapters in this volume vividly show this.

It took the international community a while to realize that culture is a basic need as it was put in an international conference organized by the Prince Claus Fund in The Hague in 2006, in which possible responses to cultural emergencies following natural disasters, conflicts, and wars were explored; culture is both "the basis from which people derive a sense of identity and security" and "the cement that holds a society together" (Chronis 2006: 15). One hopes that the recently adopted UN declaration will have further implications on how these insights are actually implemented. The grassroots are usually the ones most affected by violent conflicts and it is they who are the main actors in collective reconciliation efforts that are often heavily influenced by local cultural mechanisms. It required an important 'change of paradigm' initiated by academics and peace-building practitioners such as Lederach (1997) and Bar-Tal and Bennink (2004) to acknowledge that the broader structural and sociocultural concerns and contexts, in which the violence is embedded, have to be considered as well for a successful reconciliation process that has to take place from the top-down and from the bottom-up at the same time; high-profile reconciliation initiatives discussed earlier have to go hand in hand with or complement grassroots initiatives and the other way around too. Since a lot has already been written on the top-down part of the story, this volume's central focus is on such grassroots initiatives and the tensions arising out of top-down and bottom-up approaches as for example discussed in Avonius' chapter.

In case state initiatives or institutions are missing or not functioning properly, the grassroots have to take over. Galtung (2001: 17) therefore argued for a massive participation of the common people in conflict resolution "as subjects, not only as the objects of somebody else's decisions and deeds". Since many of the contemporary so-called ethnic or religious conflicts are about identity, it is important to bring local culture in, not only as a conflict issue, but also as a means for reconciliation. This does pose a major challenge to outside people involved in or supporting local peacemaking, since this requires in-depth research and knowledge of local authority structures and mechanisms, justice, and gender roles, to mention some important fields. It is much easier to provide emergency relief and reconstruct buildings than the social and cultural fabrics of a society in conflict (compare Green & Ahmed 1999). There is also an urgent need to detach reconciliation from notions such as forgiveness, and thus from any religious overtones, in order not to risk resistance by those who are supposed to be reconciled, simply because they cannot forgive.[17]

Restorative performances

Despite the shortcomings of retributive and punitive justice, achieving 'justice' is still seen by many as prerequisite for reconciliation (Huyse 2003b: 97) locally and internationally, although with very different perceptions of what this implies. Peace academics and practitioners have therefore slowly started to widen the notion of 'justice'. Bloomfield (2006) suggested a multidimensional concept of justice, while Meitzner Yoder (2007) recommended a hybridized justice, emphasizing that different ideas about justice do not have to contradict each other, but can be complementary. These models entail broader conceptualizations of justice that do not only consider individual guilt and punishment, but also justice without formal punishment (such as truth telling and reparations), and restorative justice that is often based on traditional mechanisms of conflict resolution. Local justice mechanisms are increasingly used to cope with the aftermath of more large-scale conflicts, be it in Rwanda, East Timor, or Bougainville (Boege 2006: 5; Buckley-Zistel 2005; McWilliam 2007a) especially in situations where retributive justice and truth commissions are out of reach (Huyse & Salter 2008; IDEA 2006b).[18] The main features of non-state traditional restorative justice mechanisms that are so popular in many 'traditional' societies in Africa and Asia, are their focus on the restoration of the victim, the communities affected and social cohesion, and the reintegration of the offenders into the communities, elements that mere punitive justice mechanisms usually ignore. The main goal of these mechanisms is to restore the relationship between the victims' and the perpetrators' communities, thus initiating the important process of identity transformation and relationship-building. The present and the future are in focus, not the past. Both sides have to actively participate in the reconciliation process. Culture, that includes cultural values and local decision making mechanisms, is a determinant factor.[19] Traditional justice mechanisms are more flexible than formal justice since they are usually not based on written law, but on negotiations and consensus; but their adaptability and transferability have their limits. Kari Telle's contribution in this volume analyzes traditional justice mechanisms on the island of Lombok. In 'Swearing innocence: performing justice and "reconciliation" in post-New Order Lombok', she outlines the dynamics of a collective oath-taking ordeal called *garap* – one of the ways in which Sasak Muslim communities in Central Lombok resolve the issues that arise after theft – that some of the recently emerging crime-fighting groups active in Central Lombok have incorporated into their charters. The analysis of these 'everyday forms of reconciliation' offers insights into cultural assumptions regarding justice and peace, where the identification of culprits and talking about past violations does not seem to be necessary. Telle uses these findings to test the limits of this 'ritual technology' when transferred to novel settings, and also to question assumptions such as the therapeutic aspect of truth telling that is so prevalent in the literature on reconciliation. The limits and difficulties of transferring traditional justice mechanisms to settings that don't reflect the sociocultural context they are usually rooted in are addressed in more detail in the section '"Traditional justice" under scrutiny'.

Traditional rituals are important in many post-conflict societies to reintegrate offenders, soldiers or members of the former militias into the community, be it in East Timor, Northern Uganda, or Mozambique.[20] Bräuchler in her case study (this volume) describes a slightly different situation, where a whole village that was totally destroyed during the Moluccan conflict and whose population was chased away wanted to return. Only after long negotiations with the neighboring village that was mainly responsible for their exodus and a carefully planned (invented) return-ceremony that drew heavily on cultural symbols and rituals from both sides, were they able to finally return to their traditional land. Important for the success of such restoration and reconciliation processes is the traditional arbitrators' or other mediating figures' knowledge of the sociocultural embeddedness of the conflict and the parties involved (see also Stevens 2001: 28). More generally we can argue that this is exactly why the involvement of people on the ground, the grassroots – local people who know the sociocultural context and who will have to live with the results of any conflict resolution and reconciliation efforts – is so significant for their sustainability. Besides their participatory and their communal character – the community taking responsibility for its members (Boege 2006: 9) – these justice systems are usually praised for their accessibility to rural people (in terms of both distance and language), their cost-effectiveness, their context-sensibility, and, of course, their restorative character. They do not depend on the state to get active, they are process-oriented and they also address the emotional needs of a society after conflict.[21]

Reconciliation most probably fails if it is restricted to a symbolic and abstract realm. As Rigby (2001: 189) suggested, it must be "embodied and lived out in new relationships between people at all levels of society."[22] Kelman (2004) argued that a change in the warring parties' identities is the foundation for peace. During conflict, the negation of the other is an inherent part of one's own collective identity. Following Kelman, reconciliation processes have to aim towards the removal of such negation and the acceptance of the other group's identity, with both sides ideally moving towards a more shared identity. This should not imply a replacement of each group's core identity with such a common identity, which might be rather counterproductive and create new conflicts, but that each side revises its own identity in a way that it can at least acknowledge "the legitimacy of the other's narrative without necessarily fully agreeing with" it (Kelman 2004: 119). According to Ellis (2006) the most important means for this negotiating or recategorization processes (Gaertner & Dovidio 2000) is the transformative potential of communication. Ellis considers a change in communication patterns and forms of discourse, the rewriting of narratives, and the reinterpretation of symbols as essential to widen the involved parties' identities, to reinterpret one's relationship with 'the others', and thus to enable reconciliation. Reconciliation initiatives should provide spaces where people can talk about their perceptions of each other and the conflict.[23] Such communicative transformations on the grassroots level can be supported in various fields such as educational institutions and media (see Leksana this volume), NGOs (see Sulistiyanto & Setyadi this volume), and other projects fostering the renegotiation of relationships (for women's initiatives, e.g. see Subagya this volume) (Ellis 2006: 145, 151, 165). On an analytical level, peace practitioners therefore put the emphasis on reconciliation as a process of relationship-building, and not an outcome (Lederach 1997: 151); a process "through which a society moves from a divided past to a shared future" (Bloomfield 2003b: 12).[24] Based on their experiences in post-conflict settings they realized that it needs to be a long-term, voluntary, deep, broad, and inclusive process in the sense that it has to involve not only 'facts' but also aspirations and emotions; it has to involve the entire society and to address the attitudes and beliefs that underpin violent conflict in a community or communities in conflict; and it should not be imposed upon the people.[25]

Symbols and rituals play an important role in peace-building and reconciliatory justice.[26] They are typically ingredients in restorative justice processes and are essential for relationship-building and identity transformation. Symbols and rituals are culturally determined and give expression to how a community sees the world and 'the other'. Hence they are important both for the creation of conflict lines and for closing these gaps. While a substantial amount of research has been done on the former, far less work has been devoted to the latter (Schirch 2001: 147). In contrast to more high-level and abstract reconciliation initiatives, symbols and rituals also focus "on emotional and cognitive reordering" (Ross 2004: 209) and "the psychological and cultural dimensions of conflict" (Schirch 2001: 145). Several chapters in this book describe rituals that aim to provide an inclusive space for both sides of a conflict in search of a common identity that enables them to put the violent past to rest. Rituals can also act as educational means for reconciliation "by enacting the desired transformed state of coexistence" (Schirch 2001: 157). Following Ross (2004: 211–6), cultural performances are another kind of rituals that can facilitate transformation processes. The performing arts, such as conflict theater, playback theater, or theater dialogue, are increasingly used worldwide to educate and "engage the public in the act of reconciliation" (Daly & Sarkin 2007: 92).[27] Barbara Hatley in her chapter on 'Social reconciliation and community integration through theater' depicts theater as a medium of social communication and community integration. In her study, it provides a space for the renegotiation of identities of opposing sides of the 1965–66 anti-communist massacres and for integrative shows put on in various neighborhoods of Solo following the 1998 communal violence in the city, thus promoting reconciliation between polarized social groups. Analyzing the narrative form, bodily images, language, and music of these performances, along with their social context and audience responses, this chapter reflects critically on the potential strengths of such events as sites of reconciliation, and their limitations.

Looking at the grassroots level and at culture opens rich resources for the human rights and reconciliation discourse in finding locally grounded tools for protecting and restoring humanity and achieving reconciliation (Bloomfield 2003a: 46; Woodiwiss 2004: 179). But, as outlined already, we also have to be aware of potential shortcomings. As Chua (2004: 22) has stated, individuals in communitarian societies should be given the right to exit, in cases where they are not willing to pay the price any more in exchange for collective well-being. As discussed earlier, traditional approaches to conflict resolution and reconciliation are not applicable in all circumstances. But there are also innovative ways to adapt traditional mechanisms to new circumstances (compare Culbertson & Pouligny 2007). As Boege (2006: 11) argued, "when conflicting parties are not tied together by shared values and interdependence, both aspects need to be created for conflict management agreements to be more than just punctual exercise". In 'Mobilizing culture and tradition for peace: reconciliation in the Moluccas', Birgit Bräuchler shows that the invention of new communicative means and rituals that build on traditions of both sides of a conflict can be another way to widen and transform conflicting identities and create the shared realities and responsibilities Bloomfield, Kelman, and Lederach were promoting. As underlined by Schirch (2001: 154), they can "be improvised and constructed by conflict interveners and/or the people involved in a conflict". What is important is that they are sensitive to cultural norms. Bräuchler analyzes the challenges and problems coming along with the revival of tradition for peace in the post-conflict Moluccas and explores the more general question of whether culture can be an effective means to build inter-religious bridges and to foster reconciliation. Through an ethnographic analysis of a traditional village union claiming to be the key to peace in the Moluccas, she argues that the incorporation of cultural aspects and local ritual approaches to conflict resolution did enable the local anchoring of peace initiatives and thus contributed to successful reconciliation. Only through this ritual were the Kariu people, who had to flee during the violence, reinstalled as *adat* people, which in the Moluccan context is tantamount to re-acknowledging their full humanity. But Bräuchler also warns against a rash identification of religion as a dividing and *adat* as a unifying force. *Adat* rituals not only unified people after this conflict, local traditions also formed the basis for the development of divided memories that were invoked to legitimize the use of violence during the conflict.

'Traditional justice' under scrutiny

More generally, researchers and practitioners have identified disadvantages of traditional justice mechanisms and expressed caveats. Main concerns are whether these mechanisms can be transferred to other levels of society beyond the local community, where 'outsiders' who do not share the same cultural values are involved; whether they can be applied to large-scale conflicts such as mass killings and genocide, in case they usually only dealt with minor crimes and offences; and that local standards and values might not be in line with international human rights.[28] Pankhurst (1999: 247) also warned against making use of these mechanisms without fully understanding their implications and the underlying local power structures. They might have been deeply damaged during colonial oppression, modernization, politicization through the state or mass violence, genocide, and civil war, during which traditional leaders or arbitrators might also have lost legitimacy and influence, or the people their trust in them (Culbertson & Pouligny 2007; Hamber 2003: 78, 81; Huyse 2008b; Stevens 2001: 129). Deliberate or unconscious misinterpretations or oversimplifications might have rather counterproductive effects on a reconciliation process, when, for instance, local leaders are enabled to misuse their power, thus not acting for the good of their people.[29] Others warn against perpetrators misusing cultural means for reconciliation as a pretext for an easy escape from being held accountable for their misdeeds, a prominent theme in Thufail's (2007) discussion on how the Indonesian military tried to (mis)use *islah* to make peace with the victims of the 1984 violence in Tanjung Priok (an urban district in Northern Jakarta) and in Leena Avonius' chapter in this volume (compare Forsberg 2003: 77). In 'Reconciliation and human rights in post-conflict Aceh', Avonius explores the role of the traditional justice mechanism called *peusijuek* in the reconciliation process in Aceh after the peace agreement that was signed between the Indonesian government and the Free Aceh Movement GAM in August 2005. International monitors, who were invited to watch the implementation of the agreement and the human rights situation, warned of a misuse of the ritual, which is traditionally meant to settle minor disputes, by political or military elites. Analyzing the dynamics of *peusijuek* practices in the post-conflict situation in Aceh, Avonius seeks an answer to the broader question of whether the global human rights discourse and local methods of reconciliation are compatible, and if so, how they could best be combined in peace processes.

Avonius' and Adam's contributions clearly illustrate the dilemmas arising out of practiced legal pluralism, a long-established conception in legal anthropology that can provide important insights for the human rights-culture debate and the relatively new idea of Bloomfield's multidimensional concept of justice. A main assumption of the legal pluralism approach is that people in an interconnected world have several legal sources to draw on: from the local, the national, and the international level, that is, customary, state, and international law such as human rights. Of course, actual accessibility is another question. These different systems, just as the different levels of society, do not exist in isolation; they are intertwined, possibly hierarchized depending on the sociopolitical context, the applicants' motives, and who is involved in the case at stake, and they influence each other (just like the international human rights debate influences the discourse on the local level, does the latter influence the human rights discourse, etc.). Essentializing any of those justice systems would ignore these interdependencies and risk a one-sided and distorted perspective. Legal pluralism, on the one hand, allows people to "shop for justice" (Schaerf 1997, quoted in Stevens 2001: 169), on the other hand it can create problematic legal ambivalences and uncertainties as Adam (this volume) shows. Based on an in-depth study of a community of refugees on Ambon island (Moluccas), Jeroen Adam's chapter 'The problem of going home: land management, displacement, and reconciliation in Ambon' illustrates how problems of displacement and land tenure affect processes of peace-building and inter-religious social interaction in contemporary Ambon. Adam argues that the migration of religious minorities opened opportunities for new elites to successfully negotiate access to abandoned lands and that one means of claiming access to these lands was through a revitalization of *adat* politics. Legal uncertainties arising out of the parallelity of different legal systems created problems for migrated communities to return home, which has become a source of frustration that still provokes an inarticulate religious inspired friction and has a negative impact on the reconciliation process.

Human rights advocates are also concerned about the hierarchical power structures in some traditional societies where people might not have an equal say in the conflict resolution process or traditional leaders are partial or even open to corruption and bribery. They are worried about the reinforcement of inequalities according to gender, age, or other status, and about inhuman punishments (Stevens 2001: 127–8). Chapter 8 of this volume addresses the gender concern. As the many cases of sexual abuse, rape, and forced prostitution during violent conflicts show, women are often victimized in a particularly humiliating way. After the violence, many women are left without their husbands, with deep physical and/or psychological scars, with social stigmatization, and have sometimes even been impregnated by the 'enemy'. In cases where many men have died during armed conflict, women have to take over and are in charge of rebuilding livelihoods. It is often women who get active as peace agents at the community level during and after the conflict to restore relationships with their neighbors and daily life; it is they who have to take care of their children, go to the markets, and provide the daily meals.[30] It would therefore seem to be most obvious to take their roles into account when it comes to setting up rehabilitation and reconciliation procedures (Green & Ahmed 1999: 192). Nevertheless, women are often in a disadvantaged position in both retributive and traditional restorative justice systems. They are rarely provided space to express their own sufferings, neither in TRCs nor in traditional or informal justice forums (Hayner 2002: 77; Minow 1998: 84; Stevens 2001: 2; Theidon 2007: 116–8). This has various reasons, such as the sociocultural context, that does not allow women to speak up for themselves in the public and does not include them in conflict-solving mechanisms, the dominant role of men in armed conflicts, women's socially and politically invisibility, women's shame and hesitance to talk about their pain, their lack of experience in dealing with authorities, the seeming apolitical nature of rape, or simply the ignorance or helplessness of the architects of reconciliation processes.[31] Alternative grassroots initiatives are therefore essential for women's and their dependants' physical and mental restoration and survival. Tri Subagya's chapter on 'Women's agencies for peace-building and reconciliation: voices from Poso, Sulawesi' provides some insightful material. In line with the international trend described earlier, Subagya stresses that most of the studies on violence and local conflicts in post-Suharto Indonesia have paid little attention to gender issues. Women are mostly described as passive victims and men as the ones who make war and engage in political decision making. These simple dichotomies do not reflect the important role women play during times of conflict when it comes to taking care of casualties, supporting logistics, or looking after their children. Taking the peace process in Poso (Central Sulawesi) as a case study, this chapter analyzes women's initiatives in promoting reconciliation and peace-building and argues that women's agencies essentially influence both conflict and post-conflict dynamics. Subagya therefore strongly promotes a more gendered perspective on reconciliation processes not only in Poso, but in any conflict setting.

Victim-perpetrator conceptualizations

The last three chapters of this volume deal with reconciliation initiatives in connection with the 1965–66 massacres in Indonesia, when hundreds of thousands of people were killed due to their alleged involvement in an alleged communist coup d'état, when Indonesia's first president Sukarno was replaced by the former general Suharto who had suppressed the coup, and when the so-called Old Order (*Orde Lama*), that is the Sukarno era, turned into the New Order (*Orde Baru*). Together with Hatley's chapter introduced earlier, these contributions explore a variety of approaches towards how grassroots try to cope with the aftermath of the pogrom that still invisibly divides society in certain parts of Indonesia. The 1965–66 tragedy was both a vertical and a horizontal conflict, in which the military chased and murdered the 'communists' and also mobilized their fellow citizens to join the killings. Since so many different parts of the Indonesian population were involved, there are no traditional justice mechanisms in place that could possibly provide a solution and bridge the divide. Due to the Indonesian government's silence, the grassroots have had to develop their own approaches to how to rebuild relationships, how to come to terms with the past, and how to initiate the recategorization process suggested by Gaertner and Dovidio (2000). The two dominant issues in these debates, therefore, are how to bridge the divided memories of these events and how to dissolve deeply ingrained victim-perpetrator categories.

Hornbacher and other contributors already warned against the perpetuation of the classic victim-perpetrator divide, on which a major part of the peace and conflict literature and most high-level approaches to reconciliation are based.[32] This is not to say that these differentiations do not play a role in grassroots initiatives or traditional justice mechanisms. But there are important differences in how to address or bridge the victim-perpetrator divide and try to achieve reconciliation. As Biggar (2003a: 309) rightly stated, in most conflicts there is "a basic disagreement about who the guilty perpetrators and the genuine victims really are". This is even more so when identity issues are involved. In some cases, where conflict lines and dynamics are more complex, where it was, for instance, not a vicious authoritarian regime victimizing its own people, this might not only be a matter of different perceptions of people directly involved in or affected by the violence. Under these circumstances there are just no clear-cut boundaries between victims and perpetrators, which makes it extremely difficult for common conflict resolution and reconciliation tools that are either perpetrator-oriented (e.g. retributive justice) or more victim-oriented (e.g. truth commissions). And what about conflict situations where both 'victims' and 'perpetrators' come from the same families or were former neighbors, as for example in Cambodia during the Khmer Rouge regime (Rigby 2001: 3), in Mozambique (Hayner 2002: 189), in Peru (Theidon 2007), or in many of the conflicts we deal with in this volume? Or cultures, where such a sharp divide between a human victim and an inhuman perpetrator, the good and the evil, does not exist, or responsibilities for the people's fate are shared by all (see Telle and Hornbacher this volume)?[33] It is therefore essential to pay attention to how people affected by conflict and involved in reconciliation processes understand human nature and personhood, that is 'the self' and 'others' (Avruch *et al.* 1998: 15). In other cases again, the blurring of boundaries could be a strategic move – be it culturally determined or as an innovative approach to bridge the divide – in order to cope with the past violence.[34] As participants of an international conference on 'From dealing with the past to future cooperation: regional and global challenges of reconciliation' stated, it is also important to include 'bystanders' in the reconciliation process and to consider that the roles of victims, perpetrators, and bystanders might change over time and/or that individuals might be at once victim, perpetrator, and bystander (GTZ & FES 2005).

The time factor in the studies dealing with the 1965–66 case is crucial. The people involved had more than four decades to either solidify or rethink their memories. The oppressive political atmosphere under Suharto made the latter, that is, the questioning of the official version of the past incidents almost impossible. Only after the step down of the authoritarian Suharto regime did an intense process of renegotiating local and national histories, collective memories, and identities set in; this is an important prerequisite for reconciliation and reconciliatory initiatives as they are described in Sulistiyanto's and Setyadi's, McGregor's, and Leksana's chapters. It is often argued that the past has to be dealt with properly in both inter- and intrastate post-conflict phases, otherwise unreconciled issues will come up again at one point in the future and maybe trigger further violence (Biggar 2003a, 2003b: 5; Bloomfield 2006: 9; Forsberg 2003: 80; Oberschall 2007: 227; Smyth 2003: 150). However, there are different perceptions of how to remember and deal with past violence 'properly', as already raised in the TRC section, and how much truth has to be brought to light right away (Biggar 2003a: 318). History education is an essential means for the formation of a new collective memory and as a long-term measure to maintain peace and foster reconciliation (compare Huyse 2003d: 28). This becomes especially important in such cases as 1965–66, where large parts of the population were affected. Grace Leksana's chapter on 'Reconciliation through history education: reconstructing the social memory of the 1965–66 violence in Indonesia' analyzes the role of history education in Indonesia as a means to deconstruct a unified collective memory, uncover hidden memories, and foster reconciliation. Symbols and media such as monuments, films, and books play an important role in the manipulation and the deconstruction of memory and the perception of the other (compare Ellis 2006: 19). For more than three decades the Suharto regime had implemented a single narrative of the 1965–66 tragedy, which is still alive almost a decade after its downfall and poses a major impediment to peace and reconciliation processes between people considered as 'perpetrators' and 'victims' of the bloody incident. Leksana promotes efforts in reforming history education as important means to transform conflicting values and identities, acknowledge the victim's victimhood, and achieve reconciliation. But she also discusses the difficulties coming along with this reformation process such as the problems encountered when trying to provide space for a greater variety of people to speak about their memories and their experiences. She also uncovers the fear of many Indonesians to seemingly put national unity at risk through questioning New Order myths and their hesitance to accept that their world view, including established victim-perpetrator categories, needs to be turned upside down. It is also apparent that elites that were installed under Suharto and remained powerful after his step down, want to preserve their interests by trying to prevent the reversal of the New Order's structures and value systems.

Both are important for sustainable reconciliation: to officially acknowledge the suffering and victimhood of victims and provide them relief in whatever form, and to explore the motivations of the offenders and try to reintegrate them into society. The dignity and the humanity of both victims and offenders have to be reinstalled; and this can only be done in a culturally appropriate way.[35] These are the main objectives of the initiatives analyzed by Priyambudi Sulistiyanto and Rumekso Setyadi in this volume. In 'Civil society and grassroots reconciliation in Central Java', they examine the failure of reconciliation initiatives at the national level and argue for the importance of civil society in pursuing grassroots reconciliation activities in the post-Suharto period. They focus on reconciliation activities of Syarikat, an NGO based in Yogyakarta, Central Java, which was initiated by one of the largest Muslim organizations in Indonesia, the Nahdlatul Ulama (NU). Syarikat publishes journals, books, and documentaries, organizes workshops, exhibitions, and closed-door meetings, bringing victims and those who had participated in or had firsthand knowledge of the 1965–66 tragedy together to share their personal stories. These initiatives are aimed at breaking down prejudices and (re)building relationships and at the same time involving Indonesian society in the process regardless of whether victim, perpetrator, or bystander, which might open a path for reconciliation. The chapter discusses both potential and limitations of these initiatives. Whereas the empowerment of civil society and the collective efforts of the grassroots are seen as essential for the realization of reconciliation in Indonesia, a major concern is how small-scale initiatives such as the ones analyzed in the chapter can be carried out on a larger scale that addresses society at large and involves a wide range of social, cultural, and religious organizations.

Katharine McGregor also takes Syarikat's activism as one of the main pegs for her study. Although both chapters reflect on possibilities of how to rebuild relationships and bridge the memory divide, McGregor takes these issues in a very different direction. Drawing on Abu-Nimer's work, among others, she is particularly interested in the religious aspect of reconciliation. 'A bridge and a barrier: Islam, reconciliation and the 1965 killings in Indonesia' explores alternate notions of Islamic identity and how ideas of Islam are deployed for the purposes of opposing or accepting reconciliation. In the wake of the failed 'coup' of 1965 the Indonesian army together with religious vigilantes perpetrated a wave of mass killings of alleged communists. Followers of Ansor, the youth wing of NU, were particularly active in the killings. For the duration of the New Order regime, senior members of Ansor publicly promoted their heroism as 'saving the nation from communism'. The end of the Suharto regime has, however, prompted the expression of different views from within NU on 1965–66 and thus the blurring of the victim-perpetrator boundaries. This chapter probes the reasons behind these polarized positions on reconciliation and reflects on what factors have facilitated and inhibited support for reconciliation within this complex religious constituency. One of the problems studied by McGregor that has an impact on Indonesian society at large: the rise of conservative Islamic (as well as Islamist) groups that accuse, for instance, Abdurrahman Wahid's pluralist traditions of distorting the teachings of Islam and so-called 'leftist Islam' to be communists, that criticize 'modernity' and capitalism, and that are actively carrying out their mission (*dakwah*) throughout Indonesia (compare also Barton 2005 and Sidel 2007). In McGregor's case, conservative members of NU try to preserve the image of the biggest Muslim organization in Indonesia through the denial of its members' involvement in the 1965–66 massacres and through the accusations and criticism noted earlier. Due to its dimensions, the 1965–66 tragedy requires reconciliation on a national scale. It has to include issues of reparation and rehabilitation and address justice issues, which, in the end, is only possible if the central government is willing to substantially support the process, which is still not the case in Indonesia. Nevertheless, the initiatives taken on the various levels and described in the chapters by Hatley, Leksana, McGregor, and Sulistiyanto and Setyadi are revolutionary in the sense that they would not have been conceivable under the Suharto regime. Considering the official hesitance to face up to the past, the opening up of these new spaces for reconciliation are important steps on the long road to national reconciliation. As Zurbuchen (2005b: 16) put it: "The issue of 'giving voice' to ordinary Indonesians' experiences of the past means a powerful shift in the way agency and authority are generally articulated".

'Lessons learned?'

All contributors to this volume take up issues developed in the introductory theoretical framework, analyze their implications in specific sociocultural contexts, and provide new insights concerning the questions raised: how people involved in various kinds of conflicts deal differently with past violence, with 'truth', and with the future; the different ways to deconstruct unified narratives of conflicts, to uncover hidden memories (as an alternative means of truth seeking), to reconcile divided memories, and/or to create new shared memories and realities; they uncover the complexities of victim-perpetrator conceptualizations and the (dis)advantages of identifying them, if possible; they analyze what role tradition, traditional leaders, and/or the misuse of traditional justice mechanisms play and could play; what impact land issues, human rights, and legal pluralism can have on reconciliation processes; how religion can legitimize conflict or peace; what role the individual, the community, humanity, collective reconciliation, and the notion of cosmological balance play; they challenge the neglect of women's role in conflict and reconciliation; and they explore symbols, ceremonies, and rituals as ingredients of locally rooted reconciliation processes. What becomes clear is that reconciliation cannot be a matter of *either ... or*, justice *or* truth, reconciliation *or* justice, retributive *or* restorative justice, top-down *or* bottom-up, and so on. Rather, it is a matter of pulling the right strings at the right time. One has to carefully analyze each individual setting and see what is feasible and possible; if there is simply no truth and reconciliation infrastructure at the moment in Indonesia, for instance, then, of course, people can fight for it, but they also have to think about alternatives as in what to do in the meanwhile, and how to recover and rebuild relationships on their level and with their neighbors.

In his chapter in Abu-Nimer's *Reconciliation, Justice, and Coexistence*, Galtung (2001) introduces twelve different approaches to reconciliation, including reparation, apology, theology, punishment, co-dependence, theater, joint healing, reconstruction, and conflict resolution. But he also stresses that there is no panacea, that "none of the approaches is capable of handling the complexity of the after-violence situation, healing so many kinds of wounds, closing the violence cycles, and reconciling the parties to themselves, to each other, and to whatever higher forces there may be" (Galtung 2001: 19). Sometimes it makes sense to identify and punish perpetrators right away when the sociopolitical context allows this; in other cases it is preferable, at least for the moment, to advance the idea of "cooperating to plug the holes in the boat we share rather than searching for the one who drilled the first hole" (Galtung 2001: 11). In the long run, and as Galtung would be the first to point out, structural problems, including political and economic, and root causes underlying a conflict need to be addressed in order to create long-lasting peace and sustainable reconciliation.

In all our chapters the impacts of national and international developments on the local level are obvious; often they are the ones that caused insecurity and conflict in the regions in the first place: the global 'war on terror' in Hornbacher's case; the conflicts flaring up in many places in Indonesia, which triggered a heightened need for security among the Indonesian population and led to the emergence of self-proclaimed security groups at the local level (Telle); tragedies and unrests on a national level such as in 1965–66 and in May 1998 (Hatley, Leksana, McGregor, and Sulistiyanto and Setyadi); major environmental disasters (Hatley); newly emerging radical Islamic groups that move to the outer regions of Indonesia (Adam, Bräuchler, Subagya); and the center's struggle to prevent parts of its territory, such as Aceh, to break away (Avonius). These factors, among others, also influence the initiatives on behalf of peace and reconciliation discussed in the various case studies of this volume. Exaggerated enthusiasm based on the observed increasing agency on the grassroots level is yet inappropriate. Small-scale initiatives might be threatened, their effectiveness diminished, by developments on the larger national level, be it the rise of religious radicalism or the persistence of old power structures that exert their influence when it comes to issues such as the 1965–66 tragedy, for instance, or Aceh's fight for independence. Another factor influencing Indonesians on all levels is the still precarious human rights situation (see above). As Sulistiyanto and Setyadi acknowledge in their chapter: "Only small groups of victims and participants are involved in these reconciliation events. Yet the number of human rights abuses in Indonesia runs into millions, and they are found throughout Indonesia." Many of the human rights violations can be attributed to the military that is still rarely held accountable for it. Although important reform laws have been passed in the *Era Reformasi* (e.g. TNI law 34/2004), the reforms have not been sufficiently reinforced by the current government and the military is still influential in Indonesia. The traditional dual function (*dwi fungsi*) of the military, that is, its role in the security and the political sector, was officially abolished in the post-Suharto years, but the territorial command structure still exists and guarantees the military considerable control and influence on all levels. Moreover, military business activities still run at full speed. Another reform undertaken in the post-Suharto era was the official split of the army and the police, which, on the one hand, should have helped to allow the army to focus on defense matters, but, on the other hand, led to a power struggle between the two institutions (see e.g. Honna 2008). All this has major impacts on how 'the state' deals with conflicts both on a local or national level and it inhibits an encompassing empowerment of civil society in Indonesia (including religious groupings, opposition parties, social movements, the various media groups, etc.) that still remains vulnerable to domination by those in power. The list could be continued.

As this book's case studies illustrate, the Indonesian people – in the absence or the failure of 'a reconciliation toolkit' or functioning state mechanisms – address the struggle over memory differently, dependent on the scale of the conflict, the people involved, the sociocultural setting, the history of the localities involved, and when the violence had happened. In each conflict setting, there are different versions of the history of the conflict and different interpretations of the past that have to be reconciled one way or the other. This volume can thus provide useful comparative material for future research in the field of reconciliation and transitional justice. It is, however, difficult to say how far local mechanisms can address and transform the broader political dynamics in the long run that may have created the conflicts in the first place. And it is difficult, if not impossible, to measure the impact of all these larger scale factors on the various reconciliation initiatives described in this book. This is certainly not just an issue for the contributions in this volume but for transitional justice mechanisms in general.[36] One reason is that all peace and reconciliation initiatives dealt with here are multidimensional and ongoing processes. A lot more needs to be invested and a lot more time has to pass in order to make sound judgments. Again this underscores that reconciliation must be understood as a multilayered process and that, in the long run, it is essential to address the underlying structural issues driving conflicts.

In spite of all this, as this book demonstrates, the grassroots are not doomed to inactivity. What I would like to stress in these concluding remarks is that it is most important in my eyes that peace practitioners at all levels stop seeing grassroots people in general and victims in particular as mere passive recipients of conflict, peace, and reconciliation aid, and acknowledge their agency. Pouligny, Chesterman, and Schnabel (2007: 3, 10) have argued that it is necessary "to find ways to recognize [the transformation of passive victims] ... into survivors and begin ... to see them as *actors*" and, directly linked to this, to identify and utilize local resources and "cultural competence"[37]. Internationally, researchers and practitioners are increasingly becoming aware of this, but, as suggested by the lack of publications, those working on Indonesia seem to lag behind. As this volume shows, people and organizations at the grassroots level in Indonesia take action on behalf of reconciliation and peace, often under difficult circumstances, and these initiatives often encounter or bring along problems. We have to analyze how people on the ground who become active and creatively address local and national issues, but at the same time remain embedded in their specific sociocultural context, may contribute to, or even initiate reconciliation. To develop an understanding of local perspectives on conflict, peace, and reconciliation dynamics, it is important to listen to people, try to get access to their social memories and critically uncover the complexity of identity-construction processes in both conflict and peacemaking.

It is crucial to acknowledge that culture plays an important role, not only in conflict, but also in grassroots reconciliation processes. At the same time, a proper notion of 'culture' is a prerequisite for the success of culture-oriented approaches to reconciliation: a notion that does not reify culture, does not simplify or overly harmonize it, and does not allow it to be exploited by individuals at the community's expense. Both the analysis and the development of approaches to reconciliation therefore need to rely on in-depth analyses of the preceding conflict, its aftermath, the changes it caused and the sociocultural setting in which all this took place, and analyses of possible actors and hindrances, just as this book's contributions do.

Acknowledgments

I would like to thank Kari Telle, Gerry van Klinken, Maribeth Erb, and Chua Beng Huat for their helpful comments on an earlier version of this introduction. I would also like to thank the Asia Research Institute (ARI) for giving me the opportunity to present a draft in the prestigious ARI seminar series and the audience for their constructive feedback. Thanks to Mark Selden for his feedback on a final draft.

Notes

1 See Avruch et al. (1998: 2), Darby (2003: 252), Ginty (2003: 235), Hamber (2003: 82), Huyse (2003a: 163).
2 According to Huyse (2008b: 15), in most African societies, for instance, "guilt and punishment, victimhood and reparation are viewed as collective", whereas "modern justice systems are designed to identify individual responsibility".
3 For some examples see Bertrand (2004), Colombijn and Lindblad (2002), Coppel (2006), Hüsken and de Jonge (2002), Sidel (2007), van Klinken (2007), Wessel and Wimhöfer (2001).
4 'Tradition' and 'traditional justice' are put in inverted commas here in order to indicate that, although these elements and mechanisms are considered to be traditional, they are nonetheless continuously changed, adapted, or reinvented one way or another. The inverted commas will be omitted in subsequent usage.
5 For the development of transitional justice mechanisms compare also Teitel (2000).
6 Compare Rigby (2001). For a comprehensive analysis of truth and reconciliation commissions worldwide, see Hayner (2002).
7 See Bloomfield (2006: 18–9), Fischer and Ropers (2004: 11), Galtung (2001), Huyse (2008b: 3). According to Lederach (1997) the four elements of reconciliation are truth, mercy, justice, and peace. In a reconciliation handbook of the International Institute for Democracy and Electoral Assistance, reconciliation is promoted as an umbrella term for the "over-arching process which includes the search for truth, justice, forgiveness, healing and so on" (Bloomfield 2003b, 2006: 11). Bar-Tal and Bennink (2004) provide a more extensive list of reconciliation methods that includes apology, truth and reconciliation commissions, public trials, reparations payments, writing a common history, education, mass media, publicized meetings between representatives of the groups, the work of NGOs, joint projects, tourism, and cultural exchanges. In parallel, John McDonald and Louise Diamond developed the concept of multi-track diplomacy, thus expanding track-one and track-two approaches, that differentiated between governmental and non-governmental actions, arguing that conflict resolution has to take several levels into account in order to be successful: the government, professional conflict resolution, business, private citizens, research, training and education, activism, religious, funding, and public opinion/communication (McDonald 2003).

8 For a comprehensive overview of transitional justice see e.g. Kritz (1995). See also Daly and Sarkin (2007), Merwe (2003), Minow (1998), Rigby (2001).
9 For a more extensive account of the shortcomings and risks of retributive justice in reconciliation and peace processes, see Huyse (2003b).
10 See also Hayner (2002: 81, 83), Pankhurst (1999: 343), Rigby (2001: 9).
11 For an overview see e.g. Aspinall and Fealy (2003), Bach (2003), Kivimäki *et al.* (2002).
12 See e.g. Davidson and Henley (2007), Schulte Nordholt and van Klinken (2007).
13 See e.g. Bräuchler (2008), Juwana (2006).
14 See also a publication by the International Center for Islam and Pluralism in Jakarta on the *Revitalisation of Local Wisdom* and its use for conflict resolution and peace-building in Sulawesi, Kalimantan, and Maluku (Amirrachman 2007b).
15 Since there is no universal idea about what reconciliation exactly is and implies, using the term might even turn out to be counterproductive as a report by the Deutsche Gesellschaft für Technische Zusammenarbeit and the Friedrich-Ebert-Stiftung demonstrates: "In some environments, the term reconciliation might be the last to use. It might not translate well into the culture. Furthermore, the notion that reconciliation means closure can be threatening to victims, notably when it is attached to one time initiatives and not communicated as being a slow and open process in which the individual retains the right not to reconcile" (GTZ & FES 2005: 6).
16 See e.g. Hornbacher (this volume) and Nader (1998: 41).
17 See also endnote 15 and compare Bloomfield (2006: 16, 25), Pankhurst (1999: 240). Several people have already tried to conceptualize and clarify the reconciliation concept. For an earlier attempt see Pankhurst (1999), for a more recent and more comprehensive one see Bloomfield (2006).
18 Of major impact was a report written by Stevens (2001) and published by Penal Reform International on *Access to Justice in Sub-Saharan Africa: The Role of Traditional and Informal Justice Systems* (see also, e.g. Bloomfield *et al.* 2003; Bloomfield 2006; Roht-Arriaza & Mariezcurrena 2006). Next to retributive and restorative justice, Bloomfield (2006: 21) introduced the terms "regulatory" and "social justice," the former being concerned about "the broader issue of setting fair rules for all social behavior," the latter about the fair sharing of all 'goods' in a society.
19 For the most salient features of traditional justice systems see Stevens (2001). Compare also Bloomfield *et al.* (2003), Boege (2006), and a special issue of the *Asia Pacific Journal of Anthropology* 8(1), 2007, on 'Traditional Justice in East Timor'. Despite these common features, there are also significant socioculturally determined differences in how the various mechanisms deal with the past, how they try to restore the victims, and whether offenders need to be identified and sanctioned or not. In Bougainville, for instance, a consensus about the facts and the truth has to be achieved and perpetrators can then confess their wrongdoings, apologize, and ask for forgiveness (Boege 2006: 8). In Kari Telle's study of a Sasak community on Lombok Island (this volume), the identity of the offender is not to be exposed.
20 See Babo-Soares (2004), Daly and Sarkin (2007: 85–6), Hayner (2002: 192), Huyse and Salter (2008), Tom (2006).
21 For a more detailed list of advantages and strengths of traditional and informal justice see Boege (2006: 11, 13), Stevens (2001: 126–7).
22 Although a focus on the grassroots is of essential importance, a certain leadership is nonetheless often required to mobilize the masses. According to Bar-Tal and Bennink (2004: 28) this could be "prominent figures in ethnic, religious, economic, academic, intellectual, and humanitarian circles" and it should include leaders on different levels.
23 In promoting communication as a means for reconciliation Ellis refers to Kelman (2004), but also to Varshney (2002) who argued that those communities in India that have a higher level of daily interaction between their Hindu and Muslim population compared to others are much less prone to communal violence.

24 Bar-Tal and Bennink (2004) have described reconciliation as a process and an outcome in reaction to the prevailing perception of reconciliation as a peaceful status quo after a conflict has been settled and the warring parties have been reconciled.
25 That is the very basic, but at the same time quite comprehensive definition the International Institute for Democracy and Electoral Assistance offers in their reconciliation handbook (Bloomfield 2003b: 13).
26 See e.g. Abu-Nimer *et al.* (2001: 344), Ginty (2003: 235).
27 See also, e.g. Bergmann (2007: 35) and the various projects of the Theatre Embassy worldwide, specifically in Central America (http://www.theater-embassy.org/huellas/index2.html).
28 See e.g. Boege (2006: 15), Huyse (2003b: 113, 2008a: 182–4), IDEA (2006a: 10, 2006b), McWilliam (2007b).
29 Two of the most prominent examples where international and national architects of post-conflict justice and reconciliation explicitly integrated local traditional justice mechanisms are East Timor and Rwanda. For a discussion of the achievements and shortcomings of these cases see, for East Timor, Babo-Soares (2004), Kent (2004) and, for Rwanda, Buckley-Zistel (2005), Daly and Sarkin (2007: 84), IDEA (2006a: 11), Lehmann (2003), Oberschall (2007: 222–3), Stevens (2001: 73–9), Uvin (2003), Vandeginste (2003b). For more examples where traditional mechanisms have been integrated into broader justice seeking structures after massive violence in various countries in Africa, see, e.g. Gibbs (1997: 232), IDEA (2006a), Ocen (2007), Tom (2006).
30 See e.g. Bloomfield (2003b: 13), Marantika (2007). Discussing the Madurese-Dayak conflicts on Kalimantan, Indonesia, Sukandar (2007) provides a good overview of the gradually growing body of literature not only on women as victims of conflict, but also on their roles as combatants and peace activists. Compare Bouta *et al.* (2004), Mazurana *et al.* (2005).
31 See Hayner (2002: 77–9), Huyse (2003e: 56), Kumar (1997: 23–4).
32 Although some authors advise that local reconciliation processes need to take the "complexities of victim and perpetrator identities" (Merwe 2003: 122) into account and that the "language of reconciliation" should not attempt to even further divide the societies in focus (Daly & Sarkin 2007: 70), the reconciliation literature in general does not pay enough attention to these concerns. In cases where this divide does nevertheless make sense, there is still a need to deal with both sides equally, especially in societies or communities, where they have to live together again after the violence.
33 Compare also Daly and Sarkin (2007: 78), Galtung (2001: 11). In South Africa, the *ubuntu* concept, a short form for the notion of humanity and "a person is a person through other people" (http://www.shikanda.net/general/gen3/research_page/ubuntu.htm, 23.3.2006), has helped many victims to forgive and to reintegrate the perpetrators into the communities, at least according to Archbishop Desmond Tutu (Bloomfield 2003a: 46; Rigby 2001: 10). For a comprehensive discussion of the *ubuntu* concept, see Kamwangamalu (1999).
34 Galtung, for instance, suggested that there are different options of how affected people can deal with the divide, they could either emphasize "*an actor-oriented perspective*" and individual responsibility that would make healing more difficult, or "*a structure-*" or "*culture-oriented perspective*" that enables both sides to see themselves as victims of external factors, which would make the reconciliation and healing process easier, although it might not necessarily be the full truth (2001: 5, emphasis in the original).
35 Compare Bloomfield (2006: 22), Huyse (2003c: 67, 72), Minow (1998: 146), Theidon (2007), Vandeginste (2003a: 148).
36 I thank Kari Telle for this useful comment.
37 Emphasis in the original.

References

Abu-Nimer, M., Said, A.A. and Prelis, L.S. (2001) 'Conclusion: the long road to reconciliation', in M. Abu-Nimer (ed.) *Reconciliation, Justice, and Coexistence: Theory & Practice*, Lanham, MD: Lexington Books.
Amirrachman, A. (2007a) 'Pendahuluan: revitalisasi kearifan lokal untuk perdamaian', in A. Amirrachman (ed.) *Revitalisasi Kearifan Lokal: Studi Resolusi Konflik di Kalimantan Barat, Maluku dan Poso*, Jakarta: International Center for Islam and Pluralism (ICIP).
—— (ed.) (2007b) *Revitalisasi Kearifan Lokal: Studi Resolusi Konflik di Kalimantan Barat, Maluku dan Poso*, Jakarta: International Center for Islam and Pluralism (ICIP).
Aspinall, E. and Fealy, G. (eds) (2003) *Local Power and Politics in Indonesia: Decentralisation & Democratisation*, Singapore: Institute of Southeast Asian Studies.
Avruch, K. (1998) *Culture and Conflict Resolution*, Washington DC: United States Institute of Peace Press.
Avruch, K., Black, P.W. and Scimecca, J.A. (eds) (1998) *Conflict Resolution: Cross-Cultural Perspectives*, Westport, Connecticut: Praeger.
Babo-Soares, D. (2004) 'Nahe Biti: the philosophy and process of grassroots reconciliation (and justice) in East Timor', *The Asia Pacific Journal of Anthropology*, 5(1): 15–33.
Bach, J.-M. (2003) *Dezentralisierung und Lokalregierung in Indonesien seit 1998: Der Fall Riau*, Studien zur Volkswirtschaft des Vorderen Orients 11, Münster: LIT.
Bar-Tal, D. and Bennink, G.H. (2004) 'The Nature of Reconciliation as an Outcome and as a Process', in Y. Bar-Siman-Tov (ed.) *From Conflict Resolution to Reconciliation*, Oxford: Oxford University Press.
Barton, G. (2005) *Jemaah Islamiyah: Radical Islamism in Indonesia*, Singapore: NUS Press.
Bergmann, U. (2007) 'Heute Friedenshelden von morgen fördern: Projekt zur Friedenserziehung von Kindern und Jugendlichen', *ded Brief (Zeitschrift des Deutschen Entwicklungsdienstes)*, 44(4: Postkonfliktsituationen in Afrika): 34–5.
Bertrand, J. (2004) *Nationalism and Ethnic Conflict in Indonesia*, Cambridge: Cambridge University Press.
Biggar, N. (2003a) 'Conclusion', in N. Biggar (ed.) *Burying the Past: Making Peace and Doing Justice After Civil Conflict*, Washington DC: Georgetown University Press.
—— (2003b) 'Making peace or doing justice: must we choose?', in N. Biggar (ed.) *Burying the Past: Making Peace and Doing Justice After Civil Conflict*, Washington DC: Georgetown University Press.
Bloomfield, D. (2003a) 'The context of reconciliation', in D. Bloomfield, T. Barnes and L. Huyse (eds) *Reconciliation After Violent Conflict: A Handbook*, Stockholm: International Institute for Democracy and Electoral Assistance (IDEA).
—— (2003b) 'Reconciliation: an introduction', in D. Bloomfield, T. Barnes and L. Huyse (eds) *Reconciliation After Violent Conflict: A Handbook*, Stockholm: International Institute for Democracy and Electoral Assistance (IDEA).
—— (2006) 'On good terms: clarifying reconciliation', Berghof Report No. 14, Berlin: Berghof Research Center for Constructive Conflict Management.
Bloomfield, D., Barnes, T. and Huyse, L. (eds) (2003) *Reconciliation After Violent Conflict: A Handbook*, Stockholm: International Institute for Democracy and Electoral Assistance (IDEA).
Boege, V. (2006) 'Traditional approaches to conflict transformation – potentials and limits', *Berghof Research Center for Constructive Conflict Management*. Online. Available at: http://www.berghof-handbook.net (accessed on 23 March 2007).

Bouta, T., Frerks, G. and Bannon, I. (2004) *Gender, Conflict, and Development*, Washington DC: World Bank Publications.

Bräuchler, B. (2008) 'Reflections on human rights and self-determination in Eastern Indonesia'. Unpublished manuscript

Bräuchler, B. and Widlok, T. (eds) (2007) Die Revitalisierung von Tradition/The Revitalisation of Tradition, *Zeitschrift für Ethnologie*, 132 (special issue).

Buckley-Zistel, S. (2005) '"The truth heals"? *Gacaca* jurisdictions and the consolidation of peace in Rwanda', *Die Friedens-Warte*, 80(1–2): 1–17.

Chronis, I. (2006) 'Culture is a basic need: responding to cultural emergencies', Conference Report, 25–26 September 2006, De Koninklijke Schouwburg, The Hague, The Netherlands: Prince Claus Fund.

Chua, B.H. (2004) 'Communitarian politics in Asia', in B.H. Chua (ed.) *Communitarian Politics in Asia*, London and New York: Routledge.

Colombijn, F. and Lindblad, J.T. (eds) (2002) *Roots of Violence in Indonesia: Contemporary Violence in Historical Perspective*, Leiden: KITLV Press.

Coppel, C.A. (ed.) (2006) *Violent Conflicts in Indonesia: Analysis, Representation, Resolution*, London and New York: Routledge.

Crouch, H. (2004) 'Political transition and communal violence', in A. Heijmans, N. Simmonds and H.v.d. Veen (eds) *Searching for Peace in Asia Pacific: An Overview of Conflict Prevention and Peacebuilding Activities*, Boulder and London: Lynne Rienner Publishers.

Culbertson, R. and Pouligny, B. (2007) 'Re-imagining peace after mass crime: A dialogical exchange between insider and outsider knowledge', in B. Pouligny, S. Chesterman and A. Schnabel (eds) *After Mass Crime: Rebuilding States and Communities*, Tokyo and New York: United Nations University Press.

Daly, E. and Sarkin, J. (2007) *Reconciliation in Divided Societies: Finding Common Ground*, Philadelphia, Pa.: University of Pennsylvania Press.

Darby, J. (2003) 'Borrowing and lending in peace processes', in J. Darby and R.M. Ginty (eds) *Contemporary Peacemaking: Conflict, Violence and Peace Processes*, Basingstoke, Hampshire: Palgrave Macmillan.

Davidson, J.S. and Henley, D. (eds) (2007) *The Revival of Tradition in Indonesian Politics: The Deployment of Adat from Colonialism to Indigenism*, London: Routledge.

Ellis, D.G. (2006) *Transforming Conflict: Communication and Ethnopolitical Conflict*, Lanham: Rowman & Littlefield.

Fischer, M. and Ropers, N. (2004) 'Introduction: Berghof handbook for conflict transformation', *Berghof Research Center for Constructive Conflict Management*. Online. Available at: http://www.berghof-handbook.net (accessed on 23 March 2007).

Forsberg, T. (2003) 'The philosophy and practice of dealing with the past', in N. Biggar (ed.) *Burying the Past: Making Peace and Doing Justice After Civil Conflict*, Washington DC: Georgetown University Press.

Gaertner, S.L. and Dovidio, J.F. (2000) *Reducing Intergroup Bias: The Common Ingroup Identity Model*, Philadelphia: Taylor & Francis.

Galtung, J. (2001) 'After violence, reconstruction, reconciliation, and resolution: coping with visible and invisible effects of war and violence', in M. Abu-Nimer (ed.) *Reconciliation, Justice, and Coexistence: Theory and Practice*, Lanham, MD.: Lexington Books.

Gibbs, S. (1997) 'Postwar social reconstruction in Mozambique: reframing children's experiences of trauma and healing', in K. Kumar (ed.) *Rebuilding Societies after Civil War: Critical Roles for International Assistance*, London and Boulder: Lynne Rienner.

Ginty, R.M. (2003) 'The role of symbols in peacemaking', in J. Darby and R.M. Ginty (eds) *Contemporary Peacemaking: Conflict, Violence and Peace Processes*, Basingstoke, Hampshire: Palgrave Macmillan.

Green, R.H. and Ahmed, I.I. (1999) 'Rehabilitation, sustainable peace and development: towards reconceptualisation', *Third World Quarterly*, 20(1). 189–206.

GTZ (Deutsche Gesellschaft für Technische Zusammenarbeit GmbH) and FES (Friedrich-Ebert-Stiftung) (2005) 'Regional report working group: Southeast Asia', paper presented at the International Conference on From Dealing with the Past to Future Cooperation: Regional and Global Challenges of Reconciliation, Berlin, 31 January–2 February 2005. Online. Available at: http://www.gtz.de/de/dokumente/Regional-Report-SE-Asia-en.pdf (accessed on 10 May 2006).

Hamber, B. (2003) 'Healing', in D. Bloomfield, T. Barnes and L. Huyse (eds) *Reconciliation After Violent Conflict: A Handbook*, Stockholm: International Institute for Democracy and Electoral Assistance (IDEA).

Harrison, G. (1999) 'Conflict resolution in a "non-conflict situation": tension and reconciliation in Mecúfi, Northern Mozambique', *Review of African Political Economy*, 26(81): 407–14.

Hayner, P.B. (2002) *Unspeakable Truths: Facing the Challenge of Truth Commissions*, New York and London: Routledge.

Honna, J. (2008) 'The peace dividend: with no internal wars to fight, Yudhoyono can afford to reform the military', *Inside Indonesia*, 92(April–June).

Hüsken, F. and de Jonge, H. (eds) (2002) *Violence and Vengeance: Discontent and Conflict in New Order Indonesia*, Saarbrücken: Verlag für Entwicklungspolitik.

Huyse, L. (2003a) 'The international community', in D. Bloomfield, T. Barnes and L. Huyse (eds) *Reconciliation After Violent Conflict: A Handbook*, Stockholm: International Institute for Democracy and Electoral Assistance (IDEA).

—— (2003b) 'Justice', in D. Bloomfield, T. Barnes and L. Huyse (eds) *Reconciliation After Violent Conflict: A Handbook*, Stockholm: International Institute for Democracy and Electoral Assistance (IDEA).

—— (2003c) 'Offenders', in D. Bloomfield, T. Barnes and L. Huyse (eds) *Reconciliation After Violent Conflict: A Handbook*, Stockholm: International Institute for Democracy and Electoral Assistance (IDEA).

—— (2003d). 'The process of reconciliation', in D. Bloomfield, T. Barnes and L. Huyse (eds) *Reconciliation After Violent Conflict: A Handbook*, Stockholm: International Institute for Democracy and Electoral Assistance (IDEA).

—— (2003e) 'Victims', in D. Bloomfield, T. Barnes and L. Huyse (eds) *Reconciliation After Violent Conflict: A Handbook*, Stockholm: International Institute for Democracy and Electoral Assistance (IDEA).

—— (2008a) 'Conclusions and recommendations', in L. Huyse and M. Salter (eds) *Traditional Justice and Reconciliation after Violent Conflict: Learning from African Experiences*, Stockholm: International Institute for Democracy and Electoral Assistance (IDEA).

—— (2008b) 'Introduction: tradition-based approaches in peacemaking, transitional justice and reconciliation policies', in L. Huyse and M. Salter (eds) *Traditional Justice and Reconciliation after Violent Conflict: Learning from African Experiences*, Stockholm: International Institute for Democracy and Electoral Assistance (IDEA).

Huyse, L. and Salter, M. (eds) (2008) *Traditional Justice and Reconciliation after Violent Conflict: Learning from African Experiences*, Stockholm: International Institute for Democracy and Electoral Assistance (IDEA).

IDEA (International Institute for Democracy and Electoral Assistance) (2006a) 'Reconciliation and traditional justice: learning from African experiences', Workshop report, Pretoria, 26–27 September 2008. Online. Available at: http://www.idea.int/conflict/ traditional_justice.cfm (accessed on 8 January 2008).
—— (2006b) 'Reconciliation and traditional justice: learning from African experiences', project description. Online. Available at: http://www.idea.int/conflict/traditional_ justice.cfm (accessed on 3 July 2007).
Jacobsen, M. and Bruun, O. (eds) (2000) *Human Rights and Asian Values: Contesting National Identities and Cultural Representations in Asia*, Surrey: Curzon.
Juwana, H. (2006) 'Human rights in Indonesia', in R. Peerenboom, C.J. Petersen and A.H.Y. Chen (eds) *Human Rights in Asia: A comparative legal study of twelve Asian jurisdictions, France and the USA*, London and New York: Routledge.
Kamwangamalu, N.M. (1999) 'Ubuntu in South Africa: a sociolinguistic perspective to a pan-African concept', *A Journal of Cultural Studies*, 13(11): 24–41.
Kelman, H.C. (2004) 'Reconciliation as identity change: a social-psychological perspective', in Y. Bar-Siman-Tov (ed.) *From Conflict Resolution to Reconciliation*, Oxford: Oxford University Press.
Kent, L. (2004) 'Unfulfilled expectations: community views on CAVR's community reconciliation process', August 2004, Dili, East Timor: Judicial System Monitoring Programme. Online. Available at: http://www.jsmp.minihub.org/Reports/jsmpreports/ CAVR_Reports/cavr_report_2004_e.pdf (accessed on 29 March 2006).
Kivimäki, T., Jacobsen, M. and Kartasasmita, P.S. (eds) (2002) *Democracy, Decentralization, Identity and Conflict in Indonesia*, Helsinki and Copenhagen: CTS-Conflict Transformation Service.
Kopong Medan, K. (2006) 'Peradilan Rekonsiliatif: Konstruksi Penyelesaian Kasus Kriminal Menurut Masyarakat Lamaholot di Flores, Nusa Tenggara Timur', unpublished PhD thesis, Universitas Diponegoro.
Kritz, N.J. (ed.) (1995) *Transitional Justice, Vol. 3*, Washington DC: United States Institute of Peace Press.
Kumar, K. (1997) 'The nature and focus of international assistance for rebuilding war-torn societies', in K. Kumar (ed.) *Rebuilding Societies After Civil War: Critical Roles for International Assistance*, London and Boulder: Lynne Rienner.
Lederach, J.P. (1997) *Building Peace: Sustainable Reconciliation in Divided Societies*, Washington DC: United States Institute of Peace Press.
Lehmann, K. (2003) 'Ruanda – Kosten der Gerechtigkeit', *Amnesty International Journal*, August. Online. Available at: http://www2.amnesty.de/internet/deall.nsf/ AlleDok/59A518E0DAD93195C1256D6C004FC48E?Open (accessed on 17 March 2006).
Malik, I., Pattinaja, M., Putuhena, S., Yakob, T. *et al.* (eds) (2003) *Breaking the Violence with Compassion: BAKUBAE*, Jakarta: Civil Society Alliance for Democracy (YAPPIKA).
Marantika, L. (2007) 'Peran strategis perempuan untuk perdamaian di daerah konflik', in A. Amirrachman (ed.) *Revitalisasi Kearifan Lokal: Studi Resolusi Konflik di Kalimantan Barat, Maluku dan Poso*, Jakarta: International Center for Islam and Pluralism (ICIP).
Mazurana, D., Raven-Roberts, A. and Parpart, J. (eds) (2005) *Gender, Conflict, and Peacekeeping*, Lanham: Rowman & Littlefield.
McDonald, J.W. (2003) 'Multi-track diplomacy', Boulder: The Beyond Intractability Knowledge Base Project, University of Colorado. Online. Available at: http://www.beyondintractability.org/essay/multi-track_diplomacy/ (accessed on 15 January 2008).

McWilliam, A. (2007a) 'Introduction: restorative custom: ethnographic perspectives on conflict and local justice in Timor', *The Asia Pacific Journal of Anthropology*, 8(1): 1–8.

—— (2007b) 'Meto disputes and peacemaking: cultural notes on conflict and its resolution in West Timor', *The Asia Pacific Journal of Anthropology*, 8(1): 75–91.

Meitzner Yoder, L.S. (2007) 'Hybridising justice: state-customary interactions over forest crime and punishment in Oecusse, East Timor', *The Asia Pacific Journal of Anthropology*, 8(1): 43–57.

Merwe, H.v.d. (2003) 'National and community reconciliation: competing agendas in the South African truth and reconciliation commission', in N. Biggar (ed.) *Burying the Past: Making Peace and Doing Justice After Civil Conflict*, Washington DC: Georgetown University Press.

Minow, M. (1998) *Between Vengeance and Forgiveness: Facing History after Genocide and Mass Violence*, Boston: Beacon Press.

Nader, L. (1998) 'Harmony models and the construction of law', in K. Avruch, P.W. Black and J.A. Scimecca (eds) *Conflict Resolution: Cross-Cultural Perspectives*, Westport, Connecticut: Praeger.

Oberschall, A. (2007) *Conflict and Peace Building in Divided Societies: Responses to Ethnic Violence*, London and New York: Routledge.

Ocen, J. (2007) 'Can traditional rituals bring justice to northern Uganda?', AR No. 123, 25 July, London: Institute of War & Peace Reporting. Online. Available at: http://iwpr.net (accessed on 29 August 2007).

Pankhurst, D. (1999) 'Issues of justice and reconciliation in complex political emergencies: conceptualising reconciliation, justice and peace', *Third World Quarterly*, 20(1): 239–56.

Pouligny, B., Chesterman, S. and Schnabel, A. (2007) 'Introduction: picking up the pieces', in B. Pouligny, S. Chesterman and A. Schnabel (eds) *After Mass Crime: Rebuilding States and Communities*, Tokyo and New York: United Nations University Press.

Pouligny, B., Doray, B. and Martin, J.-C. (2007) 'Methodological and ethical problems: a trans-disciplinary approach', in B. Pouligny, S. Chesterman and A. Schnabel (eds) *After Mass Crime: Rebuilding States and Communities*, Tokyo and New York: United Nations University Press.

Rigby, A. (2001) *Justice and Reconciliation: After the Violence*, Boulder: Lynne Rienner Publishers.

Roht-Arriaza, N. and Mariezcurrena, J. (2006) *Transitional Justice in the Twenty-First Century: Beyond Truth versus Justice*, Cambridge and New York: Cambridge University Press.

Ross, M.H. (2004) 'Ritual and the politics of reconciliation', in Y. Bar-Siman-Tov (ed.) *From Conflict Resolution to Reconciliation*, Oxford: Oxford University Press.

Ruth-Heffelbower, D. (2002) 'Indonesia: out of one, many?', *The Fletcher Forum of World Affairs*, 26(2): 223–38.

Schirch, L. (2001) 'Ritual reconciliation', in M. Abu-Nimer (ed.) *Reconciliation, Justice, and Coexistence: Theory & Practice*, Lanham, MD: Lexington Books.

Schulte Nordholt, H. and van Klinken, G. (eds) (2007) *Renegotiating Boundaries: Local politics in post-Suharto Indonesia*, Leiden: KITLV Press.

Sidel, J.T. (2007) *Riots, Pogroms, Jihad: Religious Violence in Indonesia*, Singapore: NUS Press.

Smyth, M. (2003) 'Putting the past in its place: issues of victimhood and reconciliation in Northern Ireland's peace process', in N. Biggar (ed.) *Burying the Past: Making Peace and Doing Justice After Civil Conflict*, Washington DC: Georgetown University Press.

Stevens, J. (2001) *Access to Justice in Sub-Saharan Africa: The Role of Traditional and Informal Justice Systems*, London: Penal Reform International. Online. Available at: http://www.penalreform.org (accessed on 3 July 2007).

Sukandar, R. (2007) 'Negotiating post-conflict communication: a case of ethnic conflict in Indonesia', unpublished dissertation, Ohio University.

Teitel, R.G. (2000) *Transitional Justice*, New York: Oxford University Press.

Theidon, K. (2007) 'Intimate enemies: reconciling the present in post-war communities in Ayacucho, Peru', in B. Pouligny, S. Chesterman and A. Schnabel (eds) *After Mass Crime: Rebuilding States and Communities*, Tokyo and New York: United Nations University Press.

Thufail, F.I. (2007) 'Transactions in the reconciliatory forum: islah and the legacy of state violence in Indonesia', paper presented at the Conference on In Search of Reconciliation and Peace in Indonesia and East Timor, Asia Research Institute, National University of Singapore, 18–20 July.

Tom, P. (2006) 'The Acholi traditional approach to justice and the war in northern Uganda', Boulder: The Beyond Intractability Knowledge Base Project, University of Colorado. Online. Available at: http://www.beyondintractability.org/case_studies/acholi_traditional_approach.jsp?nid=6792 (accessed on 29 August 2007).

United Nations (2007) *United Nations Declaration on the Rights of Indigenous Peoples*. Online. Available at: http://www2.ohchr.org/english/issues/indigenous/declaration.htm (accessed on 10 December 2007).

Uvin, P. (2003) 'The *Gacaca* tribunals in Rwanda', in D. Bloomfield, T. Barnes and L. Huyse (eds) *Reconciliation After Violent Conflict: A Handbook*, Stockholm: International Institute for Democracy and Electoral Assistance (IDEA).

van Klinken, G. (2007) *Communal Violence and Democratization in Indonesia: Small Town Wars*, London and New York: Routledge.

van Zyl, P. (2005) 'Dealing with the past: reflections on South Africa, East Timor and Indonesia', in M.S. Zurbuchen (ed.) *Beginning to Remember: The Past in the Indonesian Present*, Singapore: Singapore University Press.

Vandeginste, S. (2003a) 'Reparation', in D. Bloomfield, T. Barnes and L. Huyse (eds) *Reconciliation After Violent Conflict: A Handbook*, Stockholm: International Institute for Democracy and Electoral Assistance (IDEA).

—— (2003b) 'Rwanda: dealing with genocide and crimes against humanity in the context of armed conflict and failed political transition', in N. Biggar (ed.) *Burying the Past: Making Peace and Doing Justice After Civil Conflict*, Washington DC: Georgetown University Press.

Varshney, A. (2002) *Ethnic Conflict and Civic Life: Hindus and Muslims in India*, New Haven: Yale University Press.

Wessel, I. and Wimhöfer, G. (eds) (2001) *Violence in Indonesia*, Hamburg: Abera.

Woodiwiss, A. (2004) '"Community in the East": towards a new human rights paradigm', in B.H. Chua (ed.) *Communitarian Politics in Asia*, London and New York: Routledge.

Zurbuchen, M.S. (ed.) (2005a) *Beginning to Remember: The Past in the Indonesian Present*, Singapore: Singapore University Press.

—— (2005b) 'Historical Memory in Contemporary Indonesia', in M.S. Zurbuchen (ed.) *Beginning to Remember: The Past in the Indonesian Present*, Singapore: Singapore University Press.

2 Global conflict in cosmocentric perspective
A Balinese approach to reconciliation

Annette Hornbacher

Global conflict and the demand for a universal ethics: basic remarks

The economic entanglement between different parts of the world not only creates a new situation of inter-cultural contact but of conflict as well. As a consequence of this process many Western politicians as well as philosophers such as Habermas (2005) have contended that only a common *ethos*, or universally accepted ethical norms, can adequately respond to the present challenges of globalization and guarantee peace and reconciliation in a multicultural world.[1] The appeal to preserve 'Western values' formed on the basic principles of humanistic enlightenment ethics and its corresponding worldview has been intensified in the wake of Islamist terror and its threat to the modern ideal of a global civil society. In what follows, I would like to examine this claim from an anthropological point of view, that is to say, from a Balinese perspective. I will focus particularly on the Balinese interpretation (and practical management) of the global conflict between Western liberalism and Islamist terror which were retraced to local concepts of reality and responsibility.

It is not my intention here to defend an abstract cultural relativism. What I am suggesting is that in some cases not the claims of universal ethical values but rather the re-interpretation of global conflict with regard to local traditions can offer possibilities for peacefully resolving, or reconciling, or even – as in Bali – preventing a violent clash between opposing religions, worldviews, and ideas of human co-existence. Moreover, the Balinese contextualization of inter-religious conflict within local cosmology offers a new perspective on the issue of reconciliation in general because it does not restrict the discourse on terrorism to a question of victims and perpetrators (the victim-perpetrator binary being a prevailing assumption in international reconciliation debates), but rather transforms this moral opposition into the Balinese framework of cosmological balance. It thus empowers the victims by ascribing them responsibility and agency. Recognizing that local traditions of de-escalation can be effective not only in local but also in global conflict would seem all the more important because – after decades of cultural relativism and after radical, postmodern critique in the field of theory – today even anthropologists like Rabinow (1986: 258) have stressed the idea of a 'cosmopolitan' "ethos of macro-interdependencies", claiming that only a commonly shared liberal *ethos* can face the challenges of a cosmopolitan world. This argument is more than a matter of theory but has important consequences for global policy because it implies that in a global world, conflict reflects universal problems and can consequently be described along universal principles and managed by universal strategies. This assumption does not merely imply that – in end effect – all societies share the same patterns of behavior and ethical norms but insinuates that different concepts of reality and humanity either play no role in conflict management or they are the same the world over. Regarding the example of Bali to follow, I would like to challenge both assumptions as presupposing – in both theoretical and ethical respects – a Western model, the epistemological validity and practical value of which seems debatable precisely in a cross-cultural context.[2]

Anthropocentric versus cosmocentric concepts of ethics

While I hardly wish, of course, to criticize the idea of humanism, I do want to recall from a cross-cultural point of view, that the modern identification of ethics and humanism stands in stark contrast to non-Western traditions of individual responsibility. These non-Western traditions of individual responsibility are not restricted to human subjects alone, but include beings for which categories compatible with the worldview of Western Enlightenment are difficult to identify. Among these are ancestors as well as the souls of the unborn and spirits of natural phenomena which are seen as equal counterparts to human beings because they too are equipped with agency and consciousness and form an essential part of human social life and ethics (Schiller 1997: 78).

The problems that result from the implementation of a seemingly cosmopolitan, but in fact anthropocentric and Eurocentric, ethics have been discussed with respect to debates on indigenous land rights in Melanesia and Southeast Asia where holy places, individually formed landscapes, plants, or animals can all be seen as the meaningful expressions of equal but non-human agents which must be respected by human beings because they constitute the creative powers of primeval times in the individual manifestations of nature (Narokobi 1999; Suasta & Connor 1999).

While I have discussed these differences between an anthropocentric and cosmocentric *ethos* in greater detail elsewhere (Hornbacher 2005a), here I would like to contrast the universalistic claims of modern anthropocentric ethics with Balinese conflict interpretation following the Islamist terror attack on the World Trade Center in New York in 2001 and the Balinese conflict management following Islamist bombing attacks in Kuta, Bali, in 2002. Both were last guided by local cosmological concepts and explicitly aimed towards a peaceful solution, articulated in contrast to both the idea of Islamist jihad and to a 'war on terror' under the banner of Western liberalism.

Balinese image or Balinese *ethos*?

I argue that the obvious willingness of most Balinese to manage this global conflict peacefully was neither the outcome of universal ethical principles nor the consequence of a politically instrumentalized stereotype, but rather the consequence of a re-interpretation of this global conflict on the terms of Balinese cosmology and responsibility. This process can be understood as a reflexive attempt to mediate and reconcile local traditions and identity with threatening problems of global modernization by explicitly avoiding the alternative of religious fundamentalism and Westernization. In this interpretative rearticulation of religious conflict nothing less has been negotiated than Balinese identity and Balinese agency with respect to the opposing forces of national Islam and the international economy.

In order to understand the dimension of this conflict for Bali, we have to recall that the international clash of these opposing interests increasingly threatens Balinese identity: While Bali's Hindu population represents a minority within Indonesia, the world's largest Muslim society, on which it politically depends, Bali's relative wealth is based upon global tourism. Tensions between Western liberalism and fundamentalist Islam, together with the threat of Islamist terror, seriously affect Bali both economically and politically. It is thus extremely interesting that the Balinese society, rather than siding with one of the opponents, engaged with and reflected on this conflict by reaffirming local concepts of responsibility and conflict management and by reassessing local religious traditions, including the idea of the whole world as a flexible balance of opposing cosmic forces.

To illustrate the role of these local concepts in many debates as well as in social practice, it is not necessary to construct a systematic 'Balinese ethic', which to my knowledge does not exist. One may speak instead of a Balinese *ethos* as a flexible set of theoretical and practical attitudes.[3] Referring to local traditions, this *ethos* was triggered for the first time by the circumstances of Islamist terror and the Western 'war on terror'. To illustrate the discourse of this *ethos*, I will refer to numerous discussions in which I have been involved during my fieldwork, as well as to theater and dance performances in the context of temple ceremonies dealing with Islamist terror in Indonesia – and particularly in Bali – in a predominantly ironic and parodic fashion, each of them commenting upon religious violence in terms of local mythology and cosmological traditions.[4]

The aim of the following considerations is threefold. First, I would like to contrast the theory that global conflict needs universal ethical values for purpose of peace-building and reconciliation with Balinese conflict interpretation and cosmological reconciliation. Second, I would like to examine the role of Hindu-Balinese concepts concerning conflict and individual responsibility in comparison with and contrast to the monotheistic notion of 'Evil', as this notion played a crucial role as a moralist guideline in Western policy against terror as well as in Islamist terror. Finally, I would like to outline some practical consequences of Balinese conflict interpretation using the example of the peaceful handling of the Islamist bombings in Bali, 2002.

Balinese Hindus between Indonesian Islam and Western modernity

I became actively involved in discussions about religious conflict interpretation and individual responsibility during my fieldwork on ritual dance-drama in several

South Balinese villages. The following interpretation reflects these circumstances and the perspective of my interlocutors. In other words, this means that my interpretation mirrors a 'bottom-up' view and not the perspective of an academic and urban minority. Yet the people with whom I discussed ethical problems and conflict solutions were scarcely drawn from a homogeneous class: they ranged instead from university students in Denpasar to illiterate housewives providing ritual offerings for their families, from the taxi driver in the tourist business to the school teacher of Hinduism, noting indeed that all of my interlocutors were Hindus. Owing to this same discussion framework, it is my intention neither to explain Islamist terror in Indonesia nor the Western 'war on terror' in terms of political theory but much rather to focus on the interpretive appropriation of national and international forces and occurrences by the Balinese with respect to their local cosmology. It is consequently not an explanation of Islamism submitted for discussion here but instead the interpretative appropriation of these seemingly 'global,' that is, 'objective' facts by means of local traditions. I suggest that this intellectual appropriation of global facts, as reflected in local knowledge and practice, reveals what I have called a Balinese *ethos*, characterized by its attempt to de-escalate – or balance – the national and global tensions between Islamism and the 'war on terror'.

Nevertheless, it appears that this *ethos* was not only restricted to the villages where I conducted fieldwork but also corresponded with the peaceful situation in most locales in Bali during the difficult years around Suharto's resignation and the fiscal crises. This same explicitly peaceful engagement with religious conflict merits attention inasmuch as it may be distinguished from mutually aggravating forms of inter-religious violence which began in many places of Indonesia during the final years of the Suharto regime and which were further aggravated during the fiscal crises and the years following his resignation. Notorious inter-religious conflicts, with differing degrees of violence, took place particularly between the Muslim majority and Christian minorities in Java, Sulawesi, Maluku, and Lombok. The tensions in question are by no means restricted to Islamist terror which still remains an exception in Indonesia's religiously pluralistic society. They start however with the fact that – and in spite of the officially legislated religious freedom characterizing the Indonesian state – religious minority groups have been marginalized via an orthodox understanding of Islam, itself differentiated from the same syncretistic and pluralistic Islam for which Indonesia became famous.[5] Given today's increasing Islamization of the Indonesian society, religious minority groups are only allowed to build places for their worship if the dominant society does not object. Satisfying this requirement has become increasingly difficult for Indonesian Christians. In a course of fourteen years, some 600 churches have been burnt down in several parts of Indonesia and following Suharto's resignation, violent riots occurred, claiming thousands of victims in several islands, despite the traditionally pluralistic coexistence of different religions in this region (Barton 2005: 74–5; Sidel 2007).

In the time that I started fieldwork in 1998 and 1999, violent clashes between Christian and Muslim Indonesians were regularly reported in the newspaper and on television, and Balinese friends living in Lombok warned me against visiting them because they judged the situation around Mataram as being too dangerous: a church had been burnt down in an act of revenge, in retaliation to inter-religious conflicts in Maluku where thousands of people had died. The purposeful de-escalation of conflict in Bali must be understood in the context of these inter-religious tensions and requires further examination. I argue that it is insufficient to explain this behavior as the outcome of an essentially peaceful 'Balinese character', as some Balinese opinion leaders have proclaimed with an eye to the tourist industry. Yet, given the peaceful handling of the conflict it seems likewise unsatisfying to turn this argument on its head by claiming that Balinese de-escalation was no more than the expression of a politically – and hence implemented from the 'top-down' – Balinese stereotype or image designed for the tourist industry and state control.[6]

Rather, the de-escalation was the consequence of an effort to negotiate, to display, and even to re-construct a particularly modern Balinese identity, asserting its superiority vis-á-vis the Islamic-Christian axis of violence and counter-violence. I consequently suggest that confronted with the alternative between mutually intensifying forms of religious violence in Indonesia and between jihad and the 'holy war on terror' globally, most Balinese emphasized that their own Hindu-Balinese tradition, with its conception of cosmic balance, offered a better option for the purposes of national as well as international conflict management. This means, in other words, that the Balinese *ethos* can be regarded as a form of local identity created in critical opposition to national and international forms of conflict management.

This critical re-construction of a specifically Balinese identity and agency became evident to me immediately following the terrorist attack on New York on 11 September 2001 (now better known as 9/11), when spontaneous and manifestly novel declarations of solidarity were articulated in Bali towards Western visitors. Balinese whom I had never met before, now approached me in the streets of local villages as well as in the capital itself for the sole purpose of offering their own assurances to me that the Balinese in general abhor any kind of religious coercion and religious terror in particular. They showed their solidarity with the victims of New York, declaring, to my surprise, that, owing to its tolerance, Balinese Hinduism would be closer to Christianity than Islam, Indonesia's majority's religion.[7] A student who approached me in the street of Denpasar voiced her displeasure about new riots in Lombok and Sulawesi, saying with a sigh, "Why do these Muslims always cause trouble?" A young man went still further and questioned the basic principle of Indonesian religious policy by openly doubting that the Muslim god Allah could be identified with *tuhan*, the official Indonesian term for God, because he found that in Indonesian religious policy as well as in global debates *Allah* functioned as a term of exclusion and even legitimated violence which to him was incompatible with Indonesia's religious pluralism in the name of one God (*tuhan*) who can be referred to by different names.

This explicit distancing not only from terrorism but also from Islam, the religion of the Indonesian majority, was a remarkable, but at the same time unsettling new development, paralleled during these years by separatist tendencies in the *Bali Merdeka* (Bali freedom) movement. This movement was fueled in 1999, after Suharto's resignation, by the fact that Megawati, then minister in Habibie's parliament and later president, had prayed in her Balinese grandmother's temple although she herself was Muslim, and had in consequence "been accused of being an unfaithful Muslim and thus not capable of leading predominantly Muslim Indonesia" (Hitchcock & Darma Putra 2004: 222). This produced a strong Balinese solidarity with Megawati as well as a reaffirmation of Balinese religious-cultural identity within Indonesia although the *Bali Merdeka* movement itself did not develop into a strong political force.

This public debate about Balinese-ness, or *kebalian*, is not completely new. Its origins, as Picard (1999) has shown, can be traced back to the 1920s. But it has been revived after the fall of Suharto's New Order regime and is currently developing into new forms and increasingly worrying tendencies of Hindu-chauvinism, which are not discussed here (Ghindwani 2005; Picard 1999; Titib 2005). The discourse concerning Balinese cultural identity can be paralleled with similar reconstructions of local *adat* (custom) in many parts of Indonesia. However, in the case of Bali, it is less guided by concepts of local law than by religious and spiritual traditions which are increasingly re-interpreted with reference to the Indian origin of Hinduism while, on the other hand, a new interest in the re-construction of local Balinese traditions arose only in recent years (Ardika & Darma Putra 2004; Darma Putra & Windu Sancaya 2005; Sutaba 2002; Wiana 2002).

This attempt to re-confirm Balinese identity is paralleled by a growing ambivalence – if not hostility – towards Islam which became particularly evident following the Islamist bombings in Kuta (2002) and in Jimbaran (2005) and it has its roots in the late 1980s. In these years, President Suharto in search of voters supported the Islamization of Indonesian society which penetrated bureaucratic and scientific institutions of the country with the help of the Indonesian Association of Muslim Scholars (ICMI). According to the late Balinese anthropologist I Gusti Ngurah Bagus, it was during these years that Indonesian Hindus – most of them ethnically Balinese – felt marginalized in Indonesia for the first time. Their ambivalence was triggered by the marginalization of Balinese Hinduism which included the making of "derogatory" Islamic statements "about the Hindu religion" and insulted the feelings of "the Hindu community" (Bagus 2004: 88). This statement implies not only that Balinese identity has been, in essence, defined with respect to religious traditions, it also reflects a recent shift of Indonesian Islam from a traditionally syncretistic and pluralistic practice which is based on local forms of ancestor and nature worship, to a more 'purified' and thus universalistic Islamic doctrine. In social practice, this means that culturally and ritually integrated undogmatic variants characteristic of traditional Indonesian Islam and ranging from folk traditions with multi-religious rituals to Javanese mysticism, are increasingly replaced by rigid and sometimes violent forms of orthodoxy.[8]

In this process, the religious policy of the Indonesian state has a key function because it forces the re-interpretation of traditionally pluralist religious practice according to the official guidelines for religion (*agama*), including profession of monotheism, a holy book and a prophet, and therefore encourages the reconstruction of local traditions in the image of a purified Islam (Picard 1999; Ramstedt 2004).

This policy has had a great impact on Balinese Hinduism which was forced to adapt its flexible blend of Hindu-Buddhist philosophy and local ancestor and nature worship to the ideal of scriptural monotheism because it was denied the title of an officially respected religion for a long time. But in spite of this adaptation, many Balinese Hindus experience their identity as if on a dangerous tightrope between the opposing demands of national religious policy and the influences of a materialist worldview connected with globalization and Western liberalism. This leads to conflict especially where both influences are directly linked as in Bali's tourism industry which – due to Balinese ritual life – is flourishing, and attracting, in consequence, a growing number of Muslim labor migrants. However, these migrants adapt to the social and cultural duties of Balinese village life only to a limited degree, resisting, for example, the demands of mutual neighborhood assistance (*gotong royong*) which builds a solid pillar of social coherence but evolves around local rituals. The Muslim migrants evade this socioreligious solidarity with reference to their religion (*agama*), which they feel to be superior to what they see as merely local *adat* or custom. The official Indonesian concept of religion guided by Islam thus implicates religious hierarchies which, for some Balinese, link the feeling of economic exploitation with slights against their religious-cultural identity. Beyond this, a growing number of Balinese jealously defend their prosperity against the migrant workers from Java – many of them small food vendors in the streets of tourist spots – by propagating populist propaganda like: "Javanese are selling *bakso* [a Javanese soup] in order to buy Balinese *sawah* [ricefield] while Balinese are selling *sawah* to buy *bakso*", which insinuates the exploitation of Bali by poor Javanese migrants. The growing ambivalence vis-à-vis Muslim migrants now emerging has in some cases led to Balinese attacks which coincide with religious groups, but which – at least as regarded from a Balinese point of view – are not based on theological motives.[9]

Monotheism, theodicy, and the 'war on evil'

This complex ambivalence towards Islamic Javanese migrant workers doubtless played an important role in the Balinese showing of solidarity with Western-Christian victims of Islamist terror in 2001. Yet, in spite of this, there was no Balinese identification with the West in general, nor with the Western interpretation of or management of Islamist terror. Instead, sharp criticism of the Western way of dealing with this conflict began rather quickly. The basis of this critique was President Bush's assertion that the terrorist attack was not directed against the USA but against the "values of civilization" in general, requiring a "coalition of the willing" to eradicate "Evil" (Bush 2002). This thesis provoked open revulsion in my local environment, because people did not share the conviction that the way of life of Western modernity was to be the epitome and measure of 'civilization' in general. The decisive principle of the enlightenment *ethos* was specifically rejected in the light of its social consequences. The autonomy of the individual was interpreted by contrast as the epitome of being uncivilized. To prove this a local man explained to me that a society building homes for the elderly so that their children might lead an autonomous way of life was not even human, but at best the expression of greedy egotistic demons (*raksasa*) and of a destroyed society (*masyarakat yang rusak*). In these discussions, not only the basic norms of modern Western society were criticized and rejected, but similar opposition was caused by the Western idea that secular liberalism and Islamist terror could be opposed like 'Good' and 'Evil' and that the latter ought to be combated by violence, that is, by war. While I am not claiming that the Balinese abhor any kind of violence, the point I would like to bring up for discussion is that the Balinese way of dealing with violence is neither based on the basically monotheist concept of 'Evil' nor on the thesis that 'Evil' should be fought against or could be overcome by any 'holy war'.[10]

This issue is of interest with respect to theories of a cosmopolitan 'world ethos', which suggest that the notion of 'Evil' is a universal religious and ethical fact (see Küng 1991). In Bali however, this very notion caused difficulties in translation and even resistance. In advance, it is worth noting that the moral judgment of a person as being evil (*jahat*) is well-known, in contrast to Geertz's (1966) former assumption that the Balinese have no idea of ethics at all but reflect human action in merely aesthetic terms. However while moral judgments about evil persons certainly exist, they are not equivalent to the idea of an abstract and transcendent entity 'Evil' as such, which, as the opposite of the 'Good', is closely connected with the monotheist idea of an almighty creator god who is, by definition, nothing but good. From this monotheist presupposition a new concept, politics, and representation of religion arises, to which Assmann (2000) attested in his revealing analyses concerning the beginning of monotheism in Egyptian society. According to Assmann, the problem brought up by monotheism is its claim for universal truth linked with the problem of theodicy, that is, the need to harmonize the fact of destruction and of suffering with the idea of an almighty and good creator God. The way to deal with this fundamental contradiction is the assumption of a 'counter' god or devil who is, as the transcendent representation of 'Evil' as such, responsible for destruction and directly opposed to the good creator, and who has to be fought by man in order to protect divine creation. Theodicy can thus be seen as the theological basis for 'holy wars', and as Miller (1996) has shown, the idea of 'holy wars' which overcome 'Evil' in favor of the 'Good' is closely connected with the monotheistic claim of absolute truth.

Balinese Hinduism, however, in spite of its forced adaptation to the model of monotheism, lacks the idea of a morally good creator god just as it lacks the idea of absolute Evil or a fight for ultimate salvation. The malevolence of human witches (*leyak*), who are the paragon of evil persons, is not traced back to a metaphysical entity named 'Evil' as such who takes hold of the human mind, but in banal human feelings such as envy. Fear inducement from a Balinese point of view is therefore not the morally questionable motivation of a witch but only the supernatural efficacy of their agency, that is, their magical ability to instrumentalize the spiritual – but morally neutral – power (*sakti*) of the cosmos, and to use it for destructive purposes in harming others. The Balinese concept of spiritual power (*sakti*) which is implied in this interpretation is linked to traditional cosmology and particularly to the idea of a balance of polar principles which influence the visible or material (*sekala*), and invisible or intellectual as well as spiritual (*niskala*) dimensions of reality. This Balinese cosmology penetrates public debate about rituals as well as politics and about health, natural disasters, and conflicts of all kinds to date (Barton 2005: 9–10; Hornbacher 2005b; Wiener 1995).

Although this cosmic power relation is normally invisible and has to be interpreted by specialists in the case of disease or conflict, it finds a public representation in the ritual drama of *Calonarang*. Here the destructive witch, *Rangda*, brings pestilence and disaster to the island and has to be balanced out in a fight by the benevolent demon *Barong*, both of them represented by dancers wearing the huge masks and costumes of the temple. The crucial point in this ritual fight lies in the fact that it does not aim at destruction of *Rangda* as the incarnation of Evil or towards ultimate deliverance from death, but at a temporary balance of the opposing powers in the interest of earthly life and its renewal. This means that *Barong* and *Rangda* belong together as polar forces and are sometimes said to be a married couple in anger; they do not destroy but rather protect each other.[11] From a Balinese point of view, *Rangda* is as holy as *Barong* and therefore cannot be said to be 'Evil' in the moralistic sense of monotheism; like the mask of *Barong*, the *Rangda* mask is a revered object of prayer at Balinese temples. Similarly, in the case of local conflicts, a *Calonarang* performance might be given to exorcise what is interpreted in the community as the temporary rampant forces of destruction, but such a performance is never against Evil per se – which makes no sense in this framework of cosmology and conflict – but rather it aims at the restoration of balance.

Such a fight for the balanced restoration of destructive and constructive forces would have been – in the debates of my Balinese partners – the adequate political answer to the terror of New York. To them, it was incomprehensible and even grotesque that one could – or should – eradicate 'Evil' worldwide, and on top of it by using more violence! When the newspaper's headline announced the Western 'war on Evil', the villagers gathering around the *Bali Post* were laughing out noisily before they tried to convince me not to go back into a world whose leaders obviously were misjudging the situation and had no convincing answer to conflicts of such global range. In their eyes, the tragedy of 9/11 did not primarily reveal an 'axis of Evil' – which would imply that general human vices like envy could be geographically restricted – but was rather a sign of the whole world out of balance, for the restoration of which – due to his global power (*sakti*) – the president of the USA had the greatest responsibility.

The Balinese debates thus re-interpreted terror into the frame of their cosmological concept of balance and connected it with local strategies of dealing with witchcraft and conflict in general. As in the case of witchcraft, the villagers made a claim for conflict management which did not focus on the morally bad intentions of the perpetrators, but rather on the strengthening of powers which could rebalance the whole situation. This interpretation of human conflict, not solely in moral terms but in the context of a cosmic power play, has far reaching consequences for the Balinese idea of individual responsibility; from this follows that for the restoration of balance, not only the perpetrator but also the victim has to take responsibility, because he is also perceived as an active part of a disturbed balance and can prove his agency only by strengthening his constructive power and so by overcoming his role as a victim.

Such a creative commitment for the restoration of global balance was expressly expected of President Bush, because as a leader with globally effective power he should be able to protect the balance of the world. The fact that President Bush was only crying at 'ground zero' was announced in the *Bali Post* with a headline *Bush menangis* (Bush cries) and commented upon with open laughter in the village. His reaction proved that the most powerful man in the world was unable to control even his own feelings and all the more unable, obviously, to control the world. A few days later, the fact that Bush was advocating a war against 'Evil', which – regarded from a Balinese point of view – would only further disturb the balance of the world, led to the judgment: *Bush juga jahat* (Bush is evil too).

The Balinese concept of cosmic balance between ideology and practice

Let me summarize some interim findings: the Islamist attack in New York as well as the Western 'war on terror' were carefully re-interpreted in terms of Balinese cosmology, which commented upon global violence and its ethical legitimization with respect to their position in a cosmic framework of destructive and constructive forces. This interpretive appropriation of global conflict is not based on the idea of universal moral values of humanity, but rather contextualizes human conflict and moral fault within the framework of a specifically Balinese cosmology according to which human agency can never be judged by the moral motivation of the human individual alone, but depends upon non-human power relations.[12] Accordingly, the explicit motives, actions, and thus the moral principles of a person are only one aspect of a complex cosmic balance of different powers or agencies, which in the end unfolds between material and spiritual agents: *sekala* and *niskala*.

This means that – in contrast to the idea of a global "world ethos" (Küng 1991) – the Balinese *ethos* cannot be discussed independent from its cosmological implications and from a corresponding idea of reality as a relation of heterogeneous forces and interests in which human and non-human agents participate and have to be balanced out. What is ethically appropriate cannot be said with regard to universal human values but only with respect to the invisible agents of this relationship which is articulated, among other things, in natural phenomena affecting humans. The same applies the other way round as well; human action is said to have consequences for the invisible or cosmic dimension of reality. In consequence individual responsibility pertains here – different from the Western or anthropocentric ethic – not only to human subjects but to the complete cosmic field in which human action takes place. This implies that in this case reconciliation cannot be restricted to intersubjective forgiveness and agency, but rather extends to the relation between humans and non-human reality which in Western terms could be called 'nature'. One example may explain a practical consequence of this sense and range of responsibility: a man approximately 60 years old, emphasized that humans are responsible not only for their fellows but also for the invisible spirits which are dwelling in particular places of the world and can be felt (*terasa*) with a special sensibility.[13] He remembered a day where he was ordered to cut down one of the huge trees, which are often revered as the dwelling places of spiritual beings in Bali. At night he had a dream where the soul of the tree appeared and warned him against continuing. He said he had to respect the wish of this *niskala* being and so stopped his work to avoid a conflict and the risk of being harmed.

From a modern worldview, it seems obvious of course that this cosmology as well as the *ethos* linked to it is merely a kind of cultural ideology so to speak, which – in the face of global conflicts – inevitably fails and cannot be maintained in a modern world. This assumption, however, stands opposed to the Balinese dealing with a severe Islamist bomb attack which struck only one year after the tragedy of New York, in October 2002 in a crowded tourist spot of Kuta. This 'bom Bali' planted by Javanese Islamists was no longer a case for a merely theoretical and distanced interpretation, but had serious human and economic effects for Bali and demanded practical reaction. The 'bom Bali' can thus be seen as a touchstone for the cosmocentric Balinese *ethos*.

While in Java, Maluku, and Sulawesi, violence under the banner of religion had provoked revenge, the deliberately peaceful handling of the Islamist assault, not only by Balinese politicians and opinion leaders, but by most of the Balinese population was all the more remarkable in the face of the smoldering socio-economic tensions between Balinese and Muslim migrant workers. The very few attempts of revenge that had been made immediately after the attack could be easily suppressed and did not find any support in the society. This situation was surprising, especially since the damage in Bali was immense. More than 200 people were killed in Kuta, among them many Balinese, and everyone was aware that this strike was aimed not only at Western tourists but also at Balinese Hindus, whose right to exist was openly denied by one of the leading Javanese figures of the Islamist terror group *Jemaah Islamiyah*, Abu Bakar Ba'asyir, on Indonesian TV only few weeks after the bombings. The Balinese tourism industry was paralyzed for months and numerous people lost their jobs and livelihood.

In spite of all that, purification rituals were performed and peace declarations were held across the whole island of Bali, particularly at Kuta, where the tragedy had occurred. To understand this peaceful conflict management in Bali it is not sufficient, in my view, to refer to Balinese politicians and their interest to present the island as a reliable partner for tourism business (Santikarma 2005). The strategic motivation of politicians and businessmen does not explain why so many Balinese, among them even people who did not profit from tourism, completely agreed that the first goal was to restore the disturbed balance, while in Lombok a similar strategic rhetoric was much less effective. I am suggesting that in order to understand such conflict management we should not confuse official policy and the economic interests of some opinion leaders with the local interpretation and motivation of a Balinese majority, who in fact explicitly wanted to keep or rather to restore peace for two main reasons. First, they explained that a de-escalation and above all a ritual purification were in accord with their interpretation of reality, that is, with Balinese cosmology. A second motivation could be found in the fact that many Balinese considered their own Hindu-Balinese religion and *ethos* as being explicitly opposed to the violent clashes between Muslims and Christians in other parts of Indonesia and to the idea of jihad in general. This can be interpreted as an attempt to 'invent' – as a politically marginalized minority – a superior Hindu-Balinese identity. While it has become en vogue to state that everything – particularly social identities – are 'invented' or 'constructed',[14] the interesting point here is not the fact that tradition is invented, but rather that it can be invented in very different ways. These so called 'inventions' depend not only upon group interests, but also upon the intellectual traditions and conceptual frameworks the actors have at hand.[15]

In any case we should keep in mind that this sociological interpretation is missing the most important point for Balinese actors to whom the purification rituals held all over the island were neither strategies of identity politics nor were they understood merely symbolically. They argued that these rituals had an immediate and concrete effect which could be grasped in very different but also concrete ways. The first evidence for the success of this Balinese conflict interpretation and its ritual management was to be seen – according to many of my interlocutors – in the fact that directly after the rituals had been performed, almost all culprits were apprehended.[16]

The second evidence was found in a sign from *niskala* which confirmed that the balance of powers was going to be restored after the rituals: in the midst of the

Figure 2.1 'Ground zero' in Kuta, Bali, a few weeks after the bombing in 2002: the small shrine and tree miraculously survived the explosion (Photo: Jochen Schönleber)

Balinese 'ground zero' – a huge area of about 300 square meter where the bomb had destroyed and burned down every building and which was then, in November 2002, a desert like field of dust and ashes – one single building had been untouched; a small shrine for a god, and directly leaning onto this shrine, a small young tree with green budding leaves had miraculously survived the all consuming fire. People not only from Bali, but also from other Indonesian islands came to worship this place and to make offerings to it.

But during those weeks, the ritual purification of violence was only one aspect of a far-reaching attempt to re-interpret the disaster in the framework of local cosmology and to find an adequate answer to it. For months there was intense reflexive introspection in various media, mainly in theatrical and discursive forms. Every temple festival I visited during that time would reflect in the form of ritual dramas the Balinese's aversion to Islamism and the increasing tensions they felt vis-á-vis Javanese migrants out of economic and political reasons. Here the conflict was – according to the tradition of Balinese dance drama – laughed away, by ironically criticizing the perpetrators in countless local improvisations.[17]

Of special importance were newly emerging myths, which introduced a new interpretation of the disaster by attributing partial responsibility to Balinese society. These myths spread not only orally, but also via mass media like newspapers and TV and they directly connected the growing influence of the modern, materialist worldview on Bali with the disruption of cosmic balance and with the success of the Bali bomb incident. One myth talked about a group of young Balinese men who had killed a huge turtle coming out of the sea at the south coast which was said to be a goddess because she was going directly to one of the most important Balinese sea-temples.[18] Instead of 'feeling' (*merasa*) that this creature was not just profitable food to be sold at the market but rather a sign from the *niskala*, the young men killed it. The consequences of this blasphemous act were inevitable. When the young men tried to sell the meat at the market of the district town Gianyar, everybody felt threatened and ran away, because people had claimed to see a goddess standing next to the corpse of the turtle or – according to another oral version – the meat smelled like a human being. The same happened at the market of the capital Denpasar, and now two of the men had become seriously sick and had consulted a local priest because they had felt something strange and uncontrollable was going on. The priest's interpretation was quite clear. According to him the inability of the young Balinese to perceive and to respect the presence of the sea goddess in a natural being had caused an imbalance between the forces of the material world and those of the spiritual world whose agency was now to be felt by human suffering. He advised the young men to bring back the rest of the turtle to the sea temple where the goddess had wished to go and to prepare a huge cremation ceremony for it – like for a Brahmin priest – to free the goddess from her decaying condition so she might go back to the invisible dimension of the world (*niskala*).

This myth blamed the young Balinese for disturbing the cosmic balance due to the increasing influence of a global, or better, a Western worldview, which – from this perspective – is seen as one-sided and materialistic. A similar interpretation applies to another myth that sprung up after the bombing which directly linked human fault to the Kuta disaster. Like the first one, the second myth circulated in oral communication including TV reports. According to this myth, a priest from another important temple at the south coast (*Pura Luhur Uluwatu*) met a beautiful but angry goddess of the sea who demanded 200 followers a few weeks before the terror attack. The priest understood that the goddess wanted human sacrifice and was shocked; he argued that all the villagers nearby prepared offerings and worshipped the gods. When the bomb in Kuta killed 202 people – among them many Balinese who had worked in the tourist business – a few months later, the priest remembered the goddess' words and spoke about the incident on TV.

This interpretation of the Islamist attack as the result of divine anger due to Balinese faults gave a new direction to local debates about Islamist terror. Now it was not only considered as the guilt of Javanese terrorists but instead Balinese discussed their own responsibility – although not guilt; to them the plans of the terrorists – like the evil intentions of a witch – can only be accomplished in an imbalanced world. In accordance with this complex interpretation, a village priest had asked me after the Bali bombing: "What wrong did we do? Where have we disturbed the balance that on our island such a catastrophe could happen?"

To him, as to other people around me, the conflict was much too complex to be resolved by the logic of revenge or by explanations which were restricted to individual moral fault: it mirrored an imbalance which was a consequence of modernity and thus part of Balinese agency as well as responsibility.

The range of responsibility: concluding remarks

I would like to emphasize that my interpretation of the peaceful Balinese *ethos* of cosmic balance is not meant as a universal solution for global conflict; rather I am suggesting that universal ethical principles as well as the politically influential idea of a 'world ethos' are insufficient in practice, because even global conflicts have to be managed locally. In the case of Bali, the purposeful de-escalation of inter-religious conflict was not the result of that kind of principles but rather the outcome of a cosmocentric re-interpretation of conflict which was based on a local concept of reality. On the other hand, this local religious tradition too has its own limits. Serious and repeated disturbances might result in even blood sacrifices for the sake of ritual purification. In Balinese history the most extreme case of such a ritual sacrifice is the *puputan* (literally 'finishing'). In 1908 the last Balinese court of Klungkung, faced with the superior military Dutch power, destroyed itself in such a ritual. The king and his family with hundreds of followers including babies and elderly people walked into the Dutch canon fire or killed themselves with their *keris* (ritual swords). Such a *puputan* as a culture-specific form of self-destruction does not represent, as Wiener (1995) has shown, a spontaneous rash reaction but rather the conscious attempt to prove spiritual superiority and to restore cosmic balance by means of a colossal blood sacrifice.

In line with this, I am suggesting that the *puputan* does not principally contradict the Balinese plea for peace and balance. It can rather be understood as an ultimate means to defend Balinese identity and agency even in a situation of complete disempowerment as given by contrasting the military superiority of the Dutch with the spiritual strength of the Balinese kings who transcend, as it were, the material level of this fight. This concept of *puputan* still exists today along with the willingness for harmony in collective memory. The Balinese plea for cosmic balance should consequently not be confused with banal shying away from social conflict or from violence. As in *Calonarang* performances, destruction and death are not seen as intrinsically evil but rather as the outcome of morally neutral cosmic forces, which can also purify and prepare recreation, depending on the situation.

What this meant for Balinese conflict management became apparent after a further Islamist assault in Bali in 2005, where another 20 people were killed in a restaurant in Jimbaran, another tourist spot on the south coast. The atmosphere was now much more tense; although there was still no escalation of violence, a demonstration took place in which numerous Balinese in ritual dress appeared in the capital to distance themselves loudly from jihad as a holy war against Evil, and to point instead to the specific Balinese possibility of a *puputan* should peaceful attempts prove to be insufficient to restore the balance of powers (Juniartha 2005).

The Balinese idea of cosmic balance should therefore not be confused with a 'romanticized' view of Bali as a tropical paradise with an ever peaceful or 'harmonious' people. Such essentialist claims are oversimplifications of Balinese concepts of cosmological balance albeit after the bombing even Balinese opinion leaders like politicians and anthropologists have propagated slogans like *orang Bali cinta damai* (Balinese are peace-loving) in the mass media, or have supported the commodification of peace as Bali's "cultural capital" (Geria 2004). It is all the more revealing that it was precisely one of these strategic slogans which were invented to bring back tourists to Bali – 'Bali for the world' – which caused strong resentment among many Balinese and triggered an ongoing debate about Balinese identity 'beyond' its instrumentalization for foreign visitors and for economic purposes (Hitchcock & Darma Putra 2004: 221).

What I have instead tried to sketch out was the fact that underneath – or in addition to – this commodifying and strategic propaganda, a concept of reality as flexible cosmic balance between opposing forces is still valid among a majority of Balinese, and that it was not least due to this local concept of reality that Balinese society tended to actively restore peace after the Islamist bombing rather than to react with revenge or with moral indignation about the perpetrators. In contrast to the essentialist assumption of a per se peaceful and timeless 'Balinese character', I am instead suggesting that this '*ethos*' is the outcome of a self-reflexive re-shaping of identity arising from the challenge of globalization and inter-religious violence and of negotiating local agency in the face of political powerlessness. The willingness to restore peace after the devastating attack of Kuta might be seen then as a constructed Balinese identity, but nevertheless it is based on local traditions offering remarkable new possibilities for reconciliation in the Indonesian as well as in the global context of inter-religious violence. Moreover, the Balinese example questions the Western theory that the principle of humanity is the lowest common denominator of global ethics and practice and hence the only way to create peace and harmony between different religions and cultures.

In the case of the 'bom Bali' it was not a 'world ethos' of humanity, but the local cosmology that enabled the Balinese to reconcile the unresolved global conflict between modern liberalism and Islamist terror by transferring it to the context of a common cosmic responsibility. The conceptual framework of cosmic balance – in spite of its own limits – offered a way to handle the conflict constructively, because its emphasis was not on the principle contradictions between Western modernity and Islamist fundamentalism but more on the Balinese's willingness to modulate and negotiate the threatening influences and demands of modernity with respect to the situation. In this shift from principle moral contradictions to a cosmocentric responsibility, the discourse of guilt – with its implied opposition of 'victims' and 'perpetrators' – was transformed at least partially into a debate concerning the Balinese ability to reconcile tradition and modernity by strengthening local agency in a field of opposing global powers.

This reflexive reassessment can be seen as the creative and viable attempt of a politically powerless and religiously marginalized group to retain their concept of reality, responsibility, and agency even under the hegemony of global modernization; it challenges Western scholars to critically reflect upon the assumption that a global society inevitably needs universal ethical principles in order to reconcile inter-religious and cross-cultural conflict.

Notes

1 However, from an anthropological point of view, 'globalization' is neither radically new nor restricted to modern Western society, particularly if seen as cross-cultural contact by means of long distance trade or migration (see also Wolf 1982). In particular, the Southeast Asian trade relations between India and China which have for 2000 years intensively influenced and shaped local cultures and societies in this region could similarly be termed a form of globalization. On the other hand, Castells (2000) reminds us that globalization today is not the intensified process of cross-cultural contact much less a civilizing force, but rather a paradoxical phenomenon that should be understood in terms of a world which is without borders with respect to information technology and market economy, and which socially at the same time excludes masses of actors around the world who participate in this process only as marginalized, overexploited slaves. Obviously, the same radical exclusion also takes place in tribal societies that are unable – or unwilling – to accept the ideological premises of this process.

2 I have argued elsewhere that the concepts of a global *ethos* as well as of ethical universalism originate in the Western Enlightenment tradition and are consequently defined with respect to the human subject for whom alone reason, dignity, and agency are reserved (Hornbacher 2006). Correspondingly, all of these conceptions can be described as humanistic or 'anthropocentric', a point which is by no means evident in cross-cultural comparison.

3 My approach is partially congruent with Bourdieu's concept of *habitus*, which he too interprets as *ethos*. Like Bourdieu I will argue that this *ethos* is not a systematically describable object of theory but rather a dynamic potential that generates different forms of agency according to the situational requirements (Bourdieu 1999: 100). But while Bourdieu argues that the *habitus* is therefore always unconscious, I am suggesting that the threat of Islamist terror led to a conscious reassessment of this very *ethos* in Bali, which can be seen as a reflection of local agency and identity in the face of contesting forces.

4 This was accomplished in theater by sometimes quite subtle aesthetic means: in one shadow play performance (*wayang kulit*), for example, the set of puppets was split. While the gods and heroes were taken from a Balinese puppet set, the demons and villains had been taken from a Javanese set with a slightly different aesthetic, indicating to the insider audience that the destructive forces, which are part of the old Javano-Balinese cosmology, were now coming from Java. This was of course a critical Hindu comment upon the Islamist Bali bombers who although Javanese were still part of Balinese cosmology (see Hornbacher 2005b).

5 It is worth noting that since the foundation of the Indonesian state, the Indonesian society has struggled with Sukarno's idea of *Pancasila* which is based on the affirmation that all monotheist world religions are equal. This religious pluralism has been opposed from the very beginning by orthodox Muslim groups claiming that this would legitimate polytheism, which begins – in their view – with the Christian concept of trinity (for historical details of this debate, see Ramstedt 2004).

6 This interpretation has been offered by Santikarma (2005), suggesting that because thousands of people have been killed in Bali as communists during the military coup with which Suharto's New Order regime had been established in 1965, it would be impossible and hypocritical to attribute peacefulness as a core value or essential feature of Balinese tradition. I think, however, that the alternative inherent in this argument is misleading because, as I show later, from a Balinese point of view, destruction is not necessarily opposed to balance but can rather be seen as part of a struggle for cosmic harmony.

7 Such a declaration in favor of Christianity clearly implies that Christian fundamentalism, which influences not only many parts of Latin America and Africa but also has a key ideological function in the US-American 'war on terror' and consequently in global politics, is largely unknown among the Balinese.

8 For the history of pluralist and mystical Islam see Ricklefs (2007). For new tendencies of locally implemented shari'a in the era of post-Suharto decentralization, see Salim and Azra (2003), and for the active support of radical Islamist groups by political leaders of Indonesia like former Vice-President Hamzah Haz and Human Rights Minister Yusril Izha Mahendra who have "openly and vigorously campaigned for Ba'asyir", one of the masterminds of *Jemaah Islamiyah*, see Barton (2005: 78).

9 This becomes evident with regard to examples such as the following: in a south Balinese village close to the place where I conducted fieldwork, a Muslim migrant from Java had been integrated over the course of many years without any problems because he accomplished the duties of mutual neighborhood assistance (*gotong royong*), joining all ritual duties. He even showed respect for the local deities in the temple which was evident to the villagers by the fact that he became possessed by the deity of this temple during the ritual. This mutual acknowledgment between the Muslim migrant and the local deity was highly appreciated by the Balinese villagers, who, incidentally, never doubted or challenged the man's confession of Islam. This example can illustrate the difference between a pluralistic Indonesian Islam which is integrated through Indonesian ancestor and nature worship and a 'purified' or orthodox Islam which abhors this form of syncretism as pagan or – as a young orthodox Muslim in Lombok had explained to me – as simply *mad*. To him the followers of these traditional forms of Islam were just "orang gila" (mad men) who did not understand the doctrine of the Qu'ran (personal communication, August 2007).

10 It is thus in my view not helpful to play the communist killings from 1965 against the peaceful Balinese dealing with Islamist terror today, which suggests that violence always has the same meaning. This argumentation implies an essentially peaceful 'Balinese character' but it fails to note that the Balinese interpretation of violence is changing with respect to the situation (Santikarma 2005).

11 Once a *Barong* performer went into trance during the performance in a South Balinese temple and fell down to the ground during the fight. It was *Rangda* herself who helped him to get up again and to continue.

12 This is of course the opposite concept to a Kantian ethics of consciousness based only on ethical principles.
13 From a Western perspective the word *merasa* (to feel) which plays a key role in Balinese dealing with *niskala* has the complex property of merging perception, feeling, and reflection attributed in Western thought to different and even opposing fields of physical reality, subjective emotion, and human intellect.
14 This, of course, applies also to radical Islam claiming to represent a 'purer' and thus more original form of religion.
15 While I have tried to focus in this chapter on the important role of religious concepts, offering alternative models of modernity, several scholars concentrate on strategic or political questions when dealing with religious violence, claiming that religion is just the banner of a violence which originates from identity issues (see Sidel 2007: 7–9). I am suggesting instead that the critical and reflexive search for identity in a rapidly changing modern world does not merely mirror demands of modern society but sometimes also reflects a criticism of modern worldviews by means of religious tradition.
16 Some people claimed that the Javanese culprits were only detected because of the Balinese rituals, which were the only significant difference between the case in Bali and America, where Osama-bin-Laden could not be found even after one year.
17 I have elaborated in detail on this argument in my book *Zuschreibung und Befremden* (Hornbacher 2005b), where I have analyzed among others several performances with respect to their local interpretation of the 'bom Bali'. One general feature of these dramatic performances was the ironic way of negotiating this national conflict which supported the de-escalation of the conflict and strengthened the Balinese identity and position by laughing at Islamic masterminds, which in one case were represented as ridiculous elderly transvestites and homosexuals seducing attractive young men, which could be understood as a critical comment of the rigid sexual mores of radical Muslims and their abhorrence of women.
18 I owe special information about this myth to Garrett Kam, I Made Sukawati, Ni Made Reni, and I Ketut Jiwa.

References

Ardika, I.W. and Darma Putra, I.N. (eds) (2004) *Politik, Kebudayaan dan Identitas Etnik*, Denpasar: Fakultas Sastra Universitas Udayana & Balimangsi Press.
Assmann, J. (2000) *Moses der Ägypter. Entzifferung einer Gedächtnisspur*, Frankfurt am Main: Fischer.
Bagus, I.G.N. (2004) 'The Parisada Hindu Dharma Indonesia in a society in transformation: the emergence of conflicts amidst differences and demands', in M. Ramstedt (ed.) *Hinduism in Modern Indonesia. A Minority Religion between Local, National and Global Interests*, London: Routledge.
Barton, G. (2005) *Jemaah Islamiyah: Radical Islamism in Indonesia*, Singapore: Singapore University Press.
Bourdieu, P. (1999) *Sozialer Sinn: Kritik der Theoretischen Vernunft*, Frankfurt am Main: Suhrkamp.
Bush, G.W. (2002) 'State of the Union address', 29 January. Online. Available at: http://transcripts.cnn.com/2002/ALLPOLITICS/01/29/bush.speech.txt/ (accessed on 27 February 2005).
Castells, M. (2000) *End of Millennium*, Oxford: Blackwell.
Darma Putra, I.N. and Windu Sancaya (eds) (2005) *Kompetensi Budaya Dalam Globalisasi*, Denpasar: Fakultas Sastra Universitas Udayana & Pustaka Larangan.
Geertz, C. (1966) 'Person, time and conduct in Bali: an essay in cultural analysis', Yale Southeast Asia Program Cultural Report Series 14.

Geria, I.W. (2004) 'Mengamankan kapital kultural kedamaian', *Bali Post*, 1 June.
Ghindwani, H.D. (trans) (2005) *Hindu Agama Universal – Bunga Rampai Pemikiran dan Kisah Swami Vivekananda*, Jakarta: Media Hindu.
Habermas, J. (2005) *Zwischen Naturalismus und Religion – Philosophische Aufsätze*, Frankfurt am Main: Suhrkamp.
Hitchcock, M. and Darma Putra, I.N. (2004) 'Bali after the bombs: local values and inter-communal relations', in I.W. Ardika and I.N. Darma Putra (eds) *Politik Kebudayaan dan Identitas Etnik*, Denpasar: Fakultas Universitas Udayana & Balimangsi Press.
Hornbacher, A. (2005a) 'Anthropozentrische Moral – Kosmozentrisches Ethos', *Sietar Magazin*, Chemnitz.
—— (2005b) *Zuschreibung und Befremden. Postmoderne Repräsentationskrise und verkörpertes Wissen im balinesischen Tanz*, Berlin: Reimer.
—— (ed.) (2006) *Ethik, Ethos, Ethnos. Aspekte und Probleme interkultureller Ethik*, Bielefeld: transcript.
Juniartha, I.W. (2005) 'Balinese up demand on bombers execution', *Jakarta Post*, 11 October.
Küng, H. (1991) 'Für eine universale Weltethos Erklärung', paper presented for the UNESCO, Paris. Online. Available at: http://www.humanistische-aktion.de/weltetho.htm (accessed on 4 February 2004).
Miller, R. (1996) 'Divine justice, evil, and tradition: comparative reflections', in T. Nardin (ed.) *The Ethics of War and Peace. Religious and Secular Perspectives*, Princeton: Princeton University Press.
Narokobi, B.M. (1999) 'Human rights and wrongs – die melanesische Erfahrung. Der Fall Papua Neuguinea', in J. Hoffmann (ed.) *Begründung von Menschenrechten aus der Sicht unterschiedlicher Kulturen*, Bd. II, Frankfurt am Main: Verlag für interkulturelle Kommunikation.
Picard, M. (1999) 'The discourse of kebalian: transcultural constructions of Balinese identity', in R. Rubinstein and L. Connor (eds) *Staying Local in the Global Village. Bali in the Twentieth Century*, Honolulu: University of Hawaii Press.
Rabinow, P. (1986) 'Representations are social facts: modernity and postmodernity in anthropology', in J. Clifford and G. Marcus (eds) *Writing Culture. The Poetics and Politics of Ethnography*, Berkeley: University of California Press.
Ramstedt, M. (2004) *Hinduism in Modern Indonesia. A Minority Religion between Local, National and Global Interests*, London: Routledge.
Ricklefs, M.C. (2007) *Polarising Javanese Society: Islamic and Other Visions*, Singapore: National University of Singapore Press.
Salim, A. and Azra, A. (eds) (2003) *Shari'a and Politics in Modern Indonesia*, Singapore: ISEAS.
Santikarma, D. (2005) 'Monument, document and mass grave: the politics of representing violence in Bali', in M.S. Zurbuchen (ed.) *Beginning to Remember: The Past in the Indonesian Present*, Singapore: Singapore University Press.
Schiller, A. (1997) *Small Sacrifices. Religious Change and Cultural Identity among the Ngaju of Indonesia*, New York and Oxford: Oxford University Press.
Sidel, J.T. (2007) *Riots, Pogroms, Jihad. Religious Violence in Indonesia*, Singapore: Singapore University Press.
Suasta, P. and Connor, L. (1999) 'Democratic mobilization and political authoritarianism: tourism developments in Bali', in R. Rubinstein and L. Connor (eds) *Staying Local in the Global Village. Bali in the Twentieth Century*, Honolulu: University of Hawaii Press.

Sutaba, I.M. (ed.) (2002) *Manfaat Sumberdaya Arkeologi Untuk Memperkokoh Integrasi Bangsa*, Denpasar: Upada Sastra.
Titib, I.M. (ed.) (2005) *Dialog Ajeg Bali. Perspektif Pengamalan Agama Hindu*, Surabaya: Paramita.
Wiana, I.K. (2002) *Memelihara Tradisi Veda*, Denpasar: BP.
Wiener, M. (1995) *Visible and Invisible Realms. Power, Magic, and Colonial Conquest in Bali*, Chicago: The University of Chicago Press.
Wolf, E. (1982) *Europe and the People Without History*, Berkeley: University of California Press.

Part II
Restorative performances
'Traditional justice', rituals, and symbols

3 Swearing innocence
Performing justice and 'reconciliation' in post-New Order Lombok

Kari Telle

Introduction

In the post-Suharto period, civilian 'security' groups dedicated to fight crime and enforce justice have been a visible and volatile presence on the island of Lombok. The violent ways in which some crime-fighting groups have dealt with alleged criminals has obscured the fact that other groups draw upon 'traditional' practices for resolving conflicts and disputes. The renewed interest in using longstanding ritual formats, like collective oath-taking, to counter crime and lawlessness is part of a broader return to 'tradition' (*adat*) on Lombok that has been enabled by the changed political climate in Indonesia since 1998. This chapter examines an oath-taking ceremony called *garap* that Sasak Muslims in Central Lombok turn to for resolving issues related to 'intimate theft': theft of which they suspect that someone in their own community is culpable. *garap* is usually arranged in connection with theft, but the practice may also be adapted to settle other grave offences, including homicide. That two out of the five crime-fighting groups operating in northern Central Lombok have incorporated the *garap* rite into their charters suggests that this institution, far from being a relic of the past, is deemed to be highly relevant for curing contemporary social ills. By examining the performative dynamics of this ordeal, which is steeped in the symbolism of death and rebirth, I will show how expressive culture can facilitate the passage from conflict to conciliation and thereby serve to restore social relations.

As a formal agreement to mend ruptures in social relationships following violations against persons and property, *garap* is oriented towards generating a sense of reconciliation. But this communal mechanism of administering justice operates in ways that are at odds with the assumptions that inform the policy-oriented literature on conflict-resolution and peace-building. In this literature the processes held to promote reconciliation often hinge on theological or psychological notions, such as confession, repentance, and forgiveness. In a seminal study of confession in law and literature, Brooks (2002: 2) notes the centrality of the confessional model in Western culture, and argues that "confession of wrongdoing is considered fundamental to morality because it constitutes a verbal act of self-recognition as wrongdoer and hence provides the basis of rehabilitation". Brooks also warns that the constant call to admit guilt amounts almost to a tyranny of confession today.

While the confessional model pervades Euro-American conceptions of law, morality, and popular culture, the therapeutic effects of truth telling and the restoration of civil dignity by way of memory should not be assumed (Alcinda 2005; Feldman 2003).[1] If confessional speech has become a measure of authenticity in Western culture, people in other cultures and religious traditions may not value speech and the importance of 'speaking guilt' in the same manner. The globalization of knowledge in the burgeoning field of transitional justice, and the accelerated sharing of information and analysis between so-called transitional societies (van Zyl 2007) makes it timely to question the assumption that confessional speech as part of the truth-seeking endeavor promotes reconciliation. One problem with approaching conflict-resolution and reconciliation in these terms is that the individual becomes the locus of rights and responsibilities, hence the tendency to "privilege the individual over the community" (Daly & Sarkin 2007: 68–9) in these approaches.

Turning to the Sasak practice of *Garap*, we find a strong preference for depersonalizing conflicts and turning their resolution into a communal matter. Nothing illustrates this better than the fact that no one is ever accused of having committed a 'crime' in the course of *Garap*. I take the refusal to name suspects as the key to the conciliatory logic of this juridico-religious practice that aims to 'cleanse' a moral community, be it a village or the members of a voluntary association, of anger and mutual suspicion arising after cases of 'intimate theft'. Rather than calling for admissions of guilt, *garap* pivots around the declaration of innocence, a process that entails the public affirmation of key moral values. Both restorative and retributive forms of justice are administered in this communal practice. That is, *garap* allows a place for charity as well as for expressions of righteous anger and the settling of accounts. The main argument I will make is that the administration of both restorative and retributive justice, articulated in a religious language, is what makes *garap* seen as a powerful mechanism for resolving conflicts and restoring the trust required to co-operate on collective projects. As such, *garap* is an example of how 'local' or 'traditional' forms of justice often balance the need for coexistence with the moral demand for condemnation (Theidon 2006). Being concerned with the micro-politics of conflict and its resolution, the chapter highlights the multi-sensory and embodied aspects of performing justice; how achieving a 'sense of justice' to a large extent hinges on effective and transformative performance.[2] Before I explore the practice and recent attempts to tailor it to novel circumstances, it is necessary to introduce some salient features of the social and political landscape in post-New Order Lombok.[3]

Reformasi, rioting, and the specter of crime

The island of Lombok lies just east of Bali and is home to roughly 2.5 million inhabitants. The Sasak, who make up about 90 percent of the total population, refer to the island as 'the Sasak world' (*gumi Sasak*). In so doing they lay claim to a deeper connection to the island than the other groups, such as the Balinese, Chinese, Arabs, and Javanese, who together make up about 10 percent of the population. Since the collapse of the New Order regime in 1998, Sasak claims to autochthony status combined with appeals to 'majoritarianism' have become more strident. As in other parts of Indonesia, 'tradition' and the idea of 'localism' have gained new political value in the *Reformasi* era (Davidson & Henley 2007; Schulte Nordholt & van Klinken 2007). The new politics of 'tradition' is coupled with an increasingly important global politics of rights, but it is also animated by uncertainty as to collective identities and their boundaries in the new political landscape of decentralization and increased regional autonomy. The social unrest and violence that plagued several regions of Indonesia in the early *Reformasi* period have also had some impact on the situation on Lombok. In January 2000, at the height of the lethal conflicts in the Moluccas (see Adam and Bräuchler this volume), a perceived threat to the position of Muslims took the form of an anti-Christian riot.

The riot, which began immediately after an Islamic rally (*tabliq akhbar*) in the provincial capital of Mataram held in support of Muslim victims of the violence in eastern Indonesia, targeted Christian places of worship, private homes, shops, and offices belonging to Christians and Chinese. For members of the Chinese community, the riot sparked memories of the anti-communist pogroms of 1965–66 in which they were heavily targeted, hence those who could, hastily fled the island.[4] The riot spread rapidly to the tourist destinations of West Lombok and into the hinterland of Central Lombok, leaving a trail of damaged and burnt-out buildings. The rioting petered out after the police announced that they would 'shoot on the spot'. Official records report seven deaths and 54 severely injured (Kristiansen 2003).[5] External provocateurs were blamed for instigating the riot, but no formal charges were made.[6] What is more noteworthy is that the organizing committee for the *tabliq akhbar* included political and religious figures who have been closely associated with the new vigilantism in post-Suharto Lombok, in the form of so-called civilian 'security' groups (B.I. *pamswakarsa*) (MacDougall 2007). While Lombok has not had a protracted conflict cast in ethnic or religious terms, the riot combined with other signs of militant Islamic mobilization have made religious minorities more concerned about their status as minorities.[7]

The transition to *Reformasi* entailed far-reaching changes in the organization and understanding of 'security'. Since 1998, the police has achieved more autonomy while the military has lost its former near-monopoly on the "securitization" (Wæver 1995) of society. Under the New Order, 'security' was, as Bubandt (2005: 282) noted, "more than anything else a bureaucratic attempt to calculate the threats and dangers from within civil society to the state (as the true representative of the people)". The armed forces had a 'dual function' to defend against foreign enemies and a mandate to maintain regime stability and guide the development of society. This implied a focus on surveillance and the routine evocation of threats posed by internal enemies, both political and criminal (Anderson 2001; Barker 1998; Dwyer & Santikarma 2007). At the same time, the state relied on civilian proxies and criminal gangs to carry out some of its dirty business (Ryter 2002; Schulte Nordholt 2002). It has been argued that the regime operated in ways analogous to a criminal gang, employing and normalizing violence and extortion as state practice (Lindsey 2001). With the post-Suharto shift from state-secured development towards democratization and regional autonomy, 'security' has slipped beyond state control, becoming increasingly invested in private and civilian hands.

Lombok is one of many places in Indonesia were the decentralization process has been accompanied by an upsurge in paramilitary and vigilante activity (Sidel 2006; Wilson 2005). My doctoral fieldwork commenced in August 1997 just as the Asian economic crisis was beginning to be felt in rising prices, growing unemployment, and a preoccupation with crime. Of particular concern were the growing incidents of violent burglaries that occurred during the last year of the Suharto regime and in the transition period (Cederroth 2001; ICG 2003).[8] As this growth of organized banditry occurred in a milieu marked by widespread cynicism regarding the interest of the police and the official justice system in prosecuting lawbreakers, the situation was ripe for the emergence of popular initiatives to combat crime (Telle 2005). Most groups began as neighborhood patrols, but some of the groups in East Lombok rapidly evolved into militias controlled by Islamic religious leaders with ties to high-level politicians. In the early *Reformasi* era, many provincial governments saw civilian 'security' groups (*pamswakarsa*) as "a 'grassroots' security system capable of replacing Suharto's top-down military style of authoritarian rule" (MacDougall 2007: 286). On Lombok, popular initiatives to combat lawlessness were welcomed as "a new form of 'people's power'" (MacDougall 2007: 287) embodying the participatory spirit of *Reformasi*.[9] Over time, the new vigilantism, while masquerading as a move to curb crime, has become the lucrative intersection where criminal and political interests converge.

Also in Central Lombok, a rural and relatively poor district, people responded to the crisis-related wave of theft and violent burglaries by organizing patrol and 'security' groups. A striking feature of local developments is the renewed interest shown in *adat*-based conflict-resolution formats. One example of this trend is that the *garap* ordeal has been incorporated into the charters of Tigabersatu and Tunjung Tilah, two of the crime-fighting groups operating in Central Lombok. These groups combine the work of patrolling neighborhoods at night (*ngeronda*) with the challenging task of recovering the stolen property of members who have been robbed.[10] Needless to say, the latter endeavor does not always succeed and unsuccessful searches for stolen goods are likely to place the group under stress. Faced with the challenge of keeping such groups together, and of ensuring that their members do not engage in lawless activities, the leaders have turned to *adat*-based formats of justice.[11] The renewed interest in communal or 'local' justice has been enabled by a shift in the position local government has taken towards 'tradition' (*adat*). If under the New Order 'tradition' was often stigmatized as an obstacle to progress, then local officials have recently portrayed 'local wisdom' as a vital resource in the making of a new social order. That some politicians try to benefit politically by clothing themselves in 'tradition' should not, however, detract our attention from the earnest search among ordinary Sasak men and women to find ways to resolve conflicts and counter violence by invoking ancestral idioms and rituals. Speaking of a similar 'return to tradition' on the eastern Indonesian island of Sumba, Hoskins (2005: 145–6) points out that "ancestral idioms of shared moral standards and power are turned to precisely because the dislocations and uncertainties of modern times have made them especially relevant".

Garap and the problem of 'intimate theft'

It is tempting to see the revival of *adat*-based formats of justice and conflict-resolution in Indonesia as a response to the shortcomings of the legal apparatus. But it is worth stressing that even a well-functioning legal system could not respond to, much less resolve, the kind of concerns being addressed through a practice like *Garap*. This community-based institution may thrive in "the shadow of the law" (Spyer 2006: 209), yet it operates according to a very different logic than the criminal justice system, which rests on the premise that offenders should be identified, tried, and punished for their misdeeds. While this oath-taking practice has retributive elements, the dramaturgy of *garap* underlines its restorative focus: the twin objective is to restore social agency to victims and to heal fractured communal relations. Because Sasak persons are not conceived as existential isolates but as embedded in webs of affective relations, these objectives are intimately connected. One consequence for dispute resolution that follows from this 'relational' view of the person is that society is likely to be more concerned to deal with the effects of a person's behavior than with its motivations.

Garap is a highly institutionalized practice that is performed at the request of those who feel themselves to be victims of a crime, usually theft. When compared to physical violence that destroys life and limb, theft might be dismissed as a relatively trivial offence.[12] But if we are to understand other life-worlds, we better accept that "conflicts are, in every sense of the word, cultural events" (Lederach 1991: 166). As Avruch (1991) and others have noted, images, metaphors, and 'conflict talk' yield rich insight into ethno-conflict theory and praxis. In Central Lombok, theft which is attributed to a so-called 'neighborhood thief' (*maling gubuk*) is said to produce a putrid stench (*bais*). This smell, which is the smell of a corpse, is particularly intense when the thief is not caught in the act but manages to slip away. The Sasak often express moral indignation through olfactory metaphors; various practices that are symptomatic of disorder are said to 'stink', and to be difficult to keep secret because they reek. If we follow the trail of 'foul smell' that is said to escape after 'intimate theft', it becomes apparent that stealing is seen as having affinities with much-feared covert forms of violence, such as sorcery (*ilmu seher*) and witchcraft (*ilmu selaq*). As I have discussed elsewhere (Telle 2003), the 'neighborhood thief' is in some ways conceived as a witch (*tau selaq*), a figure of evil who saps their victims of blood and vitality. Unlike witches, whose nefarious acts do not prompt collective efforts at redress, the thieves who prey on fellow villagers are seen as deviant figures whose anti-social behavior demands a firm collective response.

What makes 'intimate theft' so problematic is not primarily the loss of material objects but the fact that theft is an intrusive act that breeds fear, animosity, mistrust, and suspicion. Much as physical violence generates "a psychology of insecurity" (Schulte Nordholt & van Klinken 2007: 26) that lingers long after the violence has stopped, theft erodes trust and threatens to undo the relations which fashion a sense of community. Whether a local thief runs off with a couple of chickens or absconds with a motorbike, this intrusive act impairs the victim's ability to engage productively with others. The 'neighborhood thief' threatens to rob a precarious moral community of its spirit of mutuality and exchange. Effectively, 'intimate theft' upsets the most elementary distinctions on which the social order is based, distinctions between 'insiders' and 'outsiders', 'friends' and 'enemies'. The smell of putrefaction escaping after theft is itself symptomatic of this ambiguity; it is death-like, characterized by elusiveness, formlessness, and the ambiguity of inside and outside. Implicit in this olfactory imagery is a notion of the community as a body, an organic whole with porous boundaries that are vulnerable to rupture. As one man commented with a mixture of shame and disgust after a break-in occurred near his house in July 2001: "Now this neighborhood really stinks [*bais gubuk*]. The stench is smelled far away, it cannot be sealed off." When people call for *garap* to be held, the aim is to 'purify' and reconstitute the social body by reaffirming distinctions that are vital to personal as well as communal well-being.

Swearing innocence and drinking soil

Cast as a rite of purification, *garap* entails pledging an oath of innocence before witnesses and drinking water mixed with soil that is taken from the tomb of a Muslim saint. The practice draws much of its religious authority from its close association with Wali Nyato, a figure who is reputed to have brought the religion of Islam to southern Lombok and whose tomb located on a hilltop near the village of Rembitan is a popular pilgrimage site. While this saint is said to reside in Mecca, the spiritual center of Muslims worldwide, he is believed to return to Lombok on Wednesdays and Saturdays, when the site is packed with hundreds of people from all over the island who gather to pray and to make or fulfill vows. Soil to be used for the purposes of oath-taking or healing is only removed when the site is 'filled' (*teisi*) with spiritual presence; indeed, it is strictly forbidden or taboo (*maliq*) to remove soil at other times. As a result, *garap* may only be carried out on Wednesdays or Saturdays. These temporal and material links to the revered figure of Wali Nyato serve to invest the practice with religious authority reaching back to the origin of Islam on the island.[13]

Steeped in the imagery of death, *garap* is built around a demonized 'Other', who must be revealed and brought to justice, in order for victims and the broader community to thrive. The central ritual act in this process is the swearing of an oath (*sumpah*) in order to determine a person's innocence or guilt. The kind of justice promoted through this ordeal belongs in the transcendental realm, hence suspects need not be named or identified during the rite itself. *garap* exploits the most powerful linguistic resources that the Sasak command, that is, an oath sworn before human and invisible spiritual witnesses. Among 'traditionalist' Muslims, the swearing of an oath is widely understood to activate a form of divine justice.[14] In the case of *garap*, the oath is voiced by local authority figures who speak and act in the name of the community at large, a community that includes both the living and the deceased. *garap* often takes place in the cemetery, and my Sasak companions agree that the severity of the ordeal, the symbolism of which is modeled on the burial ceremony, is most intensely felt when it takes place among the ancestral graves.

The etymology of the term *garap* is uncertain, but people explained that it means 'to dig', 'to search for something that is hidden', or 'to grope for something in the dark'. While the image of searching for something 'in the dark' suggests that the endeavor is difficult and might fail, *garap* is carried out with great certitude. People are adamant that if the culprit or his collaborators participate in the ordeal, they will be 'struck' or 'hit' (*kenaq*) by a curse. That is, sooner or later, those who commit perjury will exhibit bodily signs that reveal their true identity. These symptoms are varied, but the most commonly cited sign is that the abdominal area begins to swell, becoming big and bloated. "It's almost like being pregnant", a young mother explained. It is not only the distended belly that attracts attention, but also the foul putrid scent (*bais*) that seeps out from the body. Both the smell and the swelling belly indicate that an irreversible process of putrefaction has been set in motion. For the thief and his partners, concealment yields to disclosure in a visual and an olfactory mode; they are literally pregnant with death. The curse is said to be so potent (*mandiq*) that it may affect their offspring for no less than seven generations. This frightful scenario indicates that a strong element of vengeance, articulated in a religious language of accountability, is integral to this oath-taking ordeal.

Without underestimating this emphasis on supernatural retribution, I will nonetheless suggest that *garap* is a privileged occasion in which moral values are voiced and reaffirmed. During my fieldwork I have come across several local skeptics, men and women who doubt that transcendental forces are being activated in the course of *garap*, yet who vigorously defended the practice on the grounds that it is a public occasion where the community speaks 'with one voice', condemning those who reject the moral values being expressed in the ceremony. These points resonate with the findings in Just's (2001: 107) study of justice and morality on the neighboring island of Sumbawa, in which he persuasively argued that "the act of constructing moral narratives, presenting them publicly, and making them authoritative is *the* defining characteristics of the Dou Donggo legal process". The Sasak practice of *garap* operates according to a similar logic: the focus is less on uncovering the intentionality and the particular facts of a particular offence than to use it as an occasion to express and enact moral narratives.

In much of Central Lombok, *garap* and the process leading up to its performance is regarded as the most refined (*alus*) yet effective way of dealing with problems related to 'intimate theft'. In other words, this judicial process appears to satisfy their sense of justice. What, then, do local people emphasize about this process? For one, my Sasak companions stress the indirect and non-accusatory qualities of the entire process, highlighting the role of intermediaries. If those who have been robbed or harmed in other ways want to call for *garap*, the first step is to contact a *klian*, a neighborhood official, sometimes referred to as the 'father of the community' (*aman kanoman*), who is called to mediate conflicts among neighbors.[15] At no point in the meeting between the injured party and the *klian* are suspects to be identified by name, only the hamlets where they are believed to reside will be indicated. The cultural value placed on avoiding accusations relates to the "specter of vengeance" (Girard 1972) as the naming of suspects or perpetrators might invite further retaliation, for instance in the form of sorcery. What is important for the victims is to avoid becoming further entangled in a destructive relationship. This concern is grounded in ideas of the person as embedded in a matrix of social relations and a conception of conflict as akin to disease. Notions of flow and blockage figure centrally in Sasak understandings of disease and conflict. In both instances the curative process entails straightening out 'twisted' (*bengkok*) relations. Given these assumptions, involving a third party and leaving the name of offenders unsaid are culturally valued strategies for reducing the potential for further conflict.

What also makes *garap* seem an effective mechanism for resolving conflict is that it grants the culprit a chance to retrace his steps without being stigmatized or shamed in public. *garap* is always announced minimally one week before the ordeal is due to take place, and throughout this time it is possible to return the stolen goods while being granted anonymity. Such transactions are conducted via a go-between, who contacts the *klian*, or one of the Islamic officials in the village, the *kyai*. Most villages in Central Lombok have several *kyai*, who collectively are responsible for conducting all major life-cycle rituals. Known as the 'mother of the community' (*inan kanoman*), the *kyai* occupies a symbolically feminine ritual office associated with Islam. The *kyai* perform vital ritual functions and tend to enjoy great respect, which explains why they are deemed the most trustworthy person to conduct such secretive negotiations. As long as the goods are returned or replaced by an equivalent, there will be no further repercussions, though a small fine (*denda*) or some form of compensation is likely to be involved. When such an agreement has been reached, the announced *garap* performance is simply called off.

From this account we see that numerous established procedures – openings towards reconciliation – precede the actual performance of *garap*. Only when these mechanisms have been exhausted will the announced *garap* ceremony be carried out, and also then is the procedure marked by indirectness. The best way to ensure that no one feels accused is by casting a wide net around those who are to be included in the ceremony. This is achieved by involving an entire administrative village subsection (*dusun*), which in the densely populated areas of Central Lombok is likely to include several hundred households. The ordeal may be organized on a smaller scale, and by using well-established territorial markers, such as roads and irrigation channels; the chance of someone feeling stigmatized is reduced. In sum, the farther apart victims and suspects live from each other, the wider the circle of people who are called on to participate. Though it is often said that *garap* serves to 'cleanse the neighborhood' (*besuq gubuk*), the notion of 'neighborhood' is highly elastic.

The basic principle is that at least one member from each domestic unit (*kuren*) located within the designated area is obliged to take part in *Garap*, with the husband usually acting on behalf of his wife and dependants. Women are not obliged to participate, but they can and frequently do represent their spouse and children. To the extent that someone emerges as a suspect, the person incriminates himself by not having a legitimate excuse to be absent or by not having family members who are willing to pledge the oath of innocence on his behalf. When someone is missing without a legitimate reason, *garap* will be postponed for another week, a procedure that may be repeated up to three times. If someone fails to show up for the third time, the village administration will deliberate on the appropriate course of action. In such cases two scenarios may follow. One, local officials, including the village head, the *klian*, and the *kyai* may decide to turn the person over to the police. Given the strong preference for settling disputes without involving official institutions and the pervasive distrust of the police, this option is not entirely satisfactory. Consequently, a more likely outcome of the deliberation is to condemn the person who has refused to take the oath to leave the village for a period. While many aspects of 'local' or 'traditional' justice were abandoned during the New Order period, temporary banishment remains an *adat*-based sanction in many Sasak communities.

Swearing innocence

To give a sense of the performative dynamics of *Garap*, I will discuss an ordeal that was held in the village of Bon Raja in July 2001 to settle the issues that arose after a pair of heirloom daggers and several antique cloths went missing from a house and a neighbor emerged as a suspect.[16] The ceremony was to take place in the neighborhood prayer house (*santren*) on a Wednesday afternoon, and by the time I arrived some 200 men from the ward of Sukadane were crammed together in the compound and prepared to pledge their innocence by 'drinking soil' (*ngenem tanah*). Seated up on the porch, Amaq, the old farmer and virtuoso flute player who had called for *garap* seemed tired and withdrawn. Since the break-in two weeks earlier, he had lost his appetite and felt listless, alternating between insomnia and excessive sleeping. These symptoms of being startled (*tenjot*) worried the family because a person in this state is especially vulnerable to visitations by harmful spirits and is liable to fall sick. For this reason, the family had asked a local healer to prepare medicine (*sembeq tenjot*) to make him regain his balance and to protect him against the very serious, indeed potentially deadly, condition that may occur when the soul is dislodged from the body.

Garap was on the verge of being postponed for another week when it became apparent that one man, a well-known troublemaker with a violent demeanor, was conspicuously absent. The absence did not come as a total surprise. At a religious gathering in the neighborhood some days earlier, this man had announced that he would rather move out of the village than to take part in the ordeal. When the *klian*, speaking through a microphone, asked if people were willing to proceed despite this absence, a handful of men shouted that he was "welcome to leave, but should drink first." As nobody voiced any objections, this loud response appeared to express shared sentiments, and two men were sent to convey this collective opinion. While the man was not home, his wife was 'brave enough to guarantee' (*bani tanggung*) her husband's innocence. As the young woman made her way into the crowded compound, eyes downcast and her hand covering the mouth, people muttered that she was ashamed (*lile*) by her partner's dirty work. The man seated next to me whispered: "I pity her. If only she knew how she will suffer by drinking on his behalf and feigning ignorance, she would not have come." Whatever her motivations for participating were, her presence as the representative of the household meant that the *garap* ordeal could be carried out.

By this time, a man designated by the *kyai* had already brought the basket with the soil from Wali Nyato's grave into the prayer house in a sling made from a white funeral shroud, carefully shielding the basket with an umbrella. Deceased babies are carried to the cemetery in this manner. The first glimpse those who are gathered get of the soil is apt to prompt memories of premature deaths. Such memories are likely to be quite personal as rates of infant mortality on Lombok are among the highest in Indonesia (Hay 2001). The babies who are buried soon after birth epitomize the frailty of life. It is this frailty – how easily the life force pales, leaving the body cold and still – that is evoked by the soil carried in a sling. The tools for digging and closing graves, such as a long rod, shovels, and a bucket made from buffalo hide are also obligatory *garap* paraphernalia. These grimy tools prepare an emotional space within the participants. When I asked why these tools must be present, I was told that they would be needed should someone 'die immediately' (*mate terus*) after taking the oath. Such comments are made with a keen awareness of the props that will have a dramatic effect, but the ubiquitous presence of objects and substances associated with corpses and burials does indeed serve to create a somber somewhat tense atmosphere. The sense that people may be brought to death as a function of pledging the oath is conveyed through material objects and reinforced in speech.

That the act of drinking the soil may be tantamount to ingesting death is explicitly stated in the brief speech that precedes the *garap* oath. Before the *klian* began to speak, he ordered two men to cut some branches from a nearby banyan tree and to find a twig of *kelor* leaves. Serving symbolic as well practical functions, these leaves are an integral part of any *garap* ordeal. Leaves from the tall and impressive banyan tree, which is associated with power and traditional leadership, are folded into simple spoons. As for the tiny *kelor* leaves, it is important to note that these leaves are instrumental in marking the transition from life to death. Specifically, a twig of *kelor* leaves is used to splash water that has been blessed by a *kyai* onto the body of a person who has ceased breathing to inform her that she is dead. Another function of this 'naming water' (*aiq pemaran*) is to postpone the onset of putrefaction and thus prevent the nauseating smell of decomposing flesh from escaping prior to the burial. *Kelor* leaves wilt quickly after they are picked, and this phenomenal property informs their usage in *garap* where they are iconic of the swift demise awaiting those who take a false oath.

Now that all the required items had been fetched and placed on top of a raised tray along with the soil and the water jar, the *klian* grabbed a microphone and said:

Figure 3.1 The *garap* rite. The *klian* administers the potion consisting of water mixed with soil from the tomb of Wali Nyato, using a banyan leaf as a spoon. Desa Beber, Central Lombok, 1997 (Photo: Kari Telle)

Anyone who has seen, heard, or has any knowledge of the theft may still step forth and report. But once I open this basket with soil and mix these two substances in this earthenware bowl, then it is too late.

Explaining that he himself accompanied by another *kyai* from the village had travelled all the way to Rembitan in southern Lombok earlier in the day to fetch the soil, he noted that the soil's effects (*pemuru' tanah*) would be particularly potent since it was fresh from the source. He continued:

This soil is not just like any other piece of dirt but a very special precious substance (*barang mulia*) whose qualities are such that those who are guilty, or implicated in the theft, will surely suffer (*kenaq sangsara*). Not everyone who is 'struck' by *garap* will 'die at once' (*mate terus*). Rather, the person may suffer one mishap after the other, lose his sense of direction, never find well-being or feel pleasantly 'cool' (*embel bau*) and healthy. In fact, the effects of swearing falsely may be felt for as long as seven generations (*pituq turunan*). But those of you who do not know anything about the theft should not be afraid to drink this substance, because it will enhance and heal you (*eat kerisa'm*). You will be healed of all kinds of ills. The soil truly becomes a medicine that cures (*jari oat*).

He then asked if everyone wanted him to 'open the soil'. Many of the men assembled replied, "Open!" Now the *kyai*, who was seated cross-legged next to the white bundle, began to pray. After a brief invocation and another prayer in Arabic, he carefully removed the funeral shroud from the soil while two men lifted it up so it formed a canopy. Taking the dry clump out of the basket, he put it into a bowl and poured water over, stirring with a branch. Thereafter the *klian* stated the name of the person who had wanted to arrange the ordeal and enumerated the missing items: Two heirloom daggers and ten pieces of antique cloth. Grabbing the twig of *kelor* leaves and waving it in the air, he swore:

> If there are people among those who drink this water who have stolen these things, or who know about the theft, may they wither and shrivel up (*raraq*) like these *kelor* leaves.

Beckoning to Amaq to come forth to drink first since he was the one who had called for *Garap*, he then fed the *kyai* and thereafter himself. This drinking order suggests that those who arrange the ordeal should be the first to suffer the consequences should they be implicated or duplicitous. One by one, the men stepped up into the prayer house, bowed down and gulped down the potion, most of them muttering a brief prayer as they did so. Towards the end, the woman who represented her husband got up to be fed. After all those who were obligated to take part had their turn and their names were ticked off on lists compiled by representatives from the neighborhood, approximately 20–25 women, men, and children from other sections of the village surged forward, requesting to be fed this potent substance, hoping to be cured of their physical ailments and other afflictions. The crowd quickly disbanded while the two men who led the performance followed Amaq to his house where they shared a meal accompanied by prayers.

From this brief description, we see that themes of death and destruction are intermingled with those of cleansing and regeneration. The potion that the participants must drink encapsulates this symbolic 'doubleness': it has the capacity to heal, but it may also harm. Although *garap* is directed towards overcoming the disruptive forces unleashed by theft and to restore social agency to the victims, it is the imagery of death that is most prominent. Symbolically violent techniques are invoked in order to enable the victims as well as the members of the broader community to overcome their anger and anguish. Various discursive forms, including formal speech and prayer, are harnessed to these ends, but it is above all the act of swearing that has life-enhancing and death-dealing potency. The oath that is voiced in *garap* is formulaic and has an almost object-like fixity. Spoken in the context of a public rite, it is especially potent *(mandiq)* or efficacious in Austin's (1962) sense of a performative utterance. The Sasak term *mandiq* refers to forceful speech, but certain weapons, especially the blade of antique daggers (*keris*), are also characterized as such. For those who have called for the ordeal to be held, the pledging of the oath can thus be likened to a declaration of independence that cuts – like the piercing blade of a *keris* – a destructive relation that restricts their social agency, thereby facilitating their reintegration into the flow of social relations. Also the community as a whole is 'cleansed' in this ordeal that promises to 'cool' those who are affected by the offence and to inflict a curse on those who commit perjury. Effectively, healing and harming is combined in a single process.

Going through *Garap*, people are brought uncomfortably close to substances and objects associated with death, and I will argue that the transformative efficacy of this practice hinges on this multi-sensorial experience of being exposed to residue and reminders of death. For rituals to be persuasive to their participants, they must be habituated to them, and this habituation is partly found in the "bodily substrate of the performance" (Connerton 1989: 71). The performative aspects of justice should not be underestimated: the *garap* ordeal draws much of its affective power from being modeled on a burial ceremony. Those who go through *garap* have witnessed many burials and know that when they take the oath they are positioned just like the deceased who is to be lowered into the earth, never to be seen again. This message is conveyed through the funeral shroud which forms a canopy – literally a sky (*langgit*) – over both the scene of the burial and the moment when the oath is administered. Whenever a person is to be buried, the bier is held high until it is lowered into the grave. At this time, the shroud covering the body is lifted up to form a protective enclosure until the grave is completed. In *garap*, the soil is wrapped and held like a dead baby. When the oath is administered the shroud is lifted up to form a canopy over the person who is fed by the *klian*, or 'father of the community', while the *kyai*, or 'mother of the community', witnesses the act. Thus suspended, the shroud envelops both moments, and reveals their unity. The message displayed before the eyes, spoken into the ears, and forced down the throat of the participants is that committing perjury is like receiving a death sentence.

Once *garap* has been carried out, the offence prompting the performance should be 'forgotten'. In my experience, people avoid referring to the matter partly because continued reference is considered unseemly and disruptive. One metaphor that is used is that repeated references would be 'like scratching a wound' and thereby preventing the healing process. This willingness to 'forget' hinges, I believe, on the conviction that justice has been served. Again I stress the performative aspects of justice: this conviction does not so much hinge on 'belief' in the putative effects of the oath, rather it is more of an embodied 'sense of justice'. From watching and talking to men and women about this ordeal, it seems clear that most people are apprehensive about, and feel repulsed by, taking soil from a tomb into their body. Several men noted that they felt anxious and nauseous, and were about to vomit. Others said that they felt like spitting out the murky water that feels strangely 'cold' (*enyet*), like death. But people are not in a position to refuse to drink, and this provokes what I will call a feeling of disgust. Disgust, as Miller (1997) made clear, is a visceral emotion that simultaneously expresses condemnation. A complex sentiment, disgust conveys "a strong sense of aversion to something perceived as dangerous because of its power to contaminate, infect, or pollute by proximity, contact, or ingestion" (Miller 1997: 2). Miller (1997: 9) suggests that the bodily force of disgust "presents a nervous claim of right to be free of the dangers imposed by the proximity of the inferior". As disgust arises from a recognition of having been in contact with something that defiles, the assertion of superiority is ambivalent. This analysis can shed some light on the performative dynamics of *Garap*, a ritual that fosters a sense of disgust yet provides the means for people to purify themselves of matter that threatens their integrity. Being uncomfortable to go through, the ordeal nurtures a sense of aversion to the acts that caused the performance to be held in the first place. Consequently, this community-based institution also serves to foster a sense of how people ought to act in a village world.

Experimenting with *Garap*

As I noted earlier, the community-based practice of *garap* has witnessed a renaissance in the *Reformasi* period, being adapted to the needs of several supra-local crime-fighting groups. Formed at a time of great uncertainty, groups like Tunjung Tilah and Tigabersatu, which combine night patrol activities with coordinated searches to recover stolen property, emerged in response to a wave of theft that was seen as symptomatic of a deeper social and moral crisis. Membership in these groups also entails the obligation to perform religious work in the form of the recitation of Islamic prayers in connection with the funerals of members. Willingness to take part in *garap*, also known as *sumpah adat*, is another condition for obtaining membership. By drawing upon longstanding conflict-resolution formats, like the institution of *garap*, the leaders of these groups have found acceptance for these novel social formations that nonetheless are seen to further the revival of 'tradition'. With the aid of these associations, *garap* is also introduced into new settings, a situation that may create conflicts as the interests of these supra-local groups may collide with those of local village authorities and the population at large.

When these groups call for *garap*, it means that their members have failed in their mission to retrieve stolen property, and the performance is a final effort to 'finish' the case. What needs to be understood is that if a thief makes off with someone's cow or motorbike, it does not necessarily mean that the original owner has been fully dispossessed. On Lombok, thievery often operates according to the logic of kidnapping and other forms of extortion (see MacDougall 2007). Stolen goods may be recovered provided that the owner is willing to redeem (*tebus*) the goods from 'middlemen' who are in the business of buying stolen, literally 'crooked' property (*barang bengkok*). Groups like Tunjung Tilah and Tigabersatu often mediate in such thief-victim relationships, and through a combination of negotiation and threat they can significantly reduce the cost. But they may also fail to retrieve stolen goods, and in such cases *garap* can be held in order to put the case to rest. The following case, recounted by a Tigabersatu member, vividly illustrates that the performance of *garap* may provoke surprising admissions of complicity and guilt. In late 2005, after a month-long search for a stolen cow, Tigabersatu leaders called for *garap* to be held in a hamlet in Desa Pengenjek, a village in the fertile central plain. Just as the *klian* was about to administer the oath, the head of the local Tigabersatu unit admitted to the group's main leader that the cow was hidden in a nearby tobacco oven. It turned out that his own son had served as the 'middleman' but since the father was prepared to return the cow, *garap* was called off. Although many members were shocked by this admission of double play, the man has remained the head of the local unit. In response to my question as to why he was not expelled or lost his leadership position, I was told that a core principle in Islam as well as Sasak tradition is that faults may be forgiven up to three times. Others noted that the man had 'learned his lesson' and henceforth could be trusted. Yet the fact remains that cases where those who 'fight crime' are found to be complicit in theft and shady dealings with thieves serve to discredit the legitimacy of such groups (see Telle 2009).[17]

In the area of Central Lombok where these groups emerged, *garap* has de-facto status as customary law which means that local residents are obliged to participate whenever the ceremony is arranged in the village. But these supra-local groups, whose membership spans various villages and districts, also recruit members from communities where this practice has never been part of the local justice system. While formal permission to arrange the ordeal may be secured from village authorities, local residents may loathe participating in a ritual that is imposed from 'above', having no precedence in local custom. More fundamentally, locals may object to taking part in a ceremony that is held at the request of groups that are active in the turbulent field of crime-control and 'security' provision. While these groups enjoy relatively widespread popular support, other Sasak villagers are deeply skeptical about such home-grown initiatives to tackle crime, and would rather see them disappear. In a situation where the moral legitimacy of such groups is in doubt, the performance of *garap* clearly has the potential to cause, rather than curb, conflict.[18]

The difficulties of adapting a community-based institution like *garap* to the needs of sectarian interest groups involve more than issues of cultural precedence and legitimacy. In the course of being adapted to suit the interests of crime-control groups, whose membership extends across village and districts boundaries, the practice has undergone subtle yet important changes. Both groups will call for *garap* to be arranged after cases of theft when their members have been unsuccessful in tracking and returning stolen goods to their rightful owners, usually within one month after the offence occurred. This scenario is, of course, very different from a situation where the 'victims' of theft simply report to a local official, requesting *garap* to be held. Entailed in such a request, as I explained earlier, is an invitation to settle the matter peacefully in private provided that the culprit agrees to return the goods or provides some form of compensation. In sum, the practice appears to have acquired a more confrontational and adversarial tenor, which is perhaps inevitable when it is carried out in the name of crime-fighting groups. While the performance of the *garap* ordeal may cement relations among the members of these supra-local groups, there is a real danger that such performances could exacerbate local tensions because the interests of these groups may well clash with those of other local residents.

Conclusions

If we think of practices for overcoming past violence as located in the space "between vengeance and forgiveness" (Minow 1998), *garap* would seem to belong closer to the vengeance pole that is associated with retributive justice than with unconditional forgiveness. Both retributive and restorative forms of justice are administered through this ordeal, and I have suggested that it is this combination that causes *garap* to be viewed as an effective mechanism for dealing with cases of 'intimate theft' and for restoring communal relations to normalcy. As an ordeal, the practice of *garap* has some similarities with a trial, the paradigmatic form of retributive justice, except that the retributive aspect is articulated in the religious language of divine justice. The ordeal gives expression to deeply held assumptions regarding the nature of cosmic order itself, where every deed, positive or negative, has its corresponding return.

What is striking about *garap* as a practice for administering justice is the importance attached to keeping the names of suspects hidden and avoiding accusation and confrontation. This reflects a strong cultural disposition for resolving problems by indirection, a value that has been noted in many Indonesian societies (Bowen 1993; Just 2001). We have seen that scant attention is paid to uncovering the actual 'facts' of the offence in question, just as no efforts are made to scrutinize the 'deeper' motivations that might have prompted the offence. The dynamics of the *garap* ordeal suggests that the resolution of certain conflicts in the Sasak Muslim context does not require that suspects be publicly identified, nor does it hinge on the verbal act of 'speaking guilt' (Brooks 2002). Confessional speech, in the sense of a public proclamation of guilt and repentance, simply plays no part in this communal justice practice. This can be related to a deep skepticism regarding speech in Sasak culture, where words and things must be transacted together in order for actions to be authoritative and 'weighty' (Telle 2000). Speech does, however, play an important role in this ritual, but those who are called to speak are authority figures who speak in the name of the moral community, articulating its core values. The purpose of arranging this ordeal is not merely to resolve a particular offence by acknowledging the harm done to particular victims, it is also to express and reaffirm key moral values through a collective multi-sensorial performance.

As we have seen, the *garap* ordeal pivots around the public swearing of innocence. Although people sometimes speculate about whether someone took a genuine oath or not, just as confessional speech is always haunted by the specter of falsehood (see Brooks 2002), Sasak Muslims tend to insist that the capacity to discern 'the truth' is ultimately beyond human powers. This deeply ingrained religious sensibility, a humble acknowledgment of human limitations, is matched by the widely shared cultural assumption that one can never fully know the 'inside' of an other person's heart. In my view, these cultural and religious assumptions are elements enabling the reintegrating of offenders and the reconstruction of communal bonds. The restorative process is, however, tied to a retributive sense of justice in the form of accountability and supernatural punishment. The logic of this ordeal is such that 'offenders', by failing to respond to the invitation to settle the issue in private, are perceived as rejecting both the victim's and the community's desire for reconciliation. This refusal is, if anything, far more problematic than the original offence. The message being communicated through *garap* is that a person who violates another person can be pardoned as long as he/she is prepared to offer a replacement or some form of compensation. Those who cannot be fully (re)integrated are those who are perceived to go against the 'community' itself. That is the stark message being articulated in this ordeal. While the performance of *garap* serves to normalize social relations, those who commit perjury are condemned to suffer.

In this chapter I have discussed a conflict-resolution format where confessional speech and truth telling on the part of culprits is not part of the process of performing justice. This silence on the part of the suspects contrasts with the emphasis accorded to various forms of truth telling, including confession, as a central element of how reconciliation processes tend to be envisaged in the fast-growing literature on transitional justice (Gloppen 2005; Hayner 2001). My intention is not to question the value of uncovering suppressed memories or voicing long-silenced truths, though I would like to caution against what I call the tyranny of confession. The globalization and apparent success of certain transitional justice initiatives, like the South African Truth and Reconciliation Commission, carries the danger that one model is uncritically transplanted to other contexts (see van Zyl 2007). In the case of South Africa, 'reconciliation' was the explicit goal of the truth-seeking endeavor, though not all truth commissions have been framed around this admittedly elusive notion (Hayner 2001). The globalization of peacemaking initiatives centered on uncovering 'truth', makes it timely to ask to what extent this reflects the preoccupation with confession in modern Western culture, where confession has become a "dominant form of self-expression; one that bears special witness to personal truth" (Brooks 2001: 9). If taking verbal responsibility for one's acts has become integral to Euro-Christian notions of morality and disciplinary practices, we should not assume that people in other religious traditions accord the same value to 'speaking guilt'.

Notes

1 The assumption that truth telling is key to reconciliation figures prominently in debates on transitional justice; for good overviews, see Gloppen (2005) and Hayner (2001).
2 For a good account of performance-centered approaches in anthropology, see Laderman and Roseman (1996).
3 This chapter builds on 17 months of fieldwork in the district of Jonggat, Central Lombok between 1994 and 2006. An additional three months of research had been carried out in the Mataram area. Terms in brackets are Sasak terms except where I indicate that Indonesian (B.I.) is used.
4 Estimates of the number of victims killed in 1965–66 are uncertain. The historian Robert Cribb (1990: 25) notes that "in Lombok, local memories report 50,000 killings in early 1966".
5 For insightful accounts of the riot and its aftermath, see Avonius (2004: 62–106) and ICG (2003).
6 Some analysts pointed to the involvement of Eggy Sudjana, the chairman of Persaudaraan Pekerja Muslim Indonesia (PPMI), but no charges were made.
7 One expression of this sense of insecurity is the formation of civilian defense groups along religious lines. Since 2000, both the Hindu Balinese and local Buddhists have established such groups.
8 The number of criminal cases registered in civil courts doubled between 1997 and 1998. For statistics on crime and employment trends connected to the monetary crisis, see Kristiansen (2003).
9 According to Colombijn (2002: 305), "Lombok may be the worst place in Indonesia as far as mob justice is concerned", a claim he qualified by noting that several reported cases of so-called mob justice were "summary executions by Pam Swakarsa, patrol groups hired to provide protection".
10 By May 2007 Tunjung Tilah had 1,100 registered members, whereas Tigabersatu, organized into 63 units, boasted about 6,500 registered household heads. The latter group has members in Central and West Lombok.
11 The term *adat*, usually glossed as 'customary law' is derived from Arabic (*āda*). For a good discussion of how colonial legal policies served to reify the distinction between local custom and Islam, see Hefner (2000).
12 I agree with Heald (1999: 73–4) that anthropologists largely have treated theft as a self-evident offense with a direct relationship between delict and accusation. Consequently,

scholars have missed the implications of calling someone a thief; why thieves are seen as more of a problem in some societies than in others, and why one might have 'witch-crazes' as well as 'thief-crazes'.

13 Islam was brought to Lombok in the sixteenth century. In Central Lombok, the majority of the population are 'traditionalist' Muslims. For accounts of the politics of Islamization, see Telle (2000, 2007) and McVey (1995).

14 Oath-taking is a well-known, if also controversial, conflict-resolution strategy in Java and Madura. During the anti-witchcraft campaigns in Banyuwangi in 1998–99, Nahdlatul Ulama-affiliated *kyai* (expert of Islamic religion) began to administer *sumpah pocong*, special oaths to be sworn by those accused of being witches. Also people who feared they might be lynched by a mob asked to go through the ceremony, which involves being bathed and wrapped in funeral garb, to convince people that they did not practice sorcery, see Sidel (2006: 152–3).

15 The *klian*-ship used to be a symbolically 'male' *adat*-office associated with governance. Under the New Order, the *klian* became incorporated into the village administration, becoming responsible for registering marriages and land transactions at the sub-village level.

16 Parts of this section appeared in Telle (2003). The village name is a pseudonym.

17 Bujak, a group originating in Ubung (Central Lombok) whose history can be traced to the mid-1980s which specialized in returning stolen goods gradually lost its support as it became known to collaborate with criminals.

18 For a poignant discussion of how reconciliation ceremonies intended to reconcile pro-integrationist militia groups and supporters of East Timorese independence became a prelude to murder, see Fox (2002).

References

Avruch, K. (1991) 'Introduction: culture and conflict-resolution', in K. Avruch, P.W. Black and J.A. Scimecca (eds) *Conflict Resolution: Cross-Cultural Perspectives*, New York: Greenwood Press.

Alcinda, H. (2005) 'Healing and social reintegration in Mozambique and Angola', in E. Skaar, S. Gloppen and A. Suhrke (eds) *Roads to Reconciliation*, Lanham, MD: Lexington Books.

Anderson, B.R.O'G. (2001) 'Introduction', in B.R.O'G. Anderson (ed.) *Violence and the State in Suharto's Indonesia*, Ithaca, NY: SEAP Publications.

Austin, J.L. (1962) *How To Do Things With Words*, Cambridge, Massachusetts: Harvard University Press.

Avonius, L. (2004) 'Reforming Wetu Telu: Islam, adat and the promises of regionalism in post-New Order Lombok', PhD dissertation, University of Leiden.

Barker, J. (1998) 'State of fear: controlling the criminal contagion in Suharto's New Order', *Indonesia*, 66: 7–42.

Bowen, J. (1993) 'Return to sender: a Muslim discourse on sorcery in a relatively egalitarian society', in C.W. Watson and R. Ellen (eds) *Understanding Witchcraft and Sorcery in Southeast Asia*, Honolulu: University of Hawaii Press.

Brooks, P. (2002) *Troubling Confessions: Speaking Guilt in Law and Literature*, Chicago: Chicago University Press.

Bubandt, N. (2005) 'Vernacular security: the politics of feeling safe in global, national and local worlds', *Security Dialogue*, 36(3): 275–96.

Cederroth, S. (2001) 'Patterns of modern fundamentalism: the case of Lombok', in O. Törnquist (ed.) *Political Violence: Indonesia and India in Comparative Perspective*, Oslo, Sum Report, No. 9: 33–8.

Colombijn, F. (2002) 'Maling, Maling! The lynching of petty criminals', in F. Colombijn and J.T. Lindblad (eds) *Roots of Violence in Indonesia*, Leiden: KITLV Press.
Connerton, P. (1989) *How Societies Remember*, Cambridge: Cambridge University Press.
Cribb, R. (1990) 'Problems in the historiography of the killings in Indonesia', in R. Cribb (ed.) *The Indonesian Killings of 1965–1966: Studies from Java and Bali*, Clayton, Victoria: Monash Papers on Southeast Asia.
Davidson, J.S. and Henley, D. (eds) (2007) *The Revival of Tradition in Indonesian Politics: The Deployment of Adat from Colonialism to Indigenism*, London: Routledge.
Daly, E. and Sarkin, J. (2007) *Reconciliation in Divided Societies: Finding Common Ground*, Philadelphia: University of Pennsylvania Press.
Dwyer, L. and Santikarma, D. (2007) 'Speaking from the shadows: memory and mass violence in Bali', in B. Pouligny, S. Chesterman and A. Schnabel (eds) *After Mass Crime: Rebuilding States and Communities*, Tokyo and New York: United Nations University Press.
Feldman, A. (2003) 'Strange fruit: the south African truth commission and the demonic economies of violence', in B. Kapferer (ed.) *Beyond Rationalism: Rethinking Magic, Witchcraft and Sorcery*, Oxford and New York: Berghahn Books.
Fox, J.J. (2002) 'Ceremonies of reconciliation as prelude to violence in Suai, East Timor', in C. Coppel (ed.) *Violence in Asia*: *Comparative Perspectives*, Oxford: Oxford University Press.
Girard, R. (1972) *Violence and the Sacred*, Baltimore: John Hopkins Press.
Gloppen, S. (2005) 'Roads to reconciliation: a conceptual framework', in E. Skaar, S. Gloppen and A. Suhrke (eds) *Roads to Reconciliation*, Lanham, MD: Lexington Books.
Hay, C. (2001) *Remembering to Live*: *Illness at the Intersection of Anxiety and Knowledge in Rural Indonesia*, Ann Arbor: University of Michigan Press.
Hayner, P.B. (2001) *Unspeakable Truths: Confronting State Terror and Atrocity*, New York and London: Routledge.
Heald, S. (1999) *Manhood and Morality: Sex, Violence and Ritual in Gisu Society*, London and New York: Routledge.
Hefner, R.W. (2000) *Civil Islam: Muslims and Democratization in Indonesia*, Princeton: Princeton University Press.
Hoskins, J. (2005) 'Calling on the ancestors to stop crime: ritual performance in an age of intermittent violence', in P.J. Stewart and A. Strathern (eds) *Expressive Genres and Historical Change: Indonesia, Papua New Guinea and Taiwan*, Aldershot: Ashgate Publishing.
ICG (International Crisis Group) (2003) *The Perils of Private Security in Indonesia: Guards and Militias on Bali and Lombok, Asia Country Report*, No. 67.
Just, P. (2001) *Dou Donggo Justice*: *Conflict and Morality in an Indonesian Society*, Lanham: Rowman & Littlefield.
Kristiansen, S. (2003) 'Violent youth groups in Indonesia. The cases of Yogyakarta and Nusa Tenggara Barat', *Sojourn*, 19(1): 110–38.
Laderman, C. and Roseman, M. (1996) 'Introduction', in C. Laderman and M. Roseman (eds) *The Performance of Healing*, New York and London: Routledge.
Lederach, J.P. (1991) 'Of nets, nails, and problems: the folk language of conflict-resolution in a Central American setting', in K. Avruch, P.W. Black and J.A. Scimecca (eds) *Conflict Resolution: Cross-Cultural Perspectives,* New York: Greenwood Press.
Lindsey, T. (2001) 'The criminal state: *premanisme* and the new Indonesia', in G.J. Lloyd and S.L. Smith (eds) *Indonesia Today*: *Challenges of History*, Lanham: Rowman & Littlefield.

MacDougall, J.M. (2007) 'Criminality and the political economy of security in Lombok', in H. Schulte Nordholt and G. van Klinken (eds) *Renegotiating Boundaries: Local Politics in Post-Suharto Indonesia*, Leiden: KITLV Press.

McVey, R. (1995) 'Shaping the Sasak: religion and hierarchy on an Indonesian island', in B. Werlen and S. Wölty (eds) *Kulturen und Raum*, Zürich: Rüegger.

Miller, W.I. (1997) *The Anatomy of Disgust*, Cambridge: Cambridge University Press.

Minow, M. (1998) *Between Vengeance and Forgiveness: Facing History after Genocide and Mass Violence*, Boston: Beacon Press.

Ryter, L. (2002) 'Youth, gangs, and the state in Indonesia', PhD dissertation, University of Washington.

Schulte Nordholt, H. (2002) 'A genealogy of violence', in F. Colombijn and J.T. Lindblad (eds) *Roots of Violence in Indonesia*, Leiden: KITLV Press.

Schulte Nordholt, H. and van Klinken, G. (2007) 'Introduction', in H. Schulte Nordholt and G. van Klinken (eds) *Renegotiating Boundaries: Local Politics in Post-Suharto Indonesia*, Leiden: KITLV Press.

Sidel, J.T. (2006) *Riots, Pogroms, Jihad: Religious Violence in Indonesia*, Ithaca and London: Cornell University Press.

Spyer, P. (2006) 'Some notes on disorder in the Indonesian postcolony', in J. Comaroff and J.L. Comaroff (eds) *Law and Disorder in the Postcolony*, Chicago: Chicago University Press.

Telle, K. (2000) 'Feeding the dead: reformulating Sasak mortuary rites', *Bijdragen tot de Taal, Land-en Volkenkunde*, 156(4): 771–805.

—— (2003) 'The smell of death: theft, disgust and ritual practice in Central Lombok, Indonesia', in B. Kapferer (ed.) *Beyond Rationalism: Rethinking Magic, Witchcraft and Sorcery*, Oxford and New York: Berghahn Books.

—— (2005) 'Decentralization and the privatization of security on Lombok', paper presented at the Center for Human Rights Conference on Democratization and Human Rights in Indonesia, University of Oslo, Voksenåsen, 9–10 March.

—— (2007) 'Nurturance and the specter of neglect: Sasak ways of dealing with the dead', in M. Janowski and F. Kerlogue (eds) *Kinship and Food in Southeast Asia*, Copenhagen: NIAS Press.

—— (2009, in Press) 'Seduced by security: the politics of (in) security on Lombok', in J. McNeish and J.H.S. Lie (eds) *Development and Security* (Critical Intervention Series), Oxford and New York: Berghahn Books.

Theidon, K. (2006) 'Justice in transition: the micro-politics of reconciliation in postwar Peru', *Journal of Conflict Resolution*, 50(3): 433–57.

van Zyl, P. (2007) 'Dealing with the past: reflections on South Africa, East Timor and Indonesia', in M.S. Zurbuchen (ed.) *Beginning to Remember: The Past in the Indonesian Present*, Singapore: Singapore University Press.

Wilson, I.D. (2005) 'The Changing Contours of Organised Violence in post-New Order Indonesia', Working Paper, No. 118, Perth: Asia Research Center, Murdoch University.

Wæver, O. (1995) 'On security', in R. Lipschutz (ed.) *Securitization and Desecuritization*, New York: Oxford University Press.

4 Social reconciliation and community integration through theater

Barbara Hatley

Introduction: theater and reconciliation

Theater is widely recognized internationally as a powerful medium for education and social transformation. In the first instance theater performances attract and engage viewers as sites of enjoyment and entertainment. By involving the emotions and senses they provide experiential "learning by doing ... more usable and readily accessible than other kinds of learning" (Soule 1998: 41). Through theater's "mirroring effect" audiences identify with stage action, while its "aesthetic distance" allows them to continue to observe and analyze (Scheff 1979: 57). Legendary pioneer of socially engaged theater, Augusto Boal, argues that the "aesthetic space" of theater facilitates both awareness and transformation.

> In life we tend to make and fix images for ourselves which then influence us and we cannot modify. But the aesthetic space allows democratic interchange, allows us to say 'OK, that's the way things are but that's not the way things should be, and now I am going to create an image of how I want the world to be'.
> (Boal 1996: 49)

This capacity to bring people together in potentially socially transforming experience serves as the basis for the use of theater in situations of communal conflict. Theater activities are employed in these contexts to bring together members of groups associated with a current or past conflict to promote improved social relations between them. In some cases the goal is 'social reconciliation' understood in terms of active social bonding between direct participants in the conflict; "the restoration of broken relationships or the coming together of those who have been alienated or separated from one another by conflict, to create a community again" (Assefa 1993: 9). Theater activities with this aim are reported from sites such as school classrooms in war-torn countries, such as Israel and Northern Ireland, involving pupils from both sides of the conflict (Fyfe 1996; Schonman 1996). More often the form of reconciliation aimed at is a more general one of "a kind of relationship between parties which is founded on mutual legitimacy" (Rouhana 2004: 175), "mutual acceptance of the other's nationhood and humanity" (Kelman 2004: 112). The key element in the process is that of recognizing the right to exist of the other party and the reality of their experiences. Theater assists in this process by representing these experiences, providing community members with a site for "telling and listening to each other's stories, and developing more complex narratives and more nuanced understandings of identity" (Cohen 2004: 6). Workshops where members of refugee communities tell their individual stories and share collective experiences with local residents, or members of settler societies like Australia discuss their experiences of racism towards indigenous people, provide examples of such activities (Dennis 2003). The following discussion first reviews the way theater has been used as a medium of social reconciliation internationally, examining some common formats and approaches. The focus then turns to the use of theater in socially divided communities in Indonesia, documenting what forms such theater has taken, and attempting to assess how successful it has been. In addition, the discussion extends beyond performances with an explicit reconciliatory function to others without a specific goal, where local communities simply join together in shared celebration of their local culture. The broadly integrative, inclusive effect of such shows could be a useful introduction or adjunct, I would suggest, to more targeted processes of social reconciliation.

Approaches and techniques

A technique widely used by theater practitioners working in divided communities is that of playback theater, in which a group of actors, sometimes professionals, often community members, perform accounts of experiences told by audience members.[1] Encouraged by a facilitator, people in the audience tell stories from their own lives, and then choose the actors to play different roles. The performers stage an improvised recreation of the story, which is then discussed by the group. Practitioners suggest that such theater "opens up a safe, reflective and creative communal space between neighbors and fellow citizens" and "develops a range of values and abilities relevant to reconciliation" (Hutt & Hosking 2006: 32). They report instances where this method has been employed successfully in ethnic Indian and indigenous Fijjan communities after the 2000 Fijian coup, in India among people of different castes, and among whites and Maoris in New Zealand. However, they also acknowledge its limitations: that it can reach only small groups, not mass audiences; that it is relatively untested with combined audiences from deeply alienated social groups, and; that actors who have experienced traumatic life events are sometimes re-traumatized by performing stories of similar suffering (Hutt & Hosking 2006: 30, 32).

In addition to their direct use with fractured communities, theater techniques are also mobilized to train members of these communities to carry out social reconciliation work. A typical context is a workshop, often held over several days. The description given by Richard Barber, a community theater worker based in Thailand, of a ten-day workshop he and his partner facilitated in Sri Lanka for Young Ambassadors for Peace, a grassroots conflict resolution organization, provides a good example (Barber 2007). The participants included eight young Tamil women making their first trip outside the Jaffna peninsula, six Sinhalese young people, and six Muslim Sri Lankans. The program moved from play activities, aimed at breaking down barriers, building trust, and "forming a creative, participatory, democratic space" (Barber 2007), to an extensive mapping process. Participants first sketched out the geography of Sri Lanka, then traced the physical features of areas of conflict, drew a spider web chart of lines of social conflict, and constructed historical timelines of key events and trends as contested by different groups. This facilitated the identification or naming of the problem, and led to exercises where situations of conflict were concretely imaged on stage, then discussed, causes identified, and alternate scenarios played out. The final part of the workshop involved developing strategic plans and brainstorming ideas which would then be implemented by the participants in their respective communities and in joint activities. Initial sessions of play, social mapping, and physical imaging, recognized techniques used in such contexts (Hutt & Hosking 2006: 34–5), were combined into a specific format which evidently worked very effectively in inspiring and enthusing participants.[2] Among the planned outcomes were a peace workshop module co-facilitated by members of each group, a multi-ethnic peace tour team which would hold one-day workshops across the conflict areas, and Tamil language classes for Sinhalese youth in Colombo. Subsequent developments illustrated a common problem with such cultural approaches to social reconciliation: a broken ceasefire agreement stopped the peace tour taking place, in the way political realities outside their control often intrude on the plans of peace workers. But the workshop had illustrated how quickly and successfully theater activities can forge common bonds across divided groups and mobilize creative energies among young people already involved in reconciliatory work.

As is clear from the earlier descriptions, the standard format of social reconciliation theater derives from European theater models. Playback theater shows close connections with Western psychodrama, in its methods and the training of its practitioners (Hutt & Hosking 2006: 35). Barber (2007: 4) describes as "ironic" the Western educational mindset of training programs which produces, even in Sri Lanka, workshop spaces set with rows of chairs rather than the bare floors of traditional Asian societies. Yet descriptions of this type of theater emphasize its openness to incorporation of local cultural forms: singing, dancing, and traditional ritual greetings (Hutt & Hosking 2006: 29). Using elements from their own performance cultures along with new theatrical techniques helps familiarize the process for participants. Local theatrical genres moreover can provide a rich store of resources for expressing and communicating ideas.

The Indonesian context

In Indonesia the use of theater in social reconciliation would seem to present certain challenges along with extensive opportunities. Some techniques practiced internationally could be alienating and discomforting to local communities. For individuals to come forward publicly to recount personal experiences, particularly if their stories are likely to offend or embarrass others present, would seem to contradict the collective social norms common in Indonesian societies. On the other hand, the notion of performances as sites of significant social communication is long-entrenched. Performing arts in many Indonesian societies contribute to religious rituals, mark key events in local social life, and give expression to community identity. Many ordinary community members have some artistic skills and are pleased to perform; local people constitute appreciative and knowledgeable audiences. Difficulties such as that of a school teacher in Northern Ireland, instructed to use drama in the classroom as a medium of education and social reconciliation with reluctant male students from stern Protestant backgrounds who regarded drama as mere "pretence" (Fyfe 1996), are hardly likely to occur.

Indeed theater as a medium of social development has a well-established history in Indonesia. In the 1980s and early 1990s, a widespread movement termed *teater rakyat*, 'people's theater', saw theater practitioners working together with NGO organizations using theater as a medium for community development and social empowerment. Drawing on international models of the theater of liberation, particularly that of the Filipino group PETA (Philippines Educational Theater Association)[3] which had toured Indonesia and invited actors to the Philippines for workshops, they adapted these techniques to local social contexts. Workshops were held in village communities and with groups such as urban factory workers and shop assistants, encouraging participants to articulate issues of concern to the group, to dramatize them in simple improvisations using local performance styles, and to contemplate solutions. For various reasons, including the limits on such activities imposed by an authoritarian political regime, and disappointment when aroused aspirations for social change could not be realized, *teater rakyat* as a general movement gradually faded. Among specific groups, however, such as factory workers and plantation workers (Bain 2003; Bodden 1997b), theater activities continued as a mode of awareness and confidence building, and strengthening of group identity.

Recently, in the context of trauma resulting from natural and man-made disasters, theater has contributed significantly as a medium of psychological healing and restoration of community identity. In Bali after the 2002 bombings, humorous clowning skits, *bondresan*, publicized the availability of treatment for those suffering from post-traumatic stress disorder, and eased the pain of loss through laughter (Palermo 2007). In Yogyakarta after the 2006 earthquake, local actors, many themselves homeless, quickly mobilized to stage rudimentary performances at neighborhood level, to sustain the spirits of their fellow citizens through the experience of trauma and displacement, and help rebuild community solidarity and cultural pride (Hatley 2008).

Given this background, it seems likely that organizations working for social reconciliation in regions of Indonesia affected by post-1998 inter-ethnic and inter-religious conflicts might use theater in their work. Indeed there is some documentation of both training workshops and community-level activities in these areas. A residential workshop was held outside Makassar in January 2002 by a local non-governmental organization (NGO) FORLOG (*Forum Dialog Antarkita Sulawesi Selatan*, South Sulawesi Forum for Inter-Communal Dialogue), in collaboration with a Yogyakarta-based peace center and a Dutch NGO, where incidents of conflict in Sulawesi, Ambon, and Papua were dramatized and possibilities of resolution discussed.[4] A people's theater festival sponsored by FORLOG took place later that year.[5] Richard Barber mentioned that a group of Moluccan Christian and Muslim women who had attended a theater workshop in Canberra similar to the Sri Lanka example later organized a peace workshop in Maluku applying the same module (personal communication 2007). A festival of Moluccan ethnic music in Ambon in May 2005, organized by the Baku Bae Peace Movement, a coalition of local NGOs, involved 100 performers from senior citizens to school students. It reportedly brought about moving reunions between people long separated by communal unrest, and celebrated shared identity and community in a far more effective way than formal reconciliation measures based on unfamiliar cultural models (Iskandar 2005).

Such reports are too few and too scattered, however, to give a sense of how widely and frequently such activities take place. Moreover they are generally very brief, intended for those involved in the field rather than for public dissemination and scholarly research. They provide insufficient detail about the identity of performers and workshop participants, and the composition and reactions of audiences to give a sense of how these events worked and what form of reconciliation was aimed at and achieved. Given their very localized nature, it would also be difficult to appreciate the meanings of such activities in their community context without an informed understanding of social groupings and cultural practices in that area. The following discussion therefore focuses on Java, particularly the central Javanese cities of Yogyakarta and Solo, where I have a longstanding familiarity with the local theater scene and its sociocultural context. Central Java has not been prominently involved in recent ethnic and religious conflicts in Indonesia. Indeed the citizens of Yogyakarta, reputedly living harmoniously and securely in a sense of protection by the popular Sultan and governor, proudly describe their city as an abode of peace.[6] Yet in May 1998, in the midst of the political unrest leading up to Suharto's fall, the neighboring court city of Solo saw several days of street riots and attacks on Chinese people and property similar to those which took place in Jakarta. Both cities have experienced violent incidents such as attacks on prostitution areas and entertainment centers by fundamentalist Islamic groups. And historically Central and East Java were key sites of the most devastating communal violence experienced in independent Indonesia, the massacres of hundreds of thousands of Communist Party members and suspected sympathizers in late 1965 and 1966 (see McGregor, Leksana, and Sulistiyanto & Setyadi this volume).

Since the resignation of Suharto and the demise of the New Order regime made it possible to speak openly about these events, cultural activities such as films, art exhibitions, and theater performances have been used to bring together people from both sides of the 1965–66 conflict, and educate the wider public about this history. Four performances addressing by various means the events of 1965 and their aftermath are briefly reviewed later. Although none of the performances involved direct participation by audience members in onstage action, nor face to face interaction between representatives of opposite political viewpoints, each had the clear intention of increasing awareness of the full dimensions of the conflict and extending humanitarian understanding. Then the discussion turns to performance activities which were prompted by the communal violence and social unease of May 1998, but do not directly address this issue, nor aim for an explicit social outcome. Comparing the dramatic approaches of this range of performances, their social contexts, and their apparent audience impact, I reflect on their role, and that of theater more generally in Java/Indonesia, in both facilitating direct social reconciliation and in achieving more amorphous community-strengthening effects. The argument is not that Indonesian theatrical performances have an in-built socially integrative function. On the contrary, the stage can be a site for potent expression of opposing, combative political perspectives, especially when other modes of political debate are blocked. Satirical representations of historical and legendary Javanese kings were widely employed, for example, by modern theater groups to critique New Order power-holders, who responded by intermittently banning their plays (Bodden 1997a; Hatley 1993). And even performances held to celebrate local community can instead reveal an absence of local social solidarity in neighborhoods characterized by sharp class divisions (Hatley 1982). Rather I am suggesting that because theater has such a deeply ingrained role in Javanese-Indonesian communities, in bringing people together, in marking social events, and in celebrating local identity, it has particularly useful potential as a medium of integration.

Healing and strengthening the group

The words *Temu Rindu, Menggugat Senyap* (Come together in longing, challenge loneliness), emblazoned on a cloth banner, greeted participants arriving at an historic event held in Yogya in July 2005, a reunion of women victims of the 1965–66 violence. Two elderly former women prisoners, who gained comfort and support from one another's company, developed the idea of holding the gathering to create a sense of solidarity and strength among fellow women survivors. Syarikat (*Masyarakat Santri untuk Advokasi Rakyat* Muslim Community for People's Advocacy), a human rights organization connected with the Islamic mass organization NU (Nahdlatul Ulama), and PUSdEP (*Pusat Sejarah dan Etika Politik*, Center for History and Political Ethics), a research center of Sanata Dharma Catholic University, had worked together to organize the event. Given the differing religious affiliations of the two groups, such collaboration in itself arguably symbolizes the theme of social integration.[7] Over 500 women from cities and towns throughout Central Java attended. PUSdEP researcher Yustinus Tri Subagya, who was present at the meeting, describes emotional encounters between women who had not seen each other since their release from prison 20–25 years earlier, who didn't know their friends were still alive, and/or who had been too fearful to socialize during New Order times (Subagya 2005: 3–6). They talked and ate together, spoke publicly about their experiences, and sat on the floor around a 'stage' area where those who wished came forward to read a poem, dance, or sing. The climax of the program was a short performance of the Javanese popular melodrama, *ketoprak*.

The show was directed by Kadariyah, the legendary prima donna of the communist-associated *ketoprak* group Krido Mardi,[8] who had directed numerous all-female *ketoprak* plays in prison with other former women prisoners as actors. Kadariyah also played the main role, that of a woman whose young daughter has been made pregnant by a rich, elderly, polygamous official. As Kadariyah berated and ridiculed the official for his immoral, exploitative behavior, audience members responded with delighted laughter. Subagya reports that the woman sitting next to him confirmed the reality of this picture of men of the traditional Javanese aristocratic/bureaucratic class exerting their power over social inferiors. A king in his own household, a high-ranked official could indulge himself sexually outside the home without sanction. Then she went on to speak of her experiences when she was arrested 40 years ago for membership of the communist-affiliated women's group Gerwani. She had been fondled and groped by interrogators, and forced to appear naked with other detainees. Accounts by former women political prisoners and interviews with women accused of communist affiliation reveal that sexual exploitation by those with authority over them (military and civilian officials, prison guards) was a widespread experience (Pohlgren 2004).[9] Against this background it seems likely that other audience members watching the show may have been reminded of their personal experiences. The performance may have provided the group with shared validation of their own sexual violation years ago, and perhaps a degree of cathartic release. The event also displayed the acting abilities of group members, among other skills they are still able to contribute to society. It seems to have succeeded admirably in celebrating and strengthening the shared sense of identity of its audience of women political survivors.

Displaying diversity, accepting difference

In contrast to the performance just described – staged at a private gathering, directed to a single social group – the one which occurred in South Blitar in 2002 to mark the anniversary of the migration of the prophet Muhammad from Mecca to Medina was a big, public, inclusive event. South Blitar had been a stronghold of the Indonesian Communist Party (PKI) before 1965, and communist resistance continued there until 1967, as NU youth collaborated with the military in conducting widespread killings. In 1968 the Trisula monument was erected by the military in the town of Blitar to commemorate the extinction of the PKI. The New Order government regularly conducted political indoctrination in the regions, and former PKI areas were deeply stigmatized. But in 2002 at the instigation of Syarikat members, a mediation meeting was held between former PKI and NU communities. Through discussions they came to the conclusion that serious conflict between them in the past had begun only after September 1965 as a result of deliberate provocation by the military. They then jointly organized and funded a celebratory performance which has been described as a "symbolic cultural reconciliation event" (Wajidi 2004: 84). Each community presented its chosen art form: NU villagers staging *kentrung*, storytelling accompanied by drum music, while the ex-PKI group performed *campursari*, a blending of traditional gamelan and other styles of music with solo singing and joking repartee. Crucial to the meaning of the event, analysts suggest, was its location, right in front of the military monument. This structure, which had previously served as a reminder of the victimhood of the PKI communities and of NU's links with the triumphant military, now took on a totally new significance. In the words of one observer, "The monument has become a witness of social reconciliation ... Although there was no public testimony like in South Africa, the truth has nevertheless been revealed" (Asvis Warman Adam, quoted in Wajidi 2004: 84). In terms of the format and experience of the performances, each group in witnessing the other's presentation arguably acknowledged both its cultural distinctiveness and its legitimate participation within a shared local community. Their experience might be seen to parallel on an intuitive level the kind of "identity change", the revision of previous attitudes, which Kelman (2004: 120) regards as central to social reconciliation.

In a deliberately constructed way, the event can be seen as invoking the inclusive ideal of community-level performances as staged for 17 August, Indonesian Independence Day. A neighborhood concert, a *malam kesenian*, ideally held on a Saturday night soon after the big day, has long involved local people of all ages and interests in performing on stage, celebrating their participation within the community and wider nation. Independence Day parades through the main streets performed a similar role at city level. Events of this kind that I have witnessed in recent years seem to have been marked by a heightened social inclusiveness. Previously marginalized ethnic and social groups have enthusiastically joined in. Troupes comprising both ethnic Chinese and Javanese perform Chinese dragon and lion dances, leotarded ladies doing aerobics and devout Muslim youths playing religious music appear as contiguous acts on neighborhood stages, and dreadlocked buskers playing excruciating heavy metal music are warmly thanked by local officials for their participation (Hatley 2004: 89). One might see here the impact of the ideology of democratic participation, at a time of increased democratization of the political system. It seems possible, moreover, that the political unrest and communal conflict of post-Suharto years has strengthened awareness of the importance of symbolic expressions of social inclusiveness. Certainly there was a significant decline in local performance in the immediate post-Suharto years, which actors attributed to a climate of fear and uncertainty produced by the ethnic and religious conflict occurring at that time. Communities were said to avoid staging public events where incidents of inter-group friction might arise. By contrast the greater political stability and cessation of major communal conflicts since 2003 has allowed performances to revive, perhaps with a heightened appreciation of their inclusive potential.

Recalling epic history, representing local violence

Neither of these performances discussed so far that aimed at addressing problems and reconciling differences stemming from the anti-communist killings and imprisonments of 1965–66 depicted on stage the actual events of the time. Presented for specific audiences very aware of their purpose, they had no need to announce their topic; rather than playing out literal narratives, they worked through allegory and symbolism. Conditions were very different at two other performances addressing the political events of 1965 and their aftermath staged in Yogyakarta in 2005. One, held in celebration of the anniversary of the founding of the regency of Bantul, south of Yogyakarta, was performed in Bantul town square on a huge stage with spectacular costumes and effects by 300 local actors, dancers, and musicians, and later broadcast on the Yogyakarta state television station TVRI. Entitled *Bang-bang Sumirat*, 'The Red Light of Dawn', this *ketoprak* was set in a mythical kingdom where conditions resembled those in Indonesia in 1965 and depicted events paralleling the supposed coup attempt and its aftermath. The other performance *Jarang Sungsang*[10] was staged by the modern theater group, Teater Gadjah Mada, from Gadjah Mada University at the Yogyakarta Arts Center before audiences consisting mainly of theater enthusiasts, students, and journalists. Set among a group of village youths, it dramatized the brutal killing of the son of a PKI victim through aggressive, acrobatic movements and furious beating of the accompanying *lesung*, a rice-stamping trough struck by wooden poles, modeled on the early *ketoprak* form, *ketoprak lesung*. The two performances contrasted sharply in terms of size, dramatic aesthetic, and context of organization. What linked them was the fact that each of the directors set out to publicly address the issue of the political events of 1965 and the following anti-communist violence, presenting an alternate perspective to standard views. Both shared a concern which accords with one aspect of the agenda of theater for reconciliation, that of "developing more complex narratives and more nuanced understandings of identity" (Cohen 2004: 6). Yet in both cases audience members were unaware of this agenda, with little or no prior knowledge of the theme of the show. The actors, too, came to know the content of the performances only through the process of rehearsals.

Bondan Nusantara, director and scriptwriter of *Bang-bang Sumirat*, a very active and well-known Yogyakarta *ketoprak* figure, is the son of Kadariyah, the famous communist-linked actress mentioned earlier. During the long New Order years, he worked as a director for elite patrons, staging many huge, spectacular *ketoprak* shows, a few cautiously critical of the regime. Right at the end of the period he formed his own group performing politically satirical skits. Now with Suharto gone and with the populist-minded district head, bupati, of Bantul giving tacit agreement, he dared to play out on the *ketoprak* stage the long-forbidden narrative of the events of 1965–66. Gati Andoko, director of *Jaran Sungsang*, reports that the play is based on the real-life story of a young man deranged by the killing of his parents in the 1965–66 violence. During the 1980s, at the time of the so-called 'mysterious killings' of people with criminal associations,[11] this man, seen as a dangerous outsider and threat to the community was murdered by his own neighbors, incited by a powerful local figure who wanted to take over the man's land. Gati had known the young man well, and suffered greatly from feelings of guilt about not having spoken out about his murder. This performance gave him the chance to do so.

Elsewhere I have described in some detail the format of these performances (Hatley 2006); here I will do so more briefly, and then attempt to give some idea of their likely effectiveness in communicating with audiences. *Bang-bang Sumirat* commences with spectacular fighting scenes involving the troops of Bantala Warih (Indonesia) and Malaya Bumi (Malaysia), and a grand court audience where the fictionally-named Prabu Tuk Gungung (President Sukarno) listens to reports from officials and military leaders, including Karno Tanding (head of the PKI, Aidit) and various generals. A high-ranking military officer Haryo Tratap (Suharto) announces that there has been a coup and that Karno Tanding (Aidit) is to blame. Different groups of soldiers fight one another. Haryo Tratap (Suharto), standing high at the back of the stage, gives an order. Ordinary people arrayed below him start attacking one another, and soldiers drape a huge red cloth over them, creating a red, seething mass. When the melee quietens, bodies lay strewn across the stage. A madman appears, announcing, "Those who portrayed themselves as heroes have transformed into monsters."[12] Haryo Tratap/Suharto turns around, his face a hideous demonic mask with fangs and wild hair. "Wake up!" says the madman to the people, who stir into consciousness, "Learn from what has happened!"[13] He exhorts them to avoid taking revenge, but to look instead to the bright light of dawn, the *bang-bang sumirat* of the title. "A new time has come, a time full of glorious hope."[14] Actors flood onto the stage as the performance comes to an end.

It is hard to tell how widely the allegory of the performance was appreciated. Actors surely understood the reference of the characters and the events they were representing, and the bupati of Bantul, a politically astute former newspaper editor,

Figure 4.1 Bang-bang Sumirat: Haryo Tratap/Suharto in monster mask (Photo courtesy: Bondan Nusantara, scriptwriter and director of the production)

clearly knew and approved. Many with connections in artist and activist circles would have heard in advance about the content of the show. Journalists would have known, although their press reports made only oblique reference to a social lesson about reconciliation. Some analytically minded viewers perhaps picked up on the depictions as referring to key political actors. But uninitiated, unsophisticated audience members might not have grasped these clues. They may have had trouble recognizing the richly-attired monarch Prabu Tuk Gunung as their populist first president, Sukarno. The aesthetic format of the show, that of the grand *ketoprak kolossal* of New Order times, seemed at odds with, and may have muted the impact of its pro-people message. Yet viewers certainly would have been shocked by the sight of a noble warrior transformed into a demon, accompanied by commentary from the madman about self-proclaimed heroes who turn out to be monsters, suggesting association with Suharto and the military. Similarly, the final words of the performance about the need to embrace reconciliation and look to the future were clear and direct.

In contrast to the mythical, allegorical ambience of *Bang-bang Sumirat*, the idiom of *Jaran Sungsang* is brutally, forcefully here-and-now. As the play opens, a group of young village men and women pound vigorously on a *lesung* in the center of the stage, then stop to converse.

Points of disagreement involve both verbal and physical expression of aggression: slaps, kicks, handstands, and somersaults. One young man, Sugeng, is clearly

Figure 4.2 Jaran Sungsang: Violent pounding of poles in a wooden trough, *lesung*, opens the performance (Photo courtesy: the Gadjah Mada Theater Group)

disturbed, striking at his face intermittently, clutching to his chest a rattan hobby-horse. When someone labels his behavior as that of a communist (*dasar* PKI), he screams hysterically. One of the group sits the others down in a row on the *lesung* and recounts to them Sugeng's history: how his mother and father were both killed by a crowd of villagers at the time of the PKI killings and their severed heads placed on bamboo poles in front of his house. As a witness to the killings, Bu Lurah, the wife of the village headman, is denounced for her failure to speak out about these horrific events. She is accused, using the English expression, probably for dramatic effect, of the "crime of silence". Sugeng, the victim, comforts her, however, endorsing the need to forget rather than constantly recall the horrors of the past. Sugeng performs a stunningly wild, acrobatic dance with the hobby-horse, becoming entranced, staggering through the audience and finally collapsing on the *lesung*. The village head, Pak Lurah, labels him a menace who must be 'dealt with', must be killed, and incites the group to do so, pounding him with the wooden poles of the *lesung*. When they come to their senses, the young people are devastated with grief. "*Jangan mati kang!*" (Don't die brother!) pleads one. Another races about declaring "Sugeng has been killed. Why isn't anyone saying anything?"[15] A young girl, her face smeared with her own tears and the blood of the murdered Sugeng, laments, "All events have witnesses. What I regret is that I witnessed this event."[16]

Figure 4.3 Jaran Sungsang: Sugeng, beaten to death by the group, lies across the *lesung* (Photo courtesy: the Gadjah Mada Theater Group)

To me this performance, although I only watched it on video, seemed most impressive and moving. I imagined that its audience members would have likewise been struck by the powerful drama of the play and the awesome tragedy of its theme. Some would have appreciated the complex issues addressed within the simple, spare setting of the show: the horror of the 1965–66 violence, the suffering of its victims, but also the pain of remembering, and contestation and confusion about the past among later generations, leading to the danger of repeating its inhuman cruelty. They might have been impressed by the populist aesthetic, appropriate to the village setting and the image of socialist/populist politics, and by the way aggressive interactions between the actors conveyed a sense of pervasive violence in society, fitting conditions at the time of the 1965–66 killings. For many youthful, urban audience members, the description of the violent attacks on communists in villages in 1965–66 would have been shocking and eye-opening. I imagine that both the brutality of the stage violence and direct use of the forbidden term 'PKI' would have stirred much comment.

Enquiring about the performance among friends and acquaintances who had seen it, however, I encountered different kinds of reactions. They talked only about technical aspects of the production, particularly its acrobatic movement, not its themes. Asked whether he found the play *mengerikan* – 'frightening' or 'horrifying' – an experienced actor from another group said he had been fearful that the actors might injure themselves in their violently energetic moves. Of the violence of the actions being depicted, however, nothing was said. The director, Gati Andoko, reported journalists crying as they spoke with him after the show, and family members of PKI victims who thanked him fervently, saying they felt "*terwakili*" (represented). The young student actors who participated in the production said they had learnt a great deal about the unjust stigmatization of PKI victims, about the need to avoid stereotyped judgments, and about the importance of speaking out about the truth. But in general those watching the show did not seem to have had the same experience, at least by their own account.

Those I spoke to offered various explanations for this phenomenon. Some said that communism and the events of 1965 remained such taboo topics that audience members reacted with denial to the presence of these themes. At the same time, for young viewers growing up in an environment where such things were never discussed, Sugeng's story might not have evoked any particular associations. They might not have appreciated its grim reality, viewing it instead simply as dramatic fiction. Teater Gadjah Mada's public image, as not having any particular political connection, may have hampered recognition of its message. And an emphasis on highly skilled acrobatic movement may have distracted attention away from the content of the play.

Comparing the four performances that evoked the legacy of the 1965–66 killings, we get a clear sense of their efficacy as sites of social reconciliation. The first two examples, the *ketoprak* staged for former women political prisoners, building confidence and shared identity within a marginalized social group, and the Blitar event, bringing two previously hostile groups together, appear to have been quite successful. The two public performances, *Bang-bang Sumirat* and *Jarang*

Sungsang, likewise worked well for their directors and performers, as immediate participants, but their reception by and impact on audiences appear uncertain, variable, and hard to gauge. The implication might seem to be that even in Java, with its rich, shared theatrical traditions and widespread staging of performances to mark community events, theater as an integrative, conciliatory medium requires performers and audience members who are informed and committed participants. Engaging an unknown, unprepared body of viewers with this reconciliatory process is difficult and unpredictable.

Yet if different issues of social division are considered, and the notion of 'reconciliation' is extended to include an inherent acceptance of other social groups as fellow members of a local community, examples come to mind of other performances which do seem to have been successful in actively involving and arguably 'integrating' together large public audiences.

Sharing fun, celebrating community

Mention was made earlier of the way community concerts held to celebrate Indonesian Independence Day can function as symbolic expressions of social inclusiveness. For one theater group based in Solo, creating a sense of egalitarianism and inclusiveness through such performances has become a deliberate mission. The group *Gidag-Gidig*, formed in 1978, had long been performing *ketoprak* on Independence Day for the people of the neighborhood surrounding their rehearsal space, as well as staging avant garde modern plays in theater centers. After the violent ethnic and class-based attacks which took place in Solo in May 1998, *Gidag-Gidig* decided to take their *ketoprak* shows on the road. Performances bringing communities together in shared enjoyment and entertainment were vitally important at this time of intra-group tension and potential hostility, but often fear of public disturbances stopped local people from organizing them. *Gidag-Gidig* sought permission to perform in several *kampung* neighborhoods where they had personal connections and where there was a felt need for community solidarity. Since then they have performed numerous times in different parts of Solo for Independence Day.[17]

In August 2004 the group staged six performances in different locations of the story *Jaka Karewet*.[18] The title figure of the play is a village youth in the time of the ancient Javanese kingdom of Majapahit, who was able to make himself invisible with a magic charm. He goes to court to try the fine food there, and causes much disruption with his playful tricks, but eventually becomes hilariously drunk at a banquet set up to trap him, gets caught, and is sentenced to death. Then it is discovered that Jaka is the king's son by a former royal concubine sent home to her village. He is welcomed into the palace along with his mother and grandparents. However Jaka Karewet and his family turn down the offer of a luxurious life among the nobility to return to the familiarity and neighborly solidarity of their village home. The egalitarian content of the tale was reinforced by an exuberant, folksy performance style. As in *teater rakyat,* the reinvented folk theater used as a medium of social development in the late 1980s, all performers sat together playing musical accompaniment, with individual actors dancing on stage to take part in the action when required. I attended two of these performances: one in the residential neighborhood of one of the group's leaders, watched by an audience of local residents; the other in the Solo state prison. Both were hugely entertaining, actively involving the audience, who shouted out comments on stage action and responded eagerly to references by the actors to local people and events.

In terms of a theme or 'message', Jaka Karewet's depressing village poverty and his yearning to taste delicious elite food, although portrayed humorously, might have conveyed some empathy with the deprivations of the poor. Portrayal of court officials as ludicrous, puffed up figures, quaking with terror at Jaka Karewet's playful antics, arguably satirized the notion of the superior qualities of the rich and powerful. And the decision of Jaka Karewet and his relatives to leave the court, returning to live in the village where they felt at home, presumably validated *kampung* life in general and the identity of the particular community watching the show. Equally or more importantly, the show illustrated how vital and dynamic live performance can be. The local references from the stage and the responses from the audience created a sense of shared enjoyment and engagement. Whether or not local people felt more positive about their community in the following days, as they recalled and recounted the high points of the performance, they certainly had fun together during the show.

That this effect could be achieved even in a setting which was not a community as such but a conglomeration of people with no interest in being together, with no attachment to the locality, that of the Solo jail, surprised even the performers themselves. Actors were apprehensive before the event. Would the audience laugh and participate or simply sit there sullenly? "Don't talk about crime," the directors warned. "Don't talk about sex. Don't say things like 'This place is okay to visit, but I wouldn't want to live here.'" Their fears turned out to be totally unfounded. The big crowd of 300–500 men and about 20 women were fully engaged from the very start of the show. An older woman called out several comments during the director's introduction. While Jaka spoke of his troubles, reporting that "it is hard to get food" (*panganan rekasa*) they were quiet, listening seriously. But when Jaka announced he was going to the *kraton* to taste delicious food, voices from the crowd called out "*Malinga! Malinga!*" (Steal it!). "Oh, no, I couldn't do that," Jaka replied. But during a mimed ride to the city by oxcart, he did a brilliant rendition of succumbing to temptation. He glanced sideways into the basket of the woman sitting next to him, then looked away, rolled his eyes, sat on his hands, and blinked meaningfully in the direction of the audience members who had suggested stealing. Finally his hand darted into the basket and emerged with some money which he stuffed into his pocket with a sly grin. The performers also broke their self-imposed prohibition on sexual suggestion. The king of Majapahit, embracing his long-lost concubine, grinned at the audience and remarked that he was faring much better than they.

The huge enjoyment of the show by the jail audience indicated that such events can work in mixed, diverse, ad hoc groups as long as there is a basic linguistic and cultural background in common. Shared participation in such a fun event and inclusion in the intimate style of the performance are likely to have had the effect of bringing people closer together, opening up new conversations. The willingness of the theater group to perform in this setting, to include the inmates in their humorous interchanges, may well have contributed to a more positive self-image. The actors, in their turn, were agreeably surprised at the apparent success of the performance and the smooth running of the whole event. They gained a more positive impression of prison inmates and conditions than they had previously held. The event can be said to illustrate 'social reconciliation' in a broad sense of fostering community integration through shared enjoyment, laughter, and cultural celebration.

That the same show could also be experienced as 'speaking to' particular issues of hardship and conflict was illustrated when Gidag-Gidig performed *Jaka Karewet* as entertainment for villagers in Bantul badly affected by the 2006 earthquake. As Jaka spoke of going to the palace to eat delicious food, voices called out from the crowd, "Yes, something other than Supermi!" in reference to the ubiquitous packets of instant noodles distributed by emergency relief teams. In the palace scene in Majapahit, a man from the audience climbed on stage to join in. Calling himself a *demang*, a village leader, he accosted the king, alias the present-day Sultan of Yogyakarta, with the slowness of delivery of government relief funds (Hainindawan, personal communication November 2006). Laughing together at these humorous local interventions in the story arguably relieved some of the stress of their problems for audience members, gave them an increased sense of their grievances being aired and voices heard.

Conclusion

The Indonesian performances explored and analyzed in the preceding discussion have not involved social reconciliation of the most explicit kind, bringing together alienated parties in a communal conflict and attempting to rebuild social bonds. Nor has the main focus been on theater activities in those Indonesian societies where communal conflict has been most intense in recent years, although the scattered reports of its use in such contexts indicate important directions for future research. Instead, I have drawn on examples from Central Java, from performances I have watched, live or on video, and from discussions with directors, actors, and audience members, to give a sense of both the specific 'conciliatory' and more general 'integrative' potential of theater in these settings.

Along with performances which have worked effectively to strengthen the shared identity of a group and symbolize harmony for divided communities, in ways reminiscent of international models of theater for reconciliation, we have looked at another phenomenon: theater as an inclusive, integrative medium at neighborhood level, for public audiences, open to all. Here performances using a familiar dramatic idiom interspersed with much humor engage closely with large audiences of ordinary people. More crafted performances with specific political agendas, the Bantul *ketoprak* and the play *Jaran Sungsang*, although likewise drawing on known Javanese theatrical imagery, seem not to have communicated as fully and directly as these local shows. These examples illustrate the vital importance of audience expectations of the event. Javanese community performances show an impressive potential for communication within their local cultural environment.

Applying this model in other regions, in fractured communities, to promote broadly integrative effects, would involve identifying and mobilizing an equivalent shared local cultural idiom. In Java and Bali, with their rich range of theatrical and musical forms, such an approach seems likely to work more smoothly than in societies without strong local performance traditions. The shared entertainment medium might sometimes be popular music or dance. The example of the peace concert in Ambon suggested the power of regional musical forms to bring local communities together in Maluku. Events like these, involving shared collective participation, lessening the sense of distance and difference between communities, might be followed by more explicitly reconciliatory activities by peacemaking groups. Clearly theater cannot be drawn on in every case as a medium of social integration. But in Indonesia where communities so often mark significant happenings with a performance it is certainly a promising option to explore.

Notes

1 Developed initially in the 1970s in the United States by psycho-dramatist Jonathan Fox, playback theater is now practiced by companies in more than 30 countries, which hold regular workshops, and in some cases longer residential courses (Hutt & Hosking 2006: 5).
2 Drawing on the experience of this workshop and similar projects conducted in Thailand, India, Hong Kong, and Australia, Barber (2008) has produced a toolkit setting out in detail the techniques used by Makhampom, the theater group with which he works, in theater activities directed towards the resolution of social conflict.
3 For a discussion of the history of PETA as a politicized theater movement and its workshop method applying liberation theology and Paulo Freire's "pedagogy of the oppressed" to social reality in the Philippines, see van Erven (1992) and (2000).
4 The title of the report based on this workshop is *Laporan Narasi Pelatihan Pemberdayaan untuk Rekonsiliasi. Kerjasama antara Forum Dialog Antarkita Sulawesi Selatan (FORLOG) dengan Pusat Pengembangan Perdamaian (PSPP) Jogjakarta dan SOW Belanda, Tanjung Bira, 20–24 Januari 2002.*
5 Photos and brief details of a festival of traditional music and theater, described as a "campaign for peace" (*kampanye perdamaian*) which took place in Gowa in South Sulawesi on 14 September 2002 can be found at http://www.geocities.com/forlog/pestagowa.htm (accessed on 12 January 2008). A list of FORLOG's activities including other performance events such as an inter-religious music concert can be found at http://www.geocities.com/forlog/aktifitas.htm (accessed on 12 January 2008).
6 An iconic display of this phenomenon was the huge peaceful rally of one million Yogya residents in the city square, addressed by the Sultan, on 20 May 1998, the day before Suharto resigned. Maryanto (1998) described the peaceful, celebratory atmosphere of this event. In more recent years the Sultan's popularity waned somewhat as his plans for radical modernization of Yogyakarta alienated both displaced poorer residents and the historically aware middle class. However the 'myth' of peaceful Yogyakarta under the protection of his leadership continues.
7 Syarikat was formed with the aim of making reparation for the reputedly widespread involvement of NU youth in the 1965–66 anti-communist violence by working for reconciliation between victims and perpetrators. Their methods include research on the

causes and consequences of the conflict in particular areas, mediation between the victims and community groups, and organization of discussions on ways to overcome differences and implement cooperation. Based in Yogya, Syarikat has branches in 18 other cities in Java (see Sulistiyanto & Setyadi this volume). PUSdEP focuses attention on instances of political violence, the politics of their historical construction, and efforts at reconciliation. While PUSdEP holds frequent academic seminars and book discussions, and Syarikat's major work is more community-based, both organizations have an interest in cultural activities such as films, performances, and art and photographic exhibitions. On various occasions they have worked together to organize and promote such activities.

8 Krido Mardi was the administrative base and star troupe of the organization BAKOKSI (*Badan Koordinasi Ketoprak Seluruh Indonesia*, All-Indonesia Coordinating Body for Ketoprak), which was connected with the leftist arts and culture organization LEKRA (*Lembaga Kebudayaan Rakyat*). Some individual performers were members of LEKRA.

9 See also *Kado untuk Ibu*, a documentary film by Syarikat, 2005 (see Sulistiyanto & Setyadi this volume).

10 The term means literally a horse born in an unnatural position, a breach birth. Figuratively it suggests in various ways the situation of the young man, Sugeng, a misfit in his community who derives a sense of pleasure and identity through performing the hobby-horse dance *jaran kepang*. Gati Andoko mentioned the origin of the play to me in conversation in July 2005.

11 These killings, given the acronym Petrus, took place between 1983 and 1985, and resulted in the deaths of over 5,000 people. They were sponsored by the state, and carried out as a military/intelligence operation (Bourchier 1990: 177).

12 *Sing maune ngaku satriya malik dadi buta babrah.* (Javanese language dialogue.)

13 *Ayo, toh, tangia, tangia! Sinauna marang lelakon.*

14 *Bangkit jaman anyar, jaman sing kebak pengarep-arep mulya.*

15 *Sugeng dibunuh. Kenapa tidak ada yang bicara?* (Indonesian; the language of this performance was Indonesian, interspersed with occasional Javanese expressions.)

16 *Semua peristiwa ada saksi. Yang aku sesali peristiwa ini mesti kusaksikan.*

17 I have described *Gidag-Gidig*'s performances of *Jaka Karewet* in more detail in a study of theater in its social context in Central Java (Hatley 2008). The following text provides some similar observations to those made in the book.

18 The play's director, Hainindawan, reported in 2004 that he had adapted the tale from a text written by nineteenth-century Javanese king Pakubuwono VI during his exile in Ambon, and included in a book by American scholar Nancy Florida, *Menyurat yang Silam, Menggugat yang Menjelang* (an Indonesian translation of *Writing the Past, Inscribing the Future,* Florida, 1995). But Hainindawan, along with the skilled actors of the *Gidag-Gidig* group, have given the story a distinctive cast. While Pakubuwono VI's Jaka Karewet sees acceptance at court as a dream come true, and gratefully takes up a position there, his *Gidag-Gidig* counterpart prefers life in the village.

References

Assefa, H. (1993) *Peace and Reconciliation as a Paradigm*, Nairobi, Kenya: ACIS.

Bain, L. (2003) 'NGO theater in the post-New Order', *Inside Indonesia*, 76: 29–30.

Barber, R. (2007) 'Conflict resolution in Sri Lanka – a case study', unpublished report.

—— (2008) *The Art of Peace: A Toolkit of Theater Art for Conflict Resolution*, Bangkok: Makhampom Foundation.

Boal, A. (1996) 'Politics, education and change', in J. O'Toole and K. Donelan (eds) *Drama, Culture and Empowerment*, Brisbane: Idea Publications.

Bodden, M. (1997a) 'Teater Koma's *Suksesi* and Indonesia's New Order', *Asian Theater Journal*, 14(2): 259–80.

—— (1997b) 'Workers' theater and theater about workers in 1990s Indonesia', *Review of Indonesian and Malayan Affairs*, 31(1): 37–78.

Bourchier, D. (1990) 'Crime, law and state authority in Indonesia', in A. Budiman (ed.) *State and Civil Society in Indonesia*, Clayton, Victoria: Center of Southeast Asian Studies, Monash University.

Cohen, C. (2004) *Creative Approaches to Reconciliation*, Boston: Brandeis University.

Dennis, R. (2003) 'Place and purpose: playback theater and social change', *The International Playback Theater Network*, XIII(2) January.

Fyfe, H. (1996) 'Drama in the context of a divided society', in J. O'Toole and K. Donelan (eds) *Drama, Culture and Empowerment*, Brisbane: Idea Publications.

Hatley, B. (1982) 'National ritual, neighborhood performance: celebrating tujuhbelasan', *Indonesia*, 34: 55–64.

—— (1993) 'Constructions of "Tradition" in New Order Indonesian Theater', in V.M. Hooker (ed.) *Culture and Society in New Order Indonesia*, Kuala Lumpur, Singapore and Oxford: Oxford University Press.

—— (2004) 'Global influence, national politics and local identity in Central Javanese theater', *Review of Indonesian and Malayan Affairs*, 38(2): 63–100.

—— (2006) 'Recalling and re-presenting the 1965/1966 anti-communist violence in Indonesia', in A. Vickers and M. Hanlon (eds) *Asia Reconstructed: Proceedings of the 16th Biennial Conference of the ASAA, Wollongong, Australia*, Canberra: ASAA & RSPAS, The Australian National University.

—— (2008) *Javanese Performances on an Indonesian Stage: Contesting Culture, Embracing Change*, Singapore: NUS Press in association with Asian Studies Association of Australia.

Hutt, J. and Hosking, B. (2006) 'Playback theater: a creative resource for reconciliation', a working paper of *Recasting Reconciliation through Culture and the Arts*, Boston: Brandeis University.

Iskandar, F. (2005) 'Cegah konflik lewat musik, catatan tertinggal dari ekshebisi musik etnik di Ambon', *Radio Vox Populi, 19 Mei 2005*. Online. Available at: *Ambon Berdarah On-Line*, http://www.go.to/ambon (accessed on 12 January 2008).

Kelman, H.C. (2004) 'Reconciliation as identity change: a social-psychological perspective', in Y. Bar-Siman-Tov (ed.) *From Conflict Resolution to Reconciliation*, Oxford: Oxford University Press.

Maryanto, D. (1998) 'Orphans no more', *Inside Indonesia*, 56: 21–2.

Palermo, C. (2007) 'Towards the embodiment of the mask. Balinese topeng in contemporary practice', unpublished PhD thesis, School of Asian Languages and Studies, University of Tasmania.

Pohlgren, A. (2004) 'A fragment of a story: gerwani and tapol experiences', *Intersections: Gender, History and Culture in the Asian Context*, Issue 10.

Rouhana, N. (2004) 'Identity and power in the reconciliation of national conflict', in S. Eagly, R. Baron and V.L. Hamilton (eds) *The Social Psychology of Group Identity and Social Conflict*, Washington DC: American Psychological Association.

Scheff, T.J. (1979) *Catharsis in Healing, Ritual, and Drama*, Berkeley: University of California Press.

Schonman, S. (1996) 'The drama and theater class battlefield', in J. O'Toole and K. Donelan (eds) *Drama, Culture and Empowerment*, Brisbane: Idea Publications.

Soule, L. (1998) 'Performing identities (empowering performers and spectators)', in

C. McCullough (ed.) *Theater Praxis: Teaching Drama through Praxis*, London: Macmillan Press.

Subagya, Y.T. (2005) 'Breaking the silence: *ketoprak* social healings of the past violence in rural Java', paper presented at the Workshop on Art, Culture and Political Change since Suharto, University of Tasmania, December.

van Erven, E. (1992) *The Playful Revolution*, Bloomington and Indianapolis: Indiana University Press.

—— (2000) *Community Theater: Global Perspectives*, London: Routledge.

Wajidi, F. (2004) 'NU youth and the making of civil society', in H. Samuel and H. Schulte Nordholt (eds) *Indonesia in Transition: Rethinking Civil Society, Region and Crisis*, Yogyakarta: Pustaka Pelajar.

5 Mobilizing culture and tradition for peace

Reconciliation in the Moluccas

Birgit Bräuchler

Introduction

Analyzing the challenges and problems coming along with the revival of tradition for peace in the post-conflict Moluccas, this chapter explores the more general question of whether culture can be an effective means to build inter-religious bridges and to foster reconciliation.[1] The rising number of so-called ethnic and religious conflicts worldwide and the frequent failure of internationally established means of reconciliation triggered debates on alternative means for reconciliation and alternative dispute resolutions. The consideration of traditional conflict resolution mechanisms is one option. This immediately raises the question of what we actually refer to when we talk about 'tradition' and 'culture'. The concept of 'culture' has been questioned even by anthropologists (see e.g. Ortner 1995). We are confronted with anthropologists inventing culture (Wagner 1981) at the same time as "we are faced with a real world in which ethnic identification ... seems to be more highly mobilized than at any point in our recent history" (Mahmood & Armstrong 1992: 3–4). Through an ethnographic analysis of a traditional village union claiming to be the key to peace (*kunci perdamaian*) in the Moluccas, this chapter argues for a flexible and agency-oriented notion of culture and shows that the incorporation of cultural aspects and local ritual approaches to conflict resolution enable the local anchoring of peace initiatives and thus successful reconciliation. Nevertheless, the reader is also warned against a rash identification of religion as a dividing and *adat* – tradition and customary law – as a unifying force. *Adat* rituals not only unified people after the conflict, but traditions also formed the basis for the development of divided memories that were invoked to legitimize the use of violence during the conflict. The revival of tradition has to be analyzed against the broader sociopolitical backdrop in which it takes place.

The Moluccan conflict and the revival of tradition

In January 1999 a quarrel between an Ambonese Christian bus driver and a Buginese Muslim passenger in Ambon town – a pretty common incident in the area that is usually quickly settled – became the trigger for a long-lasting bloody conflict.[2] What first looked like an ethnically inspired conflict very soon turned into what many observers unthinkingly called a religious war. Due to the strategic use of religious symbols to mobilize the masses by spreading rumors of important religious buildings being burnt down and an influx of jihad forces from Java from mid-2000 onwards, religion became the main dividing factor in the conflict. This led to a rigorous social as well as geographical divide of Moluccan society along religious lines (Christians versus Muslims). There were thousands of fatalities and hundreds of thousands had to flee, Christians as well as Muslims, locals as well as migrants. For a long time, the Indonesian government stated that the Moluccan people should resolve their conflict themselves (that did not keep them from sending troops to the area though). Only in 2002 did it make a serious effort and organize a peace meeting in Malino (Sulawesi), where peace negotiations with regards to the conflicts in Central Sulawesi (see Subagya this volume) had taken place before. Thirty-five Christian and thirty-five Muslim representatives from the Moluccas were invited to the meeting. The resulting peace agreement put at least an official end to the fighting, but, in fact, there were various major incidents that occurred after MalinoII such as the attack on Soya village around the end of April 2002, and incidents such as bomb threats and actual bombings occurred even years thereafter. The main difference is that the masses are fed up with fighting and do not want to get involved any more. They had suffered in all aspects – social, economic, and education – and want to live a better life now. Although the culprits of these more recent incidents are individuals being paid by people who still have an interest in perpetuating unrest in the Moluccas, such cases unfortunately prompt influential newspapers such as *The Jakarta Post* to report an "Ongoing conflict in Ambon" (14 May 2007). These continuous latent and open security threats in the Moluccas make the active search for sustainable peace and reconciliation even more urgent.

The many Moluccans, from various backgrounds and various places, to whom I have spoken over the years seem to agree that it was not the government, not the big politicized peace events such as MalinoII, and definitely not the military and the police that ended the conflict, but the people themselves. They were in search of something that could provide them material to rebuild the bridge between the two communities: the call for a revival or strengthening of *adat* became louder and louder. The most prominent examples of traditional concepts used to reconcile the warring parties and construct a unifying Moluccan identity (something that was, in fact, never there before), are the *raja* and *pela*. *Raja* are the traditional village heads, whose reinstallation was enabled by the new decentralization laws in Indonesia: Law No. 22 and 25 of 1999 and Law No. 32 of 2004 (UU 22&25/1999 and 32/2004). *Pela* are traditional alliance systems in the Central Moluccas that bring two or more villages together in pacts, irrespective of their religion, to help each other in times of crisis, to build religious buildings, and to organize big events.[3] *Pela* partners generally refused to attack each other during the conflict. What is clear is that the Moluccan population is in search of peace, peace in a positive sense that goes beyond the mere absence of war and violence (Galtung 1969); peace that enables the reunification of society and prevents such large-scale violence from happening again.

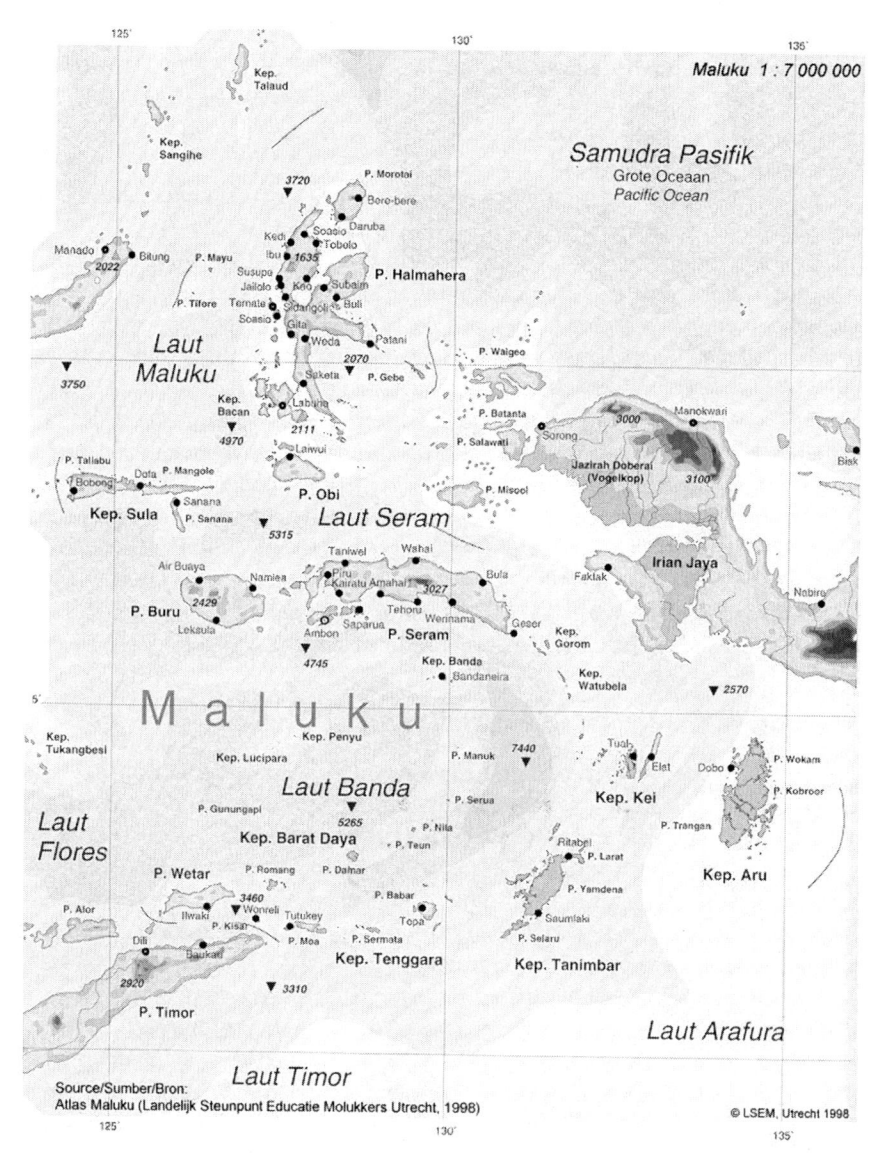

Map 5.1 Moluccas (Province of Maluku and Maluku Utara)

But why should *adat* be a means to achieve this? What probably immediately comes to one's mind is that *adat* in the Indonesian context is often abstractly projected as representing the ideal society of the past, harmony, and authenticity (see e.g. Henley & Davidson 2007: 4). As Li (2007: 337) suggested, "to invoke *adat* is to claim purity and authenticity for one's cause". Revival activities could be seen as attempts to re-enact such an authentic, coherent, and autonomous culture of the past (compare Rosaldo 1989: 217). But, as the past has shown, too often "the idea of *adat* as a guarantee of peace and harmony is misleading not only as a prescription for the future, but also as an interpretation of the past" (Henley & Davidson 2007: 33). Henley and Davidson therefore try to expose the current *adat* movement as the result of a wishful thinking, as a desperate attempt to overcome "disorder, individualism and distrust" (2007: 33).

The revival of *adat* and tradition in the Moluccas is part of an international and national trend.[4] As the edited volume by Davidson and Henley *The Revival of Tradition in Indonesian Politics* (2007) clearly shows, *adat* "gained new currency in battles over identity and resources" in Indonesia (Bourchier 2007: 123), but the *adat* movement has a highly ambiguous character, being at the same time "progressive and reactionary, emancipating and authoritarian, idealistic and manipulative" (Henley & Davidson 2007: 18).[5] Having said this and being aware of all the drawbacks of and criticism against the revival movements in Indonesia, it is no solution to simply wave the revival of tradition aside as either mere political instrumentalization and ideology or nostalgic localism. This is similar to the discourse on the concept of culture which cannot be dismissed easily either. Just as culture and categorizations play an essential role in constructing social realities (Mahmood & Armstrong 1992: 1), the revival of *adat* and the hope that it may serve as a peace agent are real. And, as Mahmood and Armstrong (1992: 8) argued, "in social life what people accept as real is real in its consequences".

Oral histories and the reconciliation of divided memories

The Moluccas are home to rich oral traditions and retelling some of the stories involved in my case study is essential for understanding the basic conflict and peace narratives. According to Portelli (1998) oral history is interesting precisely because it is always partial and always implies taking sides. Comparing different oral histories – rather then consulting so-called historical facts – therefore leads to "the confrontation of their different partialities" (Portelli 1998: 73) and, in our case, can tell us a lot about the perception of the conflict by and the different interests of the parties involved. What and how a group remembers is a selective process and very much depends on the present–past interface. The perception of the past is always influenced if not determined by the present, and the other way round, interpretations of the past – the social or collective memory of a group – shape its present behavior and legitimize the present social order.[6] As the journal issue "The Revitalisation of Tradition" (Bräuchler & Widlok 2007) shows, worldwide tendencies to revive traditional institutions and law never seem to be attempts to actually revive the past, but are conscious future-oriented strategies. Interestingly, flexibility and adaptability to changing circumstances and local needs were already seen as the main survival strategies of *adat* in Indonesia by those who were the first to actually document *adat* law, Cornelis van Vollenhoven and his Dutch crew (Fasseur 2007: 58). According to van Vollenhoven, "any codification of *adat* law … might stifle a harmonious development of native customs and institutions" (Fasseur 2007: 61). And even worse, defining *adat* as a culture with specific traits is automatically doomed to sharpen "distinctions between cultural insiders and outsiders, increasing the potential for horizontal conflict and violence" (Bourchier 2007: 124); this is an issue that is causing major problems in the recent revival of tradition trends all over Indonesia.

Talking about the past, it is not the historical facts that matter, but the meaning that is attributed to them. As Portelli (1998: 67) explained: "Oral sources tell us not just what people did, but what they wanted to do, what they believed they were doing, and what they now think they did". The same historical event might have totally different meanings for two groups and therefore legitimize different responses in the present. Accordingly, it is less important to know what actually happened in the recent conflict I am talking about, more important is how it is interpreted and narrated by the different groups involved, which determines their future action and possible peace initiatives. The question this chapter therefore deals with is how "divided memories" (Giesen 2004) can be reconciled; memories that were not only divided through the conflict, but actually look back on a long history of separating factors. Due to the increasing number of so-called ethnic conflicts where culture is 'purified' and an instrumentalist discourse where traditions are politicized and 'used' for specific means, untrained observers often tend to forget that cultures are not homogeneous, incontestable, and static unities with a fixed set of objective criteria, but rather processual, fluid, and constantly changing in response to various influences (Guthmann 2003: 107; Pottier 2003: 20). Collective identities, as Mahmood and Armstrong (1992: 11) argued, have to be seen as "an aspect of the human cognitive process of categorization". They are processes of reciprocal identification, in which the borderlines between two groups are constantly (re)negotiated (Barth 1969; Melucci 1995).

According to Avruch (1998) and Lederach (1995, 1997) no conflict can be understood, let alone sustainably resolved, without taking its cultural context into account. Culture on the one hand, is often mobilized for conflict, but according to Lederach (1997: 94), also provides "the greatest resource for sustaining peace in the long term". Lederach (1997: 151) regarded reconciliation as a process of relationship-building. It is a communicative process, in the course of which narratives have to be developed that enable all involved to cope with the painful past and the projection of a common future in the present. We are in search of symbols, narratives, and rituals that can be mobilized to enable the former warring parties to imagine themselves as a united entity. This becomes possible because people are not trapped in their collective memories, but they are rather able to reshape, adapt, and reinvent them (Ortner 2006). It requires an agency-oriented approach and a non-essentialist notion of culture that allows social practices to shape, reinvent, and restructure social relations and conflict lines.[7] Agency can shift focuses and meanings in identity construction that re-enables peace, but it can only be effective when it builds on cultural traits or conflict resolution mechanisms that are intelligible to the people concerned and consistent with the cultural background of a group and its (recreated) social memory (compare also Connerton 1989: 6).

Narratives have to be rewritten and symbols reinterpreted or created, in other words, a recategorization process has to take place (Gaertner & Dovidio 2000) that enables the integration of 'the other'. In the Moluccas efforts to revive or strengthen *adat* are reconciliatory attempts to build inter-religious bridges and a common unifying identity. These initiatives can be interpreted as attempts to widen the identities of the involved parties (Ellis 2006; Kelman 2004), and to replace collective memories divided by conflict experiences with a revived, reconstructed, or reinvented "cultural memory" and relevant "figures of memory" in the form of symbols and rituals that accentuate an imagined unity of the warring parties and thus enable peace (Assmann 1999; Assmann & Czaplicka 1995: 129). It is against this backdrop that we have to analyze our case study in order to appreciate the reconciliatory potential of reinvented traditions.

The local setting: Hatuhaha and Kariu[8]

The very general and popular depiction of the Moluccan conflict as a religious war is in line with predominant discourses on the rise of religious fundamentalisms worldwide and a national scenario, where an increasing number of church burnings was reported and inter-religious violence was erupting in many places. However, it ignores the complexity of the conflict factors and dynamics in the Moluccas and fails to account for a number of important micro-dynamics. The following discussion therefore takes a closer ethnographic look at one particular case: the Hatuhaha union on Haruku island and its neighboring village Kariu. The idea is to deconstruct oversimplified conflict images and go beyond the typical primordialism-constructivism opposition to try to see *adat* in its lived context, a context that is

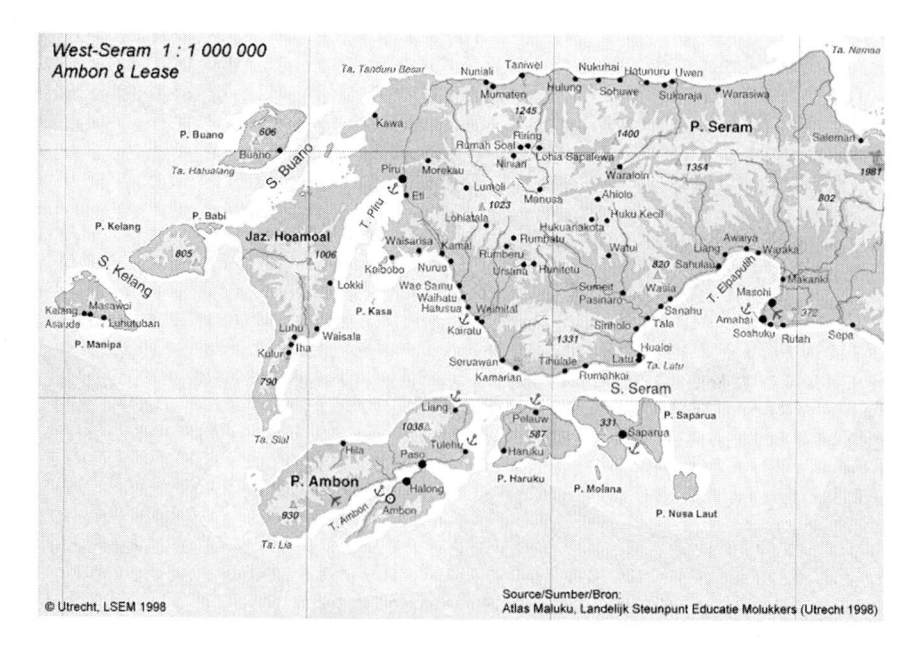

Map 5.2 West Seram, Ambon, Lease Islands

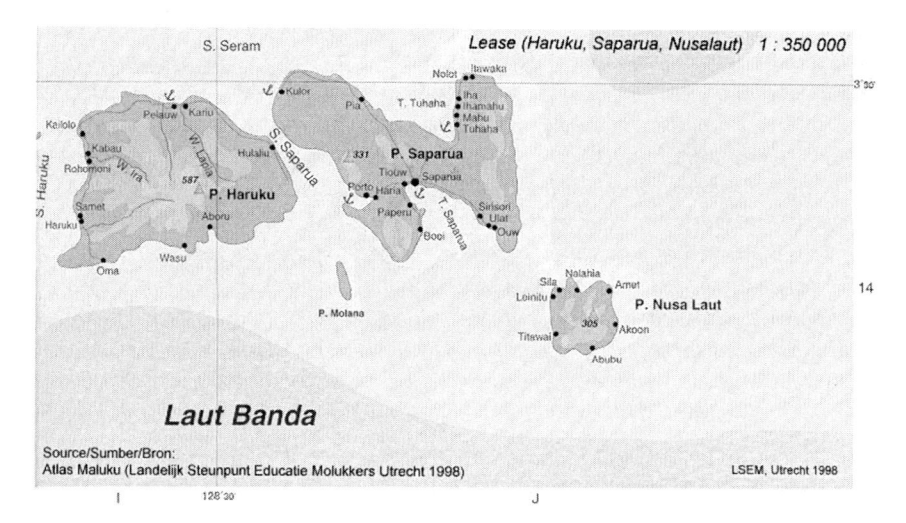

Map 5.3 Lease Islands

constantly changing and in which it becomes both a source for local identities as well as a political instrument. Investigating the mobilization of tradition for peace in this particular setting, I will discuss its feasibility as an approach to reconciliation.

Haruku is an island neighboring Ambon. The northern half is inhabited by Kariu village and *Uli* Hatuhaha, which consists of five, formerly Muslim villages: Rohomoni, Kabau, Kailolo, Pelauw, and Hulaliu (Hulaliu now being Christian). *Uli* are traditional Moluccan village federations, but most of them were eradicated under the Dutch who did not want any overarching structure to exist that might challenge their power. *Uli* Hatuhaha is one of the very few *uli* still functioning today, at least on an *adat* level.[9]

The five Hatuhaha villages were formerly located in *Hatuhaha Amarima Lounusa* (literally 'Five villages on a rock gather on the island') on Alaka mountain on Haruku, where the villagers had jointly converted to Islam.[10] The Alaka fortification was one of the strongholds of anti-colonial resistance.[11] Hatuhaha people often describe their union using an analogy to the human body, the five villages comprising different parts of it; none can exist without the other and each one of them has its specific task to keep the system running. As spokesperson, Hulaliu had to approach the colonial powers about their constant pestering and efforts to convert the Hatuhaha people to Christianity. On that mission, Hulaliu gave in and entered Christianity at the end of the sixteenth century. According to the Hatuhaha people's interpretation, Hulaliu had sacrificed itself and thus saved its brothers from conversion. This reinforces them in considering Hulaliu still to be part of their *adat* union even after it had converted, and in involving them in joint Hatuhaha ceremonies and activities such as the restoration of the Hatuhaha mosque. In the first half of the seventeenth century the Dutch finally forced all of them to settle at the coast. Only when it comes to *adat* rituals, the organic unity is still functioning and the respective villages and their *raja* still perform specific roles. Nevertheless, the harmonious Hatuhaha unity is promoted to the outside until today, but is at the same time torn by internal conflicts, power struggles, and religious quarrels, especially Islam internal ones. This led to the split of one of its villages, Pelauw, in the 1930s. The followers of a more traditional Islam called Islam Hatuhaha remained in Pelauw, while the followers of a more orthodox Islam (Islam Syariah) moved to Ori, which became a *dusun* (village part) of Pelauw (east of Kariu).[12]

Due to the Muslim-Christian composition of the Hatuhaha union and peace initiatives taken such as a peace procession organized in Ambon town beginning of 2002, when things were still quite tense, Hatuhaha people claimed to be the symbol for a Muslim-Christian reunification and the key to peace in the Moluccas, which does not go undisputed. Another reason why I chose the Hatuhaha case is because it combines several traditional elements used in revival and peace initiatives throughout the Moluccas and will thus tell us a lot about current dynamics in the Moluccas in general.

What lies just between Pelauw and Ori, but is not part of Hatuhaha, is the Christian village Kariu. Kariu often compared its situation with Israel during the conflict, being entrapped in a Muslim dominated area, although occupying its original land. Just like Hatuhaha, Kariu people claim to originally come from Seram. According to the narrative of one of the *adat* elders of Kariu, they were the first settlers on Haruku. While they first lived together in one place called *Amaira* (big village), they soon spread out over the island and established twelve *aman* (local term used for village before the colonial period). Mid of the seventeenth century Patti Elihin (or Pattirajawane) decided to gather all the settlements in the mountains (*negeri lama*) and establish the village Kariu (local term for 'to gather') at the coast.[13] Kariu directly converted to Christianity from animism.

Hatuhaha people do not claim to be the first settlers on the island, but they claim to be the first ones to have occupied the land at the Northern shore of Haruku. According to them, Kariu people then were nomads and therefore never belonged to any overarching federation or owned any land; they only came down to the coast when the Verenigde Oost-Indische Compagnie (VOC) asked them to settle at fort *Hoorn* that the Dutch had built in 1655 next to Pelauw to control the Muslim Hatuhaha people.[14] This leaves us with two conflicting claims towards the same piece of land – with two seemingly incompatible social memories – and implies various follow-up conflicts. Whereas Kariu, for instance, claims that it had allocated parts of its traditional land (*petuanan Kariu*) to those Pelauw people that had to leave the village in the 1930s (now living in Ori), Pelauw claims that Kariu occupies land that traditionally belongs to Hatuhaha. Just as there were conflicts between and within the Hatuhaha villages in the past until now, there were also conflicts between Kariu and Pelauw. Both populations were expanding, which led to increased daily conflicts and finally made the *raja* of Kariu at the beginning of the 1930s, *Raja* Jacob Pattirajawane, decide to relocate Kariu village a bit further up the coast (to the east) to prevent further conflicts. The two villages have since then lived in relative harmony, exchanging (or selling and buying) fish, field crops, and palm wine (*sageru* is an essential part of any *adat* ceremony in Pelauw, but the wine is mainly produced by Kariu people), and by maintaining daily social relationships (also many Kariu teachers worked in Pelauw schools before the conflict).

Another *adat* alliance playing into the conflict scenario is the *gandong* relationship between the four villages, Kariu (Northern Haruku), Hualoi (Southern Seram), Aboru (Southern Haruku), and Booi (Saparua).[15] It is believed four brothers once departed from Seram, shared the strains of a long and difficult journey, and founded these four villages. Whereas *pela* is usually based on an incisive incident in the past such as wars or accidents, *gandong* is based on common descent and ancestry, and thus considered to be even stronger than *pela*.[16]

Local conflict dynamics

Without having this background in mind, it is not possible to grasp the local conflict and peace dynamics. I will try to show how these social memories played into the conflict pattern and complicated the simplifying 'grand narrative' of a religious war. It is most obvious how changing circumstances on an international, national, and local level changed the prioritization of certain identity aspects and resulted in the neglect of others. Still, there seems to be no easy pattern in the inter-relationship of religion and *adat* in the Moluccan conflict. Religion became a major dividing factor, in some cases supported by *adat* and different interpretations of history, in other cases opposed by shared traditions. The Hatuhaha case illustrates the complex inter-relationship between *adat* and religion in the Moluccas and how they have been intermingling and competing with each other for the Moluccan people's identity for centuries.

The Moluccan conflict broke out in Ambon town on 19 January 1999. By August 1999 the conflict had spread over the whole of the Moluccas, including the Southeastern and the Northern Moluccas. A lot of pressure was built up on both sides, the Muslim and the Christian community, to take revenge. The first violent incidents outside of Ambon occurred in Kairatu on Seram and resulted in the burning down of dozens of houses on the Muslim side. Many Hatuhaha people live in Ambon town and Kairatu, and got involved in these first clashes. Moreover, many Hatuhaha people claim that they were brave pioneers in the conflict (and, later on, in the peace-building process). That's why it took less then a month for the conflict to extend to the neighboring island of Haruku. A visit by Saleh Latuconsina, Governor of the Moluccas at that time, who is himself from Pelauw, could not prevent that. On 14 February 1999, one of our protagonists, Pelauw, and its Muslim allies attacked the Christian village Kariu.[17] Christian Hulaliu tried to come to the aid of its co-religionist Kariu, but in vain. Kariu was razed to the ground. While it was good neighborliness and economic interdependencies that shaped the relationship between Pelauw and Kariu before the conflict, it was the different religious background and the missing *adat* link, that is, Kariu's branding as 'non-Hatuhaha', that were in focus during the conflict. Kariu people fled to Hulaliu and Aboru village in South Haruku, which is both Christian and their long-standing *gandong* partner. The Muslim village Hualoi did not join their co-religionists in attacking Kariu, but rather came to Aboru to help Kariu people out with clothes and food, thus also fulfilling their obligations as *gandong* of Kariu. In December 1999, Pelauw and its Muslim allies attacked Hulaliu, but broke off after a short while. The strong Hatuhaha union traditionally binding Muslim and Christian villages together stumbled and people were killed on both sides during the attack, but – and this is how the Hatuhaha people themselves see it – the union ultimately withstood the strong religious challenge (compare also Uhi 2004).[18] In the Kariu case it would seem that the absence of a shared cultural background with its neighboring Muslim village became a fatal factor and contributed to its annihilation. In the Hulaliu case, on the other hand, *adat* seemingly became its savior.

Reinventing and reviving tradition for peace

There would be plenty of stories to tell, how *adat* was used to foster peace all over the Moluccas. This section will focus on the Repatriation Ceremony of the Kariu Refugees (*Acara Pemulangan Pengungsi Kariu*), where *gandong* relationships and the re-enactment of the traditional Hatuhaha union played an important role. The repatriation ceremony thus gives expression to a broader range of *adat*-inspired peace initiatives and the complexity of the revival process. What follows is, first, an outline of the repatriation ceremony, then an analysis thereof, and finally some conclusions.

Acara Pemulangan Pengungsi Kariu

Kariu people were expelled from their village in February 1999. Some of them fled to Hulaliu in the east, some to Ambon island, and the majority to Aboru village on the south coast of Haruku. Due to the strong position of Muslim Hatuhaha people in the conflict as well as in Ambonese politics and economics, the chances for Kariu to return home were considered to be quite low and Pelauw people were very hesitant to receive Kariu back.[19] After living almost two years in quite cramped conditions, Aboru allocated a place called Tihunitu in the eastern part of their territory to the Kariu refugees. The Kariu people built very basic houses and stayed there until their eventual return in 2005, after more than six years and three months in exile. From 2003 onwards the government had given refugees in the Moluccas the choice of repatriation, relocation, or transmigration (Pemerintah Provinsi Maluku 2003). For the Kariu refugees in Tihunitu there was no doubt: they wanted to go back home to their *negeri adat*, to their *adat* land.

The actual repatriation was initiated by the Repatriation Team of the Kariu Refugees (*Tim Pemulangan Pengungsi Kariu*, TPPK). It was set up in October 2003 by Pieter P. from Kariu, who is also head of the Coalition of Moluccan Refugees (*Koalisi Pengungsi Maluku*, KPM). Together with *Yayasan Pengembangan dan Pemberdayaan Masyarakat* (YPPM), a local NGO in Ambon, he had put a lot of effort into bringing people from the Muslim Hatuhaha villages and Kariu together, to arrange first visits and to revive cautious attempts to exchange food again.[20] In October 2003 YPPM had managed to get all *raja* from Haruku island together, including the Hatuhaha and Kariu ones, to (re)activate a *raja* forum called Forum Latupati Haruku that had been formerly in charge of improving communication between villages and anticipating conflicts (mainly over land), but definitely did not function any more during the conflict. The first decision taken by this re-established forum was that Kariu should return to its *adat* land. All *raja* signed an agreement. After many mediating efforts by the government, NGOs, *raja* from the neighboring villages, KPM and TPPK, and other local figures, and after Pelauw people had received compensation for the many clove trees that were destroyed – although not all of them in the Kariu-Pelauw conflict – Pelauw finally agreed to allow Kariu back and got involved in the discussions on how to organize the repatriation ceremony. The Jesuit Refugee Service (JRS), an international Catholic organization, facilitated the repatriation ceremony and preceding negotiations.[21]

What Pieter considered to be essential for a successful and peaceful repatriation was the local anchoring of the process. He therefore worked in close cooperation with a large number of Kariu *adat* figures. Pelauw representatives were also part of the team. The main question was how to sustainably return the Kariu people and what kind of *adat* to use. Pelauw representatives wanted to re-enact the coming down of the Kariu people from the mountains to the beach, where the former would wait and welcome them, thus reinforcing their dominant position and their version of history. The TPPK saw this as an unnecessary arousal of antagonistic sentiments. On the other hand, they also did not want to use religion as leading principle to repatriate Kariu people, as was suggested by the *Majelis Jemaat Kariu* (the Protestant congregation in Kariu), since this would have automatically excluded Pelauw. After long negotiation processes, they decided to make use of *adat* that was supposedly carried out when Kariu had moved away from Pelauw in the 1930s, thus re-enacting the time when Kariu people first settled down on this particular land in the past. All people involved then agreed on the following procedure.

In October 2004 Hatuhaha (in particular Pelauw) and Kariu people came to the devastated site of Kariu village and started cleaning it. A month later, the first stone was laid. In June 2005, the Kariu refugees could finally go back home. Representatives of the *gandong* villages Aboru, Booi, and Hualoi had come to Tihunitu in order to pick up the Kariu refugees and accompany them back to their *adat* land. The *raja* of Hualoi, who traditionally is the oldest brother of the *gandong* and therefore has to take care of his younger siblings, was the last one to leave Tihunitu after they had prayed together in the temporary church. People from Hualoi were explicitly asked to wear their traditional Muslim clothes, in a gesture of reconciliation and solidarity for the Muslim neighbors of Kariu. The first stop was in Hulaliu, where people got together in the *baileo*, the traditional *adat* house. Kariu and Hualoi people officially thanked Hulaliu for sheltering Kariu refugees for several years and the Kariu people were officially released. After that, the journey continued and the crowd entered Ori (*dusun* Pelauw) and finally got to the Kariu border. Following the example of the 1930s, the lord of the land (*amanupu* or *tuan tanah*) of Kariu ceremonially 'opened the door' of Kariu by cutting young coconut leaves put up at the village border. In Kariu the Hatuhaha *adat* union (*persekutuan adat*) was already waiting to receive Kariu back in a tent that was erected where the former *baileo* had been. Important government representatives such as the governor, the vice governor, and members of parliament joined as well. Several speeches, all emphasizing the reconciliatory potential of *adat*, were given and prayers said together. Pelauw had prepared food, so everybody could join in *makan patita*, that is, the traditional way of putting food on a long table and then enjoying it together during communal ceremonies. For key parts of the ceremonies, the local language (*bahasa tanah*) was used by *adat* officials and 'traditional' clothes were worn throughout.[22]

Analysis of the repatriation ceremony

Considering the perception of the Moluccan conflict as a religious war, it was important to emphasize that the Kariu people did not explicitly return as Christians, but as *adat* people who returned home to their *adat* village (*negeri adat*); a recategorization of the former enemy had to take place. Wherever possible, the architects of the (re)invented repatriation ceremony included well-known *adat* elements in order to widen identities and create commonality, but in a way that each individual group involved could also preserve its specific identity and its specific interpretation of history and the conflict. All this should stay untouched by the reconciling repatriation ceremony. Jointly undergone *adat* ceremonies not only build up bonds and create a new and shared repatriation history, but at the same time impose responsibilities on those involved: the responsibility to maintain their shared reality, a good relationship, and peace. It was also important to include all parts of society, that is, not only the *adat* communities of the two villages, but also government representatives, religious figures, and security forces. All of them were witnesses and active participants in the repatriation ceremony, which makes them part of this 'social (*adat*) contract'. This could also contribute to overcoming the problem discussed earlier (see the 'Oral histories and the reconciliation of divided memories' section), that is, the potentially exclusive character of revived or reinvented traditions.

As we have seen, various influential traditions played a role in the repatriation procedure: *gandong*, the Hatuhaha union, *adat* functionaries, and the *raja*. Hualoi, the Muslim *gandong* partner of Kariu, became both a supporter and protector of its younger (and Christian) *adat* sibling as well as a mediator between the two religions. Hulaliu – being itself Christian and part of the traditional Hatuhaha union – became both a supporter and protector of Kariu as its co-religionist as well as a mediator between two separate *adat* units and social memories. And finally, the re-enactment of the Christian-Muslim Hatuhaha union set an example for a broader fraternization of Christians and Muslims in the Moluccas. These initiatives are part of a much wider network of reconciliation efforts that is very much linked with genealogical, *adat*, and religious ties in Moluccan society. That is where the importance of the detailed analysis of this particular case study lies. It helps to illustrate that Moluccan people's identities are not only based on localities, but also networks; their villages are as much a source for their collective identity as their interlinkage with other villages (on other islands), be it by *pela*, *gandong*, or other types of *adat* alliances. If we were to add more and more case studies, we would finally see that they all are somehow linked with each other, just as all members of Moluccan society are. It is this dual identity structure that has to be re-strengthened or revived for a better and more sustainable (re)integration of Moluccan society. That would be another step towards overcoming the exclusivity of (revived) localized traditions. Moreover, as I was told by many *adat* figures, people have to become aware again of much more general implications of *adat*, that is to emphasize living together (irrespective of religious and village affiliations) and being interdependent and to show respect to outsiders and immigrants.

Having said this, it would be very optimistic and overly idealistic if one would consider a two- or three-day ceremony to be sufficient to create sustainable peace and the event definitely has to be put into context. The repatriation ceremony, in the end, was only the tip of the iceberg. Multiple peace efforts, such as meetings and trainings organized by NGOs, the regional and district government between 2003 and 2005 at various locations on Haruku and Ambon, involving politicians, security forces, *adat* and religious figures, *raja*, youth, and ordinary village people from all over Haruku, had taken place before.[23] *Raja* installation ceremonies that were postponed due to the conflict also became important peace events by bringing Muslims and Christians together. The peace efforts on Haruku were preceded by an internal reconciliation process of the Hatuhaha union in February 2002, where the four Muslim villages had visited Hulaliu and pled for the re-establishment of their *adat* union that was almost destroyed, supposedly due to outside influences. Hulaliu was taken by surprise, but then accepted the offer.[24] Together they then organized a peace rally to Ambon town, passing through Muslim as well as Christian areas, which was still an extraordinary exception by that time. Hatuhaha therefore claims to be the key to peace (*kunci perdamaian*) in the Moluccas; a statement that was enforced by the governor, who had publicly emphasized that without Hatuhaha, there can be no peace in Maluku (*Tanpa Hatuhaha, Maluku tidak bisa aman*). Although the role of Hatuhaha as peace pioneer is highly contested by non-Hatuhaha people, who argue that strategically located villages such as Tulehu on Ambon island played a much bigger role in the reconciliation process, there is definitely something in it. Due to the key role of Hatuhaha people in the conflict and in Moluccan political landscape they definitely play an important role as peacemakers.

The Repatriation Ceremony of the Kariu Refugees needed a lot of strategic thinking and preparation and gives insight into the immense complexity of the reconciliation process in the Moluccas. The essential principle behind the ceremony was the local anchoring of the peace process through the use of *adat*, thus emphasizing the cultural dimension of reconciliation. Next to the *adat* elements described earlier, Pieter and his team also tried to re-raise awareness of other (Christian-Muslim) *pela* alliances Kariu and the Hatuhaha villages are involved in, and ties between two particular families in Kariu and Pelauw (Pattiwaellapia and Tualeka), who claim to have either a common migration background or even ancestry (compare Pattiwaellapia 2005). Where *adat* links were missing (such as between Kariu and Pelauw) other traditional bonds had to be rebuilt: former interdependencies in various sectors such as economy (exchange of field crops, palm wine, fish, etc.), health, and education (e.g. bringing Kariu teachers back into schools in Pelauw). Pieter involved strategic figures such as members of parliament that come from Kailolo or Pelauw in order to get in touch with influential representatives or accepted spokespersons at the village level. The goal was to address and involve the majority of the population concerned in the whole peace process.[25] He also spoke to representatives of the synod and the Indonesian Ulama Council (*Majelis Ulama Indonesia*, MUI) in Ambon town so that they on their part could exert influence on their communities on Haruku. Moreover, KPM tried to raise awareness on a national level by sending reports to the government in Jakarta and organizations such as the National Commission for Human Rights (*Komisi Nasional Hak Asasi Manusia*, KOMNAS HAM). Pieter thus aimed to develop a multi-level approach with which he wanted to set an example that could be applied to other cases.

Closing the circle

What can we conclude from these analyses? Is it possible to create an inclusive *adat* or is that a contradiction in terms? Is the mobilization of tradition for peace a feasible approach to reconciliation or rather an irrational attempt to put the fire out by adding fuel to the flames? As this case study shows, there is no easy answer to that and a simplistic revival of local traditions without taking the broader sociopolitical and socioeconomic context into account will most probably not provide a solid basis for reconciliation. Traditions have to be reconstructed in such a way that they integrate local communities, but not through the emphasis of their exclusivity (the 'othering' of those not being part of the reintegrated community), which would have the potential of creating new conflict lines. Sustainability of peace requires multi-level agency, which means that all levels of society – people in the villages as well as politicians – have to get actively involved in the decision-making and negotiation part, thus becoming the owners of the peace process. Reconciliation efforts do not take place in a power vacuum. Taking existing power structures such as the dominant position of Hatuhaha people in this case study into account is a necessary means to enable reconciliation, although justice (or better, its interpretation by dominant human rights discourses) might not be served right away.

What we have to do is to analyze under which circumstances the revival of *adat* and the hopes in *adat* as peace agent *become* real (see earlier).[26] When the state fails to solve internal conflicts in its territory, when there is not sufficient (or no) trust in the security forces due to their involvement in the conflict, when there is no law enforcement, no unveiling of the truth,[27] then people have to try to help themselves and find a way to cope with the past violence and enable a peaceful coexistence again. *Adat* is something people in the Moluccas can obviously identify with, besides religion. *Adat* might not have been the right means to stop the violence, but it seems to be effective in rebuilding social relationships, which is an essential foundation for sustainable peace. Another mechanism of how people in the Moluccas try to cope with the violence they experienced, to construct an acceptable past for all of them, and to re-establish relationships with their neighbors is not to look for the truth as such, but to blame people from outside the Moluccas to be the agent provocateur and the ones behind the conflict. It is a common saying in both Christian and Muslim villages that the conflict would not have happened if there were no influence from the outside (*pengaruh dari luar*).

Notwithstanding the structural determinants and the importance of all other peace initiatives taken on Haruku island as important preparatory steps, it seems that only the sophisticatedly planned *adat* ceremony finally enabled the return of the refugees not only by inspiring them and their neighbors with enough confidence and by reinstalling the Kariu people in their place of origin on their *adat* land, but also by providing an integrative *adat* structure. This has the potential to shape a common social memory that will offer guidance for future actions and a collective identity that can accommodate them all: the religious and the religious 'other', one *adat* group, and the 'other' *adat* group. As Ross (2004: 209) argued, reconciliation works through "emotional and cognitive reordering, which enables the development of a new relationship between former enemies" and he considers the symbolic and ritual dimension of reconciliation to be crucial for its success. In particular he promotes "the need for inclusive (new and transformed) symbols and rituals" (Ross 2004: 216). The ceremony I described in my case study definitely strives to be one such instance. Its goal is exactly what Ross (2004: 217) envisages to be the purpose of these symbolic actions and rituals: "acknowledgement of a past and the image of a different future".

As the case study showed, collective memories clearly shape conflict lines, but can also overcome them through the revival, the re-strengthening, or even a reinvention of local traditions. Symbols, narratives, and rituals shape collective identities and become the fundaments for divided memories, but they are also the means for unification and the building up of shared rituals and realities. The prerequisite is to de-essentialize collective identities – it does not matter whether based on religion or *adat* – both from an analytical and a local point of view. Borrowing from a "socially legitimate currency of memories" (Connerton 1989: 3), the (re)created or (re)invented *adat* ceremony in our case study seems to have provided local legitimization to all other peace initiatives. It enabled lived reconciliation in public space, and accredited *adat* space, thus not only granting people new rights to unite, but also imposing responsibilities on all involved. Listening to Moluccan people's recollection of the reconciliation process so far, it is that kind of locally grounded ceremony that will shape their social memories in the long run, not NGO workshops or government-initiated peace talks. Just as the narratives of the legendary Hatuhaha union, the arrival of the first Kariu people on Haruku, and the foundation of the various *pela* alliances and *gandong* partnerships structure and determine the collective memories of those groups, the newly created or reinvented *adat* ceremony or pact will be remembered, and can hopefully contribute to a long-term peaceful relationship.

Nevertheless, as the coordinator of the Repatriation Ceremony of the Kariu Refugees warned, the *adat*-laden ceremony was an important and necessary step to enable collective reconciliation, but it cannot prevent individual feelings of revenge or injustice (e.g. due to unequal compensation after the conflict and unsolved land issues) coming to the surface again. At the moment, the desire for harmony and the collective repatriation euphoria are still strong enough to silence those individual feelings, but internally in the villages, people do talk about such issues and great care has to be taken to not let them regain the upper hand as had almost happened beginning of 2008, when a youngster from Pelauw village fell off his motor scooter while passing through Kariu. The following interpretations by Kariu and Pelauw villagers of how this incident could have happened differed and almost led to violence. This could only be prevented by the intervention of locally influential figures. For a couple of days, children were taken to their schools in the neighboring village by a minibus, since walking was considered to be too dangerous due to the heated-up situation. According to Pieter, post-repatriation efforts have to focus on physical and moral reconstruction and economic empowerment, and the Indonesian government has to support all of these.

Our case study clearly shows that peace in the Moluccas still rests on shaky foundations. Constant efforts have to be made, making reconciliation not a status to be achieved, but a continuous process. In the long run the main underlying problems of the Moluccan conflict such as imbalances in power structure, social inequalities and injustices, and the role of security forces, adherents of the former regime, but also the current government need to be addressed.[28] In the long run reconciliation and positive peace (Johan Galtung) have to go along with structural changes that aim for social and political justice and balance, including education opportunities, economy, and bureaucracy. Moreover, the government has to find a way to solve the constant land issues in the Moluccas that have caused many problems and conflicts over the last centuries. What is most important when it comes to the revival of traditions for peace is to critically examine the traditional concepts in question, their history, and the motives of actors involved in the process, and to make sure that all levels of the population affected are involved in every stage of the reconciliation process. In order to avoid one-sided political manipulation or instrumentalization of (reinvented) collective identities and traditions, it is an essential step along the path to find out who is speaking for whom and who claims to represent whom.[29] A de-essentialization of collective identities and oversimplified conflict patterns has to go along with an emphasis on the complexity of conflict, identity, and peace dynamics. The different dimensions of collective identity have to be taken into account and we have to be aware of both their integrative as well as their exclusivist potential.

Academics and peace activists on all levels have to get active on many fronts, but the revival, the reinvention, or the mobilization of tradition, that is, the cultural dimension of reconciliation, and the agency of the populations concerned should definitely be taken into account in any peace process. Incorporating cultural aspects and local approaches to conflict resolution enables the local anchoring of peace initiatives and thus contributes to their sustainability. What is most important for this end: we have to listen to people's oral histories, and try to get access to their social memories – both constructed by a selective interpretation process of the more distant past and recent conflicts – but we also have to carefully follow how narratives in the villages develop and change, in order not only to better understand a conflict but also to prevent future conflicts. Emergency relief is one matter, the sustainability of conflict resolutions and reconciliation is another. Not only academia, but above all also policymakers and peace activists have to invest more in that kind of research and support local peace initiatives that build on integrative traditional structures. Beyond all its particularities, there is a lot to be learned from the Hatuhaha-Kariu case.

Acknowledgments

I would like to thank the Asia Research Institute (ARI), National University of Singapore, for supporting the research project underlying this chapter. A first version was presented at the conference on *In Search of Reconciliation and Peace in Indonesia and East Timor* in July 2007 at ARI. I would also like to thank the KITLV in Leiden for offering me a fellowship in 2007 during which I could both discuss and revise this paper. I am very grateful for the helpful feedback I got both at ARI and the KITLV. I would especially like to thank Maribeth Erb, Kari Telle, Henk Schulte Nordholt, Gerry van Klinken, Tamrin Tomagola, and Jim Schiller for their comments.

Notes

1 In this chapter I am mainly concerned with the Central Moluccas. If I talk about the 'Moluccas', I refer to this particular area unless otherwise stated.
2 For a more detailed conflict analysis and references see, among others, Bräuchler (2003, 2005); see also Adam, this volume, endnote 3.
3 Whether these traditional concepts are used simultaneously by certain individuals, business people, or politicians to jump onto the bandwagon and use *adat* for their interests, is another question. I have discussed the problems and challenges coming along with the reintroduction of the *raja* elsewhere (see e.g. Bräuchler 2008). Here I am concerned with other challenges and problems of the mobilization of tradition for peace.
4 For the international level see, e.g. the International Labour Organisation's Convention No. 169 on Indigenous and Tribal Peoples in Independent Countries (1989), most recently the UN Declaration on the Rights of Indigenous Peoples (2007), and Bräuchler and Widlok (2007). For the foundation of The Indigenous Peoples' Alliance of the Indonesian Archipelago (*Aliansi Masyarakat Adat Nusantara*, AMAN), and its evaluation see e.g. Acciaioli (2007), AMAN (1999), and Moniaga (2007).
5 Unfortunately the Moluccan province and Papua are not covered in this otherwise very rich and informative volume. On decentralization, conflict, and the revival of tradition in the Central and Northern Moluccas see, e.g. Bräuchler (2007 and forthcoming publications) and for Papua, Timmer (2007).
6 See Connerton (1989), Halbwachs (1985), Popular Memory Group (1998).
7 Compare Ortner (1999: 186), Parker (2005: 225).
8 The following is based on participant observation in the region and interviews I had conducted from 2006–2008 with *raja*, *adat* and religious figures, and people from Kariu and the Hatuhaha villages as well as with the coordinator and members of the Repatriation Team of the Kariu Refugees and other individuals and organizations involved in the peace process in this particular area. I want to thank them all for their hospitality, their time, their help, their patience, and their friendship.
9 For one version of a settlement history/myth of Haruku, see Sopacua *et al.* (1996).
10 For a short description of Islam in the Moluccas and the specificities of Hatuhaha Islam,

see Bartels (1994: 158–93). For sketchier descriptions of Islam Hatuhaha, see also Kraemer (1927) and Radjawane (1964).
11 See e.g. the Alaka war I and II in Bartels (1994) and Lestaluhu (1988).
12 For a detailed analysis of this event and its underlying causes, see Chauvel (1980).
13 *Patih* or *putih* was one of the titles used for village heads after the arrival of the colonial powers. The status of *patih* was below *raja*, but above *orang kaya*.
14 Compare van Fraassen and Straver (2002: 97–9), Valentijn (1856: 99), van de Wall (1928: 205).
15 *Gandong* derives from the Indonesian word *kandungan*, that is, uterus.
16 For an extensive treatise on *pela*, see Bartels (1977).
17 I will not deal with the question who actually initiated the Kariu-Pelauw incident, since interpretations from both sides are rather contradictory. For one possible, though not necessarily authoritative, version see Human Rights Watch (1999).
18 This interpretation is obviously meant to overcome differences and promote peace. It could be challenged by those who claim that Pelauw only withdrew because Hulaliu got support from the outside and thus became too strong. But then, again, the *raja* (Effendy Latuconsina) and other *adat* figures from Pelauw had warned their people against attacking their brothers and sisters in Hulaliu. The failure of the attack is seen as an intervention by the upset ancestors. According to the *raja* of Pelauw, the ancestors also took care that at least some of those who had asked for permission to attack Hulaliu had since suffered misfortune (interview with Effendy Latuconsina, compare also Titaley 2004: 58). There would be more examples of conflicts with other neighboring villages and among the Muslim villages of the Hatuhaha union themselves, but that would go beyond the scope of this chapter.
19 When Akib Latuconsina from Pelauw was elected as governor for Maluku in 1992, the term OPEK emerged and was unofficially utilized to refer to the phenomenon of more and more **O**ri, **Pe**lauw, and **K**ailolo people getting into influential positions. Just to give some examples: After Akib, Saleh Latuconsina was elected as governor and in 2003, Muhammad Abdullah Mehmed Latuconsina was elected as vice governor. Abdullah Tuasikal from Pelauw was re-elected as *bupati* of Maluku Tengah in 2007. Ruswan Latuconsina, the older brother of the current *raja* of Pelauw, was head of the *Dewan Perwakilan Rakyat Daerah* (DPRD), the regional parliament, from 1982 until 1997. And in 2006 Olivia Latuconsina was elected vice mayor of Ambon town and the list could be continued. Besides, Suaidi Marasabessy played an influential role in the Moluccan conflict, both as Chief of the General Staff of the Indonesian Military (Kasum Tentara Nasional Indonesia, TNI) and as a Kailolo person. But Hatuhaha people are not only strong in the political domain, but also in the economic sector. Many Hatuhaha people, for instance the *raja* of Pelauw and Kailolo, are building contractors. It is obvious that they have advantages when it comes to the assignment of government projects. Besides, it is a well-known fact that Kailolo people dominate the market in Ambon town. One reason for the 'rise of Hatuhaha people' is the improved access to education for Moluccan Muslims much more generally after independence. But Hatuhaha people also use *adat* to explain their dominant positions: Pelauw has always been in charge of leadership in the traditional Hatuhaha union and Kailolo was in charge of the economy. Moreover, based on an old song (*kapata*) Kailolo even claims that it originally was Ambon, or better *Apon* (interviews with *adat* elders in Kailolo; see also Valentijn 1856: 134).
20 The KPM's main objectives are how to involve refugees in the planning of aid programs and to act as mediator between the government and refugees. KPM was founded in 2004 by several local NGOs; all team members are volunteers. I would like to express my sincere thanks to Piet for sharing ideas and information on the repatriation process of the Kariu people with me. Without him and YPPM, Kariu people might even not have returned by now. I would also like to thank Abdulgani Fabanjo, head of YPPM, for all the valuable insights into YPPM-initiated or -facilitated projects.
21 In October 2005, for instance, JRS had invited ordinary villagers as representatives from

each Hatuhaha village and Kariu to a conflict management and peace workshop in Waiheru on Ambon, after which a team was built that was responsible for maintaining an amicable relationship between Hatuhaha and Kariu (*Tim Peduli BakuBae Hatuhaha dan Kariu*) by preventing any small-scale inter-individual dispute from developing into a large-scale conflict.

22 Due to its being an integral part of the Hatuhaha *adat* union, Hulaliu is one of the very few Christian villages in the Central Moluccas that, to date, maintain and preserve the local language (*bahasa daerah*).

23 Large parts of the population were not aware of these; for them, peace and reconciliation rather came naturally (*secara alami*), without interference from the outside, due to the revival of daily economic, educational, and social ties (compare Varshney 2002).

24 Describing the process that was also heavily laden with *adat* symbols would go beyond the scope of this chapter.

25 If I have used peace and reconciliation interchangeably in some cases in this chapter, I am not referring to peace in the negative sense, that is the mere absence of violence (compare Johan Galtung), but in the sense of rebuilding sustainable peaceful relationships, thus reconciliation.

26 I thank Henk Schulte Nordholt for raising this thought in our discussions.

27 In fact, part of the Malino peace agreement was the establishment of an Independent National Fact Finding Team (*Tim Penyeledikan Independen Nasional*, TPIN). However, the results are kept under lock and key until today by the Indonesian government.

28 Some efforts are already made in this direction. The mayor of Ambon town, for instance, is currently reorganizing the government structure and evaluating the possibilities of affirmative action according to religious affiliation, that is, to fill future vacancies in a way that creates 'religious balance' in the city's bureaucracy (see Palijama *et al.* 2007). According to Tamrin Tomagola, who was involved in the evaluation team, these affirmative action plans encountered quite some resistance among the Christian bureaucrats who had become used to getting preferential treatment in the Dutch colonial period. I thank Pak Tamrin for this information.

29 Another problem, with which I have not dealt with in this chapter, is how to integrate and to deal with migrants from outside the Moluccan *adat* system. This is a very relevant topic that needs to be explored in detail.

References

Acciaioli, G. (2007) 'From customary law to indigenous sovereignty: reconceptualizing masyarakat *adat* in contemporary Indonesia', in J.S. Davidson and D. Henley (eds) *The Revival of Tradition in Indonesian Politics: The Deployment of Adat from Colonialism to Indigenism*, London: Routledge.

AMAN (Aliansi Masyarakat Adat Nusantara) (1999) *Menggugat Posisi Masyarakat Adat Terhadap Negara. Prosiding Sarasehan Masyarakat Adat Nusantara, Jakarta, 15–16 Maret 1999*, Jakarta: AMAN.

Assmann, J. (1999) *Das kulturelle Gedächtnis. Schrift, Erinnerung und politische Identität in frühen Hochkulturen* (2nd edn), München: Beck.

Assmann, J. and Czaplicka, J. (1995) 'Collective memory and cultural identity', *New German Critique*, 65: 125–33.

Avruch, K. (1998) *Culture and Conflict Resolution*, Washington DC: United States Institute of Peace Press.

Bartels, D. (1977) *Guarding the Invisible Mountain: Intervillage Alliances, Religious Syncretism and Ethnic Identity among Ambonese Christians and Moslems in the Moluccas*, Ithaca: Cornell University.

—— (1994) *In de Schaduw van de Berg Nunusaku: Een Cultuur-historische Verhandeling over de Bevolking van de Midden-Molukken*, Utrecht: Landelijk Steunpunt Educatie Molukkers.

Barth, F. (1969) 'Introduction', in F. Barth (ed.) *Ethnic Groups and Boundaries. The Social Organization of Culture Difference*, Bergen-Oslo: Universitetsforlaget.

Bourchier, D. (2007) 'The romance of *adat* in the Indonesian political imagination and the current revival', in J.S. Davidson and D. Henley (eds) *The Revival of Tradition in Indonesian Politics: The Deployment of Adat from Colonialism to Indigenism*, London: Routledge.

Bräuchler, B. (2003) 'Cyberidentities at war: religion, identity, and the Internet in the Moluccan conflict', *Indonesia*, 75: 123–51.

—— (2005) *Cyberidentities at War: Der Molukkenkonflikt im Internet*, Bielefeld: transcript.

—— (2007) 'Ein Comeback der Tradition? Die Revitalisierung von *Adat* in Ostindonesien/A comeback of tradition? The revitalisation of *adat* in Eastern Indonesia', *Zeitschrift für Ethnologie* (Special issue, B. Bräuchler and T. Widlok (eds) 'Die Revitalisierung von Tradition'/'The Revitalisation of Tradition'), 132: 37–57.

—— (2008) 'Reflections on human rights and self-determination in Eastern Indonesia'. Unpublished manuscript.

Bräuchler, B. and Widlok, T. (eds) (2007) 'Die Revitalisierung von Tradition'/'The Revitalisation of Tradition' (special issue of the *Zeitschrift für Ethnologie* 132).

Chauvel, R. (1980) 'Ambon's other half: some preliminary observations on Ambonese Moslem society and history', *Review of Indonesian and Malaysian Affairs*, 14(1): 40–80.

Connerton, P. (1989) *How Societies Remember*, Cambridge (UK) and New York: Cambridge University Press.

Davidson, J.S. and Henley, D. (eds) (2007) *The Revival of Tradition in Indonesian Politics: The Deployment of Adat from Colonialism to Indigenism*, London: Routledge.

Ellis, D.G. (2006) *Transforming Conflict: Communication and Ethnopolitical Conflict*, Lanham: Rowman & Littlefield.

Fasseur, C. (2007) 'Colonial dilemma: Van Vollenhoven and the struggle between *adat* law and western law in Indonesia', in J.S. Davidson and D. Henley (eds) *The Revival of Tradition in Indonesian Politics: The Deployment of Adat from Colonialism to Indigenism*, London: Routledge.

Gaertner, S.L. and Dovidio, J.F. (2000) *Reducing Intergroup Bias: The Common Ingroup Identity Model*, Philadelphia: Taylor & Francis.

Galtung, J. (1969) 'Violence, Peace, and Peace Research', *Journal of Peace Research*, 6(1): 167–91.

Giesen, B. (2004) 'Noncontemporaneity, asynchronicity and divided memories', *Time & Society*, 13(1): 27–40.

Guthmann, T. (2003) *Globalität, Rassismus, Hybridität: Interkulturelle Pädagogik im Zeichen von rassistischem Diskurs und hybrider Identität*, Stuttgart: *ibidem*-Verlag.

Halbwachs, M. (1985) *Das kollektive Gedächtnis*, Frankfurt am Main: Fischer Wissenschaft.

Henley, D. and Davidson, J.S. (2007) 'Introduction: radical conservatism – the protean politics of *adat*', in J.S. Davidson and D. Henley (eds) *The Revival of Tradition in Indonesian Politics: The Deployment of Adat from Colonialism to Indigenism*, London: Routledge.

Human Rights Watch (1999) 'Report on violence in Ambon', *A Human Rights Watch Report*, 11(1)(C), March.

International Labour Organization (ILO) (1989) 'Convention No. 169 on indigenous and tribal peoples in independent countries'. Online. Available at: http://www.unhchr.ch/html/menu3/b/62.htm (accessed on 5 August 2006).

Kelman, H.C. (2004) 'Reconciliation as identity change: a social-psychological perspective', in Y. Bar-Siman-Tov (ed.) *From Conflict Resolution to Reconciliation*, Oxford: Oxford University Press.

Kraemer, H. (1927) 'Mededelingen over den Islam op Ambon en Haroekoe', *Djawa* 7(2): 77–88.

Lederach, J.P. (1995) *Preparing for Peace: Conflict Transformation Across Cultures*, Syracuse, NY: Syracuse University Press.

—— (1997) *Building Peace: Sustainable Reconciliation in Divided Societies*, Washington DC: United States Institute of Peace Press.

Lestaluhu, M.R.L. (1988) *Sejarah Perlawanan Masyarakat Islam terhadap Imperialisme di Daerah Maluku*, Bandung: Al-Ma'arif.

Li, T.M. (2007) '*Adat* in Central Sulawesi: Contemporary deployments', in J.S. Davidson and D. Henley (eds) *The Revival of Tradition in Indonesian Politics: The Deployment of Adat from Colonialism to Indigenism*, London: Routledge.

Mahmood, C.K. and Armstrong, S.L. (1992) 'Do ethnic groups exist? A cognitive perspective on the concept of cultures', *Ethnology*, 31(1): 1–14.

Melucci, A. (1995) 'The process of collective identity', in H. Johnston and B. Klandermans (eds) *Social Movements and Culture*, Minneapolis: University of Minnesota Press.

Moniaga, S. (2007) 'From bumiputera to masyarakat *adat*: a long and confusing journey', in J.S. Davidson and D. Henley (eds) *The Revival of Tradition in Indonesian Politics: The Deployment of Adat from Colonialism to Indigenism*, London: Routledge.

Ortner, S.B. (1995) 'Resistance and the problem of ethnographic refusal', *Comparative Studies in Society and History*, 37(1): 173–93.

—— (1999) 'Generation X: anthropology in a media-saturated world', in G.E. Marcus (ed.) *Critical Anthropology Now: Unexpected Contexts, Shifting Constituencies, Changing Agendas*, Santa Fe, New Mexico: School of American Research Press.

—— (2006) *Anthropology and Social Theory: Culture, Power, and the Acting Subject*, Durham and London: Duke University Press.

Palijama, R., Pentury, R. and Madubun, Y. (2007) *Format Ulang Birokrasi Kota Ambon (Draft Buku)*, Ambon: Book draft.

Parker, L. (2005) 'Conclusion', in L. Parker (ed.) *The Agency of Women in Asia*, Singapore: Marshall Cavendish Academic.

Pattiwaellapia, G. (2005) 'Hubungan Marga Pattiwaellapia di Kariu dan Marga Tualeka di Pelauw: suatu kajian teologi sosiologi terhadap sejarah bersama Marga Pattiwaellapia dan Tualeka dan implikasinya', unpublished script, Universitas Kristen Indonesia Maluku.

Pemerintah Provinsi Maluku (2003) *Keputusan Gubernor Tentang Petunjuk Teknis Penanganan Pengungsi (Nomor 413, 15 November 2003)*, Ambon: Pemerintah Provinsi Maluku.

Popular Memory Group (1998) 'Popular memory: theory, politics, method', in R. Perks and A. Thomson (eds) *The Oral History Reader*, London and New York: Routledge.

Portelli, A. (1998) 'What makes oral history different', in R. Perks and A. Thomson (eds) *The Oral History Reader*, London and New York: Routledge.

Pottier, J. (2003) 'Negotiating local knowledge: an introduction', in J. Pottier, A. Bicker and P. Sillitoe (eds) *Negotiating Local Knowledge: Power and Identity in Development*, London: Pluto Press.

Radjawane, A.N. (1964) 'Islam di Ambon dan Haruku', in W.B. Sidjabat (ed.) *Panggilan Kita di Indonesia Dewasa Ini*, Jakarta: Badan Penerbit Kristen (BPK).

Rosaldo, R. (1989) *Culture and Truth: The Remaking of Social Analysis*, Boston: Beacon Press.
Ross, M.H. (2004) 'Ritual and the Politics of Reconciliation', in Y. Bar-Siman-Tov (ed.) *From Conflict Resolution to Reconciliation*, Oxford: Oxford University Press.
Sopacua, L., Pattinama, W. and Noya, I. (1996) *Laporan Penelitian Perlawanan Rakyat Amarima Hatuhaha Terhadap Imperialisme dan Kolonialisme Portugis dan Belanda Pada Abad 16 (Perang Alaka) di Pulau Haruku*, Ambon: Balai Kajian Sejarah dan Nilai Tradisional.
Timmer, J. (2007) 'Erring decentralization and elite politics in Papua', in H. Schulte Nordholt and G. van Klinken (eds) *Renegotiating Boundaries: Local politics in post-Suharto Indonesia*, Leiden: KITLV Press.
Titaley, J. (2004) 'Amarima Hatuhaha: suatu tinjauan sosio historis dan implikasinya bagi kehidupan beragama', unpublished script, Universitas Kristen Indonesia Maluku.
Uhi, J.A. (2004) 'Hatuhaha Amarima Lou Nusa: suatu kajian sosio-historis untuk membangun teologi pluralistis yang kontekstual', unpublished MA thesis, Universitas Kristen Indonesia Maluku.
United Nations (2007) *United Nations Declaration on the Rights of Indigenous Peoples*. Online. Available at: http://www2.ohchr.org/english/issues/indigenous/declaration.htm (accessed on 10 December 2007).
Valentijn, F. (1856) *Oud en Nieuw Oost-Indien. Uitgegeven door S. Keijzer (3 Deelen)*. Tweede Deel (1–375): *Beschrijving van Amboina*, 's-Gravenhage: H.C. Susan, C. Hzoon.
van de Wall, V.I. (1928) *De Nederlandsche Oudheden in de Molukken*, 's-Gravenhage: Martinus Nijhoff.
van Fraassen, C.F. and Straver, H. (2002) *De Ambonse Eilanden Onder de VOC Zoals Opgetekend in de Ambonese Landbeschrijving (Georgius Everhardus Rumphius)*, Utrecht: Landelijk Steunpunt Educatie Molukkers.
Varshney, A. (2002) *Ethnic Conflict and Civic Life: Hindus and Muslims in India*, New Haven: Yale University Press.
Wagner, R. (1981) *The Invention of Culture* [originally published in 1975; revised and expanded edition], Chicago and London: The University of Chicago Press.

Part III
'Traditional justice' under scrutiny
Human rights, power, and gender

6 Reconciliation and human rights in post-conflict Aceh

*Leena Avonius**

Introduction

The post-conflict situation in Aceh presents us with a valuable opportunity for examining processes of reconciliation in Indonesia. The Aceh case has at least two features that invite one to examine Acehnese experiences of reconciliation more closely for lessons learned that may benefit future efforts for reconciliation elsewhere in Indonesia. The conflict in Aceh, in the aftermath of which the processes of reconciliation are now taking place, has been one of the longest separatist conflicts in Indonesia's history. It started in 1976 when the founder of the Free Aceh Movement, *Gerakan Aceh Merdeka* (GAM), Hasan di Tiro, proclaimed Aceh's independence. In its early years the conflict was mostly limited to the north-eastern parts of Aceh, but after 1999 it spread across the province. While the armed conflict mainly involved the Indonesian armed forces and the local guerrilla movement GAM, the majority of its victims were civilians. Reconciliation, then, has to take place within the complex network of relations between the central government, the national security forces, local militia groups that supported the central government, GAM combatants and their supporters, as well as the civilian population that tried – often unsuccessfully – to stay outside the conflict. As many reports on the Aceh conflict have shown, the majority of atrocities against the civilian population were committed by the Indonesian military, though GAM is also responsible for similar crimes (Amnesty International 1993, 2004; Human Rights Watch 2002, 2003, 2004; ICG 2001; Imparsial 2004; Kontras 2006; Rahmany 2004). Due to this, reconciliation in Aceh is essential for renegotiating civil–military relations in Indonesia.

The second feature that makes the Aceh case interesting is the involvement of the international community in the peace process and thus in the processes of reconciliation. So far the conflict in Aceh is the only one of Indonesia's internal armed conflicts that has been settled with the assistance of the international community.[1] The first attempt at international mediation for the Aceh conflict had failed in 2003 (Aspinall & Crouch 2003; Martin 2006), but two years later the informal peace talks in Helsinki led to the signing of the Memorandum of Understanding (MoU) between the two parties in August 2005 and to the so far successful peace process in Aceh (Crisis Management Initiative 2005). As part of the agreement, international monitors from the European Union, Norway, Switzerland, and five Association of Southeast Asian Nations (ASEAN) countries were deployed to Aceh for 15 months to monitor the implementation of the peace accord in September 2005. During these early months, the representatives of the Aceh Monitoring Mission (AMM) took part in and influenced the processes of reconciliation in Aceh.

During the first years after the Helsinki MoU, the situation in Aceh had remained conducive to peace, though several violent incidents have taken place. As expected in any post-conflict situation, crime, and especially armed robberies, has been on the rise in Aceh.[2] Violent incidents directly related to the armed conflict, including acts of revenge or violence between former GAM members and Indonesian security forces, have also taken place, though their numbers have remained limited. There is plenty of speculation whether peace will last in Aceh; many are convinced that the conflict is not likely to re-emerge in its previous form, but there are concerns that new types of conflicts might break out. The concerns are mainly regarding economic and political developments, as well as post-conflict reconstruction and the reintegration of former combatants into civilian society. However, renewed violence may also come about due to either a lack of or unsuccessful reconciliation and justice processes.

To prevent the re-escalation of conflict in Aceh it is necessary to develop mechanisms to assist the society in minimizing post-conflict tensions, to deal with past atrocities and to reconcile the victims and the perpetrators. For the purpose of dealing with the legacy of past violence, human rights courts (HRC) and truth and reconciliation commissions (TRC) have become an integral part of international models for peace processes. Particularly in relation to the latter, reconciliation methods are being sought in local cultural traditions; these indigenous methods are likely to facilitate trust-building in societies divided by years of conflict. This is also the case in Aceh, as the Helsinki peace accord determines that the mechanisms of transitional justice – an HRC and a TRC – will be established for Aceh. The Law on the Governance of Aceh (LoGA, Law No. 11/2006), the creation of which was stipulated in the peace accord, confirms the establishment of transitional justice mechanisms.

In this chapter I will not focus on the TRC process, but instead I will stress the importance of reconciliation for managing violent incidents that take place in the aftermath of the conflict. In Aceh, local reconciliation methods have been utilized in reducing the post-conflict tensions in the communities. The chapter assesses the advantages of using local cultural practices in the peace process, but it will also discuss the challenges that the use of local reconciliation methods poses for providing justice in cases of human rights violations. Particular attention will be paid to how such reconciliation methods are related to and can influence the ways international and national human rights standards are implemented in post-conflict societies. The chapter urges critical examination of local cultural traditions used for reconciliation purposes and suggests that a more thorough understanding of culture will be essential to guarantee justice and the sustainability of peace.

Reconciliation and Aceh

Reconciliation has become one of the key concepts in peace-building. Since the 1990s there is a growing body of literature on peace-building and conflict resolution processes. The number of journals, handbooks, and websites on peace-building, reconciliation, and transitional justice issues appears to be growing almost exponentially each year. In the available sources there is also a remarkable variation in the ways the terminology is understood and used.[3] In this chapter, I will look at reconciliation as one process of peace-building. Peace-building refers to the wide range of processes that all aim at transforming a society from conflict to peace. A handbook edited by the International Institute for Democracy and Electoral Assistance (Bloomfield *et al.* 2003) provides valuable insights into the complexity of reconciliation by defining it as "an overarching process, that includes the key instruments of justice, truth, healing and reparation, for moving from a divided past to a shared future." Other sources also support the idea that reconciliation is to be understood as a process (Bloomfield 2006; Lederach 1997) rather than an outcome or goal, as the latter interpretation tends to see peaceful societies too idealistically as places where social harmony and equality prevails. This distinction between a process and an end-state is also important in the context of reconciliation in Aceh, as I will discuss later.

Another important and widely agreed upon aspect of reconciliation is that it addresses the relationships of those who have been part of the violent conflict and are implementing the solutions that have ended the violence (Bloomfield *et al.* 2003). Relationships that are conflictual and built on hatred, fear, prejudice, and negative stereotypes need to be addressed and reconstructed. This rebuilding of relationships not only takes place through the formal processes of transitional justice such as HRC and TRC, but also through making changes in the everyday social practices demarcating the relationships of various actors. These changes should mean, for example, that disputes, which during conflict times were settled with violence to benefit those who held the weapons, will now be settled through peaceful processes. Whenever new social practices are formed – or old ones revitalized – there are various, often competing arguments as to which practices should be preferred over others. The challenge lies in finding a compromise acceptable to all parties and that they are all willing to implement. Inevitably, power relations are always important, since parties never have equal status or are equally empowered to put forward their views in such reconciliation processes (Wilson 2000: 78).

Current peace-building discourses are somewhat problematic in that reconciliation is often closely related to truth and reconciliation mechanisms. The Aceh MoU also only makes explicit mention of reconciliation in connection with the establishment of a TRC: "A Commission for Truth and Reconciliation will be established for Aceh by the Indonesian Commission of Truth and Reconciliation with the task of formulating and determining reconciliation measures" (Crisis Management Initiative 2005: Art. 2.3). Issues that are typically closely related to or part of reconciliation such as amnesty and reintegration are dealt with in other parts of the MoU. Nevertheless, the article cited earlier binds reconciliation to the TRC by stating that it would be a task of the commission to define the necessary measures for reconciliation in post-conflict Aceh. This, of course, does not mean that reconciliation could not or should not take place outside the TRC mechanism. Numerous reconciliation efforts have already taken place in Aceh even though the TRC is only in its planning stage. How successful or unsuccessful these reconciliation efforts are will inevitably influence the prospects of TRC in Aceh.

A problem that can arise from placing reconciliation too tightly within the TRC framework is that reconciliation is understood predominantly as a technical exercise of one particular phase of the peace process rather than an 'overarching process' as it was defined earlier. In general, if used at all, TRC is usually established some years after the violence has ceased and there has been a transformation to a new, democratic government; a commission usually functions only for a limited period of time, most commonly approximately from one to three years.[4] Then, the risk increases that those parties to the process that are not directly involved in putting up a TRC may see that reconciliation is not 'part of their job'. On the other hand, if reconciliation is understood in its wider sense it is clear that reconciliation measures must be built into a wide range of processes that take place in the peace process, starting from rearranging everyday life relations in communities and rebuilding relationships between civilians and state authorities to finding new (or revived) methods for dispute settlement and establishing truth about and ensuring justice in past and present human rights violations. It is noteworthy that reconciliation is not necessarily a process initiated by some formal action. It takes place in various forms when people try to re-establish their lives and reorganize their relations in everyday life.

Thus, those trying to learn from earlier experiences and develop improved methods of reconciliation should seek the places and spaces of reconciliation in post-conflict situations, bearing in mind that they can take various forms. In the early months of the Aceh peace process, formal efforts at reconciliation were made in the regular meetings between the representatives of the Indonesian government and GAM at the provincial and district level. These so-called COSA and DiCOSA[5] meetings were moderated by AMM monitors, whose main task in the meetings was to ensure that the two parties discussed any disputed matters at hand and came up with solutions that satisfied both sides. But there were also dozens of informal moments of reconciliation when practices that had developed during conflict times were sought to be replaced by new ones, leading to a reassessment of the mutual relationships of the persons and institutions involved.[6] While the AMM-moderated meetings were based on international models of conflict resolution, the informal reconciliation processes arose from Acehnese cultural practices. These formal and informal processes of reconciliation are inevitably interlinked and it is important to observe how they influence each other (Bloomfield 2006: 29).

In Aceh, reconciliation measures are understood to make use of local cultural traditions, or *adat*. This concerns the informal methods of reconciliation that will be discussed later as well as the future TRC mechanism. The latter is confirmed by the LoGA (Law on the Governance of Aceh) that stipulates in Article 229 that the TRC in Aceh would "take into consideration *adat* principles that are in use in the society" in its search for truth and reconciliation, and more specifically, in settling human rights violations.[7] The discussion that follows, however, will reveal that using local reconciliation methods in human rights abuses is not without problems.

Peusijuek and post-conflict incidents in Aceh

As is common in any post-conflict situation, peace in Aceh did not happen overnight after the signing of the Helsinki MoU. As stipulated in the MoU, international monitors arrived in Aceh to monitor whether both parties adhered to what had mutually been agreed upon in the MoU (Crisis Management Initiative 2005). Within days of their arrival, these peace monitors had to deal with numerous small incidents all over Aceh. Most incidents concerned the maltreatment of a civilian either by a GAM member or an Indonesian military or police official. Many cases included extortion, a widespread practice that had become commonplace during the conflict years as GAM combatants sought funding for themselves and their cause through illegal taxation (*pajak nanggroe*) or Indonesian security officers topped up their salaries via illegal means. The number of extortion cases decreased after the disarmament of GAM ex-combatants was completed and non-organic military and police were withdrawn from Aceh by the end of 2005.[8]

The incidents that took place between former GAM members and Indonesian security forces posed a more serious threat to the sustainability of peace at that early phase of the peace process. Although most such cases were fist-fights and threats, a small number of incidents did lead to fatalities. In a tense post-conflict atmosphere even minor incidents need to be attended to and reconciled as they may otherwise lead to serious clashes and even return to full-scale armed conflict. As it is commonly acknowledged in peace-building literature, it is vital that local actors play decisive roles in the reconciliation process, as it increases the local ownership in the peace process (Bloomfield *et al.* 2003; Lederach & Jenner 2002; Reich 2006). While in some cases it is necessary that outside actors such as international monitors rule on disputes, it is usually more beneficial to the process as a whole that disputes are settled at the local level, together with victims, perpetrators, their representatives, and local community leaders. Encouraging the use of local dispute settlement mechanisms also strengthens the civilian structures of the society and leads away from the conflict mindset. In these kinds of situations, local cultural practices can be helpful.

In Aceh a ritual practice called *peusijuek* became part of the post-conflict dispute settlement at the local level already at an early stage of the peace process. This ritual is organized to represent that harmony has been returned to a community after a disruptive incident.[9] *Peusijuek* closes a successful dispute settlement and shows that the situation in the community has 'cooled down'. *Peusijuek* ceremonies were organized all across Aceh to welcome back home amnestied political prisoners and former GAM combatants. They were also organized after violent conflict-related incidents had been successfully dealt with. During the first year of the implementation of the MoU, *peusijuek* was typically conducted in the aftermath of an incident in which a person was beaten up in a quarrel. Community leaders then heard the views of both parties and came together to discuss how to put an end to the problem. Usually, they proposed a solution in which the perpetrator would apologize and pay some sort of compensation to the victim, in cash or kind, or cover their medical expenses. After the compensation was received, a *peusijuek* ceremony was organized to show that the problem had now been resolved and the relation between the two parties was back to normal. In such processes international monitors had only a minimal role. They were outside witnesses to local dispute settlement processes and invited guests to *peusijuek* rituals. In the majority of smaller incidents the local dispute settlement mechanism functioned well in supporting peace in Aceh.

Local reconciliation methods tend to become problematic, however, when employed in more serious incidents that entail human rights violations. They are also problematic when used in settling cases that involve non-locals. Let me take one example to illustrate this.[10] A shooting incident in Keude village in Paya Bakong, North Aceh in early July 2006 remains one of the most serious incidents to have taken place during the first year after the signing of the MoU and involved Indonesian military and former GAM members. The events started on 3 July when soldiers at a local military post beat up and detained a former GAM member, Umar bin Ismail, who had been passing by the military post on a motorcycle. The incident was reported to the AMM district office in the nearby town Lhokseumawe, and dozens of local villagers gathered in front of the military post demanding that Umar be set free. The villagers correctly justified their claim by stating that since Aceh was no longer a conflict zone the military had no legal right to detain civilians. When AMM monitors together with the local police arrived at the military post shooting broke out suddenly. The AMM convoy and the civilians standing in front of the military barracks were shot at from several directions. In the shooting one former GAM member, Muslem bin Abdul Samad, was shot in the chest and died of his injuries. Two other persons were also injured. In the following months, the incident was investigated by various parties, including the military, the police, and AMM. The military insisted that the armed persons who started the shooting were unknown and that the military responded to the fire. Other parties stated that all evidence showed that the military did the shooting and all the others present were unarmed.

The incident has never been handled in court, nor has it been otherwise satisfactorily resolved.[11] In this chapter I do not intend to speculate about the reasons why this has not happened, but rather focus on how and why the local method of reconciliation that was recommended to be used in the aftermath of this case was turned down by the locals. In late July 2006, the Military Commander of Iskandar Muda (the military region that covers the whole of Aceh), Supiadin A.S., suggested that *peusijuek* should be organized to reconcile the heated relations between the military and the local population. An AMM representative viewed this as a positive idea, based on the organization's earlier experiences on the use of this ritual in reconciliation processes. But Umar, the young man who had been severely beaten in the military post, resolutely rejected this suggestion. "*Saya tidak mau dipeusijuek dengan TNI. Hana peureulee islah, kalheuh poh gob baro mita dame*" (I do not want to have *peusijuek* with the military. There is no need for a settlement, first they beat up someone and then ask for peace), he said to the local tabloid *Acehkita*. According to Umar, he did not want to reconcile with the TNI; what he wanted was to see justice done. Umar elaborated that enough evidence and eyewitness reports were available on the incident; he had been interviewed by AMM and he had been treated at the local hospital and health clinic for ten days due to the injuries he received during the physical abuse by the soldiers. Umar said that the Indonesian law authorities should prove that the rule of law is followed in Indonesia, and that his own assault as well as the killing of his friend Muslem should be processed according to the existing law (*Acehkita* 2006f).[12] Mario, a former GAM member who stated that he was directly shot at by a military official from a short distance during the Paya Bakong incident, repeated the words of Umar: "*Hana perlee peusijuek meunyee ngen awak nyan*" (There is no need for *peusijuek* with those people) (*Acehkita* 2006g).

In his public statement, the TNI Commander Supiadin had not even suggested that the *peusijuek* would replace the judicial processes, but that *adat* should be used in addition to it. He said: "*Nanti kita kumpul, masyarakat, TNI, GAM, korban, kita peusijuek. Tapi proses hukumnya tetap jalan. Ini dalam rangka menegakkan adat*" (We all come together later, people, military, GAM, victims, we do *peusijuek*. But the legal process will still go on. It will be done to uphold *adat*) (*Acehkita* 2006d). But the response in Aceh, by victims and their families, was decidedly negative. Human rights organizations in Aceh also shared the opinion that traditional reconciliation methods should not be used in this case. The Director of the Legal Aid Bureau Aceh (*Lembaga Bantuan Hukum*, LBH), Afridal Darmi, pointed out that the Paya Bakong incident had indications of serious human rights violations and that it should be taken to court. Director of Aceh Judicial Monitoring Institute (AJMI) Hendra Budian criticized AMM for recommending the organization of reconciliation between the local population and the military in Paya Bakong. According to him, AMM had no mandate to push for reconciliation between a perpetrator and a victim in cases like Paya Bakong when it otherwise remained so passive in its monitoring role (*Acehkita* 2006e, 2006i).

The parents of Muslem, the young man who was shot dead during the incident, told the media that one day after the shooting two high-ranking TNI commanders, the Chief of Staff of Iskandar Muda Military Region and the District Military Commander of North Aceh, had come to visit their home. The military had brought some assistance to the impoverished family. The military's gesture reflected the traditional means of handling disputes between perpetrators and victims in Acehnese communities. But the military had also brought along a letter for the family to sign. If they had signed the letter, Muslem's parents would have agreed to allow the military to remove the bullets still lodged in the body of their dead son. They would also have agreed not to lay any charges against the perpetrators. Muslem's father refused to sign, saying that he wanted justice in the case of the death of his son. He pointed out that too many unclear incidents had taken place in Indonesia already, citing the shooting of students at Trisakti University in Jakarta in the late 1990s as an example. He only promised to permit the removal of the bullets if this was agreed upon in the presence of AMM, and if the letter was rewritten.[13] In a later media report, he pointed out that an autopsy was unnecessary, as there were several eye-witnesses to the shooting (*Acehkita* 2006h).

The Paya Bakong incident shows that while the Acehnese generally have a positive attitude towards using local *adat*-based reconciliation methods in post-conflict disputes and incidents, they also insist upon the recognition of the limitations of these methods. Local reconciliation methods cannot be mechanistically used in every situation and for all disputes. The question following from this is when they can and cannot be used. The obvious but unsatisfactory answer is that it depends on the context. So, let us examine the elements in the Paya Bakong incident that may have made the victims and human rights defenders reluctant to use local reconciliation methods to settle the case.

The high military commander's suggestion to use *peusijuek* was without a doubt tactless, revealing his limited knowledge about local cultural traditions despite his ostensible willingness to uphold them. When Supiadin proposed the organization of a *peusijuek*, he was bypassing the most important part of the process, that is, reconciliation itself. Although *peusijuek* is often used to refer to reconciliation in day-to-day parlance, it is meaningless without the preceding process of dispute settlement that is done in a community meeting called *mupakat*. Therefore, the victims interpreted Supiadin's suggestion as an insincere interest in the process of reconciliation and as an attempt to arrive at the end-state, an announcement that everything was settled. If reconciliation is about truth, justice, healing, and reparation, none of this had been achieved by the time the military commander had made his suggestion.

The victims also made it clear that they believed the case should be settled through a formal court system, as several serious human rights violations had taken place. They suggested that in these kinds of cases justice can only be achieved through the formal judicial system and national law, and not through local reconciliation processes. They did not necessarily trust the national courts, as Muslem's father pointed out when he mentioned that there were human rights violations elsewhere in Indonesia that had not been resolved, but they insisted that by providing justice in the Paya Bakong case the Indonesian state authorities could show that the situation had improved and that the rule of law was followed. Umar and Mario furthermore stated that they felt that true reconciliation was not possible with TNI soldiers. Both of them were former GAM members and thus their reluctance to reconcile with the former enemy also has to be seen as a political statement from GAM. But the question whether local reconciliation methods can be used in cases that involve the Indonesian military, who are mostly non-Acehnese, is more commonly presented in Aceh both by conflict victims and peace-builders. It is one of the key questions that the drafters of the TRC for Aceh are struggling with.

Modified cultural traditions

To answer the question whether a local reconciliation mechanism can be used in Aceh to settle human rights violations, and whether it can be used in cases that involve non-Acehnese military, one needs to examine the tradition itself. In what situations has the local reconciliation process that is completed with a *peusijuek* ceremony been used historically and in Aceh today?

Peusijuek has served as part of the local mode of dispute settlement in Acehnese communities for at least a century; it was commonly used for this purpose when Snouck Hurgronje conducted research in Sumatra. Hurgronje (1985: 87–90) stated that *peusijuek* was part of a dispute settlement mechanism called *adat meulangga*.[14] In this dispute settlement mechanism the key role was held by *keuchik*, the head of *gampong* (village), who acted as a mediator between the victim and the perpetrator but also as a 'village judge'. Hurgronje pointed out that the use of this mechanism had at least two kinds of limitations, the first of which had to do with the kinds of incidents it could be used for and the second with the power position of village elders.

According to Hurgronje (1985), *adat meulangga* was never used in cases of theft, adultery, killing, or serious physical abuse.[15] There were two other methods to deal with these: revenge and paying *diyat* (reparation). In the case of killing, revenge was the most common method used and apparently acceptable, though sometimes *diyat* could be used. For the perpetrator of a homicide the only way to survive was to escape, but even if he was given refuge in another region he has lost his freedom and has to serve as a slave of a local *uleebaleng* (Acehnese territorial chief). Judging by Hurgronje's account, it appears that *adat meulangga* was most commonly used to settle minor physical assaults. But even in these cases, the injuries must have healed completely before the process could take place (Hurgronje 1985: 89). A later source points out that this method was used when residents of one village, or residents of two neighboring villages, have a quarrel or a fight. Once the dispute had been peacefully reconciled, a *peusijuek meulangga* would be organized. And if blood had been shed, the perpetrator would pay money to the victim by way of compensation (LAKA 1990: 100). Another document produced by LAKA[16] (1988: 35–6) explains that in western Aceh this was called *peusijuek leumbeng peurisee* (to lay down spear and shield), and it was used in incidents that had left someone either dead or injured. The purpose was to ward off acts of revenge that might result from the violation.

An Acehnese *adat* expert I had interviewed in late 2007 also thought that in principle the local reconciliation method ending with *peusijuek* could be used even in cases that had led to death. He further stressed that nowadays the Acehnese could not foster revenge as a means for conflict resolution since that was against Islamic teachings, and thus reconciliation was preferred. From these sources one can conclude that there is no agreement regarding what kind of violations this reconciliation method can be used for; violations that some consider falling outside the category are killing and serious physical abuse. Public opinion in Aceh also varies greatly on the uses of *adat* for serious offences. Thus, one cannot assume that this local reconciliation mechanism would always be a suitable option for reconciling post-conflict incidents in Aceh.

Another problem that diminishes the usefulness of the local reconciliation method in Aceh is related to power relations. On the one hand, what is at stake are the power relations between the formal and informal justice systems used in Indonesia. On the other hand, the mutual power relations of agencies involved in the reconciliation process or influencing it from the outside have a great impact on the credibility of the mechanism.

Hurgronje (1985: 86–7) pointed out that *keuchik* and other *gampong* leaders played key roles in *mupakat* that dealt with all village matters, including dispute settlements. But even if they functioned as 'village judges' in such cases, they did not have any judicial power. Judicial power was with the Dutch colonial courts. Hurgronje's argument illustrates well how during that period judicial power was drawn towards the colonial state and away from the indigenous leaders. Criminal law, which was established by the Dutch colonial state in 1915, was adapted without many changes by the Indonesian state after independence. According to Pompe (1987: 500), the amended Criminal Code of 1981 did not change the relation between *adat* and national law in this respect. Crimes against life and serious maltreatment are criminalized in Indonesian law, and as such belong under the judiciary power of the state.[17] Indonesian legal pluralism acknowledges *adat* as a source of justice, but this has remained a rather theoretical possibility though sometimes judges in state courts refer to *adat* in their rulings. *Adat* is used as an informal dispute settlement mechanism; and under Aceh's special status this function is also formally recognized by the provincial regulation.[18] But in the case of inconsistencies, the national legislation always takes precedence.

As in the colonial period, *adat* elders in communities do not have any formal judicial power, and generally speaking they would not have the power to deal with such serious crimes as homicide. In practice, particularly in remote areas, state authorities are not necessarily informed of crimes, and even serious crimes may be settled outside courts. This may be due to practical reasons such as long distances or high fees. In Aceh during the conflict years many judges escaped the province and courts could not function due to the lack of personnel. But it may also be due to the lack of trust in a formal judicial system that is rife with corruption and that during conflict times in Aceh was seen to be compromised by the central government's efforts to subdue the rebellion. Though some may have prioritized *adat* justice over the formal justice system, the lack of access to formal justice mechanisms has also been one of the possible reasons why the informal *adat* justice system has been used in Aceh to settle even serious crimes, including killings. According to a UNDP (2006) assessment of how people can access and how they assess various justice systems available to them, the local population considers the informal *adat* justice more trustworthy than the state court system, but they also see *adat* justice as problematic. One of its problems is that it tends to stress social harmony at the expense of individual rights.

The *adat* justice system is also influenced by the unequal power relations in society. Hurgronje (1985: 86) already pointed out in his account that *mupakat* tended to benefit powerful members of the community and those who were close to the *keuchik*. An assessment that the UNDP conducted for its post-conflict program that aims to improve citizens' access to justice in Aceh came to a very similar conclusion a hundred years later:

> [*Adat* justice system] too is not free of deficiencies. Disadvantaged groups, in particular, face challenges in accessing informal justice mechanisms due to a

lack of neutrality, unclear standards and guidelines, as well as a lack of capacity on the part of informal justice duty-bearers.

(UNDP 2006: 12)

The decisions taken by village leaders often benefit their associates or family networks, as the respondents to the UNDP team had complained (UNDP 2006: 36). What is more, in communities divided by the conflict the *keuchik* may be considered unsuitable for the role of a mediator due to his own political stance in the conflict.[19]

Traditionally, *mupakat* is understood to refer to the informal *adat*-based community meeting of a village. In the post-conflict situation, however, and particularly in relation to the more serious incidents similar to that which took place at Paya Bakong, the meaning of *mupakat* is often transformed. Reconciliation is not in the hands of village leaders, but of Muspika and Muspida, the decision-making mechanisms of the state administrative structures. These consultative forums of district leaders were created under the New Order period throughout Indonesia, and they stressed the dual military-civilian form of administration.[20] They differ significantly from the meetings of community leaders based on local cultural traditions in that the mandate of Muspika and Muspida is given by the state and not by the community members. Muspika and Muspida are formal meetings of the local military commander, police chief, and the heads of civil administration. In Muspida the representative of the state justice system is also involved. While formally the chair of these meetings is the highest civilian official of the administrative area, Muspika and Muspida were led by the local military commanders in Aceh during conflict years.

A key challenge to the usefulness of local reconciliation methods for settling post-conflict incidents in Aceh lies in the fact that the mechanism is modified in a way that undermines the credibility of the mechanism itself. Generally, the mediator in the local reconciliation mechanism is *keuchik* together with other village leaders, but in the post-conflict reconciliations the role is often taken over by the state authorities. This kind of modification goes well beyond the flexibility that is characteristic of *adat* institutions. In cases where the state authority is the alleged perpetrator of a crime, the credibility of such reconciliation efforts becomes questionable. It is, however, equally questionable whether the situation would be improved by returning the role of the mediator to village leaders, as due to their limited power position they would have none or very little influence on perpetrators from outside the community. An Acehnese *adat* expert expressed this by stating that when it comes to problems in Aceh caused by outsiders, *adat* is weak, as it is based on the respect the individuals have for the community and its leaders. One has to be part of the community in order to be bound by its *adat*.[21]

Understanding local post-conflict complexities

Recent decades have seen a growing use of local cultural traditions in peace processes and post-conflict situations, most notably in East Timor and Rwanda.[22]

Though not without problems, they have proven to be good tools for supporting the sustainability of peace and for strengthening the participation of the local population in peace-building processes. Local dispute settlement mechanisms have been helpful in settling post-conflict incidents in Aceh. A good explanation for this is that Acehnese people generally rely more on *adat* than the formal justice system for dispute resolution (UNDP 2006: 70). But it is also necessary to understand the risks that lie in making use of local reconciliation methods as part of the justice processes. Unless their functions and limitations are properly understood, local cultural traditions can be just as useful for those who wish to abuse them and avoid justice, as they are for those supporting justice.

I have illustrated some of these limitations through a serious post-conflict incident that took place in Paya Bakong, North Aceh. In the aftermath of this incident the representative of the alleged perpetrator TNI suggested that a *peusijuek* ceremony should be organized in order to reconcile the military with GAM as well as other community members. This offer was firmly turned down by the victims and their families, for they saw the suggestion as an attempt to avoid accountability. In the media statements they clearly argued that the human rights violations that had occurred during the incident should be handled exclusively by the formal justice system. While the informal *adat* justice system has been used in Aceh until today to resolve serious crimes such as homicide or serious maltreatment, there is no unanimous support to do so. People in Aceh take their complaints and grievances to *adat* elders more often than to the state courts not necessarily because they prefer the former but because they want to avoid the latter. Establishing credibility and through it public trust in the formal justice system is an important part of the peace-building process in Aceh. Using an *adat*-based mechanism may actually be counterproductive to the process of strengthening the formal justice system. And considering the existing weaknesses of the informal *adat* justice system in Aceh – the lack of neutrality, unequal access to the system, and the structural modifications that fundamentally changed the mechanism – it is questionable whether it would be able to provide justice in complex cases including human rights violations.

Paradoxically, the outsiders to Acehnese culture – Indonesian security forces and representatives of an international monitoring mission – were the ones promoting the use of local cultural traditions in Paya Bakong. The Acehnese, while utilizing *peusijuek* and the related forms of local reconciliation, were much more aware of their limitations. It is important that outside participants in peace-building, whether international or domestic, recognize and encourage the use of local cultural traditions in reconciliation. These, however, should not be used mechanistically for all occasions where reconciliation is needed; they simply need to be viewed as one alternative among many. The choice must be based on the preferences of the parties involved in the dispute, but also on the wider sociopolitical context in which the incident has taken place. The shooting in Paya Bakong took place at a time when Indonesia had just ratified the UN Human Rights Bill.[23] The Helsinki MoU also stressed the importance of adherence to this bill. There was thus new hope that impunity would be stopped and the violators of human rights would be taken to court and punished. In such a situation any gesture that might be interpreted as upholding impunity must be carefully assessed.

Exploring the wider political context of the Paya Bakong incident further explains why a local reconciliation method was considered inappropriate. A reason why the incident took place to begin with was connected to the relocation of the Indonesian military after the signing of the peace accord. The MoU had determined that all non-organic troops had to be withdrawn from Aceh.[24] After this was completed at the end of 2005, the TNI started to relocate its organic forces in Aceh and build new barracks. This has triggered several disputes in the province as local residents often rejected the relocation plans and new military barracks. In some cases, the villagers claimed that the TNI had taken over their land without any compensation. In other cases, and this happened in Paya Bakong, the relocation of the military was interpreted as a provocation. Military barracks had been built in Keude village just one month before the fatal incident took place. Paya Bakong is known to be a GAM stronghold, and the barracks were located so that they gave the military a chance to control all village traffic, as this was the only road that connected the village with the main road and the markets where the villagers sold their farm products. The military officials had built steep bumps (*polisi tidur*) on the road, forcing cars and motorbikes to slow down when passing the barracks. According to one report, they had even spread nails on the road to prevent the traffic from passing by. This created tensions and led to quarrels between villagers and the military. The villagers had already taken their complaint to the district leader (*camat*), and to AMM (*Acehkita* 2006b). Thus, what was at stake in Paya Bakong was not only the fatal shooting incident but the much broader issue of the relocation of TNI troops in Aceh.

Due to the dark history of conflict, the residents of Paya Bakong would also be least likely to easily agree to reconcile with the Indonesian military. Paya Bakong is in the vicinity of the Exxon Mobil complex, the American oil giant that has exploited Aceh's natural oil and gas reservoir for years. During the conflict years the military in this region was providing security services to Exxon Mobil. The drastic contrast between the affluent surroundings of the Exxon Mobil complex and poor Paya Bakong villages that are only a few kilometers away underlines how little the Acehnese have benefited from the natural resources of the province. Paya Bakong was classified by the TNI as a 'black' area, meaning that it was dominated by GAM and a primary target for military operation. During the military operation several serious human rights violations had allegedly been committed by the Indonesian military special troops Kostrad in the Paya Bakong district. In the beginning of 2006, after the non-organic military was withdrawn from Aceh, local residents were reported to have found two human skeletons in the location of former military barracks (*Acehkita* 2006a). According to a recent psychosocial assessment on post-conflict trauma in Aceh, some 87 percent of the people interviewed in the North Aceh regency had personally experienced combat, and 40 percent had a family member or a friend killed in the conflict (IOM 2006). These numbers are much higher than they are in most other parts of Aceh. The level of post-conflict trauma in North Aceh ranks with the post-conflict situation in places like Bosnia and Afghanistan. In this light, it seems very likely that long-term healing processes will be needed before reconciliation can proceed further.

Ifdhal Kasim, the current Chairman of the Indonesian National Human Rights Committee Komnas HAM, who himself is originally Acehnese, stated in December 2006: "Reconciliation will not be reached [in Aceh] only by organizing a *peusijuek* ceremony between previously conflicting parties in front of the political elite and wider public ..." (*Acehkita* 2006j). As important as it is to cool down the situation after an incident that threatens the peace process or to make sure that ex-combatants can return to their home villages safely, it is even more important to find long-term solutions that are based on a thorough understanding of human rights, justice, conflict history, and local culture. Although local dispute settlement mechanisms are helpful, they must be seen as only one element in a wide reconciliation process.

Notes

* The author worked for the Aceh Monitoring Mission (AMM) in 2005–2006.
1 The East Timor conflict was not an internal armed conflict, as East Timor was internationally considered to be an occupied region.
2 It needs to be noted that increasing criminality is difficult to verify as it is impossible to determine what would be a 'normal' situation in a place like Aceh that has been in conflict for decades. Before the independence struggle started in the mid-1970s, there had been mass killings of communists in the late 1960s, and before that, in the 1950s, was the Islamic rebellion. During the years of conflict few crimes were reported, and thus increased criminality may, at least to some extent, reflect increased reporting on crimes.
3 For a recent discussion on this, see Bloomfield (2006).
4 For a comparison of over 20 TRCs, see Hayner (2002).
5 COSA refers to the Committee of Security Arrangements meeting between the representatives of GAM and the Indonesian government at the provincial level, while DiCOSA refers to District Committee of Security Arrangements.
6 One could call these two lines of efforts top-down and bottom-up forms of reconciliation, or structural and cultural initiatives for reconciliation (Bloomfield 2006: 27).
7 *Dalam menyelesaikan kasus pelanggaran hak asasi manusia di Aceh, Komisi Kebenaran dan Rekonsiliasi di Aceh dapat mempertimbangkan prinsip-prinsip adat yang hidup dalam masyarakat* (LoGA Art. 229). In relation to the work of the Aceh HRC, *adat* is not mentioned. Those preparing the TRC for Aceh have to determine what this general and ambiguous sentence might mean in the practical work of the commission, and how, for example, *syariat Islam* (Islamic Law) is seen to relate to 'local culture'.
8 This does not mean that extortion stopped altogether. According to the World Bank's monthly reports based on its team's ongoing monitoring of the situation in Aceh, extortion is a continuing practice there. Most commonly extortion takes place at illegal roadside checkpoints. Another common form is to force producers of rubber and farm products to sell their products to a particular broker at a price below the market price.
9 The name of the ritual *peusijuek* refers to cooling down the community; *sijuek* is the Acehnese word for 'cool' (LAKA 1988: 35).
10 The information is based on media reports on the shooting incident in Paya Bakong, Aceh Utara. Early media reports on the incident include: Jakarta Post (2006), Kompas (2006), Serambi (2006), Acehkita (2006b, 2006c).
11 The Paya Bakong incident was closed on 16 September 2006 as an issue for the Commission of Security Arrangements (COSA). AMM, the Indonesian government,

and GAM representatives concluded that there had been "serious violations of the MoU including disproportionate use of force by the military and TNI involvement in matters of law and order which are the sole responsibility of the police." In a COSA meeting it was further stated that the criminal investigation into the death would continue as a matter of normal police and judicial procedures (AMM Press Statement on 16 September 2006). To my knowledge no further investigation has taken place.

12 Umar uses the Indonesian word *islah*, which is of Arabic origin and means dispute settlement, interchangeably with the Acehnese word *dipeusijuek* that means to go through the dispute settlement that ends up with *peusijuek* ritual.

13 See, for example, *Serambi Indonesia* (2006) and *Acehkita* (2006c).

14 *Meulangga* means to break or to violate the existing norms. Thus, it is *adat* methods that deal with violations.

15 "*Cara penyelesaiaan sengketa semacam ini tidak pernah diselenggarakan untuk peristiwa pencurian, perzinaan atau pembunuhan, ataupun dalam peristiwa penganiayaan parah*" (Hurgronje 1985: 89).

16 LAKA is the acronym for *Lembaga Adat dan Kebudayaan Aceh*, a provincial body that was set up to uphold local cultural traditions. LAKA was the predecessor of the current *Majelis Adat Aceh* (MAA).

17 After the formal implementation of *syariat* (Islamic Law) in Aceh it would also be possible for *Syariah* courts to handle *qishas/diat* crimes, that is, murder and mistreatment, as stipulated in the regional regulation *Qanun* 10/2000. So far, however, there are no specific *Qanuns* regulating these offences.

18 Regional regulation No. 7 Article 6 from 2000 states that the function of *adat* institutions is to settle social problems at the community level and mediate disputes between community members (UNDP 2006: 50).

19 In some areas, like in the western part of Aceh, *keuchiks* were often close to the military, and thus became targets of GAM action. In the GAM stronghold villages in the north the situation was often the reverse.

20 Muspika (*Musyawarah pimpinan kecamatan*, community meeting of district leaders) and its district and provincial level counterparts Muspida (*Musyawarah pimpinan daerah*, community meeting of regional leaders) were created under President Suharto's New Order rule, not only in Aceh but all over Indonesia. Under the New Order they were prime examples of the top-down rule of the governmental system and they made all important decisions in the regions and were only accountable to the central government and not to the communities. Furthermore, they illustrated the power of the military in civilian and political matters. After the fall of Suharto's regime in 1998, there has been a tendency to decentralize the government and to give provinces more freedom in determining how the regional governmental institutions are structured and how they function. Due to the conflict, Aceh has been one of the very few regions where governmental decentralization has not been realized. The current peace process is in a way bringing Aceh to the same level of reforms as other Indonesian provinces. For more information on Muspida and Muspika, see Buchori and Lay (2000).

21 Personal interview in November 2007.

22 For the case of East Timor, see Burgess (2004) and the final report by the Commission for Reception, Truth, and Reconciliation in Timor-Leste (CAVR 2005). For Rwanda, see Zorbas (2004) and Sarkin (2001).

23 In February 2006, Indonesia ratified two international covenants, the Covenant on Civil and Political Rights and the Covenant on Economic, Social and Cultural Rights, that together with the Universal Declaration of Human Rights form the Human Rights Bill.

24 The MoU distinguishes between organic and non-organic security troops. Organic troops are regular troops that are needed to uphold security in the province during peace times, while non-organic troops are the ones that have been sent to Aceh to fight against the separatist movement in special military operations.

References

Acehkita (2006a) 'Warga Paya Bakong gali kuburan di bekas pos TNI', *Acehkita.com*, 3 January. Online. Available at: http://www.acehkita.com/index.php?dir=news&file=detail&id=461 (accessed on 16 January 2008).
—— (2006b) 'Perang mulut, nembak warga dan AMM', No. 28, 10–16 July.
—— (2006c) 'Muslem "pergi" tak kembali', No. 28, 10–16 July.
—— (2006d) 'TNI ngotot jenazah otopsi korban', *Acehkita.com*, 20 July. Online. Available at: http://www.acehkita.com/index.php?dir=news&file=detail&id=1095 (accessed on 16 January 2008).
—— (2006e) 'Kronik Paya Bakong', No. 30, 24–20 July.
—— (2006f) 'Umar menolak islah', No. 30, 24–30 July.
—— (2006g) 'Saksi korban, Rasyidin: "Saya ditembak dari jarak 3 meter"', No. 30, 24–30 July.
—— (2006h) 'Siapa menabur peluru di Paya Bakong?', No. 30, 24–30 July.
—— (2006i) 'AMM di simpang damai', No. 33, 14–20 August.
—— (2006j) 'Kursi, uang dan peusijuek tidak cukup jamin perdamaian di Aceh', No. 48, 11–17 December.
Amnesty International (1993) 'Shock therapy: restoring order in Aceh, 1989–1993', *Amnesty International Report*, AI index: ASA 21/07/93.
—— (2004) 'New military operations, old patterns of human rights abuses in Aceh', *Amnesty International Report*, AI index: ASA 21/033/2004.
Aspinall, E. and Crouch, H. (2003) 'The Aceh peace process: why it failed', *Policy Studies No. 1*, Washington DC: East West Center.
Bloomfield, D. (2006) 'On good terms: clarifying reconciliation', *Berghof Report No. 14*, Berlin: Berghof Research Center for Constructive Conflict Management.
Bloomfield, D., Barnes, T. and Huyse, L. (eds) (2003) *Reconciliation After Violent Conflict: A Handbook*. Stockholm: International Institute for Democracy and Electoral Assistance (IDEA).
Buchori, M. and Lay, C. (2000) 'Assessing current political developments in Indonesia', Singapore: Institute of Southeast Asian Studies. Online. Available at: http://www.iseas.edu.sg/trends1320.pdf (accessed on 1 February 2008).
Burgess, P. (2004) 'Justice and reconciliation in East Timor: the relationship between the commission for reception, truth and reconciliation and the courts', *Criminal Law Forum*, 15: 135–58.
CAVR (Commission for Reception, Truth, and Reconciliation in Timor-Leste) (2005). *Chega!*, CAVR report. Online. Available at: http://www.cavr-timorleste.org/en/chegaReport.htm (accessed on 1 February 2008).
Crisis Management Initiative (2005) *Memorandum of Understanding between the Government of the Republic of Indonesia and the Free Aceh Movement*. Online. Available at: http://www.cmi.fi/?content=aceh_project (accessed on 1 February 2008).
Hayner, P.B. (2002) *Unspeakable Truths: Facing the Challenge of Truth Commissions*, London and New York: Routledge.
Human Rights Watch (2002) 'Indonesia: accountability for human rights violations in Aceh', *HRW Report*, 14(1)(C).
—— (2003) 'Aceh under martial law: inside the secret war', *HRW Report*, 15(10)(C).
—— (2004) 'Aceh at war: torture, ill-treatment, and unfair trials', *HRW Report*, 16(11)(C).
Hurgronje, S. (1985) *Aceh di Mata Koloniale* [Translation from the English edition *The Achehnese*, 1906, Leiden: E.J. Brill], Jakarta: Yayasan Soko Guru.

Imparsial (2004) 'Rekonstruksi negara melalui kebijakan darurat di Aceh', Imparsial's Policy Study, November.
ICG (International Crisis Group) (2001) 'Aceh: why military force won't bring lasting peace', *Asia Report No. 17*, Jakarta and Brussels: ICG.
IOM (International Organization for Migration) (2006) *Psychosocial needs assessment of communities affected by the conflict in the districts of Pidie, Bireuen and Aceh Utara*, an IOM report.
Jakarta Post (2006) 'One killed as arrest triggers violence in Aceh', 5 July.
Kompas (2006) 'Mobil AMM ditembak, seorang warga tewas', 5 July.
Kontras (2006) *Aceh Damai dengan Keadilan? Menungkap Kekerasan Masa Lalu*, Jakarta: Kontras.
LAKA (1988) 'Upacara peusijuek', unpublished papers of a conference organized by LAKA, Lhokseumawe, 8–10 January.
—— (1990) *Pedoman Umum Adat Aceh I*, Aceh: Lembaga Adat dan Kebudayaan Aceh (LAKA).
Lederach, J.P. (1997) *Building Peace: Sustainable Reconciliation in Divided Societies*, Washington DC: United States Institute of Peace Press.
Lederach, J.P. and Jenner, J.M. (eds) (2002) *Into the Eye of the Storm: A Handbook of International Peace-building*, San Francisco: Jossey-Bass.
Martin, H. (2006) *Kings of Peace, Pawns of War: An Untold Story of Peace-Making*, London: The Centre for Humanitarian Dialogue.
Pompe, S. (1987) 'De invloed van het Adatrecht bij de Toepassing van het Strafrecht in Indonesië', *Bijdragen tot de Taal-, Land- en Volkenkunde*, 143(4): 499–506.
Rahmany, D.P. (2004) *Rumoh Geudong: The Scar of the Acehnese*, Jakarta: Cordova.
Reich, H. (2006) 'Local Ownership' in Conflict Transformation Projects: Partnership, Participation or Patronage?, *Berghof Occasional Paper No. 27*, Berlin: Berghof Research Center for Constructive Conflict Management.
Sarkin, J. (2001) 'The tension between justice and reconciliation in Rwanda: politics, human rights, due process and the role of Gacaca courts in dealing with the genocide', *Journal of African Law*, 45(2): 143–72.
Serambi Indonesia (2006) 'AMM sesalkan insiden Paya Bakong', 5 July.
UNDP (2006) *Access to Justice in Aceh: Making the Transition to Sustainable Peace and Development in Aceh*. Online. Available at: http://www.undp.or.id/pubs/docs/Access%20to%20Justice.pdf (accessed on 1 February 2008).
Wilson, R.A. (2000) 'Reconciliation and revenge in post-apartheid South Africa', *Current Anthropology*, 41(1): 75–98.
Zorbas, E. (2004) 'Reconciliation in post-genocide Rwanda', *African Journal of Legal Studies*, 1(1): 29–52.

7 The problem of going home
Land management, displacement, and reconciliation in Ambon

Jeroen Adam

Introduction

Secure access to land is recognized as one of the most important prerogatives for the prevention of violent conflicts on the Indonesian archipelago (Clark 2002).[1] At the same time, land is of primordial significance in peace-building efforts and processes of reconciliation all over the country. The reasons for this are twofold. First of all, access to land has an impact on everyday livelihood strategies. Although major parts of Southeast Asia are witnessing vast and quick processes of urbanization and industrialization, agriculture still plays a major role for millions of households in the region. The Indonesian archipelago is no exception with some 43 percent of the population that is to a certain extent employed in agriculture (CIA World Factbook 2007). This means that for almost half of the total Indonesian population, land is a determining factor in the organization of their livelihood. Being denied secure and satisfactory access to land puts people in a vulnerable economic position for which they have to find alternative coping mechanisms. This can be done either by looking for alternative income-generating strategies outside the agricultural sector – very often in informal survival economies in an urban or semi-urban setting (Kamungi *et al.* 2005) – or by switching towards short-term crops that are less risk-prone. For instance, research carried out in the Eastern Democratic Republic of the Congo illustrates how populations that are confronted with insecure property rights tend to shift towards a cultivation of low-risk and seasonal crops with immediate but low profits (Vlassenroot 2006). In both cases, these adaptations result in an impoverishment of the community, especially in a context of post-conflict transition where the majority of the population has incessantly been confronted with insecurity and economic hardship.

Apart from this economic aspect, land is strongly attached with aspects of identity construction (Huggins & Clover 2005; Pankhurst 2000). Land is often perceived as the 'land of our ancestors' and the place where a community feels mentally at home. As a consequence, land evokes deep symbolic connotations bound up closely with ideas of, for instance, religion, culture, sex, and gender (Shipton 1994). The fact that people are being chased out of this mental habitat has a strong impact on the identity construction of a community, a household, and even an individual (Malkki 1995; Pederson 2003). What one sees happening is that a process of mental reconstruction unfolds about the notion of 'home' (Refslund Sorensen 2001). The inability to return to this mental construct and the restraint to rebuild a durable livelihood by being denied a secure access to land once the high-intensity violence is over causes emotional hardship and frustration and finally slows down or even blocks processes of peace-building and reconciliation (Lewis 2004). The general aim of this chapter is precisely to illustrate how problems of displacement and land management affect processes of reconciliation in contemporary Maluku (Eastern Indonesia). This will be done through an ethnographic micro study of one community on the island of Ambon, more specifically the Christian community that formerly lived in the urban neighborhood of Batu Merah in Ambon town (Ambon is the name of an island and the capital of the province of the Moluccas at the same time) and is now resettled in Kayu Tiga.[2] After an account of this case, attention will be given to the following three questions. First, the reasons that restrain the Christian community of Batu Merah from returning to their original place of living and force them to resettle in a newly established resettlement site. Second, how these problems of returning home affect issues of inter-religious interaction in post-conflict Ambon and third, how initiatives of reconciliation have tried to deal with this spatial and growing mental gap between the Christian and Muslim communities.

Displacement in Ambon

Despite the importance of land in processes of reconciliation, this often turns out to be quite problematic, since secure property rights regarding land access prove to be highly disputed in a post-conflict situation. In Ambon, one of the foremost reasons for this contestation is a massive displacement caused by a high-intensity conflict between Christians and Muslims from 1999 until 2002 and different forms of low-intensity violence afterwards.[3] At the height of this conflict, around one-third of the total Moluccan population got internally displaced.[4] Today, this massive displacement has ended and the majority of people has returned home.

Nevertheless, there are two kinds of refugee groups that still have not been able to go back. The first group consists of the many people that migrated during the conflict on an individual basis. This group can be seen as some sort of 'invisible' IDPs (Internally Displaced People) as they did not end up in big camps, but had moved/fled individually with friends or family. Many of them are currently still living with their friends/families nine years after the outbreak of the conflict. For this reason, these people have often been deprived of any assistance both from NGOs and the government. It is very hard to put any numbers on the actual size of the group as they are dispersed all over the island. The difficulty a lot of these people are facing is that their properties have been taken over during their flight by other people. For this reason, they cannot return home and are obliged to stay in their place of refuge or have to search for a new residence. Although deeply under-researched, this group will not be examined in this chapter.

A second group of refugees that has not been able to return are the people that ended up in the many resettlement camps on the Ambonese island. In most cases, all the people living in these camps had to flee during the conflict and ended up in big and visible IDP camps all over the island. When the high-intensity violence started reducing from 2002 onwards, these people were resettled in newly built sites. As a consequence, there are no official IDP camps left in Ambon today. Just as for the individual IDPs, the inability to reclaim the land and the property they owned before the conflict has forced them to start a new life in these sites. It is one of these communities that will be the subject of this chapter.

Case study: the Protestants of Batu Merah

Batu Merah is an urban neighborhood in the city of Ambon where before the conflict a minority Protestant community had lived in a majority Muslim area.[5] In 1997, one year before the outbreak of the violence, the neighborhood had consisted of some 76 percent Muslims (BPS 1997, cited in van Klinken 2007). This Protestant community gradually came to be settled there over the centuries. For this reason, the community is ethnically and culturally heterogeneous. The only factor that had united this community was their membership of the same church, Bethabara.

The area of Batu Merah was the first site of high-intensity violence between Christians and Muslims in the whole Moluccan region and proved utterly unsafe for the Protestant minority living there (Human Rights Watch 1999). As a result, the Protestant community that consisted of some 700 households was forced to leave Batu Merah. Some 200 households fled to the Christian neighborhood of

Figure 7.1 Living conditions in the IDP camp in Karpan (Photo: Jeroen Adam)

Karpan (Karan Panjang) in February 1999, one month after the outbreak of the first violence where they took refuge in an abandoned government building. The ones arriving when the building was already full had to look for another place and became dispersed all over the region. Since the people living in Karpan saw their flight as a temporary solution to cope with the insecurity, they lived together in the building itself.

However, as the violence continued, their flight took a more permanent character and families started building their own private cabins in the building itself and on the surrounding site. Living conditions during this period lacked basic provisions such as a decent sleeping place or well-functioning electricity and sanitation. Assistance from the government was meager, local and international NGOs provided food aid and basic medical care. The refugees lived in this camp for some seven years, just two kilometers away from their original place in Batu Merah, without really being able to meet their former neighbors. The community finally resettled in April–May 2006 in Kayu Tiga, a neighborhood belonging to the *negeri* (the Central Moluccan term for village) of Soya in the surrounding hills of the city of Ambon. During that period, other Batu Merah people who came to live all over the region during the conflict were resettled in Kayu Tiga as well. In total, some 500 of the original 700 Protestant households in Batu Merah are currently living in this resettlement site.

Figure 7.2 Kayu Tiga before the Protestant community came to be resettled there in 2006 (Photo: Jeroen Adam)

Apart from traumatic experiences and slumbering feelings of insecurity, the main reason the Protestants were unable to return to Batu Merah and had to resettle in Kayu Tiga, is the occupation of their houses and land by Muslim migrants. These migrants are mainly people from other parts of Maluku who took refuge in the Muslim neighborhood of Batu Merah during the conflict. From 2002 onwards, there have been attempts by the Protestants to facilitate their return to Batu Merah through informal meetings with traditional and religious leaders, local politicians, and the mediation of some NGOs. Despite these efforts, the Protestants have never been able to reclaim their houses and property, and probably will never be able to do so in the future. The causes for this failure are diverse, complex and depend often on the individual household that, certainly in an urban context, searched its own way of securing access to land. Yet, one of the main reasons that underlines most of these cases is a clash between *adat* and a semi-formal legal arrangement based on colonial legislation.[6] To illustrate this, I will use the example of the conflict between the Protestant Church and the different *adat*-based clans of Batu Merah.[7]

Before the violence erupted in 1999, the *Gereja Protestan Maluku* (GPM) or Moluccan Protestant Church owned a big plot of land in the Batu Merah area. The primary purpose of this land was for housing but some minor parts were also used for agriculture. This was a considerable source of revenue since a lot of Protestants lived on this land and paid rent to the GPM. When the Protestants left the area and their church was burned down, the presence of the Christian community disappeared and Batu Merah turned completely Muslim. This was seen by Batu Merah *adat*-based clans as an opportunity to start claiming the land of the GPM and a conflict between those actors developed. The GPM claims its access to land on the basis of colonial agreements that did not get securely formalized by the post-colonial Indonesian state. After the Indonesian independence there was a transfer of the land on which there was a military camp of the *Koninklijk Nederlands Indisch Leger* (KNIL, the Dutch Colonial Armed Forces), from the Dutch colonial government to the GPM. These claims are weakly backed as there are only written documents about the Dutch presence but not of the transfer itself. On the other hand, there are different clans in Batu Merah that try to reclaim this land. They base their title on *adat* by stating that the GPM land was originally their clan land before the Dutch took it away illegally. Central to their argument is the notion of being the original, traditional, and therefore legitimate owners of the land. The result of this quarrel is a situation in which the legal status of the land is contested by two parties. In the meantime, the Protestant community of Batu Merah has been permanently resettled in Kayu Tiga.

As a consequence, the GPM is de facto outmaneuvered although they are still planning to take juridical steps to fight for their claim. Considering the slowness of the juridical process, it looks like, at least in the near future, there will be no definitive conclusion in this dispute. Moreover, the fact that hundreds of Muslim newcomers in Batu Merah have already lived in the area for eight years and have established for themselves a livelihood and a permanent place of living, makes the replacement of these people extremely difficult. Another problem is that the settlement of these newcomers strengthens the claim of the clans since these people

Figure 7.3 Rebuilding the Bethabara church in Kayu Tiga (Photo: Jeroen Adam)

are now paying them rent, thus recognizing the clans as the legitimate owners of the land. Here it should be noted that not only Christians have problems returning to their original houses and land but Muslims who fled the area during the conflict have encountered the same problems. As Batu Merah was a very dangerous place during the conflict, different Muslim families decided to leave the area for a safer location. After the conflict, many of these families have faced huge problems to return to Batu Merah and reclaim their original property, although almost all of them finally managed to do so.

Access to land in Ambon

Although mono-religious zones already existed before the outbreak of the violence in 1999, in most parts of the city of Ambon such as in Batu Merah, Christians and Muslims lived peacefully next to each other. Since the conflict, apart from a couple of villages such as Wayame on Ambon island, Christians and Muslims are segregated. In the city itself, there is a strong divide between the Christian and the Muslim sections.

As shown in my case study, one of the main reasons for this phenomenon can be found in the issue of land management.[8] One can distinguish two sorts of land-related disputes in contemporary Ambon. The first one has to do with a prevailing legal pluralism in which the root of the conflict lies in a clash between different normative systems. Legal pluralism can be defined as "the coexistence of two or more legal systems in the same social field or setting" (Griffiths 1986). My case study on Batu Merah is an illustration of this legal pluralism. There exist different legal systems (in this case: *adat* and semi-formal state legislation) through which multiple actors stake their claims. In the end this has led to a situation of utmost legal complexity in which different parties try to claim access to land based on different legal systems. The second type of conflict can be labeled "system-internal pluralism" (von Benda-Beckmann 2002) in which different interpretations within one normative system are the reasons for competing and conflicting claims. In the Batu Merah case, it is different *adat* clans that reclaim the land of the GPM that are having fierce discussions about the borders of their respective clan land.

Because of this multitude of different land-related conflicts, I do not have the intention to point a finger at *adat* as the reason for the failure to successfully repatriate displaced communities in Ambon. One should not forget that I am only talking about one micro study and that the inability to reclaim property in Ambon cannot be solely reduced to a problem of *adat* politics but that a multitude of factors relate to this problem. A resurgence of *adat* is mainly of importance in situations where a perception existed that, according to *adat* rules, Christians had an illegitimate and unjust access to land based on Dutch colonial politics and privileges.[9] For Muslims, this is of lesser importance as they are considered to have had very few privileges under Dutch colonial rule.

We also have to be aware of the fact that contestation over land access existed long before the conflict. As von Benda-Beckmann and Taale (1996: 39) stated: "In the rich and colourful world of Indonesia's local legal systems, Ambonese property law is perhaps the most complex". Typical for Ambon is that the limited efforts of the Indonesian state to acquire control over land regulation have even been less successful than in other parts of the country. Particularly revealing in this regard is the research undertaken by Franz and Keebet von Benda-Beckmann during the 1980s in the village of Hila, situated on the island of Ambon (see e.g. von Benda-Beckmann 1994 and von Benda-Beckmann & Taale 1996). In this rather small setting they describe how three legal systems, namely, *adat*, Islamic inheritance law, and formal state law are creatively used by the villagers to claim their access to land. At the same time, different interpretations within one legal system are used to contest existing claims to land and the resources growing on it. Consequentially, land access in Hila has been highly contested for a long time and has provoked mainly Islam-internal conflicts at different levels within society (e.g. family, clan, sub-clan, ethnic migrants versus 'original' Hila people).

Adat in post-New Order Indonesia

The recent conflict in the Moluccas and related refugee and displacement issues reinforced and further complicated these conflicts. Simply stated, displacement presented a chance for different actors to claim abandoned land. In some cases, such as Batu Merah, this is done through the construction of an *adat* discourse in which aspects of history, identity, and culture are creatively mixed. To understand the strength and legitimacy of these *adat*-based claims, one cannot only focus on the regional conflict dynamics but has to take into account recent legal changes on a national level. Since the fall of the New Order regime in 1998, *adat* has gained a strong impetus in the whole of Indonesia, which is related to a nation-wide process of decentralization (Fitzpatrick 2006; Thornburn 2004). Before 1998 *adat*-based forms of resource management were only weakly backed by national legislation. The first major post-colonial land regulation was the Basic Agrarian Law (BAL) of 1960 that aimed to remove the legal dualities that sprung out of the Dutch colonial administration. This BAL is based on article 33 of the Indonesian Constitution of 1945 which says that the natural resources of Indonesia should be controlled by the Indonesian State so that these are used to the benefit of the nation. Although *adat* was recognized in itself, land administration based on *adat* titles proved to be very uncertain and subject to political arbitrariness. In article 5 it is stated that the basis of BAL "is *adat* law in so far as it is not in conflict with the National and State interests based on the unity of the Nation." Further, it is stated in Article 56 that the BAL provides for *adat* recognition "as long as they [*adat* laws] are not in conflict with the spirit and the provisions of this law." During the New Order era that started in 1966, communal *adat* rights kept on being subordinated to centralized state interests and more specifically the patrimonial lineages of the Jakarta-based elites around President Suharto (Thornburn 2004). This changed after the fall of Suharto in May 1998 when new regulations came into being that gave more autonomy to the regions and a stronger legal backing for *adat*-based forms of resource management. Of special importance in this regard are Law No. 5/1999 regarding Guidelines for the Settlement of Communal Land Rights Issues and Law No. 22/1999 regarding Regional Autonomy.

As a consequence, a multitude of different organizations sprang up or were revitalized since 1998 that stressed their particular culture and identity after the centralized features of the New Order state (Sakai 2002). Often, this was a strategy to negotiate the access to vital economic and political assets in a decentralized post-New Order Indonesia. In this regard the resurgence of *adat* should not merely be seen as backward looking but as a modern project in which answers are formulated for contemporary challenges (von Benda-Beckmann 2007). Research carried out by McCarthy (2004) on the province of Central Kalimantan illustrates how decentralization and new national legislation such as Law No. 22/1999 have put *adat* elites at the foreground of socioeconomic and political life in Indonesia; McCarthy (2004: 1211) stated: "With villages claiming corporate customary rights over lands found in village administrative boundaries, village heads and the village apparatus found themselves in a profitable gate-keeping role". Or to put it another way, since the end of the New Order a new bargaining process emerged in Central Kalimantan to get access to the forest for economic benefits and local *adat* elites saw a chance to become more proactively involved in this. This whole process ultimately gave rise to "highly volatile sociolegal configurations that create insecurity and heighten resource conflicts" (McCarthy 2004: 1200).

This example illustrates how in the field of resource management, decentralization, in contrast to the common international discourse, did not result in governance improvement but rather led to fragmentation, intense competition, and profound legal uncertainty in which local elites often manipulated existing legislation for their own benefit (Fitzpatrick 2006; Hadiz 2004; McCarthy 2004; Schulte Nordholt 2003). Different flaws and weaknesses within the numerous decentralization laws have further enforced this process. Thornburn (2004: 45) came to the following conclusion: "If land certification and transactions were uncertain and risky ventures before *Reformasi*, they have now become nigh impossible".

A similar story is ongoing in Ambon. We noticed how *adat* elites have become more daring to (re?)claim their access to land in the *Reformasi* era (the era following the New Order) and how this heightened resource conflicts. Specific to the Moluccan region is that the revitalization of (Moluccan) *adat* is perceived as a cure to heal a religiously fractured society (see also Bräuchler this volume). This common belief that *adat* can build bridges between Christians and Muslims by stressing a common Moluccan identity has put *adat* at the forefront of the societal debate and given it an utterly positive connotation. Moreover, stressing Moluccan *adat* in Ambon is seen as a positive way of underlining a collective and harmonious Moluccan identity that contrasts the popular image of a Java-based and greedy Indonesian government. Partly because of this positive belief in *adat*, the whole legal move that has been started up at the national level is now being implemented at the regional and local level at a very quick pace (after major delays due to the conflict). Of specific importance in this regard is the provincial law regarding the reinstatement of the *negeri* as the basic system of village government *(Peraturan Daerah Provinsi Maluku No. 14, 2005 tentang penetapan kembali negeri)* and the different decrees to implement this at the district level.

Interviews have revealed that both in rural and urban settings many of the *adat* leaders are exceptionally well-informed about these new regulations and are themselves in the possession of copies of these legal documents. According to them, the existence of the new regulations gives them the legal backing to claim what 'historically' belongs to them. It is therefore fair to state that the whole plethora of regulations on the national, regional, and local level has stimulated *adat* clans and figures to (re)claim access to resources such as land.

The changing nature of inter-religious interaction[10]

Although the region has been relatively stable for the last couple of years, with the formation of mono-religious zones, two problems arise regarding reconciliation and social interaction. First of all, the impossibility of returning still provokes communal friction that will not necessarily cause a renewed high-intensity conflict but nevertheless hinders unrestrained social interaction between the two communities. My case study shows how difficulties of repatriation are mainly a problem of resource management and legal uncertainty. However, local actors often interpret things quite differently. Sometimes they see behind these problems of resource management clear-cut and deliberate strategies to block the presence of their religion in their original village.[11]

Second, there is a decrease in everyday inter-religious interaction and a subsequent growing mental alienation between the Christians and Muslims of Batu Merah. Today, there are definitely contacts between the two religious communities but some side-notes have to be made. First, this social interaction only happens with Muslims that before the conflict already lived in Batu Merah. Any form of interaction between the Christians of Kayu Tiga and Muslim migrants that entered the area during and after the conflict is non-existent. Second, the social interaction itself takes a more formalized turn. People still see each other during special events such as a marriage, a festival, or a religious celebration, but this interaction has a ceremonial rather than a day-to-day character. This in itself is of course logical as the Christians and the Muslims now live at different ends of the city. Third, for children being born in Kayu Tiga, Batu Merah and the Muslims living there are only remnants of an unknown past being told and retold by their parents and grandparents. In their everyday social world, Batu Merah is of little significance and their network of friends consists mainly of Christians hailing from their camp.

Consequentially, the gap is growing between the Christians of Kayu Tiga and their former neighborhood of Batu Merah. As people told me, they no longer recognize the area they grew up in since so many new people are now living there. They no longer have the feeling that Batu Merah is their original neighborhood. In other words, they perceive the nature of their neighborhood as fundamentally different compared to the time they still lived there. During the interviews I conducted in Kayu Tiga on different aspects of displacement, the story often went that Muslims who came to live in Batu Merah during the conflict were radicalized Muslims with strong anti-Christian feelings. In their view, this has radicalized the area and altered the tolerant nature of their former neighborhood.[12] Proof of this is found in the fact that the area was the site of a strong Laskar Jihad (the military wing of an Islamist organization in Java) presence during the conflict. A visual expression of the changing nature of their place, at least through the eyes of the Christians in Kayu Tiga, can be found in the wearing of the burka by some women nowadays in Batu Merah. This perceived radicalization of Batu Merah and the people living there is also quoted as one of the main reasons that they are not able to return and are forced to settle in a new place.

This growing mental estrangement between the two religious communities is all the more regrettable since the Muslim and Christian community were in many cases indeed very close with each other. Too often, observers of the Ambonese conflict forget that for every story about religious violence in the past years, one can give a counterexample of inter-religious solidarity where Christians and Muslims protected each other in harsh times during the conflict. This was clearly the case for the Christians of Batu Merah who during their flight got economically and even physically protected by their Muslim neighbors. These inter-religious solidarity mechanisms were often based on family relationships but also friends constantly looked after each other and exchanged essential information during the violence. These mechanisms – at least to a certain extent – contained the violence. A question one can therefore pose is what sorts of everyday inter-religious solidarity mechanisms will contain the violence in a potential future conflict.

Land and grassroots initiatives of reconciliation

The initiation of institutionalized forms of reconciliation to overcome this growing mental gap is particularly meager in our case. Apart from individual initiatives in which households decided to visit their former neighbors/friends/family, initiatives of the state to reconcile Muslims with Christians are non-existent and at least for the near future, there is no attempt to form some sort of truth and reconciliation commission for the Moluccan conflict.[13] The first and foremost way reconciliation has been initiated through *adat* means is the practice of *pela*. Simply stated, *pela* is a traditional brotherhood alliance of mutual assistance between two or more villages in the Central Moluccan region and is part of central Moluccan *adat* (Bartels 1977; Huwaë 1995).[14] It is important to note that *pela* alliances exist only between individual villages (irrespective of their religious affiliations) and have nothing to do with an alliance between the whole Muslim and Christian community (Bartels 2000). Since the end of the conflict, these *pela* alliances have been used as a way to recreate mutual bonds of friendship and to stress a common Moluccan identity in contrast to religious identity. In our case, Batu Merah's *pela* relationship with the Christian village of Passo has been reinstated after the conflict through a *pela* celebration. This celebration was held for the first time in 2004 in Batu Merah and consisted of different practices that symbolically confirm the mutual bond of assistance and friendship. An example of this is the *kain gandong* or a ritual exchange of clothes between the villagers of Passo and Batu Merah. Such rituals are reserved for the original *adat* clans of the two villages. In both Passo and Batu Merah however, these 'original' members constitute a minority of the population. More important for our community in Kayu Tiga is the fact that around these rather strict rituals there is a whole range of other activities such as *makan patita* (eating *patita*) to which non-*adat* members are also invited. It is in these rather informal practices that lies the core of the reconciliation for the Christians of Kayu Tiga. For many, the *pela* celebration was the first time they visited Batu Merah after the conflict and the first time they had the feeling they were invited to their former neighborhood with an open heart (*membuka hati*). In this regard, *pela* has not only brought the villages of Passo and Batu Merah together, but has also overcome the religious differences between the Protestants and the Muslims within the village of Batu Merah itself. Certainly among the Christians who were expulsed from their original place, it is seen as an important symbolic gesture to be part of this *pela* celebration as a Batu Merah member irrespective of religion.

Nevertheless, the practice of *pela* does not touch upon the existing power relations and the issue of land management that restrain the Christian community's return to Batu Merah. It is definitely true, as Lederach (1997: 94) argued, that "the greatest resource for sustaining peace in the long term is always rooted in the local people and their culture". The *pela* celebration supports this argument as people themselves seem to have the ownership over these practices which are therefore seen as highly legitimate. For this reason, an integrated and durable strategy of peace-building should definitely involve grassroots initiatives of reconciliation as these take into account the societal relations at the micro level of society. However, studying these cultural practices of reconciliation from the angle of land management, we quickly encounter constraints regarding these initiatives, namely, the neglect of involved aspects of power politics. One of these aspects is precisely the political and legal struggles that restrain the Christian community to return home to be able to build a new and durable relationship of trust with their former neighbors. The concrete political and economic consequences of these symbolic gestures are thus particularly meager and the problems the Christian community faces regarding land management are not solved.

Conclusion

The micro study of the Christian community of Batu Merah illustrates how conflict and the subsequent displacement created opportunities to renegotiate access to certain economic assets. The case discussed here involves the issue of land but during the violence access to other economic resources such as markets, roads, or even *becaks* (bicycle taxis) was also transformed. Having this in mind and in order to fully grasp the complexity of the Ambonese conflict, we need to get insights into the complex economic transformations it invoked as these have a major impact on the outlook of the current post-conflict landscape in which some managed to ameliorate their socioeconomic position but many others are left on the losing side of the game.

These processes are not unique to the Ambonese violence as any conflict in the world involves to a certain extent a political and socioeconomic transformation. Research conducted in other contexts revealed that controlling access to land implies power over the economic and the mental well-being of people (Lavigne-Delville 2002; Pottier 2004; Vlassenroot 2004). For this reason, land is a political asset through which major parts of a population can be controlled and which strengthens one's political credibility and capacities. In addition, having ownership over land brings numerous economic benefits through the direct cultivation and selling of crops or the imposition of different sorts of taxes. All this makes controlling land highly desirable. As I illustrated for Batu Merah, situations of conflict have a huge potential to reorganize control over land. Throughout a conflict, patterns and institutions that traditionally governed the access to land are prone to deep transformations due to different dynamics such as a shift in political power or internal displacement (Huggins & Ochieng 2005; Unruh 2004). Consequentially, most post-conflict situations are characterized by tenurial uncertainty as the regular sociopolitical order is altered and patterns of control over land have changed profoundly (Huggins & Clover 2005; Unruh 2003). A situation of post-conflict, such as the one in Ambon, can therefore be described as a so-called "open moment" (Lund 1996), which denotes that there exists a potential for the reorganization of the social and political order.

Precisely because of this involvement of politics, land administration proves to be one of the most volatile and difficult aspects of peace processes all over the world (Unruh 2004). As our micro study illustrates, the capacity of grassroots initiatives of reconciliation to deal with these power politics are limited. Practices of grassroots reconciliation have the potential to build bridges in a fractured post-conflict society. However, these initiatives need to be embedded into a much broader strategy of peace-building that takes into account structural economic and political factors, and is aware of the many and complex societal transformations that occurred during the violence. As Goodhand and Hulme (1999) described, writers from a peace studies background often tend to focus too strongly on human agency and sometimes neglect the structural factors, such as the politics blocking the repatriation of a displaced community, provoking and sustaining violence, and blocking processes of peace-building. Trying to provide equitable land access should nevertheless play a primordial role in any strategy of peace-building and reconciliation as land relates both to the mental well-being of a population and the provision of a durable and sustainable livelihood. The problem is that addressing these issues will always imply a political intervention and a (probably highly unwanted) intermingling in localized, complex, and sensitive contexts. It is precisely here that one of the biggest challenges and difficulties lies for peace builders and reconciliation workers. As Augustinus and Barry (2006: 676) pointed out in their article on land management and strategic action planning in a post-conflict setting, there are no fixed and technocratic roadmaps in which "policy provides the vision" to guarantee an equitable and secure land access. These interventions will therefore always be highly improvisatory as they have to focus on the whole land management systems with all its complex societal implications, rather than on a technical formalization of cadastral sub-systems.

Notes

1 Access to land is not the same as simple ownership, but instead includes a wide range of social relationships and regulations regarding land tenure that relate to the opportunity to use, manage, and control land and its resources.
2 These data were collected through two fieldtrips that were conducted from January until March 2007 and from October until November 2007. During my research, a combination of semi-structured household interviews, focus group discussions, and participant observation was used in the resettlement camp of Kayu Tiga concerning aspects of displacement and access to land. These data were then further complemented with in-depth interviews with people that were closely involved in the organization of the camp such as community leaders, religious leaders, and NGO (Non-Governmental Organization) activists.
3 I do not intend to give a full overview on the origins and the history of the Moluccan conflict within the outline of this chapter. For an elaborate account of the conflict itself I wish to refer to ICG (2002), van Klinken (2001, 2007), von Benda-Beckmann (2003), and Schulze (2002). For accounts on the socioeconomic and political roots of the conflict, see Bertrand (2002, 2004), Goss (2004), and Pannell (2003).
4 In 1999, the Moluccan archipelago was divided into the province of the Moluccas and the Northern Moluccan province. The International Crisis Group wrote that, as a consequence of the fighting, one-third of the total population in both the provinces of Maluku and North Maluku was internally displaced (ICG 2002). Another report by the US Committee for Refugees stated that in 2002 around 422,000 of a total population of 1,300,000 people were displaced as a consequence of violence in the province of Maluku (Mason 2001). The figures that came across the official channels are particularly lower. A report published by the Indonesian National Commission on Human Rights declared

Land management, displacement, and reconciliation 151

that in the years 2002 and 2003, there were 275,091 Internally Displaced People (IDP) in the province of Maluku, which was then the province with most IDPs in the whole Indonesian archipelago (INCHR 2005). The latest figures I could find were for the last quarter of 2005. In this report by CARDI-Maluku (Consortium for Assistance and Recovery towards Development in Indonesia), it is stated that around that period there were still 15,788 households displaced for the whole Maluku province, of which 6,433 were in the city of Ambon (CARDI 2005).

5 The city of Ambon consists of 258,331 people of which there are 120,489 Muslims, 122,407 Protestants, and 15,175 Catholics. The province of Maluku consists of 1,322,908 people of which there are 798,292 Muslims, 425,490 Protestants, and 94,180 Catholics, the rest are small minority religions (Badan Pusat Statistik Provinsi Maluku 2007).

6 It is very hard to give a clear and uncontested definition of *adat* as this both refers to an institution that regulates resource management, and a much broader set of social norms where issues of identity and tradition play a central role (e.g. Biezeveld 2004). Moreover, although *adat* exists all over the Indonesian archipelago, the contents of *adat* not only differ greatly depending on the region but also depending on, for instance, class and religion. Therefore, I will not give a clear-cut definition of *adat* but refer to this as a broad set of social norms. Within these norms, identity and tradition stand central and very often there is reference to some sort of harmonious past (Davidson & Henley 2007). For interesting accounts specific to Moluccan *adat*, see Cooley (1962), Holleman (1923), von Benda-Beckmann and Taale (1996).

7 This case has been investigated by interviewing different stakeholders in the field that are closely related with this issue such as lawyers, the GPM, clan leaders, and law specialists. Written statements documenting such claims were often lacking. Where these documents existed there was a restraint to share this with a foreign researcher considering the sensitivity of the case. However, it is not my objective to engage myself in the conflict by trying to prove that the claims of one of the parties are historically more correct than the other. My first purpose is to reconstruct the discourses and beliefs that are used by both parties and to look at the actual outcomes of this clash of opinions.

8 Apart from these issues of resource management, a second feature that perpetuated the formation of mono-religious zones is the policies by the provincial and the city governments to resettle displaced communities within their own religious zone. Their strategy was mainly driven by a short-term vision on conflict management and efforts to prevent renewed violence.

9 This does not mean that Christians as such cannot own *adat* land. In Christian villages they are typically the owners of *adat* land that is uncontested as they are considered as the 'first' and legitimate owners of the land.

10 As the focus of my research is on resettlement and I also spent most of my time in the camp of Kayu Tiga, this chapter articulates in the first place the viewpoint of the Christians now living in Kayu Tiga rather than the Muslim community in Batu Merah.

11 Considering the urban nature of my case, this aspect is of minor concern here for the provision of a durable livelihood. Earlier research has revealed that for the Christian community of Batu Merah, apart from for housing, land has always been of lesser economic importance (Adam & Peilouw 2008). In all other resettlement camps in Ambon, on the contrary, communities who had made an income through farming before the conflict are now confronted with a lack of decent agricultural land. Research carried out by the author in collaboration with C-ChildS (Center for Child and Development Studies) Maluku in camps such as Kate-Kate, Liang, or Tanah Putih has shown how this presents people with economic hardship and vulnerability. A situation that is seemingly all the more painful and frustrating for them considering how people from 'the other religion' have taken over their former lands and profit from related economic benefits.

12 I want to stress that I try to translate the feelings of the Christians living in Kayu Tiga rather than my own opinion about these matters. Any definitive conclusion on the

so-called radicalization of Muslims in Batu Merah cannot be made as any objective research is lacking. Nevertheless, many interviews revealed this radicalization was a very live and strong conviction among the Christian community.

13 For more details see Bräuchler (Chapter 5) this volume, endnote 27, and Sulistiyanto and Setyadi this volume.

14 Interviews with government representatives concerned with post-conflict reconstruction in Ambon revealed that the state explicitly does not want to deal with these *pela* celebrations as they are considered a 'people's thing' in which interference of the state would only diminish the spontaneous nature of the initiative.

References

Adam, J. and Peilouw, L. (2008) 'Internal displacement and household strategies for income generation: a case study in Ambon, Indonesia', *Social Development Issues*, 30(2).

Augustinus, C. and Barry, M.B. (2006) 'Land management strategy formulation in post-conflict societies', *Survey Review*, 302(38): 668–81.

Badan Pusat Statistik Provinsi Maluku (2007) *Maluku Dalam Angka 2007*, Ambon: BPS Provinsi Maluku.

Bartels, D. (1977) *Guarding the Invisible Mountain: Intervillage Alliances, Religious Syncretism and the Ethnic Identity among Ambonese Christians and Moslems in the Moluccas*, Ithaca: Cornell University.

—— (2000) 'Your god is no longer mine: Moslem-Christian fratricide in the Central Moluccas (Indonesia) after a half-millennium of tolerant coexistence and ethnic unity', in S. Pannell (ed.) *A State of Emergency: Violence, Society and the State in Eastern Indonesia*, Darwin: Northern Territory University Press.

Bertrand, J. (2002) 'Legacies of the authoritarian past: religious violence in Indonesia's Moluccan Islands', *Pacific Affairs*, 75(1): 57–85.

—— (2004) *Nationalism and Ethnic Conflict in Indonesia*, Cambridge: Asia-Pacific Studies.

Biezeveld, R. (2004) 'Discourse shopping in a dispute over land in rural Indonesia', *Ethnology*, 43(2): 137–54.

CARDI (2005) 'Maluku Overview 2005', unpublished document.

CIA World Factbook (2007) *Indonesia*. Online. Available at: http://www.cia.gov/cia/publications/factbook/ (accessed on 7 January 2008).

Clark, S. (2002) 'Introduction', in S. Clark (ed.) *More than just Ownership. Ten Land and Natural Resource Conflict Case Studies from East Java and Flores*, World Bank, Indonesian Social Development Paper No. 4.

Cooley, F.L. (1962) *Ambonese Adat: A General Description*. New Haven: Southeast Asia Studies.

Davidson, J. and Henley, D. (eds) (2007) *The Revival of Tradition in Indonesian Politics: The Deployment of Adat from Colonialism to Indigenism*, London: Routledge.

Fitzpatrick, D. (2006) 'Private law and public power: tangled threads in Indonesian land regulation', in H. Schulte Nordholt (ed.) *Indonesian Transitions*, Yogyakarta: Pustaka Pelajar.

Goodhand, J. and Hulme, D. (1999) 'From wars to complex political emergencies: understanding conflict and peace-building in the new world disorder', *Third World Quarterly*, 20(1): 13–26.

Goss, J. (2004) 'Understanding the "Maluku wars": an overview of the sources of communal conflict and prospects for peace', *Cakalele*, Vol. 11–12.

Griffiths, J. (1986) 'What is legal pluralism', *Journal of Legal Pluralism*, 24: 1–55.

Hadiz, V.R. (2004) 'Decentralisation and democracy in Indonesia: a critique of neo-institutionalist perspectives', *Development and Change*, 35(4): 697–718.

Holleman, F.D. (1923) *Het Adat-Grondenrecht van Ambon en de Oeliasers*, Delft: Meinema.

Huggins, C. and Clover, J. (2005) 'Introduction', in C. Huggins and J. Clover (eds) *From the Ground up: Land Rights, Conflict and Peace in Sub-Saharan Africa*, Pretoria: Institute for Security Studies.

Huggins, C. and Ochieng, B. (2005) 'Paradigms, processes and practicalities of land reform in post-conflict sub-Saharan Africa', in C. Huggins and J. Clover (eds) *From the Ground up: Land Rights, Conflict and Peace in Sub-Saharan Africa*, Pretoria: Institute for Security Studies.

Human Rights Watch (1999) 'Indonesia. The violence in Ambon', *HRW Report*, 11(1). Online. Available at: http://www.hrw.org/reports/pdfs/i/indonesa/indon994.pdf (accessed on 24 February 2005).

Huwaë, S. (1995) 'Divided opinions about adatpela: a study of pela Tamilou – Siri-Sori – Hutumuru', *Cakalele*, 6: 77–92.

ICG (International Crisis Group) (2002) *Indonesia: The Search for Peace in Maluku*, Asia Report, No. 31, Brussels and New York: ICG.

INCHR (2005) *IDP's Report on Social Disaster in Indonesia*, Jakarta: The Indonesian National Commission on Human Rights.

Kamungi, P.M., Oketch, J.S. and Huggins, C. (2005) 'Land access and the return and resettlement of IDP's and refugees in Burundi', in C. Huggins and J. Clover. (eds) *From the Ground up: Land Rights, Conflict and Peace in Sub-Saharan Africa*, Pretoria: Institute for Security Studies.

Lavigne-Delville, P. (2002) 'Towards an articulation of land regulation modes? Recent issues and progress at stake', paper presented at Regional Meeting on Land Issues, Kampala.

Lederach, J.P. (1997) *Building Peace: Sustainable Reconciliation in Divided Societies*, Washington DC: United States Institute of Peace Press.

Lewis, D. (2004) 'Challenges to sustainable peace: land disputes following conflict', paper presented at Symposium on Land Administration in Post Conflict Areas, Geneva.

Lund, M. (1996) *Preventive Diplomacy: A Strategy for Preventing Conflicts*, Washington DC: United States Institute of Peace Press.

Malkki, L. (1995) *Purity and Exile. Violence, Memory And National Cosmology Among Hutu Refugees in Tanzania*, Chicago: University of Chicago Press.

Mason, J. (2001) *Shadow Plays: The Crisis of Refugees and Internally Displaced Persons in Indonesia*, Washington DC: US Committee for Refugees.

McCarthy, J. (2004) 'Changing to gray: decentralization and the emergence of volatile socio-legal configurations in Central Kalimantan', *World Development*, 32(7): 1199–223.

—— (2005) 'Between adat and state: institutional arrangements on Sumatra's forest frontier', *Human Ecology*, 33(1): 57–82.

Pankhurst, D. (2000) 'Unravelling reconciliation and justice? Land and the potential for conflict in Namibia', *Peace and Change*, 25(2): 239–54.

Pannell, S. (2003) 'Violence, society and the state in Eastern Indonesia', in S. Pannell (ed.) *A State of Emergency. Violence, Society and the State in Eastern Indonesia*, Darwin: Northern Territory University Press.

Pottier, J. (2004) *Re-imagining Rwanda. Conflict, Survival and Disinformation in the Late Twentieth Century*, Cambridge: Cambridge University Press.

Pedersen, M.H. (2003) *Between Homes: Post-War Return, Emplacement and the Negotiation of Belonging in Lebanon*, New Issues in Refugee Research, Working Paper No. 79.

Refslund Sorensen, B. (2001) 'IDPs: an anthropological perspective', in J. Mason (ed.) *Response Strategies of the Internally Displaced: Changing the Humanitarian Lens*, Oslo: Norwegian Refugee Council – The Norwegian University of Technology and Science.

Sakai, M. (2002) 'Land dispute resolution in the political reform at the time of decentralization in Indonesia', *Antropologi Indonesia*, 68: 40–56.

Schulte Nordholt, H. (2003) 'Renegotiating boundaries; access, agency and identity in post-Soeharto Indonesia', *Bijdragen tot de Taal-, Land- en Volkenkunde*, 159(4): 550–89.

Schulze, K.E. (2002) 'Laskar Jihad and the conflict in Ambon', *The Brown Journal of World Affairs*, 9(1): 57–69.

Shipton, P. (1994) 'Land and culture in tropical Africa: soils, symbols and the metaphysics of the mundane', *Annual Review of Anthropology*, 23: 347–77.

Thornburn, C. (2004) 'The plot thickens: land administration and policy in post-New Order Indonesia', *Asia Pacific Viewpoint*, 45(1): 33–49.

Unruh, J.D. (2003) 'Land tenure and legal pluralism in the peace process', *Peace and Change*, 28(3): 352–77.

—— (2004) *Post-conflict Land Tenure. Using a Sustainable Livelihoods Approach*, LSP Working Paper 18.

van Klinken, G. (2001) 'The Maluku wars: bringing society back in', *Indonesia*, 71: 1–26.

—— (2007) *Communal Violence and Democratization in Indonesia. Small Town Wars*, London and New York: Routledge.

Vlassenroot, K. (2004) 'Land and conflict: the case of Masisi', in K. Vlassenroot and T. Raeymaekers (eds) *Conflict and Social Transformation in Eastern DR Congo*, Ghent: Academia Press.

—— (2006) *Household Land Use Strategies in a Protracted Crisis Context: Land Tenure, Conflict and Food Security in Eastern DRC*, FAO Working Paper. Online. Available at: ftp://ftp.fao.org/docrep/fao/009/ag306e/ag306e00.pdf (accessed on 17 November 2006).

von Benda-Beckmann, F. (2002) 'Who's afraid of legal pluralism', *Journal of Legal Pluralism*, 47: 38–82.

von Benda-Beckmann, F. and Taale, T. (1996) 'Land, trees and houses: changing (un)certainties in property relationships on Ambon', in D. Mearns and C. Healey (eds) *Remaking Maluku: Social Transformation in Eastern Indonesia*, Darwin: Centre for Southeast Asian Studies.

von Benda-Beckmann, F. and von Benda-Beckmann, K. (1994) 'Texts in context: historical documents as political commodity on Islamic Ambon', in W. Marschall (ed.) *Texts from the Islands. Oral and Written Traditions of Indonesia and the Malay World*, Berne: University of Berne.

—— (2007) 'Ambivalent identities; decentralization and Minangkabau political communities', in H. Schulte Nordholt and G. van Klinken (eds) *Renegotiating Boundaries. Local Politics in Post-Suharto Indonesia*, Leiden: KITLV Press.

von Benda-Beckmann, K. (2003) 'Law, violence and peace making on the island of Ambon', in M.-C. Foblets and T. von Trotha (eds) *Healing the Wounds: Essays on the Reconstruction of Societies after War*, Portland: Hart Publishing.

8 Women's agencies for peace-building and reconciliation
Voices from Poso, Sulawesi

Y. Tri Subagya

The eruption of violent conflicts accompanying the decay of Indonesia's authoritarian New Order regime has received a great deal of attention from scholars. Their analyses are varied in their emphasis on a broad range of theoretical perspectives and discourses from a political economy approach to a discussion of the historical roots of violence and embedded cultural traditions (Columbijn & Lindblad 2002; Coppel 2006; van Klinken 2007). These studies, however, pay less attention to gender relations, and tend to ignore women's involvement in the violent conflicts and their aftermath. The fact that men and women have different experiences of conflict and post-conflict situations as a result of their different access to resources and justice is almost completely neglected.

Studies highlighting women's role in the conflict of Poso only began to appear in the national media, research monographs, and articles when the conflict was no longer intense. Some of these articles pinpoint the expanded roles of women at the household and community levels during and after the conflict, but the underlying local context of gender relations before the conflict is less elaborated in the analyses (Agustiana & Pakpahan 2004). Others are concerned with women's status as victims during the conflict such as their vulnerability to sexual harassment and gender-specific forms of suffering (Mangun 2002; Media Sangkompo 2004; Wijaksana 2002).

This chapter is the result of a study attempting to bring to light women's agencies during the communal conflict in Poso as well as their efforts to establish reconciliation. It unfolds women's initiatives in reweaving social ties and trust between the conflicting parties. Women strive for the reconciliation process because they need a conducive environment for reviving the social economic life of their households and society. The conflict had deteriorated their livelihood and reduced the sources of income of their households which has only added a greater burden to their traditional role as household managers. Women have to struggle for their families' survival given the limited role of their husbands as the breadwinners in the households during the conflict. Reconciliation paves the way to erode prejudice and tension so that they can rebuild their family life. In addition, it also allows them to unburden the sufferings and loss of loved ones they had experienced during the conflict which are at last acknowledged.

What I would like to highlight here is the role played by women to reintegrate their communities that have been divided during the conflict along religious and ethnic lines. The study, which includes literature review and archival data collected since 2003 as well as fieldwork conducted in Poso in 2004 and 2006, assumes that even though men and women are positioned unequally and women experience conflict in ways dissimilar to men, this does not mean women are not active in trying to effect change or to play a broader social role within conflict situations and reconciliation processes. As social agents, women and men have individual and group-based capacities and resources, which they use to process social experiences and devise ways of coping with social crisis. In this view, men and women can be seen as actors embedded in gendered power relations. While this means that women-as-a-group and men-as-a-group may experience conflict differently, it also means that women and men can have quite specific and unique ways of approaching conflict-resolution initiatives.

The growing feminist literature on violent conflict in diverse and wide-ranging localities indicate that women are not merely passive victims, but also struggle for survival in the grip of violence and its aftermath (see e.g. Butalia 2000; Moser & Clark 2001). During the conflict in Maluku, Aceh, Sambas, and East Timor, *Jurnal Perempuan* (2004) reported that women played greater social roles in everyday life interaction, whether in villages or refugee camps, due to the limited mobilization of men and the reduction in men's productive roles as a result of the conflict. Nonetheless, the various stories of the efforts of women to build peace are still not widely recognized except by aforementioned feminist researchers and practitioners. Women's voices are often unaccounted for in formal peace accords and their problems are left unattended by policy makers.

This chapter aims to describe women's roles in creating a process of social reconciliation. Social reconciliation refers to the creation of a space for the restoration of order and harmony in a community following an extended phase of distrust, prejudice, and vengeance due to communal conflict. According to Lederach (1997), social reconciliation is built on mechanisms that engage the different sides of a conflict with each other as humans in social relationships. It accounts for acknowledgment and acceptance of their past mistakes so that all parties involved can learn from what had happened in the past in order to prevent its recurrence in the future.

This is different from theological notions of reconciliation that assert the importance of atonement and forgiveness on the road to peace (Gopin 2001). Neither does the concept refer to legal approaches with emphasis on retributive justice through the court system. What these concepts are lacking is the recognition of the gendered dimensions of conflicts. One issue, for instance, is access to justice. As McKay (2000: 569) argued, the patriarchal nature of judicial proceedings, the politicization of post-conflict justice and reconciliation, and spiritual teachings that encourage women to "forgive and forget" have resulted in little public recognition of gender-based war trauma and virtually no gender justice within legal systems.

The study in hand describes women's agencies in the search for conflict resolution as well as their promotion of peacemaking through local cultural practices. Specifically, it addresses the following questions: How do Poso women perceive the conflict? How did they get involved in the peacemaking processes and what capacity do they have to carry on the peace activities? What activities do they undertake in order to promote reconciliation and social justice? And what are the constraints they face to achieving their goals? The chapter ends with a few recommendations on how the reconciliation process in Poso could be enhanced through the greater involvement of women and what these findings imply for conflict and peace studies more generally.

Women and violent conflict in Poso

Poso is one of the regions in the geopolitical landscape of post-Suharto Indonesia that has been experiencing extensive bloody violence since 1998. Administratively, Poso belongs to the Province of Central Sulawesi and is located about 205 kilometers southeast from the province's capital, Palu. Poso regency has a complex ethnic and religious population composition, made up of groups indigenous to the region as well as migrants from other parts of Indonesia. The indigenous people are Pamona, Mori, Lore, Napu, Bungku, and Ampana, while the migrants include Buginese, Makassarese, Kaili, Javanese, Balinese as well as people from Gorontalo and Minahasa. Prior to the conflict, there was already evidence of social segregation based on ethnicity and religion, particularly in relation to settlement areas and population distribution.[1] Nevertheless, for quite some time, the inhabitants of Poso claimed that they could live in harmony despite their religious and ethnic differences. While feuds among different groups or gang fights were common, they never escalated into a large-scale conflict, paralyzing the livelihood of the population.

The series of communal violence between Muslim and Christian groups were provoked by clashes between youth gangs in the town of Poso on 28 December 1998. Ethnicity and religion had been manipulated to mobilize people for the battle; the early conflict was fought out between the indigenous ethnic groups, that were associated with Christianity, and migrant groups whose religious affiliation was mainly Islam. The conflict then turned into a religious one – Christians versus Muslims – when fighters from outside Poso came to support them in the name of religious solidarity. Jihadists from South Sulawesi and Java came in 2001 and exacerbated the situation by attacking villages where the inhabitants were predominantly identified as Christians. Several military personnel, police officers, and local apparatus got involved in the conflict and segregated themselves according to their religious affiliation. The escalation of the conflict had left the community with a lack of trust in living together and loss of its sense of security, as well as with the burden of psychological trauma. The conflict has also left many dislocated from their homes, work, and businesses, and struggling to make a living, and at the same time dealing with a devastated infrastructure.

However, the communal conflicts in Poso were not simply the conflict between two different religious communities as was often reported by the local media. There were multiple factors and diverse vested interests at play in the conflict. Ethno-religious sentiments were exploited and manipulated in the political transition away from the authoritarian regime of the Indonesian New Order. Scholars have tried to explain the roots and causes of the Poso violence from various perspectives, for example, in terms of historical grounds (Aragon 2001), cultural processes in which customary traditions failed to adapt to the political transformation of the society (Ruagadi et al. 2007), political economy (Aditjondro 2002, 2004; Sangaji 2005, 2007; van Klinken 2007), and the growth of radicalism as an extension of the global terrorism network (ICG 2005, 2007).

There are no exact numbers of casualties and victims; some sources claim that more than a thousand people were killed and thousands of buildings and most of the infrastructure in Poso were destroyed.[2] Livelihood and economic activities were paralyzed as people lost their material belongings and were separated from their families and solidarity groups. While some took revenge and retaliated against those they perceived as the enemy, others, especially children, the elderly, and women fled from their neighborhoods. Most of the men remained behind to defend their village from the often anonymous group of offenders. The official Malino Peace accord of 19–20 December 2001, did not put an end to the violence, although the mobilization of the groups in an open battle declined from this point; attacks turned into underground terror. The target was no longer religious groups, but persons in public areas. There were many incidents of mysterious killings, random bomb explosions, and abductions. Only recently, the police claimed that the perpetrators of the post-Malino violence were groups connected with the Asian terrorist network of Jemaah Islamiah that backed them up with military training and automatic weapons (Tempo 2007a, 2007b).

The experiences of Poso women caught in the communal conflicts have similar patterns of gender-based violence, discrimination, and injustice found in the stories of women in other conflict areas. Seifert (1999) pointed out that women often become targets of rape and sexual torture in times of crisis and war. Violence against women is often aimed at destroying a nation's culture because women are deemed as the ones holding families and communities together. In Bosnia–Herzegovina, for example, instances of sexual violence against women were systematic, ordered acts and an important element of Serb warfare strategy. Turshen (2001) described the phenomena of sexual violence in Mozambique and Rwanda as a means deployed by the military to destroy women's economic and political assets, that is, their productive and reproductive labor power as well as their possessions such as land and livestock. In the partition of Pakistan from India, Butalia (2000) described the silence of women who had suffered from the violent conflict. Their struggles for survival and resistance against the brutality of the offenders were kept locked within their memories since the patriarchal structure of their community prevented them from voicing their grievances and demand for justice.

Although patterns are similar, the experiences of Poso women are also determined by local specificities and contexts, namely the ethnic and religious flavor of the violence as well as traditional perceptions. Like men, women viewed the roots of the violence in terms of a crack in social solidarity. Some of them stated that they recognized their neighbors either taking part in destroying their houses or else doing nothing when strangers ransacked their settlements. Most of them also remembered that only selected houses were attacked and burned down. The predominantly Christian villages were attacked by people who wore and yelled Muslim attributes. Likewise, predominantly Muslim settlements were raided by alleged Christians dressed in black shirts with red bandanas. People also witnessed the destruction of religious buildings, both mosques and churches. Some people, who previously did not know how to fight and how to use weapons, participated as combatants in line with their religious identity.

While men were obliged by their community leaders to defend their villages, women often initiated the flight from their homes and possessions, taking with them the children and elderly. Most of them had to walk for long distances and for many hours in fear and uncertainty in order to find a safe place. They had to make important decisions for their families and children in the absence of their men during this time. Nining Laganda (28 years old) was one among many who led people to flee their village, Tangkura, after it was attacked by militia in 2000. Nining took command for escaping from the violence since the men were forced to stay behind to defend their village and prevent raiders from hunting down all villagers. She recalled her story (translation by the author):

> It was a Sunday morning. Since there was a rumor that my village would be targeted for the attack, people were prepared to flee. Men were guarding the village while women, children, and the elderly went to the nearby forest or rice field to hide. I was in the rice field with my children while my husband stayed in the village. After a while, the raid did happen and several houses were burnt down.
>
> The raid went on uninterruptedly for three days, so I remained in the rice field. Then, the village headman announced that he could no longer guarantee the protection of the people who hid in the forest. Therefore, the villagers who were in the forest went back to the village to bring clothes, mattresses, and other valuables back to the forest. In short, it was indeed a frightening situation. After two days in the forest, there was a downpour. The children felt cold and cried.
>
> When we went back home and prepared dinner, two young men came and said that all strong men had to leave immediately to defend the village. All the men then left their food and went out to the village border. My father, my husband, and two of my brothers joined the other villagers.
>
> Shortly after we left home, I heard that my village was under attack. I did not know what else to do except run away with my children. We ran and ran. Then we lay prone in the paddy fields. At that time, I saw a child who had been stabbed by a barbed wire lying close to me.
>
> I asked him, "Is it painful?"
>
> He replied, "No, ... no ma'am, I just want to be here."
>
> In the meantime, people were running wildly and I heard children screaming, "Mummy ... wait for me ... mummy wait for me!" and others shouting, "Don't kill my mother ... don't kill my mother!"
>
> I shouted out loudly and instructed them to lie prone.

When the conflict was still at its height, women from time to time took risks to prevent the violence. Their tactics were sometimes hidden and often highly creative and individual. Ruaedah, a Muslim woman from Kayamanya village, for instance, tried to foil a group of youths' plan to attack a village they had considered to be a base of the enemy. Ruaedah was a respected person in the community because she was the chief of *Aisyiyah* (the women's wing of Muhammadiyah, one of the largest Muslim organizations in Indonesia) in Poso, but due to the conflict emotions were running high and the youths did not pay attention to her order to stop. So she was forced to outwit them. When she heard about their plan to attack, she invited them to drink orange juice that was mixed with valium pills. When the youths fell asleep, she asked their families to bring them home. Although it was only once, she said that at least she had prevented an open battle from happening, which might have killed a lot of people (Ruagadi 2006a).

In the grip of violence, women were even willing to become human shields to protect their community. On 10 August 2002, the villages of Sepe and Silanca were threatened with attack by a convoy of 15 military trucks that was on its way to search for missing comrades who were rumored to have been held hostage in these villages. Three women priests led the villagers to lie down along the street to their villages in order to stop the convoy and the possible violence against the villages. The action of the villagers seemed to have worked because the military commander then changed his order from door to door inspection, which could have provoked violence, to negotiation under the guarantee of the three women priests. After finding out that the rumor was not true, the military left. Nonetheless, two days later these two villages were burnt down by unidentified people (Ruagadi 2006b).

Only very rarely were women perpetrators of violence. A few of them indeed mentioned that they joined as combatants during the conflicts, even if their roles were just to give support to their men in the battle field, by providing logistics for the group in defending their villages or praying for the awakening of their bravery.

However, women were especially vulnerable in the communal conflicts because of the symbolic value attached to the female body. Women often became the targets of sexual assault as a way of humiliating their broader community as well as a way of inflicting pain and shame on women. As noted in other conflict areas, the female body has symbolic significance to her community, attacking it means humiliating the community for the incapability of its men to protect its women from threat and danger. Hence, sexual attacks against women can be one of the most sensitive aspects of a conflict as it implies psychological wounds for men, whose masculinity is put in question and who are thus marked as incompetent. For all these complex reasons, violence against women tends to be denied and underreported, not only to protect the dignity of the men but also to prevent community retaliation which would prolong the conflict (see e.g. Butalia 2000; Seifert 1999).

Media reports mentioned that a lot of Muslim women from Sintuwulembah – a village that is dominantly occupied by Christians – had been forced to undress and their intimate organs were then touched as they were suspected of hiding amulets. In 2000, some Muslim women were even raped in a *baruga* (customary house) of the Christian village Tambaro (Ecip & Waru 2001: 65). The reports of the incident named the case of Kilo Sembilan (Kilometer Nine is the name of the place where the incidents were supposed to have happened) aroused great controversy. Muslims accused the Christians of being the perpetrators and described it as cruel and immoral.[3] On the other hand, Christian groups whose militia was suspected to be the perpetrators claimed that it was impossible that they had committed those crimes because it was illegitimate and contradictory to their vows of struggle during the conflict. According to some of my key informants in Poso, the group of Christian youths who went into battle in 2000 had to keep three promises: they were forbidden to attack if they were not attacked; to loiter or to steal anything; and to harass women.

The recent investigative team of Komnas Perempuan (National Commission for Women against Violence) was not able to verify the case of Kilo Sembilan and meet the victims of the rape as it was previously reported by the local media; they only heard the stories about the sexual harassment. One of the reasons was that many Muslim women from Sintuwulembah had already moved out of the village and lived in scattered and unknown places. They declined to provide testimony of the sexual violence when the team was gathering data in 2006.

Violence against women in Poso was massive and occurred extensively even after the Malino Peace Accord, among others bomb explosions in several markets during business hours. In a social context where women dominate market activities (both as sellers and buyers), it is probable that such bombs were intentionally set to target women. There were at least three bomb explosions: the central market of Poso (13 November 2004), the market of Tentena (28 May 2005), and the pork market of Maesa, Palu (31 December 2005). On 18 July 2004, Rev. Susianti Tinulele who was preaching in Effata Church in Palu was shot dead. Furthermore, three female students who were on their way to school from Buyumboyo to Poso Town were beheaded by five persons wearing Ninja-like masks on 29 October 2005. A few days later, two other female students who were chatting on the veranda of their lodging in Kasintuwu were shot by two persons on a motorbike. These incidents added to the findings of the Komnas Perempuan's investigation that recorded 61 cases of violence against women in the whole region of Poso after the Malino agreement. The cases encompassed murder, sexual exploitation, forced abortion, sexual slavery, rape, and battering. The perpetrators were mainly identified as police and military personnel who were on duty in the region.[4]

Likewise, the barrier to overcome violence against women was related to patriarchal structures embedded in local traditions and military institutions (forthcoming report of Komnas Perempuan). In terms of local traditions, women who were victims were often intimidated by their male relatives to accept compensation through customary laws. According to customary laws, perpetrators could pay a sum of money or in some cases provide, for instance, a cow as compensation for their crime. The negotiation was made between the perpetrator and the head of the girl's or woman's family under the witness of a customary leader. The victim herself was excluded from the negotiations, because she was considered to be the responsibility of the family head. The victim and all family members have to accept the decision as long as it meets the customary requirements even if the compensation might be far from their expectations. Ironically, while women were the victims, it was the men who represented their families and who negotiated with the (male) perpetrators on behalf of these women.

In the incidents of rape or sexual harassments, women are even blamed to be the guilty ones and are accused of having flirted with the men. Such attitudes are reinforced by idioms and rumors that denigrate women as *tapol* (*tampa bapolo*), that is, women who often change partners. Victims then are often stigmatized as *Koramil* (*Korban rayuan militer*, Victims of military infatuation).[5] This idiom was popular after 2000 in the refugee camps in which a few women were engaged in more intimate relationships either with military/police officers or with their friends. These relationships carried a negative stigma after the relationship had broken, especially if the woman was left with an unwanted pregnancy. In some cases, there were reports of forced abortion (the women were under threat of being shot). A lot of the victims in fact suffered from depression and psychological stress (Media Sangkompo 2004: 13).

Several cases of women abused by members of security forces were sent to the special military court for prosecution; however, such prosecutions never met the victims' demands for justice. Even if the perpetrators were found guilty, they got impunity from their corps. Most of them were not sent to jail. Instead, they provided the victim with some financial compensation and were then assigned to other places. None were held responsible to support the victim after the prosecution. Meanwhile, the costs for attending such trials were not inexpensive for Poso people because they had to travel to Manado (about 400 kilometers north) where the nearest special military court was located. Besides the high traveling and accommodation costs that were never reimbursed, the victims had no protection while reporting their cases.

It was not only difficult, but also sensitive to unveil the violence against women for either personal reasons or because of the fragility of the ongoing peace process. There were at least four reasons why women victims remained silent rather than tell their stories. First, they would feel ashamed if their traumatic experiences were made known to the public. Another aspect here was the difficulties they faced in opening up this past wound, particularly as there was no assistance provided to help them deal with their traumatic experiences. Second, some women had moved away to other places, sometimes working as laborers abroad. Third, many spouses did not allow them to tell their past bitter experiences, preferring them to keep it a secret. Finally, people were worried that, if such cases were exposed, it might jeopardize the peacemaking processes between the communities. Another factor is also the lack of space provided by the government to search for the truth. The government has instead pursued a security approach to the violence and established reconstruction projects which by large ignore women's voices.

Gender in the formal processes of peace-building in Poso

The resolution of the Poso conflict requires an integrated approach, which goes beyond bringing together leaders from the conflicting parties in order to reach a ceasefire agreement. Strengthening the legal structure or rebuilding destroyed public infrastructure such as housing, or providing resettlement is also insufficient if such moves do not pay attention to the needs of the victims of violence and vulnerable groups. Instead peace-building in Poso should be addressed through processes of reconciliation and truth seeking. The government should both investigate what had happened and provide space for those involved to tell of their experiences during the conflict and its resolution. A commitment to reconciliation and truth seeking is needed in order to restore trust in social relationships that have been destroyed due to the conflict. Reconciliation here is not simply a matter of saying sorry or of seeking forgiveness, but implies the recognition and social acceptance of the fact of the occurrence of such a conflict (Kriesberg 2001), which implicitly suggests a process similar to truth seeking. It should thus involve all conflicting parties including victims and vulnerable groups, in order to recognize the range, the extent, and the legacy of violence. In this way, truth seeking can be considered as a stepping stone not only to understand the causes of the conflict, but also to discover ways to achieve social reconciliation (Zurbuchen 2005). Nonetheless, government-sponsored truth-seeking processes are not yet initiated in relation to the violent conflict in Poso.

Since the outbreak of violence, several attempts to end the conflict have been made with the sponsorship of the national and local governments. There were at least twelve meetings involving local leaders (mostly men), which took place from 1998 to 2000, to deliberate ceasefire and end the violence (Damanik 2003: 66–8). One peace effort at this time was meant to revive the customary or traditional idea of *To Poso* (people from Poso). This peace initiative was called *Rujuk Sintuwu Maroso* (reconciliation for strong unity) and was held on 22 August 2000 when 14 customary leaders signed a peace agreement that was to put an end to the violence and achieve consensus for building peace, which was witnessed by former President Abdurrahman Wahid. On this occasion, the ritual of *motambu tana* (burying [something] in the ground) was conducted to mark the accord;[6] there were no efforts taken for legal proceedings as there was no wish to dwell on the previous violent incidents. Unfortunately, the peace did not last long as the violence erupted again in several areas two months later.

A later, more pronounced effort by the central government to end the conflict resulted in Christian and Muslim leaders signing the Malino peace accord on 20 December 2001. Unlike the earlier *Rujuk Sintuwu Maroso* initiative, the Malino peace accord selected representatives from the religious leadership in Poso. The group of leaders attending the meetings consisted of 25 Muslims and 23 Christians. There were only four women from both delegations. At the end of the meetings, they came to a consensus of developing peace and support for social economic reconstruction. Since then, the number of inter-communal attacks has declined, but there has been no end to violence per se; as outlined before, the violence now took shape of sporadic and largely anonymous terror attacks. There were at least 157 violent incidents between December 2001 and December 2005, after Malino (Ruagadi *et al*. 2007: 241). Ironically, an increasing deployment of police and military since the Malino agreement has been unable to prevent this violence.

In many ways, the Malino accord has been unsuccessful. Its reconstruction program has resulted in rampant corruption (Aragon 2007), and its security approach has resulted in the violence taking on a vertical rather than horizontal character, as state security apparatuses increasingly exercise power over citizens and civil society in an effort to break ethno-religious solidarity.[7] The execution of three Catholic peasants – Fabianus Tibo, Marinus Riwu, and Domingus Da Silva who were accused of being leaders of Christian militia – on the eve of 22 September 2006 led to the attack on police camps in Pamona Selatan by an anonymous group of villagers. On 22 January 2007, a violent clash between some Muslims and the police, who were hunting several persons accused of having committed a series of crimes and terrors in the area, resulted in the death of 14 people including one police officer. Eleven days earlier, two civilians were shot by the police in a police raid on a village. Another police officer was killed during the mass retaliation against police brutality which this incident had provoked. Rather than reducing violence, security operations after Malino have only exacerbated the deep community wounds resulting from past traumatic experiences.

One of the reasons underlying the failure of both the *Rujuk Sintuwu Maroso* and the Malino peace accord was the failure to take into account the needs and perspectives of all the victims and survivors of the Poso conflict. This is also an issue of social injustice. For example, the Malino peace accord primarily accommodated the perspectives and interests of elites (whether traditional or religious), who claimed to represent the diverse needs and perspectives of the conflicting parties. The legal process instituted by the Malino accord has proven to be totally ineffective, with no prosecutions made in the regional court because of mass intimidation. Neither has there been any effort to seek the truth in line with the grassroots' demands to know what had really happened in their community. Moreover, meetings that took place in preparation of Malino and after were dominated by men and hence had a male bias. Not only were women less represented in the meetings, but there were also no special policies implemented to address the gender-based problems women experienced during the conflict and its aftermath.

For instance, violence against women experienced during, and in the aftermath of, the conflict, such as forced abortion, sexual slavery, and battering were never deliberated upon by the local authorities. There was no special attention to women's reproductive health in reconstruction efforts even though many health facilities were damaged during the conflict. This resulted in severe shortfalls in service delivery to women in the areas of maternal and infant health care during and after the supposed peace accord (Putranti & Subagya 2005). The government post-Malino reconstruction policies have also discriminated against female program beneficiaries at the grassroots level as only men were registered as household heads.

While government policies ignored women's needs in terms of accessing public services, women's problems became the concern of social workers and NGO activists. Here women were involved to a great extent in the delivery of services and a wide range of activities from food distribution and the building of shelters in refugee camps, through microfinance programs, trauma and psychological services, to health care provision, and water and sanitation planning. Of relevance to this study is also the extent to which women were included in non-governmental reconciliation activities and informal inter-communal dialogue.

Women's limited engagement in formal peace-building and reconstruction activities was derived from cultural expectations and stereotypes relating to women's and men's different social roles. The idealized social role accorded to women of both communities in Poso is primarily as caregiver of children and the household. The exclusion of women in formal reconciliation activities was based on the notion that men are the 'natural' leaders of their community and the household. The formal political arena was therefore perceived as a male domain, with men being seen as the appropriate representatives of the household and the community. Women were instead largely viewed as lacking leadership skills and not competent to tackle public issues. Even when women were involved in meetings, their contribution was limited to minor tasks. Another factor here was Poso women's relative lack of formal education, knowledge, and skills, with the majority of women having limited education due to the traditional roles discussed earlier. Although Poso women are not illiterate, their educational attainment is mostly elementary or up to junior high school. Only a few activists have completed their education at the senior high school or university level. This lack of education and knowledge often discouraged women from speaking up in public and from disagreeing with the dominant (male) voices from the community in public situations.

Yet, despite women's highly constrained public role in peace-building and reconciliation efforts, at the informal level the women of Poso have played an effective and significant role. Women's informal activities often addressed people's immediate needs. They also approached reconciliation with greater flexibility and resilience than more formal mechanisms. Unfortunately, due to limited institutional resources, women's activities here tended to be fragmented and parochial. Most activities were dependent on donor funds, and when donors left, many of these activities could not last long.[8] Nevertheless, and as discussed in more detail later, the involvement of women in informal reconciliation activities – albeit limited in nature and duration – points to the value of women's broader role in reconciliation activities in general. Unfortunately, women's activities in rehabilitation and reconciliation in the post-conflict situation have been submerged by the dominant discourse on conflict and resolution, which emphasizes the grand narratives of formal peace accords followed by official rehabilitation programs and reconstruction activities.

Women as actors for reconciliation

Since women are at the forefront when it comes to fostering and reviving social encounters, they played a prominent role in reweaving the social fabrics torn by communal conflict in Poso. First, women who worked for humanitarian agencies provided emergency aid during the conflict and promoted peacemaking. Other women engaged in public domains such as civil servants, traders, or farmers were quick to rebuild social relationships not only with their colleagues and clients, but also among the wider societies. Women were also noted as initiators and participants in public gatherings for reconciliation in many villages (Setara 2006).

Women contributed to the peace process in various ways at the household level. Their role in educating children provided them the chance to heal traumatic experiences and soothe the sense of bitterness. One informant reported that she continuously encourages her 12-year-old son to look to a better future by avoiding conflict and strengthening a sense of solidarity amongst people regardless of their religion and other differences. Once, she was shocked by her son's anger when he learnt that a friend of hers had a different religion. She reported that at the time he discovered this, her son picked up a knife and drove her friend from her house shouting, "You are cruel, fierce ... I hate you ... Get out of here!" The mother tried to calm down her son and told him that her friend was not like that, that he was not involved in the violence, and, more generally, that there was no principal correlation between religion and violence.

Many women also took an expanded economic role during the conflict, which later contributed indirectly to an environment more conducive to reconciliation and peace. In order to provide food for their families, many women had taken on extra work, such as working as hired laborers in the nearby farms, household servants, or engaging in market activities. With men's limited mobility outside the house because of the conflict, women often had to take long walks to the forest (to search for forest products) or sell crops from the garden of their native village in order to provide food for their families. Many shouldered the burden of being the sole protector and supporter of their families, particularly if their spouses were dead. This expanded role later proved important in giving some women greater self-esteem and confidence to take part in decision-making processes not only for their households, but also in peace and informal reconciliation-related activities.

Women in Poso have long been involved in market activities, with the market considered to be a female domain. Generating an income outside the household is considered an extension of women's primary responsibility to maintain the welfare of the household. Due to the conflict, several women who were previously focusing on agricultural activities or housework became engaged in market activities as a result of their need to earn additional cash. When the conflict was less pronounced, the markets were densely occupied by women selling agricultural products. Other women made cakes or snacks and distributed these door-to-door by themselves in their neighborhood and throughout their villages. Their varied economic encounters with different people in the market and elsewhere helped to erode prejudice and to establish a situation conducive to peace.

Women's involvement in expanded public space and economic activities was mainly motivated by their desire to protect and provide livelihood for their families and their communities, rather than a conscious attempt to move beyond a confinement to the private sphere. Nevertheless, their presence and involvement in such public spheres contributed to the development of peace in a number of informal but no less important ways. For example, through their social interaction in public arenas, women have been able to tell different community members about the everyday situation in their villages and areas. The sharing of such experiences acts as a catalyst for social reintegration by paving the way for reconciliation with regard to the decline of social trust and a sense of insecurity among the Poso people.

The conflict has also fostered women's agency at the community level especially in terms of organizing and delivering social services for the community. Several women are engaged as social workers in refugee camps and villages. They carry out humanitarian programs and are involved in trauma healing, income generating, education, and health activities facilitated by NGOs and donors. The activities and support of the organizations give them opportunities to develop skills in leadership and self-confidence in public affairs, especially for community decision-making processes.[9]

The NGO campaigns for reconciliation seem to complement rather than contradict existing women's organizations, that is *Pembinaan Kesejahteraan Keluarga* (Family Welfare Movement), *Kantor Pemberdayaan Perempuan Poso* (Poso Women's Empowerment Office), and religious organizations such as *Aisyiyah* or *Fatayat NU* (women's organizations affiliated with Muhammadiyah and Nahdlatul Ulama respectively, the largest Muslim organizations in Indonesia), and *Komisi Wanita Gereja Kristen* (Women's Commission of the Christian Church). Although such organizations have been criticized for ideologically promoting patriarchal structures (Suryakusuma 2004), to some extent they are nonetheless effective in mobilizing women to participate in grassroots social activities. Social workers and activists often cooperate with these organizations to advocate community-based programs and activities, especially in relation to women's empowerment and reconciliation.

Besides the aforementioned organizations, there are also mass organizations and networks that play an important role in supporting peace-building and facilitating education on women's rights. Some of these include *Kelompok Perjuangan Kesetaraan Perempuan Sulawesi Tengah* (KPKPST, Central Sulawesi Group for Women's Equity), *Koalisi Perempuan Indonesia* (KPI, Indonesian Women's Coalition), *Lembaga Pemberdayaan Masyarakat Sipil* (LPMS, Institute for Empowering Civil Society), and, in Tentena, *Kelompok Kajian Tana Poso* (Study Group on Poso Motherland). All the organizations were relatively newly established after the outbreak of the communal conflict and had organized various activities from supporting management of credit unions, providing training on establishing small-scale enterprise, to convening social gatherings to reintegrate the community in different refugee camps or villages where they have been segregated along ethnic and religious lines. Most of the organizations' committees and members are women who come from different ethnic and religious backgrounds. They worked together focusing on problems of women affected by the conflict. They developed activities to help them deal with their difficulties and social constraints in the public sphere in which women were discriminated against and so to obtain public services.

Conclusion

The prolonged conflict in Poso has left feelings of bitterness and suffering amongst people who lost their families or their livelihoods, or who were displaced from their homes. The violent conflict also had particular gender dimensions. As this chapter has shown, men and women experienced the conflict differently – both as victims and perpetrators – and they developed different kinds of coping strategies. There is plenty of evidence of women's expanded role in public activities both during the conflict and in their efforts to promote social reconciliation. Yet during the conflict, women were also more vulnerable to sexual violence; women were often targeted during the communal conflict precisely because sexual violence against women acted to symbolically emasculate and humiliate men for their failure to protect the women of their community. Violence against women could also provoke retaliation and thus prolong the communal conflict.

Only a few women were involved in the conflict as combatants. Rather, women attempted to prevent the escalation of violence, often silently and secretly. If they supported the battle, women helped fighters by providing logistics, preparing food, or through prayer. During the conflict, women struggled to protect their families and often made crucial decisions in relation to their survival. They were not only forced to flee their homes in order to look for safe places, but they also took on remunerative activities in order to provide food for their families due to men's limited (safe) mobility outside the home. Several women became the primary breadwinners for their families during this time.

Not only did women become dominant actors in the productive activities during the conflict, but they also contributed significantly to the social process of reconciliation. Their expanded role in the public spheres enabled them to reweave the social fabrics torn apart by the conflict. In their roles outside their homes, women have been able to mediate peace and tolerance at the grassroots level, where prejudices that support ethnic and religious divisions are often strongest. In contrast to their important role in promoting reconciliation at the grassroots level – the prominent theme of this volume – women have been less involved in the formal peace efforts. As a result, gender-specific needs and problems related to women's social identities and experience of the conflict have been ignored in the formal reconstruction policies and rehabilitation programs.

Considering the experiences of Poso women, the study suggests that the formal peace process and reconciliation should also involve women. The representation of women would reduce tension and erode mistrust of the conflicting parties because women were more flexible in interacting with other groups beyond their religious and ethnic affiliation, thus crossing the conflict boundaries. Moreover, women's perception of the conflict was different from the dominant discourse that was male biased. For women, the violent conflict brought about nothing but sufferings with the increasing tasks in the households dealing with the deterioration of livelihood. The integration of women in the official process as mediators would enhance peacemaking due to their greater roles at the grassroots level. Formal peace efforts should also pay attention to women's specific problems such as the increasing social economic burden of the household on women's shoulders, the lack of health facilities for children and maternal health care, and discrimination in access to public services and resources. To give priority to women's needs in rehabilitation programs would be fundamental for gender justice as well as for preventing women's re-victimization.

In addition to that, the reconciliation process could be supported by strengthening the women's arena to articulate their voices. The present social arena alternated the stagnancy of legal systems and the patriarchal structure of customary tradition that was disadvantageous to women. The women's arena could be made by establishing networks among the existing women's organizations that could also partly fulfill the function of a truth commission. The availability of safe public spaces for women to tell their stories of violence to relatives, neighbors, and to other ethnic and religious groups could have a therapeutic value and help women release the burden of their trauma. Women's narratives could also disclose abuses that could be used in formal legal proceedings and reforming the future of social relationship that is gender sensitive. These are some important lessons we can learn from the Poso case.

Notes

1 For a discussion of social segregation in Poso during colonialism and the construction of ethnic and religious identity see Schrauwers (2000) and Aragon (2000). In the postcolonial period, this social segregation of the society influenced the dynamics of local politics leading up to the violence in 1998.
2 It seems impossible to count the number of casualties and the amount of damage due to the wide and scattered areas of the violent incidents and the continuing sectarian tensions in the area. For estimations of casualties and material loss, see Lembah et al. (2000) who recorded 2004 deaths, 129 seriously injured people, 20 women raped and harassed, 4,338 houses burnt and destroyed, and 11 churches and 6 mosques burnt. Ecip et al. (2002) reported 267 deaths, 187 injured people, 6,984 houses damaged, 17 churches and 2 mosques burnt. Damanik (2003) pointed to 602 deaths, 57 mosques and 72 churches damaged. Al-Anshari and Suhardi (2006) show the name list of 202 Muslims who were killed in 2000.
3 There is a video film entitled *Tragedy of Poso* narrated in the Arabic language that shows the suffering of Muslims who were claimed to be the target of violence. The film therefore calls for jihad in the area. It is circulated largely outside of Poso. Such religious sentiments also appeared in the book *Tragedi Poso*, edited by Fauzan Al-Anshari and Ahmad Suhardi (2006).
4 Peer group discussion on the findings of Human Rights Watch on Women Violation in Poso 1998–2005, Komnas Perempuan, 17 February 2007.
5 *Koramil* is officially the acronym for *Komando Rayon Militer* (Office of Military Districts), but it is here used to insinuate women who have had special relationships with military personnel.
6 *Motambu tana* is an indigenous ritual to resolve conflict, for example conflict between kinship groups or ethnic alliances due to land dispute and other resource issues. In the ritual, a buffalo is killed and its head is buried which symbolizes the burial of their past conflict. After the ceremony, all parties involved in the conflict are not allowed any more to open up their past memories. In other words, they have to forget what they have done in order to forgive for the future.
7 Conclusion from a discussion in the Poso Crisis Center (local NGOs network to advocate peacemaking) on 21 January 2007.
8 The number of NGOs and grassroots activities funded by international agencies declined noticeably after the tsunami in Aceh and the earthquake in Yogyakarta, which triggered a reorientation of humanitarian relief efforts. Nevertheless, some local NGOs and social workers are still active in Poso and continue to involve women in peace-building activities.

9 There were at least eight donor agencies providing grant support for humanitarian activities under the United Nations' Office for Coordination of Humanitarian Affairs (UN-OCHA) since 2002. They run their programs in collaboration with local NGOs (OCHA Sulawesi Tengah 2004). Unfortunately, the number of women engaged in the activities was not well recorded, but several sources claimed women beneficiaries in the program. According to my informant, there were 63 NGOs in Poso during and after the conflict. Most of the NGOs employed several women for their humanitarian activities.

References

Aditjondro, G.J. (2002) 'Laporan penelitian pemekaran KODAM di Sulawesi', unpublished paper, Jakarta: NDI.

—— (2004) 'Kerusuhan Poso dan Morowali, akar permasalahan dan jalan keluarnya', paper presented at the Propatria Symposium, Jakarta, 7 January.

Al-Anshari, F. and Suhardi, A. (2006) *Tragedi Poso*, Indonesia: Departemen Data dan Informasi Majelis Mujahidin & Forum Silaturrahmi dan Perjuangan Umat Islam Poso.

Agustiana, E.T. and Pakpahan, M. (2004) *Women and Peace Building. Central Sulawesi and North Maluku*, Jakarta: UNDP and BAPPENAS.

Aragon, L.V. (2000) *Fields of the Lord. Animism, Christian Minorities and State Development in Indonesia*, Honolulu: University of Hawaii Press.

—— (2001) 'Communal violence in Poso, Central Sulawesi: where people eat fish and fish eat people', *Indonesia*, 72: 45–79.

—— (2007) 'Elite competition in Central Sulawesi', in H. Schulte Nordholt and G. van Klinken (eds) *Renegotiating Boundaries. Local Politics in Post-Suharto Indonesia*, Leiden: KITLV Press.

Butalia, U. (2000) *The Other Side of Silence: Voices from the Partition of India*, Durham: Duke University Press.

Columbijn, F. and Lindblad, J.T. (eds) (2002) *Roots of Violence in Indonesia*, Leiden: KITLV Press.

Coppel, C.A. (ed.) (2006) *Violent Conflicts in Indonesia*, London: Routledge.

Damanik, R. (2003) *Tragedi Kemanusiaan Poso. Menggapai Surya Pagi melalui Kegelapan Malam*, Jakarta: PBHI, Yakoma PGI and CD Bethesda.

Ecip, S.S. and Waru, D. (2001) *Kerusuhan Poso yang Sebenarnya*, Jakarta: Global Mahardika Netama.

Ecip, S.S., Waru, D. and Kunandar, A.Y. (2002) *Rusuh Poso, Rujuk Malino*, Makasar: Cahaya Timur.

Gopin, M. (2001) 'Forgiveness as an element of conflict resolution in religious cultures: walking the tightrope of reconciliation and justice', in M. Abu-Nimer (ed.) *Reconciliation, Justice and Coexistence: Theory & Practice*, Lanham, Maryland: Lexington Books.

ICG (International Crisis Group) (2005) 'Weakening Indonesia's Mujahidin networks: lessons from Maluku and Poso', *Asia Report*, No. 103, Jakarta and Brussels: ICG.

—— (2007) 'Jihadism in Indonesia: Poso on the edge', *Asia Report*, No.127, Jakarta and Brussels: ICG.

Jurnal Perempuan (2004) 'Perempuan dan pemulihan konflik', Vol. 33, Jakarta: Yayasan Jurnal Perempuan.

Kriesberg, L. (2001) 'Changing forms of coexistence', in M. Abu-Nimer (ed.) *Reconciliation, Justice and Coexistence: Theory & Practice*, Lanham, Maryland: Lexington Books.

Lederach, J.P. (1997) *Building Peace. Sustainable Reconciliation in Divided Societies*, Washington DC: United States Institute of Peace.

Lembah, H.S.F., Bahar, S. and Kerrololo, P. (2000) 'Kronologis konflik, akar permasalahan, dampaknya, strategi pengelolaan konflik dan prospeknya', in S. Mappangara (ed.) *Respon Militer terhadap Konflik Sosial di Poso*, Palu: Yayasan Bina Warga Sulawesi Tengah.

Mangun, N.H. (2002) 'Perempuan tulang punggung ekonomi keluarga pasca konflik (kerusuhan) Poso', *Jurnal Perempuan*, 24: 35–47.

McKay, S. (2000) 'Gender justice and reconciliation', *Women's Studies Forum*, 23(5): 561–70.

Media Sangkompo (2004) *Operasi Kelar 'Koramil' Muncul*, Vol. 4, Juni–Juli.

Moser, C.O.N. and Clark, F.C. (2001) *Victims, Perpetrators or Actors? Gender, Armed Conflict and Political Violence*, New Delhi: Kali for Women.

OCHA Sulawesi Tengah (2004) *Panduan Singkat, Kegiatan Kemanusiaan dan Pembangunan di Sulawesi Tengah*, document paper, June 4, Palu: OCHA.

Putranti, B.D. and Subagya, Y.T. (2005) *Jerat Bantuan, Jerit Pengungsi: Penanganan Kesehatan Reproduksi di Poso Pasca Konflik*, Yogyakarta: Universitas Gadjah Mada (Pusat Studi Kependudukan) and Ford Foundation.

Ruagadi, A.E.S. (2006a) 'Ibu Ruaedah: kisah sirup orson dan valium', in A. Rahmawati, M.F. Cahyono and F. de Djalong (eds) *Perlawanan Tanpa Kekerasan. Cerita-cerita dari Daerah Konflik di Indonesia*, Yogyakarta: CSPS.

—— (2006b) 'Tinagari, perempuan pemberani', in A. Rahmawati, M.F. Cahyono and F. de Djalong (eds) *Perlawanan Tanpa Kekerasan. Cerita-cerita dari Daerah Konflik di Indonesia*, Yogyakarta: CSPS.

Ruagadi, A.E.S., Waru, D., Lempadelly, S.V.E. and Agus, S.A. (2007) 'Bersatu kita teguh di tana Poso', in A. Amirrachman (ed.) *Revitalisasi Kearifan Lokal. Studi Resolusi Konflik di Kalimantan Barat, Maluku dan Poso*, Jakarta: International Center for Islam and Pluralism and European Commission.

Sangaji, A. (2005) *Rumput Kering di Balik Anyir Darah: Konteks Etno Religius dari Tragedi Kemanusiaan Poso*, Palu: Yayasan Tanah Merdeka.

—— (2007) 'The security forces and communal violence in Poso', in H. Schulte Nordholt and G. van Klinken (eds) *Renegotiating Boundaries. Local Politics in Post-Suharto Indonesia*, Leiden: KITLV Press.

Schrauwers, A. (2000) *Colonial 'Reformation' in The Highlands of Central Sulawesi, Indonesia, 1892–1995*, Canada: University of Toronto Press.

Seifert, R. (1999) 'The second front. The logic of sexual violence in wars', in M.B. Steger and N.S. Linds (eds) *Violence and its Alternatives: An Interdisciplinary Reader*, New York: St. Martin's Press.

Setara (2006) *Menebar Janji, Menuai Tagihan: Catatan Kritis dari Dialog Terbuka*, Edisi V Thn. II, Palu: KPKPST.

Suryakusuma, J. (2004) *Sex, Power and Nation. An Anthology of Writings 1979–2003*, Jakarta: Metafora Publishing.

Tempo (2007a) 'Penyergapan di Tanah Runtuh', Edisi 29 Januari–4 Februari: 24–31.

—— (2007b) 'Mohamad Basri: "Kami Ini Hanya Kerbau"', Edisi 12–18 Februari: 30–2.

Turshen, M. (2001) 'The political economy of rape: an analysis of systematic rape and sexual abuse of women during armed conflict in Africa', in C.O.N. Moser and F.C. Clark (eds) *Victims, Perpetrators or Actors? Gender, Armed Conflict and Political Violence*, New Delhi: Kali for Women.

van Klinken, G. (2007) *Communal Violence and Democratization in Indonesia. Small Town Wars*, London and New York: Routledge.
Wijaksana, M.B. (2002) 'Reruntuhan jiwa: trauma perempuan Poso', *Jurnal Perempuan*, 24: 49–62.
Zurbuchen, M.S. (2005) 'Historical memory in contemporary Indonesia', in M.S. Zurbuchen (ed.) *Beginning to Remember: The Past in the Indonesian Present*, Singapore: Singapore University Press.

Part IV
Victim–perpetrator conceptualizations
History education, civil society, and religion

9 Reconciliation through history education

Reconstructing the social memory of the 1965–66 violence in Indonesia

Grace Leksana

Introduction

Close to dawn on 1 October 1965, seven teams of soldiers boarded trucks in an isolated rubber grove south of Jakarta and headed for the houses of seven army generals inside the city. Their aim was to capture the generals, dead or alive. They were largely successful. Only one team failed to accomplish its mission; its target, the Defense Minister, General Nasution, managed to escape, leaving his adjutant, a lieutenant, to be abducted by mistake. The soldiers sped back to the grove located in an area called Lubang Buaya, next to the Air Force's Halim airbase. With three of the generals either dead or dying from wounds inflicted when they were abducted, the soldiers decided at some point later that morning to kill all of the officers and dump their corpses down a well. The organizers of this early morning action also seized the national radio station in Jakarta and announced the name of their group: the September 30th Movement (*Gerakan 30 September*, abbreviated as G30S).

This abduction and the killing of seven army officers has become one of the most important events in Indonesia's history. The army's second in command, Major General Suharto, quickly took charge of the army and attacked the G30S forces in and around the Halim airbase. He accused the Communist Party of Indonesia (PKI) of having masterminded the action and then began a wholesale campaign to suppress members of the party and affiliated organizations. Suharto's army, from early October 1965 to mid-1966, orchestrated the arrests of over one million people and the killing of hundreds of thousands. In the name of defeating the G30S, people were detained indefinitely without charge and without adequate food or medical care, leading to many deaths due to malnutrition and disease. Many prisoners were either summarily executed or disappeared. Even the some 1.5 million people who survived and were eventually released were classified as 'ex-political prisoners' and treated as pariahs. This anti-communist campaign involved many gross human rights violations and unnecessary suffering. Those who organized the repression ruled Indonesia for the subsequent 32 years and thus largely controlled what was said in public about it. They remained silent about their atrocities even while speaking of the abstract process of 'crushing of the PKI' as a glorious and noble event.

In the midst of the anti-PKI violence of 1965–66, Suharto's army overthrew President Sukarno and established a new dictatorial form of government. After becoming the de facto president in March 1966, Suharto's supporters began naming the new government as the 'New Order' and referring to Sukarno's presidency (from 1945 to 1965) as the 'Old Order'. This so-called New Order strove to control Indonesian society in all respects. The school system was redesigned as a tool of indoctrination. The goal was to create obedient subjects. I am one of those students who experienced this system. In my primary school years, from late 1980s to the early 1990s, my history teacher repeatedly told us about the villainy of the PKI, about how it was a cruel, bloodthirsty party that had to be suppressed. I was not, however, told about the horrifying violence that Suharto's army and its civilian supporters used to suppress the PKI. The suffering of my fellow Indonesians accused of being PKI was not something I was supposed to even know about, much less care about. It was assumed that whatever suffering 'the PKI' endured was nothing more than just desserts.

This so-called New Order ended with Suharto's resignation as president in May 1998. The end of the Suharto regime opened up new possibilities for making the government more democratic. This post-Suharto period has come to be called the Reformation (*Reformasi*). After 1998, a greater variety of people have been speaking up about the violence of 1965–66 and the state propaganda about that time has come under some suspicion. Facts about the arrests, mass killings, and sufferings of the victims and their families, have been revealed by the victims and by human rights activists.[1]

Only two years after Suharto's resignation, the upper house of parliament (*Majelis Permusyawaratan Rakyat*, MPR) whose members had been newly chosen through free elections, passed a law that required the government to create a Truth and Reconciliation Commission (TRC). One of the past atrocities that the TRC was expected to handle was the mass violence of 1965–66. But many politicians and government officials, accustomed to the state propaganda of the Suharto years, were wary about new information coming out about the violence. While hoping that the TRC could foster national unity through reconciliation, they had many reservations about the 'truth' side of the TRC. It took the government four years to finally draft the regulations by which the TRC would operate. Even then, the regulations (approved by the MPR as Law No. 27 of 2004) were rather vague and ill-considered. Before the TRC was formed, the Constitutional Court, through a decision in December 2006, struck down the MPR's 2004 law as unconstitutional.[2] The MPR can revise the law but it appears the consensus in the MPR is to just let the law die. After all, the politicians are not receiving a lot of public support for the TRC.

The lack of support for the proposed TRC reflects a fundamental problem regarding historical knowledge in Indonesia. Many Indonesians know so little about the violence of 1965–66 so they do not understand that atrocities were actually committed. Therefore they see little need for the TRC. All the new books that have come out from the victims since Suharto's fall have not made a major impact on the society's historical perceptions. Most people still know next to nothing about the victims' perspectives. For three decades, the regime had incessantly stated that everyone connected with the PKI (meaning millions of people) were not victims but perpetrators, collectively responsible for murdering six army generals and a lieutenant, and preparing a social revolt. The army, it was said, saved the nation from PKI terror and thus did nothing wrong. Many Indonesians have either refused to see the former members of PKI as victims or adopted a very skeptical approach towards their claims of victimhood.[3] They have had great difficulty accepting the idea that the 1965–66 violence was a humanitarian disaster, an event in which many people suffered unnecessarily. Despite all the new information about the events of 1965–66, the school system's curriculum on history has not changed in any significant way.

In order to initiate the reconciliation process of Indonesian society, we need to start with the very basic element within the 1965–66 discourse, that is, our social memory about the tragedy. The idea that the single narration of the New Order is absolute should be contested. Our memories need to go beyond the heroic narratives of the generals or the cruelty of PKI, and start to include other narratives that have been silenced for years. There should be a constant dialogue of these narratives, as a process of reconstructing our social memory on the 1965–66 tragedy. There has to be some awareness first that over one million people were indeed victims of military repression and were treated unjustly. Legal processes for reconciliation will not be enough to address the complexity of this case. I think this is where public education about the 1965–66 violence can play an important role. I see reconciliation in this case as not just a matter between victims and perpetrators – the people directly involved in a particular human rights violation – but as a broader process involving the reintegration of the victims back into the national community. Indonesian society as a whole, including the generation born after 1965, needs to reconcile with the victims. The stigmatization and demonization of the victims as 'traitors' and 'murderers' is ongoing. That kind of broader reconciliation will require the society to understand the injustices these victims experienced and the lies the Suharto regime told about historical events.

This chapter is derived from my experiences as a member of the Sekitarkita Community and the Indonesian Institute of Social History (*Institut Sejarah Sosial Indonesia*, ISSI), two organizations based in Jakarta that have been working on issues of the 1965–66 tragedy and initiating public education as part of their work.[4] We have been conducting a series of history discussions with students and working with history teachers since 2004. Based on these experiences, this chapter will address two issues. It will first examine how the New Order shaped the social memory about the events of 1965–66. Second, it will examine how history education reform in the schools has the potential to alter Indonesia's social memory about the 1965–66 events, and thus improve the chances of reconciliation between the victims and the national community. I will argue that in a context where social memory has been shaped for so long by a military dictatorship, public education can contribute significantly to the reconciliation process. I will also problematize the common victim-perpetrator dichotomy which sometimes leads to a limited understanding of reconciliation. It is important that a reconciliation process should not rely merely on legal-formal practices, but also include efforts within the social-cultural sphere at all levels, from the grassroots to the national government's policy-making process.

Constructing Indonesia's social memory

Once independence was gained in 1949, the history of Indonesia was written with one main purpose in mind: to build a sense of nationalism. As van Klinken (2005: 234) has stated, "after independence, the precariousness of the state, as most Indonesian elites soon perceived it, lent the 'history for nation building' project a sense of urgency, and raised its stakes". With the rise of the Suharto regime, the idea of nationalist historiography changed. If before 1965, the main enemy in the national narrative was Dutch colonialism, after 1965, the main enemy became a group of fellow Indonesians: those involved in the communist party. The Suharto regime, while demonizing the communists, even those of the 1920s who had rebelled against the Dutch colonial state, extolled the military as the nation's most steadfast hero. The Suharto regime designed history books so that the regime appeared as a glorious fulfillment of the nationalist movement and not as a descent into an anti-democratic, murderous military dictatorship, something early nationalists had never desired (McGregor 2007: 217). The New Order version of history was a simple story of a heroic military and a cruel communist party. One of the most important propagandists of the military dictatorship who played a key role in composing the official version of the 1965–66 events was Nugroho Notosusanto. As Head of the Armed Forces History Centre (1965–85) and Education Minister (1983–85), he was the military's main historian (McGregor 2007: 39).

The Suharto regime, in imposing its version of history, eliminated all others. Literature that contradicted the official propaganda was banned. The regime's handpicked parliament passed a resolution in 1966 to ban the distribution of any literature about Marxism-Leninism. This law still stands today. In practice, the law has justified banning all left-wing writing even if it is not strictly Marxist-Leninist. Also, it has meant banning books published before 1965, even those written during the nationalist struggle for independence. What had been classics of Indonesian literature were entered into the official black list. Pramoedya Ananta Toer, for instance, an influential, famous writer, was imprisoned for 14 years (1965–79) and all his works were banned.

In shaping Indonesia's social memory, the Suharto regime built what Pierre Nora has called "sites of memory" (Schreiner 2005: 269), places that possess the capability to store memory and to trigger acts of remembering. General Suharto recommended the memorialization of the disused well in Lubang Buaya shortly after the bodies of the seven victims were removed from it (McGregor 2007: 70). As early as 1967 the army began to work on constructing an elaborate monument at the well. The monument, known as the Sacred Pancasila Monument, shows the seven officers standing in front of a massive sculpture of Garuda, the mythical bird that is the national symbol.

Surrounding the base of the monument is a bas-relief depicting scenes of the PKI's brutality and the army's heroic acts. The army later built a museum next to

Figure 9.1 The Sacred Pancasila Monument, with the seven army officers and the national symbol – Garuda (Photo courtesy: Indonesian Institute of Social History)

the monument. Opened in 1990, the museum, called the Museum of Communist Treachery, shows dioramas that depict alleged incidents of PKI brutality from 1945 to 1965. This museum has become a compulsory destination for school field trips. Suharto used the monument as the site for an annual public ceremony. Every year on 1 October, an official ceremony was held there to reaffirm Indonesian society's commitment to Pancasila, the state's ideology. At these ceremonies, the seven army officers killed by G30S, posthumously named the Seven Heroes of the Revolution, were honored.

The army also had people to visualize the event. Every year, from 1984 to 1997, the national television screened the state's propaganda film, *The Betrayal of the 30 September Movement/Communist Party of Indonesia.* Four hours long, the film showed a horrifying depiction of the kidnapping and killing of the army officers. It also showed events that were fabricated by army intelligence agents, events that never occurred, such as women of an organization affiliated with PKI, Gerwani (*Gerakan Wanita Indonesia*), dancing and singing "Genjer-genjer" after slashing the officers' bodies with razor blades.[5] In schools, the film was often shown as a part of history class. Some universities showed it to students during their first week on campus to ensure the students were sufficiently anti-PKI.

The government ensured textbooks contained standard information about the so-called 'treachery' of the PKI. The government released the *Indonesian National History Textbook* (Sejarah Nasional Indonesia) in 1976. Consisting of six volumes, this textbook was the first comprehensive Indonesian history series to be written by

Figure 9.2 The diorama of torture located near the Sacred Pancasila Monument. One of the kidnapped generals was depicted as the victim of PKI's brutality (Photo courtesy: Indonesian Institute of Social History)

Indonesians themselves. All of these volumes are still used today as reference works for history textbook writers. The sixth volume of the book covers national history from the period of the Japanese occupation (1942–45) to the founding of the New Order. It reproduces the army's black propaganda about PKI members brutally torturing the seven army officers before killing them (Poesponegoro & Notosusanto 1984).

The *Sejarah Nasional Indonesia* volumes represent what van Klinken (2005: 235) has called the "monological project" of history: "So many internal conflicts (the seeds of change in any unconscripted history) written out of the record. So much context abandoned to see great men and glorious moments better". The Suharto regime propaganda built up an image of a courageous, heroic army on the one side and a brutal villainous PKI on the other. This dichotomy has become the standard feature of Indonesia's history writing on the tragedy, resulting in a black-and-white narrative that disregards all the social-political factors which contributed to this historical event.

Indonesia's social memory on the 1965–66 tragedy was largely formed through history education, sites of memory, visualizations of the event, and commemorations. The result is a single narrative that is believed to be the truth by many people in Indonesian society. This narrative engenders a feeling of hatred towards the PKI and everyone related to it and justifies the state's persecution of them. This single version of the 1965 incident imposed by the New Order was based on a systematic silencing of the victims. Even children of victims became affected. One former-female political prisoner from Solo, Central Java, recalled her pain on having to defend her honor before her own children. She returned home after 14 years in prison, without ever being charged, much less tried, of a crime, to find her children believing the state propaganda more than herself:

> It did not feel good, because we had to straighten things up. It was all messed up; even the children blamed their parents. Because they were still young and did not know. And the history education in schools did not tell them. They only knew: 'Whoever is involved with G30S/PKI is bad.' That is what they knew when we asked them. But the little ones ... they had already gone to the university after I got back from 14 years in the camp. So after I got back they asked, 'Mom, why did you join it? People who were involved in G30S/PKI are bad, right?' 'Who told you that?' 'School, history.' That was it. What else could I do? During that time, the government was still like that, no democracy, right? I was sad, really sad. Why didn't they understand their parents' struggle, especially of people like me who joined the [anti-colonial] guerrillas when I was young?
>
> (Sukartiningsih 2004: 108)

Rethinking reconciliation

Minow (1998: 147) has stated that "through collective steps such as prosecutions, truth commissions, memorials, and education, people wager that social responses can alter the emotional experiences of individuals and societies living after mass violence". But the question remains: who are responsible for the collective steps? How should we arrange those steps to achieve reconciliation after mass atrocities? In the case of the 1965–66 tragedy, the end of the New Order era opened up an opportunity for legal processes to deal with the human rights abuses of the tragedy. However, the government has done nothing to deal with the 1965–66 tragedy. The failure to form a TRC was a very significant failure because it was one of the few viable options available to the government. The criminal justice system in Indonesia is too weak and corrupt to handle criminal cases related to the violence of 1965–66, especially when the crimes were committed so long ago and went largely undocumented (van Zyl 2005: 333).

There has been a lot of resistance to the proposals to open up an official forum for discussing the crimes of 1965–66. The resistance has come not only from the perpetrators who, not surprisingly, do not want their crimes to be revealed. It has also come from people who were not directly responsible for the violence, but who were or are members of organizations that were responsible (see e.g. McGregor 2005). Such people have condemned proposals for reconciliation and truth telling to be merely disguised efforts to revive communism.[6] But the resistance has also come from people who are worried about what such a potentially drastic re-evaluation of history will entail for Indonesian national identity. Under the Suharto regime, the demonization of the PKI became institutionalized to the point that many Indonesians became complicit in it. It is now difficult to contemplate the idea that all the history teachers were lying, that all the commemorations were unjustified, that the displays in the national museum were false, and that the people celebrated as heroes were perpetrators of gross human rights violations. Such people believe that Indonesians will become cynical about their national identity and that it is better to sustain the old narrative, even if it is mythical. These people will admit that atrocities were committed, but they do not want them to be extensively investigated for fear that a reopening of the past will prompt the victims to seek revenge and prevent the nation from focusing on the future.[7]

In this political climate, it has been hard for the victims and their families to talk openly about their experiences. Crane (1997: 1376) working from Halbwachs' concept of collective memory, stated that "collective memory exists and is perpetuated in specific groups that exist in discrete times and places". These groups maintain a living relation to the past and it is only within such groups that any individual can remember and express personal memories. For the victims of the 1965–66 tragedy, such as the ex-political prisoners, their families, and the relatives of the disappeared, their stories of suffering belong to themselves alone. They have cultivated their own kind of collective memory. But the collective memory of Indonesia as a nation has understood their suffering to be unworthy of consideration; since they were evil perpetrators, whatever they suffered was just retribution. Reconciliation in this case will have to mean a kind of reconciliation between the collective memory of the victims and that of the nation. People who have been the victims of despotism in the past feel the need to have their pains and sorrows be properly acknowledged by the society around them (Setiawan 2004b: xxii). Their 'truth' needs to be listened to and given a place. Thus, reconciliation in this case involves everyone in the society, not just the people who were directly involved in the violence of 1965–66 as victims or perpetrators.

All of the different ways in which the events of 1965–66 have been narrated by different individuals and groups, at different times and places, contribute to what Zurbuchen (2005: 7) refers to as historical memory: "the intertwined yet discontinuous aspects of individual and social processing in shaping representations of the past in the present". She has added that "the scope of historical memory embraces not only fixed texts or other emerging 'sites of memory', but also processes of configuring memory, moments when the past can be reshaped and outcomes remain unresolved" (Zurbuchen 2005: 8). Indonesia's social memory on the 1965–66 tragedy should be geared towards a more dynamic state so that it is more open to alternative voices. Rather than trying to narrate history in a strict 'hero versus villain' framework, we should be able to think of history that respects the humanity of the different sides of the conflict. When different voices are heard, one hears different ways of narrating the events; accepted facts are rearranged and reinterpreted and new facts are brought forth. In the process, the nation's social memory can be reconstructed. What is important at this point is to create more spaces for discussion, for more information to emerge, and more opportunities for the victims to tell their stories.

The reconstruction of Indonesia's social memory will play a large role within the reconciliation process. For the 1965–66 case, the stigmatization, discrimination, and exclusion of those labeled 'PKI' continues to this day. Again, the reconciliation process has not only to take place between the victims and perpetrators but also with Indonesian society as a whole. Legal efforts, such as court trials, often reinforce this tendency to reduce the complexities of past human rights abuses into a matter of victims and perpetrators. I am not suggesting that trials should always be eschewed. I am only suggesting that trials have their limitations and should not be necessarily considered the main method of dealing with past crimes. As van Zyl (2005: 338) argued, it is important to move beyond "prosecutorial romanticism", meaning the idea that "retributive justice" is the best response to past abuses. He also stated:

> The punishment of perpetrators is crucial to dealing with the past, but it will always be insufficient response to mass atrocity, and any successful attempt to deal with the past must seek to explore other strategies to make victims whole and to prevent a recurrence of past abuse.
>
> (van Zyl 2005: 338)

One important method of reconstructing the nation's social memory is through film since the Suharto regime's film had such a major contribution to constructing the existing social memory. Until Suharto's fall, there had not been an alternative film about the events of 1965–66 produced and shown in Indonesia. No film about those events has yet reached a mass audience, but there have been many films that have been released and shown in a variety of settings. The prominent director, Garin

Nugroho, made the film *Puisi Tak Terkuburkan* (Unconcealed Poetry) in 2000 which showed how prisoners of 1965–66 in Aceh were taken out at night with sacks over their heads to be secretly executed. The excellent Australian-made film, *Shadowplay* (2002, director: Chris Hilton), is the first documentary that presents a careful examination of the mass killings. Another example is Syarikat, an organization that works on reconciling victims and perpetrators and that has put a lot of effort into film-making. It has organized a film-making competition for students about 1965–66 and has produced films on its own (see also Sulistiyanto & Setyadi this volume).

Democratization in history education

Mirroring the many political changes during the post-Suharto period that have made the state more democratic, the teaching of Indonesian history has also become more democratic. The Suharto regime had created a very centralistic curriculum which every educational institution had to implement according to technical guidelines from the central government. The last such curriculum, issued in 1994, resulted in array of problems for the students as well as the teachers.[8] Textbooks had to be used as the only references for teaching. Teachers could not provide their own input. Indeed, teachers were only supposed to get the students to memorize a pre-determined list of facts and were not supposed to encourage the students to think critically. Many officials in the school system did not like this type of education but having little choice, had to follow it. After Suharto fell, they began to propose revisions to this top-down curriculum. In 2001, the Education Department began a limited pilot project to revise the 1994 curriculum. This project uses what is called a Competency-Based Curriculum (*Kurikulum Berbasis Kompetensi*, KBK). The competency approach contains a clear statement of the minimum skills that have to be reached by students at every level of school (Mulyasa 2007: 9). In 2003, the Indonesian government, on the recommendations of the Education Department, passed a law that made this Competency-Based Curriculum into a principle for schools to follow nationwide. The law states that "curriculum on every level and type of education is to develop by the principle of diversification according to educational level, local potencies, and students" (Law No. 20/2003, article 36, clause 2). This law allows schools to make decisions on their own as to how subjects will be taught. The schools only have to be sure that the students learn certain skills.

Stemming from this initiative to de-centralize certain aspects of teaching, the Education Department has also developed since 2006 something it calls the Education Unit Level Curriculum (*Kurikulum Tingkat Satuan Pendidikan*, KTSP). According to KTSP, the development of a curriculum is to be done by teachers, principals, school committees, and educational boards (Mulyasa 2007: 21–2). KTSP gives autonomy to teachers to develop their own curriculum under the supervision of the local district or city government. Ratna Hapsari, a teacher in Public High School 6 in Jakarta and also the head of History Teacher Consultative Group in Jakarta explains:[9]

Our guidelines cover only the basic competencies. These basic competencies allow for a lot of interpretation ... we have to think about which materials are suitable to fulfill competence A, for example. So we are free to interpret. This is the positive point of the new curriculum.

Although KTSP resulted in many debates,[10] it has received general acceptance. The implementation of the KTSP has provided a basis for the reconstruction of Indonesia's social memory of the 1965–66 incident. Teachers can now decide for themselves which materials, books, and methods to use in the classroom. Students are also encouraged to become actively involved in discussions, small-scale research projects, and critical analysis of the materials presented in the class. Therefore, possibilities to discuss the events of 1965–66 have been widened. Ratna Hapsari encourages her students to search for information about the September 30th Movement from different sources:

In our teaching process in school we look at how far, how deep was the involvement of PKI in the September 30th Movement. We ask them to look for information outside the classroom, whether from electronic or printed media. So they look at documents: written documents that can be accessed by the public. They have to bring all of that information into the classroom, and we discuss it later on. They ask me: 'I got this information. Is this true? I got that information. Is that true?' So the class is really active with this kind of discussion. It is what we wanted.[11]

This learning method is also capable of changing the direction of Indonesia's history education. If previously history was just a lesson of recalling dates and names of heroes, now it has become a way to encourage critical and analytical thinking among the students. As Ratna Hapsari has stated:

Actually, history is directed more towards how the students can think critically. Think critically by comparing the existing facts. Based on these facts, what should I do in the future? So it is not only recalling this event, that event, but they also have to think critically.[12]

A student's ability to critically view historical events can be encouraged in many ways, even outside the curriculum guidelines. From October 2004 until January 2005, I was involved in an organization called Sekitarkita Community that conducted a series of discussions in several schools in Jakarta and Tangerang about the issue of human rights and the 1965–66 violence (see Komunitas Sekitarkita 2004a, 2004b). In the beginning of our discussions, we found that students had already attained other information besides the Suharto regime's single narration. For example, some students had come to believe that the G30S had been organized by Suharto to gain the presidential power.[13] Surprisingly, some students also knew about the mass killings during 1965–66, which had never been a topic included in the textbooks and government propaganda. We usually opened the discussion by screening the film *Mass Grave* which is about the exhumation of skeletons from a grave in Central Java by a victims' organization in 2000. Then one of us would provide a short review of the historical context of events. In some of the discussions, we invited a former political prisoner to accompany us and describe his/her experiences to the students. Students were always eager to ask questions during the discussions. Most of the questions pertained to the alleged stories of the PKI's brutality and the various conspiracy theories behind G30S. But the most interesting questions for us were those that pertained to the students' own process of learning. For example, some students asked about how they could determine which information to trust or how should they react to the history lessons that are still taught on the basis of Suharto-era propaganda.

A few school administrators and teachers were resistant to our proposals for in-school discussions. Given that the Suharto regime propaganda persisted for three decades and tended to focus on the 1965–66 events, it is remarkable that we did not face more resistance. One way that we approached some schools was by proposing to speak about a general issue, such as violence against women, rather than the 1965–66 violence specifically.

After holding these discussions in the schools, the Sekitarkita Community conducted a public discussion 'History in the Perspective of Students' on 29 September 2005 in one of the bookstore cafés in Southern Jakarta. Attended by several public and private schools around Jakarta, this was a forum for both students and teachers to talk about their ideas on history education in relation to the 1965–66 events. The discussion was led by four resource persons from different backgrounds: an ex-political prisoner, a highschool student, a historian, and a history teacher. Two clear conclusions emerged from the discussion. First, sources besides official government publications need to be made available to the students and discussed in the classroom. Rarely do history teachers utilize sources apart from the textbooks. Second, spaces for discussions outside of school are needed because the time for history classes during the school hours is so short and because school administrators are often unsupportive of any kind of experimentation in the classroom. Moreover, teachers spoke about their problems in teaching controversial materials (Komunitas Sekitarkita 2005: 2).

Activities to improve history education are underway. Continuing the efforts of the Sekitarkita Community, the Indonesian Institute of Social History (ISSI) has been working with school teachers.[14] In general, ISSI has been encouraging teachers to see history education as a democratic education, a process which involves debates, discussions, and critical thinking among students. Also, ISSI has been providing the teachers with materials. ISSI, in collaboration with the National Commission on Violence against Women and the History Teacher Consultative Group, organized a discussion for teachers on the theme of 'Violence against Women in National History'. Part of the discussion was about the violence against women during the 1965–66 mass imprisonments and killings. The teachers in the discussion agreed that the teacher's role is no longer as a messenger of whatever the government wants to tell the students, but rather as a facilitator who will encourage a critical analysis of historical events and their backgrounds.

The discussion concluded that methods in history education should be reformed and become independent of the sources and pedagogical guidelines provided by the government (ISSI *et al.* 2006). One lesson I have learned from my work with Sekitarkita and ISSI is that there is an urgent need to build critical historical thinking, not only among the students, but also among the teachers.

However, efforts to democratize history education will not be an easy one. Although nowadays different voices are being heard, within the present government itself there are conflicting tendencies. Some officials are open-minded, but many are Suharto-era bureaucrats who insist that the myths of that era be retained. Based on the aforementioned Law No. 20/2003, the Education Department approved a new curriculum in 2004 for national history that allowed some minor changes. One change was that different theories about who was responsible for G30S could be discussed in the textbooks. Some textbook writers began using the term G30S without the suffix that was mandatory during the Suharto years: '/PKI'. These writers left the PKI's responsibility for the movement as an open question. However, the Attorney General, a Suharto-era stalwart, responded by overriding the Education Department's curriculum. He decreed, on his own, in March 2007, that any textbook that did not use the term "September 30th Movement/PKI" (which is G30S/PKI in its Indonesian abbreviation) would be banned (Decision Letter/SK19/A/JA/03/2007 issued on 5 March 2007) (Adam 2007). He stated that the PKI's responsibility for the movement was an incontrovertible historical fact. His office reviewed a variety of textbooks and decided that 13 history textbooks for junior and high schools, published by ten different publishers, could not be used for schools. They lacked that crucial backslash and three-letter suffix. (The bureaucrats in the office were not very good readers; they mistakenly banned some textbooks that did not even cover the years 1965–66.) The police were ordered to confiscate all copies of these textbooks and destroy them. Many newspapers, magazines, and public commentators opposed the decision but it still stands today. This means that the Attorney General's office is now partly responsible for determining what is taught in the schools. Following this decision, a collaboration of history teachers, historians, and human rights activists composed and signed a petition in March 2007 against the Attorney General's decision as a form of obstacle towards democratic education. Unfortunately, the petition has had no real impact so far.

Conclusion

Since the Suharto regime imposed a single version of history upon the society and censored all others, it has been important in this post-Suharto era to open up discussions on national history to a greater diversity of perspectives. In the case of the 1965–66 violence, it has been particularly important to provide a public space where the victims can speak and feel safe about speaking. In working towards the goal of reconciling Indonesian society with the people whom it had so viciously demonized for over three decades, I do not think that it is productive to propose another singular truth to replace the Suharto regime's. The Indonesian public needs to be asked to listen to a plurality of voices. I agree with Esbenshade who, when speaking of post-communist Eastern Europe, sees social memory as a field in which many different people propose ways of understanding the past:

> Party ideologues (the state), dissident writers, intellectuals, nationalist politicians, all claim to portray or shape a 'truer' collective memory, or one more in line with 'true' collective past. In fact they are involved in creating and developing discourses – state socialist discourse, resistance discourse, discourse of intellectual responsibility, nationalist discourse – that compete to shape or take over the 'regime of (memory-) truth'.
>
> (Esbenshade 1995:87)

I do not see social memory as something in which every issue can be understood as either right or wrong. Some issues are clearly a matter of right or wrong; the Suharto regime propagated many lies. The women of Gerwani did not torture and mutilate the bodies of the seven officers captured by G30S. The PKI as an institution, with millions of members, did not organize G30S. Those of us working on transforming social memory do have to defend the truth of certain propositions, but we should not imagine that our task is limited to that. Our task is also to create the spaces in which a greater variety of people can speak about their experiences.

This is a particular task for historians, not for lawyers. Sometimes, legal advocacy for the victims reduces the exploration of past events into an investigative process of 'truth seeking'. The stories of victims, perpetrators, or witnesses are sifted and winnowed for nuggets of factual information that can be used as evidence in the courtroom. Ultimately, what we have to work on is nothing less than national identity, of what it means to be an Indonesian after such mass violence. In a condition where a very narrow version of social memory had been enforced for years, court trials and other forms of legal proceedings might not accomplish very much in changing people's conception of the past. There is not much value in trying to punish individual perpetrators when so many people were involved and when the society as a whole does not recognize that any crimes were committed. The victims of the 1965–66 violence themselves find it impossible to affix criminal responsibility on any one individual or institution. For even if one says that the late General Suharto was ultimately responsible, one still has trouble assessing responsibility of the many civilians and low-level officials who actually carried out the killings. Legal proceedings might be feasible in this case only after there is some widespread agreement on who was responsible for the violence.

This chapter has presented historical education reform as one, often underappreciated, method for reconciliation in the wake of mass violence. With the fall of Suharto in 1998, there has been a great flowering of new publications and discussions about the violence that brought him to power and the experiences of the victims. But there have also been many impediments to any major transformation of social memory and the way that national history is taught. Many people still want to cling to the old myths, as if those were essential to national unity.[15] One can at least say that Indonesians have broken out of the frozen discourse of the Suharto years and begun an ongoing process of rethinking history; a process that would be so essential for any country emerging out of mass violence, be it Argentina, Guatemala, Rwanda, or Bosnia, just to give some examples. In Indonesia, many individuals and organizations are working at the grassroots level in quiet, low-key ways to change how Indonesian history is conceptualized and taught. Perhaps we will see some dramatic changes in the future.

Acknowledgments

I would like to thank John Roosa who has contributed greatly to the editing process of this chapter.

Notes

1 There are many books written by the victims and published after the downfall of Suharto, such as Sulami's *Perempuan – Kebenaran dan Penjara* (1999), or Setiawan's *Aku eks-Tapol* (2003) and *Memoar Pulau Buru* (2004a). There are also several websites that contain alternative information on the 1965 tragedy, organized by NGOs working with the 1965–66 victims: see e.g. http://www.elsam.or.id, http://www.kontras.org, and http://www.progind.net.
2 In April 2006, a coalition of non-governmental organizations and victims' organizations appealed for judicial review of several articles in Law No. 27/2004. The intention was to "straighten out the mechanisms in the TRC so that they are fairer to the victims and enable punitive actions through court trials" (ELSAM 2006: 6). But the Constitutional Court decided to strike down the entire law (see also Sulistiyanto & Setyadi this volume).
3 For example, on 22 May 2006, a seminar in Bandung, held by INCReS (Institute for Culture and Religious Studies), the National Commission of Violence against Women, and the NGO Syarikat Indonesia, was forcibly dispersed by young toughs affiliated with various anti-communist militias. The people attending the seminar, including 60 elderly female victims, felt their lives were in danger (*Suara Pembaruan* 2006).
4 Sekitarkita Community is a civil society organization that focuses on the distribution of information on human rights, culture, and environmental issues. Information is distributed through its website (http://www.sekitarkita.com) and discussions within communities (such as discussion of the 1965–66 tragedy with high school and university students).
5 "Genjer-genjer" is a song created by M. Arif, a member of LEKRA (the Institute of People's Culture, which was accused of being affiliated to the PKI), which describes the poor condition of Indonesian people during the colonial era. Limited food supplies drove the people to eat the leaves of the genjer plant. The song became a hit in 1960s but was banned during the Suharto period because the regime claimed it was associated with the PKI (see Utomo 2003).
6 Many examples could be cited. One is the protest by anti-communist organizations on 24 April 2008 against the ad hoc team of the National Human Rights Commission which was discussing the 1965–66 human rights violations. They demanded the team to be cancelled because it was helping to revive communism (*Antara News* 2008).
7 Personal notes on discussion with the History Teacher Consultative Group, 4 May 2006.
8 Although this curriculum was promulgated in 1993 (with the Decision of Ministry of Culture and Education No. 060/U/1993 and No. 61/U/1993), its implementation started in 1994.

9 Interview with Ratna Hapsari, Jakarta, 15 May 2007.
10 The main debate regarding the KTSP is whether teachers are able to maintain and develop a curriculum autonomously. Teachers are accustomed to following government instructions. Another debate is on whether it is consistent with the government's requirement that students pass a nationwide standardized test before they can graduate from high school. See *Media Indonesia* (2006).
11 Interview with Ratna Hapsari, Jakarta, 15 May 2007.
12 Interview with Ratna Hapsari, Jakarta, 15 May 2007.
13 Although this knowledge still revolves around assigning singular 'blame' on a 'mastermind', it shows that these students had already accessed other interpretations of the movement.
14 ISSI is a non-governmental organization that started an Oral History Project of the 1965–66 tragedy in 2000. This research aimed to uncover the 1965–66 victims' life stories. A collection of essays based on these interviews has been published (Roosa *et al.* 2004). The ISSI maintains an oral history archive and a library specializing in Indonesian history.
15 A group called the Indonesian Anti-Communist Front (FAKI) violently attacked the conference of the National Liberation Unity Party (PAPERNAS) at Batu, East Java, on 4 March 2007. FAKI alleges that PAPERNAS is a communist organization. FAKI then burned a PAPERNAS flag and threatened the conference participants; the conference was cancelled. The incident took place while several armed police officers were present who took no action to halt the violence by FAKI (see http://www.ahrchk.net/ua/mainfile.php/2007/2257/).

References

Adam, A.W. (2007) 'Blunder kejaksaan agung dan departemen pendidikan nasional', *Tempo Interactif*, 15 March. Online. Availabale at: http://www.tempointeraktif.com/hg/nasional/2007/03/15/brk,20070315-95550,id.html (accessed on 18 May 2008)

Antara News (2008) 'Puluhan massa anti-komunis kembali demo komnas HAM'. Online. Available at: http://www.antara.co.id/arc/2008/4/29/puluhan-massa-anti-komunis-kembali-demo-komnas-ham/ (accessed on 18 May 2008).

Crane, S.A. (1997) 'Writing the Individual back into collective memory', *The American Historical Review*, 102(5): 1372–85.

ELSAM (2006) *Ketika Prinsip Kepastian Hukum Menghakimi Konstitusionalitas Penyelesaian Pelanggaran HAM Masa Lalu: Pandangan Kritis Atas Putusan MK dan Implikasinya Bagi Penyelesaian Pelanggaran HAM di Masa Lalu*, Jakarta: Lembaga Studi dan Advokasi Masyarakat (ELSAM).

Esbenshade, R.S. (1995) 'Remembering to forget: memory, history, national identity in postwar East-Central Europe', *Representations*, 49: 72–96.

ISSI (Institut Sejarah Sosial Indonesia), KNAKTP (Komisi Nasional Anti Kekerasan Terhadap Perempuan) and MGMPS (Musyawarah Guru Mata Pelajaran Sejarah) (2006) *Laporan Diskusi Kekerasan Terhadap Perempuan dalam Sejarah Indonesia* (*Discussion Report on Violence toward Women in National History*), Jakarta: ISSI, Komnas Perempuan dan MGMPS.

Komunitas Sekitarkita (2004a) *Laporan Program: Diskusi 'Perspektif Kemanusiaan dalam Tragedi 1965' di SMU Gonzaga*, Jakarta: Komunitas Sekitarkita.

—— (2004b) *Laporan Program: Diskusi 'Perspektif Kemanusiaan dalam Tragedi 1965' di SMUN 19*, Jakarta: Komunitas Sekitarkita.

—— (2005) *Laporan Diskusi Publik: 'Sejarah Dalam Perspektif Pelajar'*, Jakarta: Komunitas Sekitarkita.
McGregor, K.E. (2005) 'Legacy of a historian in the service of an authoritarian regime', in M.S. Zurbuchen (ed.) *Beginning to Remember: The Past in the Indonesian Present*, Singapore: Singapore University Press.
—— (2007) *History in Uniform: Military Ideology and the Construction of Indonesia's Past*, Singapore: KITLV Press.
Media Indonesia (2006) 'Di bawah sandera kurikulum (In hostage to the curriculum)', 4 October.
Minow, M. (1998) *Between Vengeance and Forgiveness: Facing History After Genocide and Mass Violence*, Boston: Beacon Press.
Mulyasa, E. (2007) *Kurikulum Tingkat Satuan Pendidikan: Suatu Panduan Praktis*, Bandung: PT. Remaja Rosdakarya.
Poesponegoro, D.M. and Notosusanto, N. (1984) *Indonesian National History: Part VI*, Jakarta: Balai Pustaka.
Roosa, J., Ratih, A. and Farid, H. (eds) (2004) *Tahun yang Tak Pernah Berakhir (The Year That Never Ends)*, Jakarta: ELSAM.
Schreiner, K.H. (2005) 'Histories of Trauma and Sites of Memory', in M.S. Zurbuchen (ed.) *Beginning to Remember: the Past in the Indonesian Present*, Singapore: Singapore University Press.
Setiawan, H. (2003) *Aku Eks Tapol*, Yogyakarta: Galang Press.
—— (2004a) *Memoar Pulau Buru*, Magelang: IndonesiaTera.
—— (2004b) 'Membangun kembali budaya rekonsiliasi', in Budiawan (ed.) *Mematahkan Pewarisan Ingatan*, Jakarta: ELSAM.
Suara Pembaruan (2006) 'Kapolri Harus Klarifikasi Pembubaran Kegiatan Mantan Tapol PKI', 23 May. Online. Available at: http://www.suarapembaruan.com/News/2006/05/23/Nasional/nas07.htm (accessed on 18 May 2008).
Sukartiningsih, J. (2004) 'When women became political prisoners', in J. Roosa, A. Ratih and H. Farid (eds) *Tahun Yang Tak Pernah Berakhir (The Year That Never Ends)*, Jakarta: ELSAM.
Sulami (1999) *Perempuan – Kebenaran dan Penjara*, Jakarta: Cipta Lestari.
Utomo, P.W. (2003) 'Genjer-genjer dan stigmatisasi komunis', *Sinar Harapan*. Online. Available at: http://www.sinarharapan.co.id/hiburan/budaya/2005/0423/bud2.html (accessed on 18 May 2008).
van Klinken, G. (2005) 'The battle for history after Suharto', in M.S. Zurbuchen (ed.) *Beginning to Remember: the Past in the Indonesian Present*, Singapore: Singapore University Press.
van Zyl, P. (2005) 'Dealing with the past: reflections on South Africa, East Timor and Indonesia', in M.S. Zurbuchen (ed.) *Beginning to Remember: the Past in the Indonesian Present*, Singapore: Singapore University Press.
Zurbuchen, M.S. (2005) 'Historical Memory in Contemporary Indonesia', in M.S. Zurbuchen (ed.) *Beginning to Remember: the Past in the Indonesian Present*, Singapore: Singapore University Press.

10 Civil society and grassroots reconciliation in Central Java

Priyambudi Sulistiyanto and Rumekso Setyadi

Introduction

On 7 December 2006, the Constitutional Court (*Mahkamah Konstitusi*) annulled the Law on Truth and Reconciliation Commission (No. 27/2004) on the grounds that it was against the 1945 Constitution and international human rights principles. This announcement ended the possibility of establishing a truth commission in Indonesia where victims and perpetrators can be brought together in a national truth-telling forum. What's left from all of this? Is there still any hope for reconciliation in Indonesia? What are other ways in which reconciliation could be pursued? Despite the failure of the Indonesian government to establish a truth commission, we believe that the reconciliation process is not dead yet. Grassroots reconciliation (*rekonsiliasi akar rumput*) activities exist and are growing rapidly outside government realms, and they have something positive to contribute to the reconciliation process. The rising number of non-governmental organizations (NGOs) – a constitutive part of civil society – increasingly works on reconciliation in many places in Indonesia together with local religious and social organizations from places such as Aceh, Java, Poso, and Ambon to Papua, thus establishing grassroots reconciliation activities. Their activities contribute considerably towards mediating between conflicting parties and also towards maintaining local political stability in the post-conflict period. There has also been a proliferation of academic works, of NGO publications, and of memoirs and personal stories of political prisoners, who were jailed during the Suharto period, which has helped significantly in disseminating a variety of accounts and views about the past, contributing to the process of historical clarification and the deconstruction of a singular version of history (see Dani 2001; Farid & Simarmatra 2004; Latief 1998; Moestahal 2002; Sasongko 2005; Zurbuchen 2002, 2005). Indonesia is not alone with respect to the role grassroots organizations are playing in the reconciliation process. Studies done by Babo-Soares (2004), Baxter (2005), Kingston (2006), and Rotberg and Thompson (2000), suggest that in countries such as South Africa, Chile, and Timor Leste, NGOs such as church groups and religious organizations, human rights organizations and victims' associations, have made a crucial contribution to the reconciliation process at the local level.[1]

The focus of this chapter is on the role of grassroots reconciliation activities in Central Java in dealing with the legacies of the 1965–66 tragedy which refer to the arrests and the killings of hundreds of thousands of members and sympathizers of the Indonesian Communist Party (PKI) and other leftist organizations in Java and Bali islands during those years. The killings followed an attempted coup led by young military officers early in the morning of 30 September 1965 in Jakarta. Seven army officers were killed. Much has been written about the origins, causes, and consequences of this failed coup and subsequent arrests and mass killings which changed dramatically the political, economic, and social scenes in Indonesia (see Anderson 1971; Cribb 1990; Crouch 1978; Heryanto 2006; Roosa 2006). Little has been written, however, about the ways in which new generations of Indonesians have tried to overcome this bloody legacy. The fall of Suharto in 1998 opened up public debate about the 1965–66 affair, generating critical and self-reflective examinations among the members of civil society.

The urgency of dealing with '1965–66' is that it is a national tragedy which caused the loss of many lives and terrible suffering among ordinary people in many parts of Indonesia. The 1965–66 affair is a dark spot in the history of Indonesia, and addressing it requires serious soul searching for Indonesians. We believe that dealing with '1965–66' is a matter of priority, because if Indonesia does not deal with it properly and with a sense of dignity, the country as a whole will not be able to learn from the past and therefore to move forward to a new chapter. Dealing with this tragedy quickly is even more crucial, as those who were involved and affected, either as victims or perpetrators, are aging. Many have already died. This makes the quest for accountability and truth seeking more difficult. By saying this, we argue that any effort to address this tragedy through political, legal, and social/cultural means at this time makes a significant contribution to the reconciliation process.

In this chapter, we want to highlight the importance of grassroots reconciliation activities initiated by NGOs especially given the absence of state-sponsored reconciliation initiatives.[2] We want to show that NGOs, which expanded rapidly since the fall of Suharto in 1998, have had a positive impact on reconciliation activities in Indonesia. We will argue that there are both promises and limitations in reconciliation activities carried out by civil society by analyzing one of its members, the NGO Syarikat (*Masyarakat Santri untuk Advokasi Rakyat*, Muslim Community for People's Advocacy), as an example of reconciliation initiatives which deserve more academic attention.[3]

Civil society and grassroots reconciliation

First of all we need to clarify what we mean by civil society. The concept of civil society is the subject of a vivid scholarly debate and is defined in different ways (Edwards 2004; Edwards *et al.* 2001). Civil society is often defined as a political space between state and society where citizens act to improve the well-being of the people. In theory, the existence and the growth of civil society has a positive impact on democracy generally as it allows citizens to take a more active role in political processes which are otherwise controlled by or in the hands of political parties and their leaders. Civil society is crucial to a democratic system because it facilitates expression of different interests and views within a society and challenges the domination of the state over its citizens. However, civil society develops in a variety of contexts and therefore its growth and expansion are very much shaped by the specific political and historical contexts of each society. The kinds of civil societies that exist in Western democracies differ from those in newly democratizing regions such as Asia, where civil societies have their own trajectories (Alagappa 2004; Lee 2004; Putnam 2003).

In countries that experience a transition from authoritarian rule to democracy, civil society plays an important if not crucial role in nurturing and facilitating the participation of citizens, through a variety of avenues, in ensuring that those who committed human rights violations in the past are brought to account. It is in this context that the relationship between civil society and the pursuit of reconciliation can be found. According to Daly and Sarkin (2007: 5), reconciliation refers to the restoration of a relationship which has fallen apart, creating very painful memories for the victims of human rights abuses. Restoring this relationship is not an easy process and it must involve as many participants as possible, hence the importance of the role of civil society. Crocker (1998: 505–6) suggested that civil society can work with the victims of human rights abuses in capacities such as enabling the victims to speak up about their past ordeals and documenting their stories. Civil society can also become involved in pressuring the government to investigate past human rights violations and to establish a truth commission. Furthermore, civil society can also assist with reparation, rehabilitation, and compensation activities for victims, at least to some extent. But, at the same time, Crocker (1998: 507–8) also warned that the role of civil society is limited. Its work is often conducted on a small and local scale. It may be limited in terms of resources, or its activities may be carried out in isolated areas and so not create much impact at the national level.

In this chapter, we discuss 'grassroots reconciliation' carried out by civil society in the context of the failure (or the lack of interest) of the Indonesian government to pursue the reconciliation agenda. We want to see civil society in as flexible a manner as possible, referring to independent NGOs that seek to promote reconciliation through work on a variety of levels and by utilizing a range of means. These organizations have the aim of empowering others and themselves for the common good. This civil society encompasses social, religious, cultural, and even recreational organizations which are active at the local level.[4] What do we mean by grassroots reconciliation? As pointed out by Babo-Soares (2004: 18) in his research in Timor Leste, grassroots reconciliation is grounded at the local level, is inclusive, involving local and ordinary people, and, as such, has a communal spirit. In this chapter, we suggest that the grassroots reconciliation process can be very broad, encompassing mutual dialogue, public forums, workshops, and cultural activities involving victims and, to a limited extent, perpetrators, as well as religious leaders, activists, and ordinary people who work together towards building a path for reconciliation. However, we also acknowledge that in this kind of reconciliation process there are some serious limitations. For instance, the quest for large-scale rehabilitation and compensation is difficult to pursue because these are the responsibility of the government.

It can be said here that a reconciliation process (of truth telling and of listening) requires the involvement of both victims and perpetrators. Unfortunately, in many cases in Indonesia, the major perpetrators of human rights abuses, in particular the members of the Indonesian armed forces and other government figures, have not been willing to participate in reconciliation processes. In this chapter we will describe, however, how in some local communities, perpetrators, including former members of Banser, have been willing to come together with victims of 1965–66 and to seek reconciliation.[5] This is reconciliation on a small scale and does not involve the major perpetrators and masterminds behind the mass killings. Nonetheless, it is significant particularly in terms of the benefits it brings to local communities in various places in Central Java where the killings took place because it has the potential for opening up ways to come to terms with the past at the national level in the future.

In comparison, the newly elected Rudd government in Australia took responsibility for past human rights abuses against indigenous Australians by offering a national apology to these people on behalf of past governments and parliaments of Australia. Through this it seeks to advance the process of national reconciliation between indigenous and non-indigenous Australians (see Dodson 2008; Kock 2008). Events of the past few years have shown that the Indonesian government, on the contrary, is as yet unwilling to put reconciliation on the national agenda in any substantive way (see Simanjuntak 2003; Sulistiyanto 2005). Given these major shortcomings, we would like to stress in this chapter that grassroots reconciliation initiatives, carried out by civil society, are of utmost importance. They are grounded firmly in society and they empower local actors to take charge of the local reconciliation process.

The failure of state-sponsored reconciliation in Indonesia

In dealing with past human rights violations, new democratic countries have pursued a range of what scholars describe as 'transitional justice' strategies. These include trials, amnesty, and truth commissions/truth telling forums (Kritz 1995; McAdams 1997). These different strategies suit different circumstances. The strategy of trials is commonly used when the new government wants to uphold the rule of law and to deliver a sense of justice by bringing the perpetrators to court (or a human rights court).[6] Bringing perpetrators to trial eliminates impunity and acts as deterrence against future human rights violations. But trials are only an option when a new democratic government and its leaders are in a stronger position than the outgoing authoritarian regime. When the new government has more or less an equal political power with the previous leaders, it cannot impose its power over them so easily. In this situation, a compromise will most likely be established, with the new government deciding to give amnesty to the perpetrators. The main reason for giving amnesty is that punishing the perpetrators of past human rights crimes may destabilize the new democratic political environment. Amnesty, although against international principles, has been used in several countries that have democratized in recent decades.[7]

In recent times truth commissions have been used alongside the trial and amnesty strategies. Truth commissions are established to give an opportunity to both the victims and the perpetrators of human rights abuses to meet, to speak publicly, and to exchange accounts of the past.[8] Although a truth commission is not a legal institution, in some cases it does have several important legal functions such as recommending or rejecting amnesty for the perpetrators and addressing issues related to the rights of the victims in terms of compensation and rehabilitation. With some criticism about their successes and failures, truth commissions were very popular as a 'third way' strategy to deal with human rights abuses that had occurred in Chile, Argentina, Peru, Columbia, El Salvador, and South Africa (see Hayner 2001).

After the fall of Suharto in 1998, Indonesia began to address the human rights abuses of the Suharto period by using the prosecution strategy, and began to explore the possibility of establishing a truth commission. The government pursued the prosecution strategy by legislating two human rights laws: the Law on Human Rights (*Undang-Undang Hak-hak Asasi Manusia*, No. 39/1999) and the Law on Human Rights Court (*Undang-Undang Peradilan Hak-hak Asasi Manusia*, No. 26/2000). These laws were introduced during the Habibie and Abdurrahman Wahid governments respectively and they incorporated partially two important new criminal concepts from the Rome Convention of 1998. These concepts are 'crimes against humanity' (*kejahatan terhadap kemanusiaan*) and 'genocide' (*genosida*). The enactment of these concepts in the prosecution strategy gives the government (with the support of parliament) the right to establish a human rights tribunal. Two human rights tribunals were established in 1999 and 2000 to try the perpetrators of gross human rights violations in East Timor following the UN-sponsored referendum in 1999 and in Tanjung Priok, Jakarta, in 1984. These trials were the subject of national and international criticism as the verdicts they delivered were disappointing and shameful, with many perpetrators escaping punishment (ICTJ 2003; Sulistiyanto 2007).

The legal foundation for establishing a truth commission was the Law on Human Rights Court (Law No. 26/2000). Articles 43 and 44 state that the government must establish a truth commission in Indonesia. This was endorsed constitutionally by the Peoples' Consultative Assembly decree (No. 5) in 2000, which states that the truth commission should be an extra-judicial institution established by law to deal with past human rights abuses. After more than three years of bickering and constant negotiations in the parliament, the Law on Truth and Reconciliation Commission (No. 27/2004) was finally enacted in the last days of the Megawati government (ELSAM 2004). As stated in this law, the government must establish a truth commission within 60 days of the parliament having passed the law.[9] Legally, the current Yudhoyono government became responsible for establishing a truth commission as well as selecting the commissioners. With slow progress, between 2005 and 2006, the Ministry of Law and Human Rights finally set up a special panel to choose candidates to be proposed to the president and parliament as the commissioners of Indonesia's truth commission.

In the middle of 2006, several NGOs, including ELSAM, Kontras, Imparsial, and the Indonesian Legal Aid Foundation,[10] and some individuals such as Raharja

Waluya Jati and Tjasman Setyo Prawiro, contested the validity of the Law on Truth and Reconciliation Commission in the Constitutional Court, which has the right to review the legality of laws (Tim Advokasi Kebenaran dan Keadilan 2006). These human rights organizations contested the articles in the Truth and Reconciliation Commission (TRC) Law because it allowed amnesty as one means to achieve reconciliation. They believed that the TRC should not include any means by which perpetrators could escape punishment or trials. More importantly, they also strongly argued that the provision of amnesty goes against international laws and conventions on human rights, and that Indonesia as a country must respect these. The Constitutional Court took up the case, which drew a lot of public attention during its review between September and December 2006. Amongst others, human rights lawyers and international experts, were invited to give their views about the law. Finally, the Constitutional Court delivered its verdict on 6 December 2006, which annulled the law. This verdict shocked the nation and took many people by surprise because there was a strong perception that Indonesia had opened a new chapter in the quest for reconciliation, and that those who had suffered human rights abuses would finally have the opportunity to tell their stories in a national truth-telling forum. The verdict caused disappointment and increased a sense of anxiety as victims' hopes for reconciliation through a truth commission were crushed and the window of opportunity for the establishment of a truth commission was closed.

The failure of state-sponsored reconciliation in Indonesia to this point must be acknowledged. Reconciliation in the post-Suharto period is a difficult process because it involves legal, political, and constitutional issues. A reconciliation process which includes revealing the truth about the past would implicate many political and military actors from the New Order government, some of whom are still attached to the current government. The remnants of the old power have not been sidelined yet. However, there is no doubt that while Indonesia still needs a truth commission and reconciliation process through state-sponsored reconciliation initiatives, it is not the only way to deal with the human rights violations that occurred during the Suharto period. Therefore, it is important that we continue to explore and implement alternative ways or forums through which the reconciliation process can be pursued in Indonesia. It is in this context that the activities of civil society organizations are crucial.

Syarikat

Syarikat was established in Yogyakarta in 2000 with the support of a group of young activists from the Muslim organization Nahdlatul Ulama (NU). Syarikat relies very much on grassroots networks throughout Java which are well established under NU and many of its members come from *pesantren* (Islamic Schools). These young activists were inspired by the wisdom and idealism of the prominent NU leader Abdurrahman Wahid who, at that time, was also the newly elected Indonesian President. Soon after he was inaugurated, Wahid publicly asked for forgiveness for the actions of NU and its affiliated organizations during the

1965–66 affair and proposed the elimination of discriminative laws applied to former political prisoners. He also called for the government to rehabilitate the victims of 1965–66 (see Budiawan 2004; Wajidi 2003). It was in this political climate that Syarikat began to establish grassroots reconciliation initiatives such as workshops, exhibitions, and closed-door meetings bringing victims and those who had participated in or had firsthand knowledge of the 1965–66 tragedy together in order to share their personal stories. These initiatives were aimed at breaking down prejudices at the grassroots level and also at building new relationships, which might open a path for reconciliation. Syarikat also publishes materials such as the journal *Ruas*, books, and documentary films with the main intentions to inform and educate the public about the need to be critical with what is promoted as historical facts by the government and about the importance of reconciliation. We will present two activities of Syarikat in more detail: a workshop conducted in 2003 and a film project of 2005.

The workshop especially was grounded in the involvement of victims and a few perpetrators (from Banser) from various localities in Central Java. The documentary film project was about the life stories of women victims of 1965–66. These grassroots activities demonstrate the strong community spirit that evolves through such local initiatives; they are also rich with cultural expressions. These cases have been chosen because of their impact as the victims' voices were heard by each other and by the public (in the case of the documentary film), restoring their dignity as human beings no different from their fellow Indonesians who had not suffered as they had in the past. Through these initiatives, the public gained a new understanding of the 1965–66 affair and the plight of the victims in the decades which followed.

First, the meaning and importance of such initiatives can only truly be appreciated when we consider that it has never been easy to organize meetings at the local level between victims and perpetrators to talk about the past. During the Suharto period such meetings were strictly forbidden and this created a culture of fear and anxiety. The barriers were such that people were afraid to initiate even simple conversations about what happened in the past in their own localities let alone at the national level. Therefore it was a significant moment when both sides met for the first time to talk about the past sufferings. Second, the use of documentary film was strategically important not just for informing the public generally but also to counter the official version of the past in Indonesia. By reaching out for a wider audience through film the public can gain a better knowledge about the plight of the victims.

The victims' forum (2003)

Syarikat organized a workshop on reconciliation and rehabilitation for the victims of the 1965–66 affair from 5–7 May 2003 in Semarang, Central Java.[11] In organizing this workshop, Syarikat received support from the National Commission on Human Rights (*Komisi Nasional Hak-hak Asasi Manusia*, Komnas HAM) and a number of NU leaders (*kyai*) from various Islamic schools (*pesantren*) in Central

Java.¹² According to Imam Aziz, the head of Syarikat, this workshop was part of the continuation of grassroots reconciliation initiatives organized by Syarikat in other places in East Java which started in 2000 (Syarikat 2003: 1).¹³ The workshop invited both victims and former members of Banser to meet and exchange their respective accounts of the 1965–66 events as they occurred in their different localities. The main goal was to break down prejudices about each other and also to build a new relationship which would open up a path for reconciliation between both sides. Many participants had firsthand knowledge about the past events; they came from various places in Central Java such as Cilacap, Batang, Kebumen, Wonosobo, Boyolali, Blora, Purwodadi, Jepara, Klaten, Salatiga, and Yogyakarta, all formerly strong bases of the Indonesian Communist Party. They had spent years in prisons or on the notorious Buru island where they had to work and to live under very harsh conditions. It is known that many thousands of followers of the Indonesian Communist Party and its affiliated organizations were killed in 1965 and 1966 in Central Java, but there are no precise numbers about how many and where the bodies were buried (Cribb 1990). The memories, trauma, and victimization experienced by those who were involved still linger in the minds of many people, especially the victims.

On the first day of the workshop, M. Billah from Komnas HAM said the attempt at reconciliation and rehabilitation of the victims of 1965–66 should be placed in the context of the democratization process in Indonesia. He described the 1965–66 affair as being like the *Mahabharata* epic involving the wars between the *Kaurava* and the *Pandava* families which ended with a tragedy for everyone. With everyone suffering greatly and both sides wanting to claim their sides of the stories as the valid one, the quest for finding the truth about who is right and who is wrong has never brought clarity about the event. He argued that the truth about the past must be revealed and those who are involved in the search for the truth must work together so that similar tragedies will not happen again in the future. He also agreed that Komnas HAM should be involved in this kind of reconciliation process and participate in the efforts to deal with the human rights abuses of the Suharto period. However, he warned that the 1965–66 affair can be forgiven but not forgotten and he also suggested that the need to rewrite Indonesian history is important, especially to inform the students in school about the facts that many Indonesians had suffered greatly during that time (see Leksana this volume).

In his opening remarks at the workshop, M. Adnan from the NU branch in Central Java emphasized the need to get rid of the culture of violence and revenge which lives on in Indonesian society. He argued that everyone must uphold the spirit of reconciliation so that the nation as a whole would become a nation of forgiveness (*bangsa yang pemaaf*) and it was in this context that this workshop was very important and crucial. He also stated that there are more than 30 verses in the Qu'ran which address the importance of mutual forgiveness (*maaf-memaafkan*). He added that an act of revenge against evil is evil itself and therefore he urged that those who promote and work towards reconciliation will be getting big rewards (*pahala*) from God. He stated his belief that a religious (Islamic) method for reconciliation is useful because it can be easily adopted by the people regardless of their backgrounds and ethnicities. Meanwhile, KH Wahid Zuhdi, from Al Ma'aruf *pesantren*, asked forgiveness for the misunderstanding that happened due to the 1965–66 affair and especially for the 'real' masterminds at the local level. He recalled that the followers of NU were involved in the destruction of the Indonesian Communist Party including physical violence and killings. He also suggested that many of those from NU were forced to act in the turbulent situation of 1965–66 and pleaded that many of them had already asked to be forgiven for their involvement. He suggested it was important to continue nurturing the spirit of brother/sisterhood (*persaudaran*) between both sides as this is also an important part of the teachings of Islam. Another prominent *kyai*, KH Syamsudin, from the NU branch in Central Java, raised similar points suggesting that Islam is a religion for bringing goodwill and prosperity to the people on earth (*rahmatan lil alamin*); therefore it regards reconciliation or *islah* (peace) very highly. *Islah* here means that human beings must pursue peace as a way of correcting past wrongdoings and also to forgive each other. KH Syamsudin suggested that *islah* can strengthen solidarity among human beings generally and not just among Muslim people (*ukhuwah watoniah*), and that this must start from the heart before reaching out to society as a whole (see also McGregor this volume).

With encouragement and moral support from a Komnas HAM commissioner and the *kyais*, participants shared their personal stories freely and openly in the workshop which was important, particularly as they were drawn from opposite sides of the past political and social spectrum: PKI and NU. The spirit of mutual understanding and of solidarity allowed them to hear each others' views and accounts and also to ask for forgiveness from each other (including the general citizenry caught in the 'crossfire'). By speaking out and exchanging views and stories, they came to terms with a better understanding about each other, which helped considerably to establish a new friendship. It must be noted here that the barriers were very high in the past between the followers of PKI and NU, but surprisingly the participants had goodwill and intentions to make this workshop successful, at least as a first step to explore ways in which reconciliation between both sides could be achieved in the future.[14] Let us share some of the personal stories here.

Sabar lived in Purwodadi in 1965. He was a teacher and is now in his late 60s and had been through a very tough and difficult time in the past. According to him, around November 1965 his house was surrounded by military troops together with village officers, but he was able to escape by crossing the river near his house. However, they arrested his wife and the children and brought them to Bulu prison in Semarang, where they stayed until 1971. He himself went to Jakarta looking for refuge in his former student's house. However, he was finally arrested and lived under harsh conditions in prison for years. Even years after his release from prison, he did not know for what reason he was arrested because he, at least to his knowledge, had done nothing wrong in the past. Ironically, according to a letter issued by the Team of Local Investigators (*Tim Pemeriksa Daerah*, Teperda), he was also cleared of any charges concerning his involvement in the 1965 affair.[15] He had been asking the government to rehabilitate him by lifting the discrimination against him in society. And as a former teacher he believed he deserved some form of proper/financial compensation as well. He also said that until today his request for rehabilitation and compensation has not been accepted by the Indonesian government. For someone like him, reconciliation at the grassroots level becomes therefore even more important.

Anjar Roeslan from Salatiga was a former middle-ranking army officer attached to the Regional Military Command IV Diponegoro overseeing Central Java province. He was arrested wrongly and jailed for 13 years because his name was similar to that of someone the government was looking for.[16] During his life in prison, he became a priest and looked after other political prisoners in a spiritual way. After he was released he became active in various victims' organizations such as the Association of Victims of the New Order (*Paguyuban Korban Orde Baru*, Pakorba) and the Research Foundation for the Victims of the 1965 Killings (*Yayasan Penelitian Korban Pembunuhan 1965*, YPKP) and advocated reconciliation and rehabilitation for the victims of 1965–66. In expressing his views about the past and the quest for reconciliation, he wrote a poem dedicated to the victims who participated in the workshop.

Tulang-tulang Kurban Tragedi '65	**The Bones of the Victims of the '65 Tragedy**
Bangsaku ...	My nation ...
Dengar suara kami	Listen to our voices
Tulang-tulang kurban '65	The bones of the '65 victims
Bukan karena tangan penjajah	Not because of the colonialist's hands
Tetapi ...	But ...
Oleh tangan bangsa sendiri	By the hands of our own nation
Yang sedang kehilangan kiblat	Which had lost direction
Demi Pancasila sakti	In the name of sacred Pancasila
Berlabel agama	Under the banner of religion
Jutaan anak bangsa	Millions of the children of the nation
Dibantai bagai binatang jalang	Were slaughtered like wild animals
Dikubur massal tanpa batu nisan	Buried en mass without gravestones
Tak bertabur bunga	Without flowers
Meski mawar melati masih	Although jasmine flowers
Tumbuh di negeri ini	Still grow in this country
Negeri yang pernah melahirkan	This country which gave birth
Pahlawan-pahlawan besar	To great patriots
Gajahmada, Imam Bonjol, Pattimura	Gajahmada, Imam Bonjol, Pattimura
Tak pernah menyerah	Who never surrendered
Meski hati menanti	Although the heart is waiting

Tulang-tulang Kurban Tragedi '65	The Bones of the Victims of the '65 Tragedy
Kini bangsa kehilangan pamornya	Now the nation has lost her dignity
Bangsaku	My nation
Dengar suara kami	Listen to our voices
Tulang yang sudah tidak bisa bicara	The bones that can no longer speak
Lewat kamu generasi penerus	Through you, the next generation
Suara kami menembus hati anak negeri	Our voices penetrate the hearts of the children of the nation
Sampai ke ujung bumi	Till the end of the earth
Berteriak ...	Shouting ...
Mana keadilan	Where is justice
Mana kemanusiaan	Where is humanity
Mana kebenaran	Where is truth
Kami muak dengan slogan	We are sick of slogans
Kami butuh kenyataan	We need action
Jangan ditunda	Don't delay
Hari ini rehabilitasi	Rehabilitation today
Hari ini rekonsiliasi	Reconciliation today
Kami berpacu	We are racing
Dengan waktu	With time

This poem implores us to listen to the voices of the victims who were silenced, through a variety of means, during the Suharto period. Their suffering is likened to that of the national heroes revered by Indonesians. Anjar calls on the current generation to recognize the suffering and sacrifice of these victims, and demands that the government urgently addresses the issues of rehabilitation and reconciliation.

Representatives of NU and Banser also shared their personal stories. Mohammad Zamazi lived in the town of Demak in 1965. He is now in his 50s and witnessed the arrest of his village head, who was accused of being a sympathizer of the PKI. According to him, in 1965 Demak was divided into two areas: the 'red' area in the eastern part of the city and the 'green' area in the west.[17] Prior to 1965–66, the tension was already very high, caused by the conflict between the supporters of PKI and those of NU, which almost created a civil war in the area. Fortunately it did not happen, but during 1965–66, Zamazi saw a group of Banser activists with the protection of military officers come to the area to arrest the supporters or sympathizers of PKI. However, he did not see any killings in the area because the senior *kyais* helped to ease the tensions by telling the supporters of NU not to take the law into their own hands. Zamazi acknowledged that those who suffered in the 1965–66 affair deserved to be treated humanely and with dignity. He also called for both sides to sit down together and to forgive each other and agreed to support reconciliation process initiatives.

Romlan R. Junaedi lived in Cilacap in 1965. He was the leader of a local NU branch. He is now in his late 60s. He experienced the turbulence in his town. He recalled that he received an order coming from Idham Chalid, the national leader of NU in Jakarta, to calm the supporters of NU in Cilacap where the local people were divided into two camps: the communists and the *Pancasila*.[18] He also acknowledged that the members of Ansor, a youth wing organization of NU, participated in arresting the members or sympathizers of PKI but he also helped to disarm the Ansor members and consequently a potentially volatile situation as part of restoring law and order in Cilacap. However, he was disappointed and disillusioned when under the New Order government NU became a subject of repression as well. He also posed a question regarding who was ultimately responsible for the 1965–66 affair: was it Aidit or Suharto?[19] This question implies his demands for interrogating the validity of the official version of the past which blamed the leaders of PKI as those responsible for the political crisis.

The workshop concluded with some collective reflections and proposed a set of recommendations for the government (Syarikat 2003). The participants recommended the need to embark on historical clarifications about 1965–66, enabling the Indonesian people (especially the younger generation) to get to know the truth about the tragedy. They recommended that the former members of PKI and NU should work together to build a better future through revealing the truth of the past. This could be done by educating the public about the 1965–66 affair through media, public forum, and social and cultural activities. They also recommended that the government should declare the 1965–66 massacres a national tragedy, which had components of basic human rights violations. More importantly, they also wanted the government to do something about their circumstances, especially the legal restrictions and social stigmatization and discrimination which had been attached to them and their families in terms of employment and freedom of movement as well as living normally in society for decades in the Suharto period. With many of them now in their 60s and 70s, this was the last thing they wanted to do in their life and there was a sense of urgency about addressing the issues related to reconciliation and rehabilitation.

The most important outcome of this workshop was that it provided a forum in which the victims could speak out about the past and share their views about what steps could be taken towards achieving reconciliation. Although the forum was small in scale, it increased the victims' sense of dignity and their hope for a better future. During the course of this workshop, accounts were presented by some perpetrators (not from the military) who had participated in the killing and the hunting of the followers and sympathizers of the Indonesian Communist Party. This was significant in the sense that these perpetrators agreed to come forward to tell their stories. In this way, the workshop was able to break down some barriers in that local community which had been there for decades and start the long process of rebuilding social relationships.

Kado untuk Ibu (A gift for mother)

In Yogyakarta in 2006, Syarikat chose the national public holiday, Kartini Day (which falls on 21 April) as a time to educate the public about the plight of women

Figure 10.1 Kado untuk Ibu: 'The voices of former women political prisoners'

victims of 1965–66 who are often forgotten and denied in the official version of events. A range of arts and cultural activities such as a painting exhibition, performances, and a seminar on reconciliation was held in this celebration. Kartini is a very important national figure and she is seen by many as someone who encouraged Indonesian women to educate themselves and to fight for their rights in the society. Syarikat believed that the spirit of Kartini could have an impact and draw public attention to the fact that some Indonesian women are still discriminated against and living in unfortunate situations. These ordinary women are former political prisoners of the New Order period. As part of this occasion, Syarikat produced and screened a documentary film as 'a gift' to these unfortunate women.[20]

The title of this documentary is *Kado untuk Ibu*. It is about four women victims, Putmainah, Sumilah, Fatmiati, and Sumarmiyati, who were jailed for several years without trials. It tells their personal stories of suffering and agony, starting from when they were rounded up in their homes, arrested, and tortured by military interrogators in prisons. They got into trouble because they were active members of, or were involved in the activities organized by, Gerwani (*Gerakan Wanita Indonesia*, Indonesian Women's Movement), the largest women organization affiliated to the PKI. In the New Order government's official accounts, the members of Gerwani were involved in the killing of the seven army officers on 30 September 1965 in Lubang Buaya, Jakarta. It is commonly claimed that the members of Gerwani participated in a so-called *Tarian Harum Bunga* (Fragrant Flower Dance) wearing very sexy clothes, after which they participated in killing the generals in a barbaric way.[21] Images of these events can be found on the walls of the Lubang Buaya museum. During the Suharto period these images were frequently disseminated and perpetuated through official speeches and mass media coverage; their credibility had never been challenged until recently.

However, the personal stories revealed in *Kado untuk Ibu* dispute and challenge the official accounts. Gerwani, according to the women in the documentary, was a women's organization that generally fought for the improvement of the well-being of Indonesian women like other women's organizations. They believe that Gerwani was a victim of the political tragedy which occurred in Jakarta in 1965 and that its members became the scapegoats for it. These women also believe that the Suharto government fabricated the stories about Gerwani members being involved in the killing of the generals in an attempt to destroy the popularity of Gerwani.

Some of these extraordinary personal stories can be found in this documentary film. Sumilah's story is a tragic one as she had been wrongly accused and had to spend many years in prison. She was only 14 years old when the village leader (*lurah*) requested her to report to the village office. After being interrogated and imprisoned in Wirogunan prison in Yogyakarta, she was then transferred to Plantungan prison, a notorious women's prison located in Kendal district, Central Java, with other women political prisoners. Sadly, after about eight years in Plantungan prison, the prison master told her that she was wrongly arrested and that the person the government was looking for was a teacher who happened to have a similar name in the village. After she was released from Plantungan prison, Sumilah returned to her village near Yogyakarta. It was later on in the village that she met the 'other' Sumilah and both of them became good friends and shared each other's personal journeys. In reflecting on her life, Sumilah raised ethical and legal issues and demanded the government to find ways to rehabilitate and compensate someone like herself and other women who had been through similar experiences.

Sumarmiyati's personal story is also sad and chilling. As a member of Gerwani, she was treated very badly in prison, particularly as she repeatedly denied the accusation of being involved in political activities to challenge the Suharto government. She revealed that her interrogators tortured her, a method which was commonly used to force those being interrogated to make false confessions as well. She explained that she was also subjected to various forms of sexual harassment and humiliated to the point that she lost her dignity as an Indonesian citizen. She was asked to show a tattoo on her body which marked her association with Gerwani. She refused to do this at first, believing that the motivation behind the order was that the interrogators wanted to see more of her body. The interrogators used their hands and feet to touch the private parts of her body and this happened repeatedly in prison. The most humiliating part was when she was asked to strip off her clothes, along with other women, and was told that they deserved to be treated like that for their association with Gerwani. In reflecting on her life, Sumarmiyati questioned the integrity and morality of her interrogators, many of whom were military officers. She had lost her respect for those who worked with the government.

Kado untuk Ibu also documents the lives and the experiences of women political prisoners living in the aforementioned Plantungan prison. This prison is located in an isolated place in Sukorejo village, Kendal district, not far from the Dieng Plateau in Central Java. It was originally built by the Dutch in 1870 and in 1929 it became a leper hospital funded by the rich plantation owner Boscha. In 1957 the Indonesian government took over the hospital from the Dutch as a result of nationalization programs and later on it was turned into a juvenile prison run by the Ministry of Justice. In 1971, the New Order government's powerful Security and Order Command (*Komando Operasi Pemulihan Keamanan dan Ketertiban*, Kopkamtib) transformed this place into the largest women's prison in Indonesia. There were about 5,000 women political prisoners in Plantungan prison, many of them 'B category' prisoners, a category for those who were members of the PKI and its affiliated organizations. These prisoners were guarded by military officers and isolated from society and had to work in various jobs such as farming, carpeting, small business activities, and others.

The accounts about living in Plantungan prison given by Sumilah, Sumarmiyati, Fatmiati, and Putmainah are saddening but at the same time also inspire a high degree of respect for those who had the courage and strength to survive under such harsh conditions. They were arrested for political reasons; they were separated from their families, subjected to inhuman interrogation methods, and finally were imprisoned for many years. There is no doubt that some women did not survive, others became angry, anxious, and suffered mentally, but at the same time many of them decided to hold on their hearts to keep them going and moving on a daily basis. The ability of these women to tell their personal stories gives us more than just 'life stories' but also a sense of their 'inner' strength which not everyone can nurture especially when it comes to dealing with suffering and uncertainty.

What do the stories in *Kado untuk Ibu* tell us? First of all, the stories offer to the public real images of women victims from Plantungan prison. This kind of material has not been available through official government sources.[22] The accounts of these women powerfully counteract the stories perpetuated by the government about the involvement of Gerwani in the 1965–66 affair, opening up a new chapter in the reconciliation process. We believe that the real and visual account in this documentary has opened up debates over the appalling and unacceptable treatment of these women by the Suharto government.

The documentary film has had several public screenings, among others in various places such as cultural buildings, cafés, and independent cinemas in the cities of Yogyakarta and Jakarta in 2005. In Yogyakarta, one of the women in the film, Sumarmiyati, also talked to the audience after the screening. The audience consisted of activists, victims, students, and also teachers, many of whom were shocked to hear of the sufferings and struggles she experienced in various jails during the Suharto period. In Jakarta, the documentary film was screened in Taman Ismail Marzuki (TIM) as part of the commemoration of the 40th year of this very prestigious cultural center. In commenting on this film, a young academic Gadis Arivia (2005) reminded the Indonesians collectively not to forget the past and also urged them to learn from the past so that this brutality and ignorance would not happen again in the future.

The potential and limitations of grassroots reconciliation

What can be learned from these two examples of grassroots reconciliation initiatives carried out by Syarikat? We encounter both a great potential as well as limitations. First, there is a lot of potential for these events to contribute to the national reconciliation process. These initiatives helped to establish different narratives to official accounts about the many human rights abuses of the Suharto period such as the 1965–66 tragedy, the Tanjung Priok killings in 1984, and the Lampung killings in 1986, often challenging popular accounts. By enabling the victims to speak up and to tell their personal stories, an accumulation of counter narratives occurs and this could have a very positive impact in educating current and future generations about the past. The more alternative narratives there are, the better we are able to uncover the truth about the past or, in Adam's (2004: 19) words, "to correct the history" (*pelurusan sejarah*). It is important that these counter narratives are also published and disseminated to the public where they can create public debate or even controversy which will be useful in enhancing the reconciliation process at a national level. Grassroots reconciliation initiatives foster the victims' right to speak out and to tell their sides of the story that were denied for years during the Suharto period. Victims are important actors in the quest for reconciliation in Indonesia because until today there is no legal or institutional national body dedicated to them. In the absence of a national truth-telling forum, victims have nowhere to go except to participate in victims' forums like the one organized by Syarikat, hence the importance of these grassroots reconciliation initiatives. To a certain degree, grassroots reconciliation initiatives can act like an unofficial truth commission because they provide a forum in which victims and perpetrators can exchange their personal stories. This function could be strengthened if those stories and accounts were compiled and later published in a report for the general public including the government and the parliament.[23]

Another point to make, however, is that grassroots reconciliation initiatives are limited, especially in terms of the scale of these activities. Only small groups of victims and participants are involved in these reconciliation events. Yet the number of human rights abuses in Indonesia runs into millions, and they are found throughout Indonesia. The question as to whether grassroots activities can be carried out on a larger scale is a difficult one. Activities on a national scale are needed that involve a wide range of social, cultural, and religious organizations in the reconciliation process. Another limitation is that grassroots reconciliation initiatives to date have been limited only to hearing personal stories and have not yet developed into collective (or national) stories of the victims which could enhance the reconciliation process at the national level. Grassroots reconciliation initiatives are also often limited in terms of resources and funding. This is particularly significant when it comes to addressing rehabilitation and reparation issues. NGOs have limited capacities to respond to the victims' right to obtain some form of rehabilitation and reparation; these are the obligations of the government. Similarly, the quest for justice through prosecution is beyond what grassroots reconciliation initiatives can offer. The potential for victims to bring their cases to a human rights court in the future is limited if not impossible. They can only pursue this course of action by putting their cases to the National Commission on Human Rights, which is the only government institution with the capacity to bring perpetrators to trial. However, this requires considerable time, effort, and financial resources.

On balance, it is not easy to know whether the aforementioned two initiatives meet the demands of victims simply because these initiatives are carried out by civil society which, as mentioned earlier, has its limitations. However, we believe that by enabling the victims to speak up and to tell their stories they meet the goal of restoring a sense of dignity and of respect to victims, while the nation as a whole revisits the social memory of the past. It is important that this can be started from the grassroots level because initiatives at this level can considerably strengthen the reconciliation process. Reconciliation does not imply that everyone can agree upon the same version of the past. The important thing is that the victims are given the right to share their stories. In this regard, these two initiatives are just the beginning of a long journey in the reconciliation process that is part of the dynamics of Indonesia's new democracy.

Conclusion

In his book entitled *The Healing of Nations*, Amstutz (2005) reminded us about the potential and limitations of national governments of, for instance, Argentina, Chile, Northern Ireland, and South Africa, in dealing with their difficult and unpleasant pasts. He called for political forgiveness which implies the need "to create the preconditions that will prevent the repetition of offences while simultaneously fostering the renewal of a community's moral and political order and the restoration of social and political bonds" (Amstutz 2005: 231–2). This requires the willingness of everyone to participate in ways in which collective healing and national reconciliation can occur from small to large scales.

This is precisely what grassroots reconciliation activities are all about as some of the activities presented in this chapter demonstrate. With the failure of the reconciliation process in Indonesia at the national level, we have argued for the importance of civil society in pursuing grassroots reconciliation activities. The two examples of grassroots reconciliation activities conducted by Syarikat in Central Java inform us a lot about the urgency to support victims to tell their personal stories about the 1965–66 affair, which is one among many events in which gross violations of human rights occurred during the New Order period. We have suggested that these kinds of activities contribute to the reconciliation process because they empower victims and produce counter narratives about the past. However, we have also shown that grassroots reconciliation activities have both potential and limitations.

The case studies show that to seek reconciliation at the grassroots level is a very complex process, but nonetheless occurring in Indonesia. Small steps that allow those who have suffered in the past to speak up can be taken independently without waiting for government assistance and leadership. In the absence of a government commitment to national reconciliation, we have argued that the actions of individuals or of local communities in initiating reconciliation activities are all the more significant. In fact, these local communities are providing leadership in the quest for reconciliation in Indonesia. These grassroots initiatives also make an important contribution to the field of peace and conflict research, as scholars and policymakers learn about them, and make comparative studies of grassroots initiatives towards reconciliation in new democracies like those in South Africa, Cambodia, and Timor Leste.

We therefore want to conclude by saying that the quest for reconciliation through a national truth-telling forum in Indonesia should not only rely on the government's legal and constitutional initiatives that have proved to be unsuccessful, especially with the failure to establish a truth commission. With this very unpromising situation the only hope we can find is to empower civil society to get involved more in grassroots reconciliation activities. We believe that only through a collective effort can the quest for reconciliation in Indonesia be realized in the years to come.

Acknowledgements

This chapter is based on Sulistiyanto's field trips to Central Java in July 2007 and January 2008 and Setyadi's experiences as an active member of Syarikat, the non-governmental organization in focus in this chapter. Sulistiyanto's last field trip was made possible by a Faculty of Social Sciences Establishment Grant from Flinders University. Thanks also to Birgit Bräuchler and Kate McGregor for commenting on the draft version of this chapter. All shortcomings are ours.

Notes

1 In South Africa, the reconciliation activities addressed the discrimination against the African communities during the Apartheid regime; in Chile, they focused on the human rights abuses committed during the Pinochet regime; and in Timor Leste, they dealt with

the legacies of violence and civil war during the Indonesian occupation period (1975–99).

2   See Giring (2004), Kontras (2006), Sekretariat Keadilan dan Perdamaian (2007), Sumarwan (2007), and Tindage (2006).

3   Previous works on Syarikat can be found in Budiawan (2004) and Wajidi (2003); see also McGregor this volume.

4   Of course we also acknowledge that there are uncivil 'civil society' organizations which act against democratic principles and civility and therefore do damage at the local level.

5   Banser is the paramilitary youth wing of Nahdlatul Ulama (NU), one of the largest Muslim organizations in Indonesia. It took part in the killing of members (or sympathizers) of the Indonesian Communist Party in Central and East Java in 1965 and 1966. For an account of the negotiations surrounding NU's role in the reconciliation process, see McGregor this volume.

6   Such trials were held for the war criminals in Germany and Japan and also for the perpetrators in former Yugoslavia and Rwanda (see Neier 1999).

7   On the Spanish experience, see Aguilar (2001).

8   There are at least four important components in a truth commission: it should focus on the past; it is established to find the truth by clarifying the whole episode of the past human rights crimes; it has power to access information in every government institution; and it has specific mandates and will end its existence after publishing the final report (see Bronkhorst 1995). However, it must be noted that each TRC has a different mandate and it depends on the political and legal contexts in which TRCs are established. Thank you to Birgit for her comments on this point.

9   For the debates on Indonesia's TRC law, see Sulistiyanto (2005).

10 ELSAM (The Institute for Policy Research and Advocacy) was established in 1993 by Abdul Hakim Garuda Nusantara in Jakarta and it became the leading advocate for the establishment of TRC in Indonesia; Kontras (Commission for Disappeared People and Victims of Violence) was founded by activists and lawyers in Jakarta in 1998 with its mandate to document the plights of political prisoners; Imparsial was also founded by a group of lawyers in Jakarta in 2000 with its main focus on human rights documentation; and the Indonesian Legal Aid Foundation known as YLBHI (*Yayasan Lembaga Bantuan Hukum*) was founded by the well-known lawyer Adnan Buyung Nasution in the 1970s.

11 The following information is based on the workshop proceedings (Syarikat 2003) and the second author's observations.

12 For instance, M. Billah (Komnas HAM), KH (abbreviation of *kyai haji*) Syamsuddin (NU), M. Adnan (NU), and KH Wahid Zuhdi (Pesantren Al Ma'ruf, Purwodadi).

13 Prior to this workshop, he traveled to many *pesantren* personally asking for the support of several *kyais* such as KH Sahal Mahfudz in Pati (Central Java), KH Mustofa Bisri in Rembang (Cilacap), KH Muchit Muzadi in Jember (Central Java), KH Abdullah Badawi in Cilacap (Central Java), KH Abdullah Faqih Langitan in Tuban (East Java), KH Abdurrahman Chudori, KH Yusuf Chudori in Magelang (Central Java), and also Buya Syafii Maarif from Muhammadiyah.

14 During the meetings there were moments when some participants cried and got upset about the past, but generally everyone got on well with each other which helped to make the workshop successful.

15 There was no precise date of the issuing of the Teperda letter. However, it can be suggested that Teperda was set up after 1965 by the local military office to investigate those who were accused to be followers or sympathizers of PKI.

16 True that the military is usually depicted as the main perpetrator, especially those who were supporting the actions taken by the Suharto camp within the military structure, both at national and local levels. In Central Java, the Suharto loyalists followed the instructions from Jakarta to arrest and even kill the supporters of PKI, and because these actions were done without proper legal procedures, many cases of wrong arrests such as those experienced by Anjar Roeslan and Sumilah occurred.

17 'Green' area refers to an area where many supporters from Islamic parties lived, while 'red' area refers to those of the Indonesian Communist Party PKI.
18 Followers of the national ideology of Pancasila.
19 Aidit was the Chairman of the Indonesian Communist Party and he was assassinated by the military in 1965 in Boyolali, Central Java.
20 For this occasion Syarikat set up a team to find out where former women political prisoners lived in Yogyakarta and also to do research in the National Archive in Jakarta. The following information is based on this documentary film (Syarikat 2005).
21 On the political history of Gerwani, see Wieringa (1999).
22 Rumekso Setyadi, who was involved in the making of this film documentary, also visited the National Archive office in Jakarta to gather information about Plantungan prison.
23 One idea suggested was that the civil society could produce their own truth commission report for the government to take actions. We believe that a number of NGOs such as ELSAM and Syarikat were in early discussions about taking this idea seriously.

References

Adam, A.W. (2004) *Pelusuran Sejarah Indonesia*, Yogyakarta: TriDe.
Aguilar, P. (2001) 'Justice, politics, and memory in the Spanish transition', in A.B. de Brito, C. Gonzalez-Enrique and P. Aguilar (eds) *The Politics of Memory*, Cambridge: Cambridge University Press.
Alagappa, M. (2004) *Civil Society and Political Change in Asia, Expanding and Contracting Democratic Space*, Stanford: Stanford University Press.
Amstutz, M.R. (2005) *The Healing of Nations*, Lanham, MD: Rowman & Littlefield.
Anderson, B.R.O'G. (1971) *A Preliminary Analysis of the October 1, 1965, Coup in Indonesia*, Ithaca, NY: Modern Indonesia Project, Cornell University.
Arivia, G. (2005) 'Kado untuk ibu, merasakan pengalaman etis?', *Kompas*, 30 September.
Babo-Soares, D. (2004) '*Nahe biti*: the philosophy and process of grassroots reconciliation (and justice) in East Timor', *The Asia Pacific Journal of Anthropology*, 5(1): 15–33.
Baxter, V. (2005) 'Civil society promotion of truth, justice, and reconciliation in Chile', *Peace and Change*, 30(1): 120–36.
Bronkhorst, D. (1995) *Truth and Reconciliation, Obstacles and Opportunities for Human Rights*, Amsterdam: Amnesty International Dutch Section.
Budiawan, P. (2004) *Mematahkan Pewarisan Ingatan, Wacana Anti-Komunis dan Politik Rekonsiliasi Pasca-Soeharto*, Jakarta: ELSAM.
Cribb, R. (ed.) (1990) *The Indonesian Killings in Java: Studies from Java and Bali*, Melbourne: Centre for Southeast Asian Studies, Monash University.
Crocker, D.A. (1998) 'Transitional justice and international civil society: toward a normative framework', *Constellations*, 5(4): 492–517.
Crouch, H. (1978) *The Army and Politics in Indonesia*, Ithaca, NY: Cornell University Press.
Daly, E. and Sarkin, J. (2007) *Reconciliation in Divided Societies: Finding Common Ground*, Philadelphia: University of Pennsylvania Press.
Dani, O. (2001) *Tuhan, Pergunakanlah Hati, Pikiran, dan Tanganku: Pledoi Omar Dani*, Jakarta: PT Media Lintas Inti Nusantara and Institut Studi Arus Informasi.
Dodson, P. (2008) 'It takes courage to apologize and it takes courage to forgive', *The Age*, 14 February.
Edwards, B., Foley, M.W. and Diani, M. (2001) *Beyond Tocqueville, Civil Society and the Social Capital Debated in Comparative Perspective*, Hanover and London: Tufts University.

Edwards, M. (2004) *Civil Society*, Cambridge: Polity Press.
ELSAM (2004) *Undang-Undang Republik Indonesian No. 27 Tahun 2004 Tentang Komisi Kebenaran dan Rekonsiliasi*, Jakarta: ELSAM.
Farid, H. and Simarmatra, R. (2004) *The Struggle for Truth and Justice: A Survey of Transitional Justice Initiatives throughout Indonesia*, New York: International Center of Transitional Justice.
Giring (2004) *Madura di Mata Dayak: Dari Konflik ke Rekonsiliasi*, Yogyakarta: Galang Press.
Hayner, P. (2001) *Unspeakable Truths*, London and New York: Routledge.
Heryanto, A. (2006) *State Terrorism and Political Identity in Indonesia: Fatally Belonging*, New York: Routledge.
ICTJ (2003) *Intended to Fail: The Trials before the Ad Hoc Human Rights Court in Jakarta*, New York: International Center of Transitional Justice.
Kingston, J. (2006) 'Balancing justice and reconciliation in East Timor', *Critical Asian Studies*, 38(3): 271–302.
Kritz, N.J. (1995) (ed.) *Transitional Justice*, Washington DC: United States Institute of Peace Studies.
Kock, T. (2008) 'Closing the gap', *The Australian*, 14 February.
Kontras (2006) *Aceh, Damai dengan Keadilan?: Mengungkap Kekerasan Masa Lalu*, Jakarta: Komisi untuk Orang Hilang dan Tindak Kekerasan.
Latief, A. (1998) *Pledoi Kol. A. Latief, Soeharto Terlibat G 30 S*, Jakarta: Institut Studi Arus Informasi.
Lee, H.G. (2004) *Civil Society in Southeast Asia*, Singapore: Institute of Southeast Asian Studies.
McAdams, A.J. (1997) (ed.) *Transitional Justice and the Rule of Law in New Democracies*, Notre Dame and London: University of Notre Dame Press.
Moestahal, A. (2002) *Dari Gontor ke Pulau Buru: Memoar H. Achmadi Moestahal*, Yogyakarta: Syarikat.
Neier, A. (1999) 'Rethinking truth, justice, and guilt after Bosnia and Rwanda', in C. Hesse and R. Post (eds) *Human Rights in Political Transitions: Gettysburg to Bosnia*, New York: Zone Books.
Putnam, R.D. (2003) *Making Democracy Work: Civic Traditions in Modern Italy*, Princeton: Princeton University Press.
Roosa, J. (2006) *Pretext for Mass Murder: The September 30th Movement and Suharto's Coup d'Etat in Indonesia*, Madison, WI.: University of Wisconsin Press.
Rotberg, R.I. and Thompson, D. (2000) (eds) *Truth v. Justice: The Morality of Truth Commissions*, Princeton and Oxford: Princeton University Press.
Sasongko, H.D.H. (2005) *Korupsi Sejarah dan Kisah Derita Akar Rumput*, Jakarta: Pustaka Utan Kayu.
Sekretariat Keadilan dan Perdamaian (2007) *Memoria Passionis di Papua Tahun 2005: Catatan Sosial, Politik, HAM*, Jayapura: Sekretariat Keadilan dan Perdamaian, Keuskupan Jayapura.
Simanjuntak, T. (2003) 'Jalan terjal menggapai keadilan: *qua vadis* komisi kebenaran dan rekonsiliasi', *Dignitas*, 1(1): 167–93.
Sulistiyanto, P. (2005) 'Reconciliation and forgiveness in the post-Suharto Indonesia', paper presented at the International Conference on Truth and Reconciliation Commission in Indonesia organized by ELSAM, Jakarta, Indonesia, 12–14 September.
—— (2007) 'Politics of justice and reconciliation in post-Suharto Indonesia', *Journal of Contemporary Asia*, 37(1): 73–94.

Sumarwan, A. (2007) *Menyeberangi Sungai Air Mata: Kisah Tragis Tapol '65 dan Upaya Rekonsiliasi*, Yogyakarta: Kanisius.

Syarikat (2003) 'Narasi Forum Semarang', Laporan Workshop Rekonsiliasi dan Rehabilitasi Masyarakat Korban Tragedi 1965/66.

—— (2005) *Kado untuk Ibu* (DVD film), Yogyakarta: Syarikat Indonesia.

Tim Advokasi Kebenaran dan Keadilan (2006) *Permohonan Hak Uji Materiil Terhadap Undang-Undang No. 27 Tahun 2004 Tentang Komisi Kebenaran dan Rekonsiliasi*, Jakarta: ELSAM-Imparsial-Kontras-LBH Jakarta-YLP Yaphi-SND.

Tindage, R. (2006) *Damai yang Sejati: Rekonsiliasi di Tobelo, Kajian Teologi dan Komunikasi*, Jakarta: Yakoma-PGI.

Wieringa, S.E. (1999) *Penghancuran Gerakan Perempuan di Indonesia*, Jakarta: Garba Budaya dan Kalyanamitra.

Wajidi, F. (2003) 'Syarikat dan eksperimentasi rekonsiliasi kulturalnya', *Tashwirul Afkar*, 15, Jakarta: Lakpesdam.

Zurbuchen, M.S. (2002) 'History, memory, and the "1965 incident" in Indonesia', *Asian Survey*, Vol. XLII(4): 561–81.

—— (2005) *Beginning to Remember: The Past in the Indonesian Present*, Singapore and Seattle: National University of Singapore Press and University of Washington Press.

11 A bridge and a barrier
Islam, reconciliation, and the 1965 killings in Indonesia

Katharine E. McGregor

In the wake of the failed coup attempt of 1 October 1965, which the army blamed on the Indonesian Communist Party (PKI), the army together with religious and nationalist vigilantes perpetrated a wave of mass killings of persons affiliated with the PKI and its affiliate organizations. Approximately 500,000 people were killed and many more were imprisoned without trial and subjected to further persecution once released (Cribb 1990: 14). For the duration of the New Order regime, the government continued to portray all communists as brutal for their alleged role in torturing and murdering the seven military victims of the 1965 coup attempt and for alleged acts of aggression against Islamic groups prior to the killings such as in the land actions of 1964, in which *pesantren* (Islamic boarding school) lands were targeted (McGregor 2007: 68–74, 100–2, 202–3). Some people thus represented the subsequent killings as a 'justifiable act of revenge'.[1]

Since the fall of Suharto in 1998, Indonesians have experienced a much greater degree of freedom to articulate alternative versions of sensitive chapters of the Indonesian past and to research and investigate past crimes against humanity. Victims, victims' groups, non-governmental organizations, and historians have begun to put forward new narratives of the events of 1965–66 in which communists and members of the broader Left have been humanized and portrayed instead as victims of the New Order regime. They have begun to research and document the killings and the suffering of former political prisoners, to uncover mass graves and in some cases demand compensation from the government. These efforts have not been universally welcomed. In some instances they have been met with violent protest.[2] A significant degree of resistance to these revised versions of the past has originated from Islamic groups or individuals, who in the past supported or participated in the violence. One source of opposition is retired members of Ansor, the youth wing of Nahdlatul Ulama (NU), one of the biggest Muslim organizations in Indonesia that played a significant role in the mass killings. At the same time, young members of Ansor and other organizations linked to NU have begun the sensitive task of promoting reconciliation between their members and victims of the violence of 1965–66.

Based on surveys of a variety of NU publications, press reports, transcripts of dialogues, and interviews with concerned parties, this chapter will probe the reasons behind these polarized positions on confronting the violence of 1965–66. I will focus here on the links between the killings and alternate notions of Islamic identity within NU and also examine how ideas of Islam have been deployed for the purposes of creating both a bridge and a barrier to achieving peace over this past. In doing so I will elaborate on a larger theme of the book of how ideas of culture, in this case ideas of Islam, can be mobilized for the purposes of bringing members of a fractured community together.

Van de Kok et al. (1991: 88), Zurbuchen (2002), Heryanto (2005), and others have all demonstrated that the 1965–66 killings are important in Indonesia not only as an event in history, but also as an element of political discourse. My research is distinguished from most works on 1965–66 by a focus on the religious dimension of the way the killings are understood in contemporary Indonesia. Purwadi (2003) has provided the most thorough analysis of the Islamic dimensions of anti-communist discourse in Indonesia. Purwadi does not, however, approach this topic from the perspective of competing notions of Islam, nor does he focus on specific resistance from within NU to re-examining this past, which has increased since the period of his research.

Nahdlatul Ulama, Islam, and the 1965–66 killings

The mass killings of 1965–66 were the combined result of rising social tensions over resources exacerbated by a failing economy, political opportunism, military direction, provocation and coercion, and the propaganda surrounding the cruelty of communists in the coup attempt. They were often the product of long-standing conflicts within local communities exploited by the military (see Robinson 1995: 273–303). In East Java we know that the sense of threat to the interests of Islamic groups escalated when communists and members of affiliated organizations began to implement land reforms in 1964 and 1965, which resulted in attempted seizures of *pesantren* lands.[3]

Fealy (1998) described how during this period the militants within NU, who were concerned about increased accommodation by NU's leadership of the system of Guided Democracy that allowed the communists a prominent role, became increasingly aggressive in their attitudes to communists.[4] Immediately after the 1965 coup attempt these militants pressured the NU leadership to join the army in accusing the communist party of orchestrating the coup attempt. On 2 October 1965, NU leaders joined the armed forces to form the Action Front to Crush the 30th of September Movement (KAP-Gestapu). Members of the armed wing of Ansor, Banser then went on to kill thousands of leftists with varying degrees of military supervision.

The fact that some Islamic groups participated in the killings does not mean that the killings were the product of 'religion' or 'religious' differences. Victims of the post-coup violence included not only communists and members of affiliated organizations, but also Sukarno supporters, particularly supporters of the leftist wing of the Indonesian National Party (PNI) and members of leftist military units. Amongst the victims were also Indonesians who would have described themselves as Muslims. In the case of Bali, Robinson (1995: 301) stressed the "manipulation of cultural and religious symbols" by enemies of the PKI including the military and other political groups as crucial to understanding the violence that took place. He gives the example of efforts to promote the Hindu derived idea of *nyupat* or voluntary execution to assuage a killer's conscience suggesting that this was promoted as an equivalent to freeing a person from their suffering and allowing them reincarnation, versus murder.

In the case of Java, Islamic concepts may have been similarly exploited by both *kyai* (Islamic scholars) or military officers for different reasons. The perception that participation in the killings was a religious duty is replicated in Rochijat's (1985) famous account of 1965–66. He wrote, "After all, wasn't it everyone's responsibility to fight the *kafir* (unbelievers)?" (Rochijat 1985: 43). Rochijat also recalled hearing the cries of '*Allahu-Akbar*' (God is Great) as NU vigilantes waged destruction on PKI property and persons. Fealy (1998: 339) noted that several *kyai* in East Java, such as Kyai Machrus of Lirboyo Pesantren, were vocal in their support of violence against communists on the basis that they were hostile infidels (*kafir harbi*) or persons who had rebelled against a legitimate government (*bughat*). The Surabaya branch of the NU Party issued a statement on 10 October 1965 stating that according to the sura Al-Baqoroh[sic.] (The Cow), verse 191, the appropriate response to the coup attempt was to "eradicate those (who had committed slander) wherever they are, and remove them from their positions as they have done, because slander is worse than this."[5] This suggests that in East Java at least some people connected the killings with religious duty or framed their participation in religious ways and more specifically on the basis that this was a 'just war' against deserving enemies. The notion of a just war ties into the widely shared perception that Islam endorses defensive violence.

In his research on non-violence and peace-building in Islam, Abu-Nimer (2003: 185) critiques an emphasis in Western scholarship, in particular, on the connections between Islam and violence, arguing that Islamic cultures in different local contexts can "encompass values and norms that promote peace-building as well as the use of force and violence". Building on Avruch (2000: 14–6) who cautioned against viewing culture and in this case Islam as either homogeneous, fixed, and/or uniform across a group or as a tradition, Abu-Nimer (2003) reminded us of the need to examine multiple ideas of Islam. Despite his anti-communist sympathies, for example, one *kyai* (the current head of Langitan Pesantren, Abdullah Faqih) forbade members of his *pesantren* from taking part in the killings on the basis that Islam forbids the taking of another life without reason and a fear that mistakes might be made as to who was to be killed.[6] Another *kyai* Choiril Bisri, who was head of Ansor in Rembang, also forbade his friends from persecuting members of the PKI and tried to dissuade the military from killing leftists on the basis that they were neighbors and only different in their ideology and if they were wrong, they should be tried according to the law.[7] It is thus necessary to examine a range of ideas of Islam evoked in this memory war, or battle to control interpretations of the 1965–66 violence.

Resistance within NU to opening this past

Until his death in 2006, Kyai Yusuf Hasyim, former head of the Tebu Ireng *pesantren* in Jombang, East Java had led resistance within NU in order to defend the idea that the 1965–66 killings were justified and to stop initiatives that would award concessions to, or political and historical accommodation to, former political prisoners. His views are shared to varying degrees by other senior members of NU who experienced the 1960s and by a broader alliance of people and organizations with strong anti-communist views. Yusuf Hasyim killed leftists following the Madiun Affair of 1948, in which he claimed he narrowly escaped being a victim of attacks on *kyai* (Islamic preachers) and *pesantren* by leftist troops. Pesindo (Indonesian Socialist Youth) troops carried out these attacks following their failed attempt to seize local government and as they fled Republican forces. Kahin (1952: 300) wrote that members of the Islamic party Masyumi, which was supported at this time by NU members, were singled out for cruel treatment including torture and execution, but he does not detail how many people were killed. Fealy (1998: 313, n24) suggested that in the clashes between communists and *santri* (devout Muslims) some estimated 8,000 people, mostly communists, had died. Hasyim's nephew, Solahuddin Wahid (2007), suggested that this experience left such an imprint on Hasyim that he then had always remained suspicious of movements that were similar to the PKI. Hasyim went on to play a key role in the armed wing of Ansor, Banser (*Barisan Serbaguna*, Multipurpose Ansor Brigade) in the early 1960s and participated in and directed Banser's killing campaigns in Java.

Several themes are apparent in the statements made by Yusuf Hasyim and his followers concerning the perceived or potential rehabilitation of former leftists since the fall of Suharto. First they argued that it was necessary to continue vigilance against the PKI because in the past they supported atheism and contributed to the political marginalization of Islam. In response to his nephew Abdurrahman Wahid's controversial proposal made while he was President to lift the ban on communism in Indonesia (TAP MPRS 25/1966), Hasyim (2000) stated his opposition on the grounds that "communists do not believe in the existence of God. They believe that there is no Almighty God. God, according to communist teachings is a made up concept or the product of a person's imagination."

He claimed that communism, because of its atheism, was thus a threat to all religions. He also asserted that in the early 1960s President Sukarno had paralyzed almost all Islamic forces, with the exception of NU and Ansor. He noted that Masyumi (which had links with the PRRI rebellions)[8] had been banned, GPI (*Gerakan Pemuda Islam*, Muslim Youth Movement) had been disbanded, and HMI (*Himpunan Mahasiswa Indonesia*, Islamic Student's Association) was threatened (Hasyim 2000). This is an exaggerated claim as organizations such as Muhammadiyah and Persis (*Persatuan Islam*) continued to thrive. In making this claim, Hasyim attempted to appeal to those who also felt that only since the closing years of the Suharto regime had Islam been once again allowed a political role. He implied threats to the future political role of Islam if groups unsympathetic to religion were again allowed political space.

Second it is clear that Hasyim and others view historical revision as a threat to the image of NU. Hasyim (2000) referred to the ban on communism as "a hard won victory for Muslims"; he implied that lifting this ban would nullify the contribution that Muslims have made to the Indonesian nation by crushing the communists. There is also a sense that by re-examining this past, NU's claim to the status of hero in this 'battle' against communism will be negated. For the duration of the New Order this role was openly celebrated. Anam (1990: 92), a former leader in the NU youth wing Ansor, for example referred to the *jasa* (merit or service) of Ansor in these actions and to Ansor as the backbone to the East Java operations to kill communists. Again drawing on religious justification and the idea of hostile infidels, Anam stated that "the communists were enemies of religion, they had to be wiped out (*diberantas*)."

The third theme advocated by those within NU who defend this violence is that the killings were more akin to a civil war than a one-sided repression of communists. Proponents of this view frequently suggest that the communists antagonized Muslims prior to the coup attempt. Former national head of Ansor, Chalid Mawardi, for example recalled in an interview how communists referred in the early 1960s to *kyai* as one of the seven kinds of "village devils" in relation to the land reform actions, and that the cultural wing of the PKI (presumably a reference to LEKRA, the People's Cultural Institute) hosted a cultural activity entitled 'The Death of God'.[9] Hasyim (2005: 16–7) also espoused the idea that Islam was under attack in the 1960s; he recalled how members of Ansor studied Hitler's *Mein Kampf* as a model for building a power base from which to "counter a threatening force". Some communist linked organizations, such as the Indonesian Farmers Union (*Barisan Tani Indonesia*), engaged in small-scale attacks on Muslim landlords during the land reforms. Claims of communist antagonism are, however, exaggerated in order to reinforce the idea that all communists were hostile and aggressive to Islamic groups and that the post-coup killings were thus part of a 'just war'.

Yusuf Hasyim not only emphasized leftist threats to Islam in the Sukarno years, he also frequently tried to remind Indonesians of 'communist cruelty' in the Madiun Affair of 1948. In 2001, for example, Yusuf Hasyim organized a photographic exhibition in Jakarta depicting the cruelty of communists in 1948 and 1965 in addition to communist cruelty in other countries. The exhibition was repeated in 2003 (Hasyim 2003). Then in 2004, Yusuf Hasyim hosted a national dialogue between NU and those who identified themselves as families of victims of the communists in 1948 (Madiun) and in 1965.[10] As noted earlier the number of *santri* Muslims killed in 1948 is unclear, but as Fealy (1998: 313, n24) noted, in *pesantren* circles the number was often exaggerated . The exhibitions were intended to stem any sympathy felt towards victims of the post-coup violence and to prevent concessions to them, whereas the 2004 dialogue focused on preventing future concessions.

A key theme in all these efforts was to reject the portrayal of former political prisoners or those who died in the mass killings, as victims and instead to suggest Muslims were the victims of communist violence. Poet Taufiq Ismail, a firm anti-communist who joined in student demonstrations of 1966 against Sukarno and the PKI with close ties to the conservative and anti-communist organization Indonesian Islamic Missionary Council (*Dewan Dakwah Islamiyah Indonesia*), made a lengthy and impassioned contribution to the 2004 dialogue with the victims of the PKI. He claimed "we are pressured to always feel guilty about what we did to them in 1965. But what they did to us in 1948, we will just whisper about it" (Dialog Ulama NU 2004). In the case of both Madiun and more clearly 1965–66, the number of leftists killed strongly outweighs the number of *santri* killed, but this did not hold Ismail back. He went on to deny the scale of the violence against the communists asking "if the purpose is to pressure the Muslim community, the number of victims will always be exaggerated" (Dialog Ulama NU 2004). Here Ismail suggested that under the guise of reconciliatory efforts, the Muslim community was again under attack, as it allegedly was in the 1960s, this time as a result of the efforts of ex-political prisoners to draw attention to this past.

Although there were differences in the individual views of the participants in the 2004 dialogue, it seems that what they feared most is the historical revision whereby NU members would be cast as human rights abusers. This would significantly threaten the institutional image of NU as a moderate organization. Those who participated in the violence have more to fear if former leftists were rehabilitated, including perhaps future prosecution. The possibility of a future Truth and Reconciliation Commission covering this violence, knocked back by the Constitutional Court in 2006, but now again under consideration by a newly appointed Human Rights Commission, has intensified concerns about prosecution in *santri* circles.

Participants in the 2004 dialogue issued a joint statement requesting the Constitutional Court to re-evaluate the decisions to allow former political prisoners to become legislative candidates and stated the need for greater awareness about the past crimes of the PKI (*Republika* 2004). Yusuf Hasyim also directly intervened in the textbook debates, discussed by Leksana in this volume, to attempt to prevent students learning about alternative versions of the 1965 coup attempt; in June 2005, he led a delegation to meet with the head of the People's Consultative Assembly to protest against the omission of the 1948 and 1965 PKI revolts from the 2004 history curriculum (*Republika* 2005). By December 2005 the National Curriculum Standardization Board decided to return to the 1994 curriculum and include accounts of the Madiun Affair as a PKI betrayal and of the involvement of the PKI in the 1965 coup attempt (*Tempo Interaktif* 2005). Hasyim also protested against the proposed Truth and Reconciliation Commission.

Alternative perspectives and counter discourses

So far I have concentrated on Islamic opposition to challenging the official version of the 1965–66 killings. Despite vehement resistance to opening this past by some within NU, the former head of NU, Abdurrahman Wahid, had taken a far more conciliatory approach to this past. Wahid's views on 1965–66 are a product of both his personal experience and his open approach to alternative ideologies. Wahid's position on this past is crucial because of not only the steps he had taken to address this, but also because of his status as grandson of the founder of NU and as a long-serving head of NU from 1984 to 1999.

In the early 1960s Wahid was studying abroad in Cairo and here he was exposed to many different ideas (Barton 2002: 87). As a staff member of the Indonesian Embassy in Cairo, he was well informed about the Left–Right polarization in Indonesia. After the coup, he was instructed to assess for communist leanings all Indonesian students studying in Cairo. Because the students were all from *santri* backgrounds and studying at renowned Islamic universities, it was fairly easy for him to defend each person even if they had been interested in leftist thinking, but the experience frightened him (Barton 2002: 87–90).

Wahid maintained a concern for the victims of 1965–66 throughout the New Order regime. In 2000, the year after he had been elected president, he floated the idea of lifting the ban on communism. This proposal caused great controversy.[11] It was in part through Wahid's inspiration that the Yogyakarta branch of Ansor founded an organization called Syarikat (*Masyarakat Santri untuk Advokasi Rakyat*, Muslim Community for Social Advocacy). Syarikat also grew out of the activities of Lakpesdam NU (*Lembaga Kajian dan Pengembangan Sumber Daya Manusia*, NU Institute for Research and Development of Human Resources), which commenced grassroots human rights training in *pesantren* in 1997 (Olliver 2004). In 2002 Lakpesdam also hosted a form of local reconciliation in the town of Blitar (East Java) where the army and Banser had crushed the last armed communists in 1968. The current head of Syarikat, Imam Aziz, previously headed Yogyakarta's Lakpesdam NU. Both these organizations deploy alternative notions of Islam to challenge understandings of the violence of 1965–66.

Syarikat focuses on the joint aims of reconciliation and rehabilitation for the purpose of building a peaceful and democratic Indonesia. Its members are motivated to prevent future conflicts by strengthening society's social fabric.[12] Imam Aziz claims that they are theologically driven by the desire to create greater justice in society, based on the view that this is one of the most important messages of the Qu'ran.[13] They are strongly oriented towards the future and achieving societal harmony. Although they use the term reconciliation to describe their work, they also focus on the goal of achieving coexistence and enhancing bonds across two groups of people that have in some cases purposely isolated themselves from the other for almost 40 years. Several international bodies such as the UNHCR (United National High Commissioner for Refugees) have begun to advocate for coexistence, which encompasses 'cooperation across' previous lines of division and programs in the fields of arts, education, and economic development (Chayes & Minow 2003: xx–xxii). Syarikat's activities include organizing meetings or collaborative projects between former members of the left and their families and the NU community, creating associations for women victims and efforts to lobby members of the parliament to address this past and in particular to end discrimination against former political prisoners and their families. They also seek to promote alternative truth telling by means of their publications, films, and photographic and object-based exhibitions. Members of Syarikat have worked together with victims' organizations to advocate for restoration of their rights and a reintegration of former leftists into society.[14]

Sulistiyanto and Setyadi (this volume) provide an assessment of the grassroots nature of Syarikat's work focusing on narrative-based initiatives like public meetings in which members of the older generation of NU and people who became victims in the post-coup period share their experiences, and Syarikat's film projects. Another aspect of Syarikat's work is to challenge existing beliefs about the killings within NU circles and especially the theological justifications for this violence.

In 2003 Lakpesdam published a special edition of its journal *Tashwirul Afkar: Jurnal Refleksi Pemikiran Keagamaan dan Kebudayaan* (Journal of Reflection of Religious and Cultural Thinking), entitled *The 1965–66 Event: Tragedy, Memory and Reconciliation*. The issue featured two articles reflecting on Islamic theological arguments for reconciliation. The first of these articles, written by Imam Aziz (2003), provides numerous citations from the Qu'ran in support of the need to acknowledge past mistakes and for reconciliation between perpetrators and victims. He quoted first from verse 32 in the sura *Al Maidah* (The Feast 5: 32)[15], to argue that Islam views the killing of others as a crime against all people. This is a significant departure from attempts to use Islam to justify the killings. Second, he cited verse 18 of *Al-Hasyr* (The Gathering [of Forces] 59: 18)[16] to demonstrate the need for Muslims to look at their faults in the past in order to build a just society. Third, he quoted from verse 160 of *Al-Baqarah* (The Cow 2: 160)[17] to argue that those who have repented and made peace and stated the truth will have their sins forgiven. This verse encourages those who had committed past violence to also repent. Finally, to justify Syarikat's mission he quoted from verse 9 of *Al Hujurat* (The Private Quarters 49: 9)[18] to claim that reconciliation is recommended in the Qu'ran. Perhaps in anticipation of many of the arguments made by Muslims who reject the idea that the PKI were innocent victims, Aziz interestingly stated that truth seeking is not just about victims stating their viewpoints. He claimed perpetrators also need to be given the chance to explain their actions in the context of defending themselves (Aziz 2003). This last statement seems to be one way in which accommodation with those on the other side of this history war might be achieved.

The second article by Abdul Moqsith Ghazali, who is Head of the Centre for Research and Development at Ma'had Aly in Situbondo and researcher for the Wahid Institute,[19] argued that the barriers to reconciliation on 1965–66 are both psychological and theological. Ghazali (2003: 25) claimed that "psychologically those who were victims of PKI cruelty still harbour anger towards the PKI, which they will not let go of". Theologically the main barrier to reconciliation in his view is that the teachings of the PKI are considered to be anti-God and that PKI members are viewed as atheist. Ghazali stressed the need to consider the case of the 1965–66 killings from the perspective of *fikih* or Islamic jurisprudence, which includes a responsibility to achieve justice for groups who have been downtrodden.

In this article he critiqued conservative Islamic groups who he felt distort teachings of Islam and promote ideas of exclusivism, fueled by classical Islamic jurisprudence. Ghazali directly tackled some of the justifications used by those who participated in, or later defended, the mass killings or continuing persecution of leftists and their families. In particular he examined the concept of *kafir*, suggesting it has broader meaning than one who does not believe in the teachings of God. Based on the writings of the Indian philosopher, Ali Asghar Engineer, Ghazali (2003: 35) suggested that *kafir* may also apply to persons of means who stand by and let their neighbors die of hunger.[20] Drawing on the work of the famous Japanese scholar of Islam, Toshihiko Izutsu, he also claimed that historically the term *kafir* meant one who was not thankful and that this social historical meaning should not be ignored (Ghazali 2003: 35). He also claimed that there is no theological justification for sanctions against an unbeliever. Ghazali (2003: 35) argued based on the sura *Al-Sadjdah* (Bowing Down in Worship 32: 25)[21] that only Allah the Creator has the right and ability to judge the faith of a person and that this judgment is not made in this world, but in the Hereafter. This directly counters claims, such as those made by Rochijat (1985) that it was a duty to kill the *kafir* and Yusuf Hasyim's suggestion that atheists are necessarily enemies of Islam. Although he did not deal with the category hostile infidels, Ghazali presented a sufficient challenge to justifications for killing communists, on the basis that people do not have the right to judge another person's belief in God or make the assumption they are non-believers. Following the lead of Syarikat, Ghazali also pointed to the cases of the Muslim communists Kyai Haji Misbach and Hasan Raid to challenge the notion that all members of the PKI were atheists.

Like Aziz, Ghazali (2003: 29–30) also implied that forgiveness must come from both sides. He also argued that reconciliation initiatives must come not only from the state, but also from organizations such as NU and Muhammadiyah. To counter discrimination against the children of former political prisoners, Ghazali made a strong case for the rejection of the idea of inherited sins within Islam. He argued first based on the sura *Al-Najm* (The Star 53: 38–9)[22] and on the interpretation of Islamic scholar Thabathaba'i in his famous exegesis *Al-Mizan*, that a person cannot be sanctioned or tried for the sins of another (Ghazali 2003: 27). Second he argued that based on the sura *Fathir* (The Creator 35: 18)[23] and Islamic scholar, al-Fakhr al Razy's reading of this, every person is born in a state of purity and no one can be punished for the sins of another person (Ghazali 2003: 27). He thus suggested that while some guilt may lie with their parents, these children cannot be punished for what their parents have done.

The choice of these authors to use the Qu'ran and theological interpretations to support the process of reconciliation can be understood as an effort to counter the claim frequently made by some Muslims that the killings were justified because the communists were a threat to Islam, and atheist. These articles demonstrate alternative uses of ideas of Islam in this memory war that support peace, and counter claim that Islam justifies the past behavior of members of Ansor. Gopin (2003: 262) observed that "for strategists of coexistence, it is critical to examine and understand how each religion promotes countervailing values", because adversaries will often use ideas of religion to "strengthen the us–them dynamic of conflict and violence wherein the members of one's own group are the righteous victims and the others are only abusers". The pattern of using ideas of Islam to 'Other' communists is central to representations of the violence of 1965–66.

This special edition of the journal *Tashwirul Afkar* is significant because of the fact that its target audience was *pesantren* or Islamic boarding schools. Because of the involvement of senior members of some *pesantren* in the killings, some *pesantren* have either formally or informally encouraged a continuing commitment to anti-communism amongst their members.[24]

The dramatically different views of people within Syarikat and Lakpesdam and some older members of NU are a product of developments within NU in the last 20 years. The founders of Syarikat are young members of NU, mostly alumni from *pesantren* and universities. They are part of a broader group of NU activists concerned with promoting ideas of civil society and democracy within NU circles (Wajidi 2004: 68). The focus of these groups can be traced back to the 1984 NU Situbondo decision backed strongly by Abdurrahman Wahid to return to the 1926 mission as a religious organization (*jamiah diniyyah*) under the guidance of *ulama* by withdrawing from politics and focusing on culture and educational tasks (Wajidi 2004: 68).

In contrast to some older members of NU who oppose opening this past because of the possible threat to legitimacy new versions of the past might pose for them, the founders of Syarikat felt that as young members of NU they had no choice but to confront NU's role in the killings, especially if they wished to be involved in a credible way in the reform and democratization movement. The founders of Syarikat shared a perception that in the post-Suharto era, Ansor had been stigmatized in activist circles and it was for this reason that they sought to investigate the role of Ansor in the killings.[25]

Importantly researchers from Syarikat acknowledge the involvement of NU in the killings and they seek to address this past. They have, however, identified different positions on the killings across a range of *pesantren* ranging from support for the violence, such as the case of Lirboyo Pesantren in Kediri, to providing a temporary safe haven for members of the PKI as in the case of Pesantren Kedunglo also in Kediri (Wajidi 2003: 71). These findings answer Abu-Nimer's call, outlined earlier, for attention not only to the connections between violence and Islam, but also to acts of non-violence or peace in different Islamic contexts. We need to understand more about what brought about these varied responses.

Responses to Syarikat and Lakpesdam NU

There have been mixed responses to Syarikat within the broader community of NU. They have support from some leaders within NU because of the moral nature of their mission, but this support is by no means comprehensive. Syarikat researcher, Rumekso Setyadi, noted that support for Syarikat tended to fluctuate.[26] The current head of NU, Hasyim Muzadi supports the idea of cultural reconciliation by which he seems to imply only non-formal reconciliation or at least a restoration of the civil rights of victims, but he claims that in his view Syarikat does not have clear aims.[27] Imam Aziz claimed that at the very least many within NU have allowed Syarikat enough space to attempt better integration between former political prisoners and broader society. He felt that most within NU want this past finished with (although I would suggest they differ in their views about how this might occur). They are willing to acknowledge NU was involved, but they reject the idea of collective guilt and want it clarified that there were also some in NU who did not participate in the violence. Aziz suggested that resistance to Syarikat is limited to a few people. This is, however, an underestimation of resistance to their somewhat risky activities. Amongst all of the NGOs within the NU umbrella, the focus of Syarikat's activities is perhaps the most sensitive.

In the last few years there has been an increasing backlash from conservative Islamic groups and individuals against what is labeled 'Islam kiri' or leftist Islam which includes critiques of, for example, capitalism. Organizations with links to Abdurrahman's pluralist tradition such as the Liberal Islamic Network (*Jaringan Islam Liberal*) have been accused of distorting the teachings of Islam by more conservative members of NU and Muhammadiyah and by groups linked to Masyumi.[28] This backlash has also had ramifications for groups within NU that have sought to address the violence of 1965–66. They too have been branded with the label 'communist' (Misrawi 2004: 4). This backlash is not confined to senior Islamic figures who lived through the 1960s, but comes also from younger figures such as Fadli Zon, the nephew of Taufiq Ismail, who joined Yusuf Hasyim to reject the 2004 history curriculum (*Republika* 2005).[29] Another younger anti-communist who frequently speaks on this topic is M. Alfian Tanjung, a founder of PINTAR (*Pelajar Islam Indonesia*, Indonesian Islamic Students) and HAMMAS (*Himpunan Mahasiswa Muslim Antar Kampus*, Inter-Campus Association for Muslim Students) and a former leader of GPI.[30]

Resistance within NU to revisiting versions of 1965–66 is particularly strong in East Java. In May 2007 *AULA* magazine, the provincial-level NU magazine in East Java, devoted most of one triannual edition to the theme of the contemporary revival of the PKI. The magazine included attacks on both Gus Dur's (another way of referring to Abdurrahman Wahid) liberalism and on organizations such as Syarikat and Lakpesdam, which some view as products of his liberalism. Alongside one article on the alleged revival of communism, the magazine printed a photograph of a man holding a poster featuring Gus Dur with a hand extending to his shoulder, guiding him (a play on Wahid's limited vision as well). The extended arm is connected to a headless figure with a body in the form of a communist flag bearing the hammer and sickle. The bottom of the poster reads www.Gus.Comunis.id as if to imply that his website (http://www.gusdur.net) is also a hotbed of communist ideas (*AULA* 2007a).

The criticisms of Syarikat and Lakpesdam NU are more explicit. Abdul Wahid Asa, the magazine editor who is deputy head of NU East Java and a member of the Finance Commission in the regional East Java parliament, recounted his experience of the aggressiveness of the PKI in the land seizures of 1964. He recalled how in these situations Ansor naturally defended the *haji* (those who had made the pilgrimage, a mark of being a *santri*) and then after the coup, crushed the PKI. The author goes on to say that 40 years later in 2007, many NU youths who had never

Figure 11.1 "Beware of the PKI": The cover image of the East Java NU publication, *AULA*, 5(XXIX), May 2007

Figure 11.2 An image accompanying one article in *AULA*, 5(XXIX), May 2007: 28

witnessed these events "blame their parents and defend the PKI. Their excuse is for the sake of human rights" (Abdul Wahid Asa 2007: 9). In a direct slight at young members of NU involved with both Syarikat and Lakpesdam, he accused them of "failure to absorb the meaning of *birrul-walidin* [Arabic for being loyal to one's parents]" (Abdul Wahid Asa 2007: 9). Abdul Muchith Muzadi similarly stated that he could not understand the attitude of the young, "because Islam – particularly NU was the PKI's foremost enemy in the 1960s" (Subhan 2007: 22). For these men it is as if those within Syarikat have betrayed their elders, if not their own parents. This suggests a widening gap in visions between some members of the older and younger generations in NU and far stronger resistance to Syarikat than Aziz[31] alludes to.

Another article in the *AULA* magazine entitled 'NU Cadres Infiltrated' referred to the shock felt by several NU leaders in East Java when they discovered that NU was linked to the Syarikat publication, RUAS magazine, which profiles the stories of former political prisoners and that the editor in chief (Imam Aziz) was a "central leader of the Lakpesdam and an important figure in LKIS (*Lembaga Kajian Islam dan Sosial*, Institute for Social and Islamic Studies)" in Yogyakarta (Subhan 2007: 19). Abdul Wahid Asa warned that Lakpesdam "had to follow NU thinking, not others, particularly communists" (Subhan 2007: 21). In 2006, Sahrasad, of

Paramadina University in Jakarta, questioned whether NU itself was becoming increasingly intolerant citing NU's support for recent fatwa issued by the conservative Indonesian Council of Ulama (MUI) declaring the Islamic group Ahmadiyah heretical and banning pluralism, liberalism, and secularism, and for the anti-pornography bill (Sahrasad 2006), which sought to curtail the rights of women and freedom of expression.

Repeating the sentiments expressed in the 2004 dialogue, the historian and former head of Ansor in East Java, Agus Sunyoto[32] is quoted in the *AULA* magazine as saying that "in the eyes of the world Muslims are now being portrayed as reactionaries, anarchists and terrorists and more sadistic than communists" (*AULA* 2007b: 32–4). He implied that Islam has taken the place of communism as a new world enemy. He cautions readers, "We should not say we are proud about the past by saying that we have already destroyed the communists, for this will lead to us being considered evil, just as the communist were in the past" (*AULA* 2007b: 34). This comment signals a key problem with those who continue to defend past violence against communists. In defending the participation of Muslim groups in past violence, these people do reinforce the idea that violence is acceptable for Muslims or endorsed by Islam. Sunyoto's fear is that this plays into the equating of Islam with terrorism.

By failing to confront the involvement of Muslims in the violence of 1965, including personal involvement, however, some within NU are missing a valuable opportunity to critique the endorsement of violence carried out by groups such as Majelis Mujahidin and The Islamic Defenders Front (FPI), that NU together with Muhammadiyah have begun warning their followers against (Syam 2007). Recent anti-communist campaigns within and beyond NU are, as indicated earlier, connected to a much wider sense of Islam being under attack worldwide. This is an idea generally more often espoused in circles linked to the former Masyumi party, such as in the Islamic Missionary Council's publication *Media Dakwah* and by the radical groups listed earlier.[33] The fact that this *AULA* publication and many of the most vocal anti-communists within NU come from East Java reflects the intensity of violence that took place in this area over 40 years ago and perhaps fears of what it would mean to confront this past. On one occasion members of Syarikat were summoned to attend a meeting with senior *kyai* and counseled not to give their support to the proposed Truth and Reconciliation Commission.

Conclusions

In this chapter I have presented two polarized positions within NU on dealing with the history of 1965–66. There are probably many within NU less vocal about this past, who represent a middle position and indeed who are traumatized by this past. It is the older members of NU, those most directly connected to, if not involved in, the killings that are most active in challenging the efforts of ex-detainees and NGOs to research and make public human rights abuses in the killings and imprisonments following the 1965 coup attempt. It is they who seek to remind the nation that Muslims were the victims of communists in 1948 and in the early 1960s in order to defend the participation of members of NU in the post-coup violence. They are unwilling to let go of the official narrative of the killings as a justifiable act of revenge, because to do so would mean foregoing a claim to heroism and one basis of legitimation for NU's contributions to the nation. These men are attempting also to defend their own pride and sense of identity. For these older members of NU, communism is linked to a long-held fear of the suppression of political Islam as experienced in the early 1960s by groups like Masyumi and for most of the New Order.

Support for anti-communism is not limited to older NU members. Perhaps as a result of the efforts of the older generation to reinforce the message of past communist brutality, there are younger Indonesians who will continue to promote this cause. Many of these young people have links to different Islamic organizations outside of NU. They, like those they follow, have used interpretations of the killings to define Indonesia as a religiously devout country and a bastion of anti-communism in an attempt to strengthen commitment to religion at a time when they feel Islam is again under attack and threatened by liberalism. The communist label is thus a way of discrediting liberal ideas.

The younger members of NU in Syarikat and Lakpesdam NU are the product of a major wave of reformist thinking within NU and they have been shaped by very different experiences to those of their parents. They are far more open to examining alternative ideologies and they are not, for example, as molded by Cold War thinking or Cold War politics as their seniors. They are also highly aware of an entrenched pattern of historical manipulation in Indonesia. Young members of Ansor and Lakpesdam NU have taken the initiative to work towards reconciliation with survivors and the families of victims because they believe this is essential in order for the youth within Ansor to recover any sense of legitimacy in the present and for the purposes of achieving future peace in local communities. For them reconciliation is partly symbolic and oriented towards achieving the Islamic goals of societal harmony between members of NU and long marginalized former political prisoners or families of former leftists. They believe that national-level reconciliation is necessary, but there is not a strong emphasis on retributive justice in their agenda to date.

Accompanying the goal of reconciliation is an understanding that particular versions of Islamic theology have to date been a barrier to creating empathy or compassion for victims of the post-coup violence and thus any kind of will for reconciliation. Islamic scholars have thus turned to the Qu'ran as a potential way of challenging those who defend the killings and those who continue to attack alleged communists. It will take considerable time for these ideas to be socialized in NU and wider Islamic circles and they have already met with some resistance, but in tackling this issue Syarikat has began to overcome a broader obstacle to any national-level reconciliation over this past. These theological arguments are important not only in the case of 1965, but also to counter more narrow interpretations of Islam that suggest, for example, that violence against non-believers or non-Muslims is acceptable. They offer important examples of how concepts of Islam can be deployed as a bridge to achieving future peace.

Acknowledgments

This research was supported under Australian Research Council's Discovery Projects funding scheme (project number DPO772760) and by grants from the University of Melbourne. I would like to thank Greg Fealy and Birgit Bräuchler for their helpful comments on this chapter and Vannessa Hearman for her research assistance.

Notes

1 This term was first used by Indonesian historian Abdullah (2000).
2 See Zurbuchen's (2002: 579–80) account of the violent disruption of the attempted reburial in 2001 of bones recovered from a Wonosobo grave. Since this other violent actions in the name of Islam against so-called communists have occurred. These include intimidation by the Islamic Defenders Front of lawyers and supporters of the 2005 class action brought against all former presidents demanding the 1966 ban on communism be lifted (Diani 2005).
3 On the land reform see Mortimer (1972).
4 Another response to the political direction of the early 1960s was the pro-*jamiah* view or support for NU's withdrawal from politics and reversion to being a socio-religious organization (Fealy 1998: 312–5).
5 Ansor Tjabang Kopra Pekalongan (1965) VI/2 Surabaja, 10 Oktober, 1965. This is my translation of the Indonesian version of this verse. This verse in the Qu'ran from *Al-Baqara* reads "Kill them wherever you encounter them, and drive them out from where they drive you out, for persecution is more serious than killing." This and all subsequent extracts from the Qu'ran are taken from Haleem (2004).
6 Although Abdullah stated this in an interview, he qualified this statement by saying that he did not prohibit alumni of the *pesantren* from participating in the killings. Interview with Kyai Abdullah Faqih, Tuban, 27 February 2008.
7 KH Muhammad Cholil Bisri, Gerakan Pemuda Ansor, profile posted on the official Ansor website, http://gp-ansor.org/ (accessed on 13 June 2007).
8 The PRRI (Revolutionary Government of the Republic of Indonesia) consisted of Masyumi and Indonesian Socialist Party members together with dissident army officers declaring an alternative government in 1958 with covert US, British, and Australian support. The revolt was crushed shortly afterwards.
9 Interview with Chalid Mawardi, Jakarta, 22 February 2007.
10 The Dialogue was called *Dialog Ulama NU Dengan Keluarga Korban PKI '48 di Madiun dan '65 di Jakarta*, hereafter (Dialog Ulama NU) and held on 12 March 2004 in Jakarta. Many thanks to Lakpesdam NU for allowing me to purchase a VCD copy of the dialogue. The following observations are based on this recording.
11 For an analysis of responses to this proposal see Purwadi (2004: 46–73) and Kasemin (2004).
12 Interview with Rumekso Setyadi, Yogyakarta, 21 May 2007.
13 Interview with Imam Aziz, Yogyakarta, 22 May 2007.
14 Interview with Rumekso Setyadi, Yogyakarta, 21 May 2007.
15 "On account of [his deed], we decreed to the Children of Israel that if anyone kills a person – unless in retribution for murder or spreading corruption in the land – it is as if he kills all mankind, while if he saves a life it is as if he saves the lives of all mankind." Aziz has taken the meaning of this *sura* quite literally which seems justified.
16 "You who believe! Be mindful of God, and let every soul consider carefully what it sends ahead for tomorrow; be mindful of God, for God is well aware of everything you do." The rest of the *sura* focuses on a duty to the oppressed and to build a just society.

17 (From verse 159) "As for those who hide the proofs of guidance We send down, after We have made them clear to people in the Scripture, God rejects them, and so do others, (160) unless they repent, make amends and declare the truth. I will certainly accept their repentance: I am Ever relenting, the Most Merciful."
18 "If two groups of the believers fight, you [believers] should try to reconcile them; if one of them is [clearly] oppressing the other, fight the oppressors until they submit to God's command, then make a just and even-handed reconciliation between the two of them: God loves those who are even-handed."
19 Ma'had Aly is an institute for the advanced study of *fikih*, Islamic jurisprudence based at the Sukorejo Pesantren in Situbondo. The Wahid Institute was founded with the support of Abdurrahman Wahid and is an organization which seeks to expand the vision and intellectual principles of Abdurrahman Wahid for moderate Islam, democratic reform, religious pluralism, multiculturalism, and tolerance amongst Muslims both in Indonesia and around the world.
20 Engineer is a Muslim activist from India who offers his own version of Liberation theology based on re-interpreting Prophet Muhammad's life.
21 "[Prophet] it is your Lord who will judge between them on the Day of Resurrection concerning their differences."
22 (From verse 36–9) "Has he not been told what was written in the Scriptures of Moses and Abraham who fulfilled his duty that no soul shall bear the burden of another, that man will only have what he has worked towards."
23 "No burdened soul will bear the burden of another: even if a heavily laden soul should cry for help, none of its load will be carried, not even by a close relative. But you [Prophet] can only warn those who fear their Lord, though they cannot see Him, and keep up the prayer – whoever purifies himself does so for his own benefit – everything ends up with God."
24 Interview with Miftahul Huda, Kediri, 29 February 2008. On the role of Gus Makshum, who trained many anti-communist youth in martial arts in 1965–66, in promoting anti-communism in Kediri see also van Bruinessen (2002: 29).
25 Interview with Rumekso Setyadi and Pak Taufiqurrahman, Syarikat, Yogyakarta, 25 May 2005.
26 Interview with Rumekso Setyadi, Yogyakarta, 21 May 2007.
27 Interview with Hasyim Muzadi, 19 May 2007.
28 *Media Dakwah*, the flagship publication for *Dewan Dakwah Islamiyah Indonesia* (Indonesian Islamic Missionary Council) ran a series in 2002 covering the 'Danger of Liberal Islam' (*Bahaya Islam Liberal*): *Media Dakwah*, January, February, March 2002. One article in 2003 centered on the head of Jaringan Islam Liberal, Ulil Abshar Abdalla, 'Orang Liberal Indonesia-Malaysia Berhadapan dangan Ulama dan Umat Islam', *Media Dakwah*, February 2003.
29 Fadli Zon works for the Institute for Policy Studies, a private organization founded by retired General Prabowo, former head of Kostrad and Suharto's son-in-law.
30 Alfian Tanjung has made a DVD on this topic entitled *Menguak Indikasi dan Sistematika Kebangkitan PKI*, by Produksi Taruna Muslim foundation.
31 Interview with Imam Aziz, Yogyakarta, 22 May 2007.
32 Agus Sunyoto is also a co-author with Maksum and A. Zainuddin of the 1990 publication *Lubang-Lubang Pembantaian: Petualangan PKI Di Madiun*; a book that also attempts to highlight past 'communist' brutality. Interestingly, given the earlier statements, he is also a co-author of the 1996 publication *Banser berjihad menumpas PKI* (Banser undertakes jihad to crush the PKI), Tulungagung: Lembaga Kajian dan Pengembangan Pimipinan Wilayah Gerakan Pemuda Ansor Jawa Timur and Pesulukan Thoriqoh Agung.
33 *Media Dakwah* espouses the idea that Muslims are victims around the world by highlighting cases of Muslim suffering in Palestine, Iraq, Afghanistan, Kashmir, and elsewhere.

References

Abdul Wahid Asa (2007) 'Lupa', *AULA*, May.
Abdullah, T. (2000) 'Menata ingatan kolektif masyarakat,' *Kompas*, 3 October.
Abu-Nimer, M. (ed.) (2003) *Nonviolence and Peace Building in Islam*, Gainesville: University Press of Florida.
Anam, C. (1990) *Gerak Langkah Pemuda Ansor: Sebuah Percikan Sejarah Kelahiran*, Surabaya: Majalah Nahdlatul Ulama AULA.
Ansor Tjabang Kopra Pekalongan (1965).
AULA (2007a) 'www.Gus.Comunis.id' (image), 5(XXIX), May: 28.
—— (2007b) 'Cari siapa yang mendanai mereka' (Interview with Drs Agus Sunyoto), 5(XXIX), May.
Avruch, K. (2000) *Culture and Conflict Resolution*, Washington DC: United States Institute of Peace Press.
Aziz (2003) 'Teologi rekonsiliasi: mengungkap kebenaran, menegakkan keadilan', *Tashwirul Afkar*. 'Special Edition: Peristiwa '65–66', No. 15: 2–7.
Barton, G. (2002) *Abdurrahman Wahid: Muslim Democrat, Indonesian President. A View from Inside,* Sydney: UNSW Press.
Chayes, A. and Minow, M. (eds) (2003) *Imagine Co-existence: Restoring Humanity After Violent Ethnic Conflict*, San Fransisco: Jossey-Bass.
Cribb, R. (ed.) (1990) *The Indonesian Killings of 1965–1966: Studies from Java and Bali*, Clayton: Monash University Centre of Southeast Asian Studies.
Dialog Ulama NU (2004) *Dialog Ulama NU dengan Keluarga Korban PKI' 48 di Madiun dan '65 di Jakarta*, (DVD Recording) held on 12 March 2004, Jakarta.
Diani, H. (2005) 'FPI members stage protest during PKI court session', *Jakarta Post*, 4 August.
Fealy, G. (1998) *Ijtihad Politik Ulama: Sejarah NU 1952–1967*, Yogyakarta: LKiS.
Ghazali, A.M. (2003) 'Membincang fikih rekonsiliasi', *Tashwirul Afkar*. 'Special Edition: Peristiwa '65–66', No. 15: 24–36.
Gopin, M. (2003) 'Religion as an aid and a hindrance to postconflict coexistence work', in A. Chayes and M. Minow (eds) *Imagine Co-existence: Restoring Humanity After Violent Ethnic Conflic*t, San Fransisco: Jossey-Bass.
Haleem, M.A.S.A. (2004) *The Qur'an*, New York: Oxford University Press.
Hasyim, Y. (2000) 'Kenapa kita menentang komunisme?', *Republika*, 29 April.
—— (2003) 'Komunis dan sejarah hitam bangsa', *Republika,* 7 August.
—— (2005) 'Killing communists', in J.H. McGlynn (ed.) *Indonesia in the Suharto Years: Issues, Incidents and Images*, Jakarta: The Asia Foundation and Lontar Foundation.
Heryanto, A. (2005) *State Terrorism and Political Identity in Indonesia: Fatally Belonging*, London: Routledge.
Kahin, G. (1952) *Nationalism and Revolution in Indonesia*, Ithaca: Cornell University Press.
Kasemin, K. (2004) *Mendamaikan Sejarah: Analisis Wacana Pencabutan*, TAP MPRS/Xxv/1966, Yogyakarta: LKiS.
McGregor, E.K. (2007) *History in Uniform: Military Ideology and the Construction of Indonesia's Past*, Singapore: Asian Studies Association of Australia in conjunction with National University of Singapore Press, KITLV and University of Hawaii Press.
Media Dakwah (2003) 'Orang liberal Indonesia-Malaysia berhadapan dangan ulama dan umat Islam', February.
Misrawi, Z. (2004) *Menggugat Tradisi: Pergulatan Pemikiran Anak Muda NU*, Jakarta: Kompas P3M.

Mortimer, R. (1972) *The Indonesian Communist Party and Land Reform 1959–1965*, Ithaca: Cornell University Press.

Olliver, C. (2004) 'Reconciling NU and the PKI', *Inside Indonesia*, 77: 24–5.

Purwadi, B. (2003) *Mematahkan Pewarisan Ingatan: Wacana Anti-Komunis dan Politik Rekonsiliasi Pasca Soeharto*, Jakarta: ELSAM.

Republika (2004) 'Ulama NU dan korban keganasan PKI buat pernyataan bersama', 15 March.

—— (2005) 'Pelajaran sejarah kembali ke kurikulum', 24 June.

Robinson, G. (1995) *The Dark Side of Paradise: Political Violence in Bali*, Ithaca: Cornell University Press.

Rochijat, P. (1985) 'Am I PKI or non-PKI?', *Indonesia*, 40: 37–52.

Sahrasad, H. (2006) 'Is NU Shifting toward intolerance?', *Jakarta Post*, 8 May, reproduced on GUSDUR.NET – Abdurrahman Wahid's official site. Online. Available at: http://www.gusdur.net/english/ (accessed on 2 June 2007).

Subhan, M. (2007) 'Kader NU kesusupan', *AULA*, May.

Syam, N. (2007) 'Gerakan Islam radikal rugikan NU-Muhammadiyah', Syirah.com, 4 July 2007. Online. Available at: http://www.syirah.com (accessed on 6 July 2007).

Tempo Interaktif (1 December 2005) Online. Available at: http://tempointeraktif.com (accessed on 15 March 2007).

van Bruinessen, M. (2002) 'Back to Situbondo: Nahdlatul Ulama attitudes towards Abdurrahman Wahid's presidency and his fall', in H. Schulte Nordholt and I. Abdullah (eds) *Indonesia: In Search of Transition*, Yogyakarta: Pustaka Pelajar.

van de Kok, J., Cribb, R. and Heins, M. (1991) '1965 and all that: history in the politics of the New Order', *Review of Indonesian and Malaysian Affairs*, 25(2): 84–94.

Wahid, S. (2007) 'Mengenang Pak Ud', 2 April. Online. Available at: http://www.tebuireng.net (accessed on 15 May 2007).

Wajidi, F. (2003) 'Syarikat dan eksperminentasi rekonsiliasi kulturalnya', *Tashwirul Afkar*. 'Special Edition: Peristiwa '65–66', No. 15: 55–79.

—— (2004) 'NU youth and the making of civil society', in S. Hanneman and H. Schulte Nordholt (eds), *Indonesia in Transition: Rethinking 'Civil Society', 'Region' and 'Crisis'*, Yogyakarta: Pustaka Pelajar.

Zurbuchen, M.S. (2002) 'History, memory and the "1965 incident" in Indonesia', *Asian Survey*, XLII(4): 564–81.

Index

Note: General topics of this volume such as grassroots and agency are not indexed. Other general topics such as culture, victims and perpetrators are partly indexed, but not all occurrences are listed (see below: not all listed).

1965–66: 1965–66 tragedy / killings / massacres / pogrom / conflict / violence 4–5, 10, 15, 18–23, 59, 81–90, 175–232; Lubang Buaya (Jakarta) 175, 178, 205; September 30th Movement (*Gerakan 30 September*, G30S) 175, 180–1, 185–8

Abu-Nimer, Mohammed 21–2, 216, 223
Aceh 4–5, 8–9, 16–17, 23, 121–37, 156, 184, 192; Aceh Judicial Monitoring Institute (AJMI) 127; Aceh Monitoring Mission (AMM) 122, 124, 126–7, 133; Acehnese Independence Movement (*Gerakan Aceh Merdeka*, GAM) 8, 17, 121–2, 124–8, 132–3; Memorandum of Understanding (MoU) / Helsinki peace accord 8, 121–6, 132–3
adat (tradition and customary law) 5, 9–10, 16, 40, 60–1, 97–118, 124, 127–32, 142–8; *adat* politics 17, 144; *adat* union *see* Hatuhaha; conflict resolution / justice 60–1, 65, 129–32; law 100, 145, *see also* customary law; movement 100; *mupakat* (*adat*-based community meeting) 128, 130–1; peacemaking / unifier / peace agent / reconciliation / building bridges 9, 97, 100, 102, 106, 108–10, 124, 127–8, 146, 148, *see also* traditional mechanisms for restoring social relationships; and religion 105–13; resource management 145; *sumpah adat* 70; *see also* Christian, Islam, revival, tradition
Africa 13
agama 39–40, 201

Allah 38, 222
alternative justice or reconciliation mechanisms, truth telling/seeking 6, 18, 22, 97, 138, 197, 220, *see also* traditional justice
Ambon (town/island, Moluccas) 17, 81, 93, 97–8, 102–6, 109–10, 138–44, 146, 149, 192
amnesty 3, 7, 123, 195–7
anthropocentric 35, 43
anthropology, anthropological, anthropologist 17, 34, 39, 48, 97, 129
Argentina 189, 196, 208
art(ists) 5, 15, 80–1, 83, 85, 87, 204, 220
Asia 13, 79, 194
authenticity (*adat*, culture) 11, 58, 99
autonomy law *see* decentralization law
Avruch, Kevin 3, 19, 61, 101, 216

Bali, Balinese 5, 9–10, 34–53, 80, 93, 157, 193, 215; Balinese agency 36, 38, 41, 47; *kebalian* (Balinese-ness) 39
Bali bombing 9, 35–6, 39, 44–9, 80
Barong 42
Batu Merah (Ambon town, Moluccas) 139–44, 147–9
Blitar (East Java) 83, 89, 220
bom Bali *see* Bali bombing
Bosnia(-Herzegovina) 133, 158, 189
bottom-up 12, 22, 37, 124n6
Bougainville 13

Calonarang (ritual drama) 42, 48
Cambodia 6, 19, 209
Chile 6, 192, 196, 208

Chinese 58–9, 81, 84
Christian (not all listed): anti-Christian riot (Lombok) 59; Christianity and *adat* (Moluccas) 106–10, 146; Christians (in Indonesia) 37; Euro-Christian notions of morality 73; Moluccan Christians 81, 97–8, 103–9, 111, 139–44, 146–9
Christian-Islamic: *adat* union (Moluccas) *see* Hatuhaha; alliances (Moluccas) *see pela*; violence *see* Islamic–Christian violence; relationship (conflict, peace and reconciliation in the Moluccas) 97–118, 138–54
civil society 3–4, 6, 21, 23–4, 34, 59, 164, 167, 192–213, 223
class divisions 82, 90
coexistence 9, 15, 22, 34, 37, 58, 110, 143, 220, 222
collective (not all listed): reconciliation 3, 5, 10, 12, 21–2, 111, 209; rights 10–11; truth 7; *see also* communal, community, identity, memory
colonial, colonialism 4, 11, 16, 103–4, 129–30, 142, 144–5, 178, 181, 201
communal: ceremonies 108; communal / community spirit 194, 198; conflict / violence / friction 5, 15, 77, 81–2, 84, 92, 146, 155–68; conflict resolution 58; inter-communal dialogue 165; justice 14, 57, 60, 72; reconciliation 4–5
communism, communists, communist coup, anti-communist killings / massacres *see* 1965–66; Museum of Communist Treachery 180
Communist Party of Indonesia / Indonesian Communist Party (PKI) 81–9, 175–88, 193, 199–200, 202–3, 205–6, 214–19, 221–4, 226
community (not all listed): Bali 42; community–individual 11, 25, 58, 130–1; community-based institution (Lombok) *see garap*; divided communities / groups 78–9, 92, 131, 156; international 12, 121; living and deceased 63; Lombok 57; moral 58, 62, 72; national 177; reconciliation 3–4; (re)integration 9, 13, 15, 77–96 (through theater) 110, 156, 167, 215; religious 5, 10, *see also* Christian, Islamic, Muslim; restoration / renewal 7, 80, 156, 208; women 155, 167; *see also* communal
compensation 64, 71–2, 107, 111, 126, 129, 133, 161–2, 194, 196, 201, 205, 214

confession / confessional speech 57–8, 72–3
conflict management 9, 15, 35, 47, 122; Balinese 35–6, 42, 44, 48; national and international 38
conflict theatre *see* theater
cosmology 3; cosmic / cosmological balance 9, 22, 34, 38, 43–9; cosmic order 71; cosmic power play 42; cosmic / cosmocentric responsibility 49; cosmocentric 35, 44, 47; cosmological dimension of reconciliation 5, 36; cosmological perceptions / concepts 9–10, 35, 42; (Balinese) cosmology 34, 36–7, 42–6, 49; cosmos 41
courts 6–7, 126–8, 130, 132–3, 156, 162, 164, 183, 188, 195; Balinese court 47; Constitutional Court 8, 176, 192, 197, 219; International Criminal Court (ICC) 6; (court) trials 6–7, 71, 162, 183, 188, 195–7, 205, 208, 214; *see also* human rights, justice (formal)
crime-fighting groups *see* security groups (civilian)
culture, cultural (not all listed) 4–5, 7, 9–13, 17, 20, 24–5, 39–40, 61, 78, 97, 100–1; cross-cultural 35, 49; (socio)cultural context / setting / system / background 3–5, 7, 9–10, 12–19, 22–5, 81, 91, 93, 101, 106, 155, 178, 216; cultural relativism 34; cultural resources / competence / capital 9, 24, 48; cultural rights 11; cultures of reconciliation 5; politicizing / essentializing / manipulation 11, 101, 215; reconciliation / peace / conflict resolution (or handling) 12–13, 15–16, 24, 57, 64, 72, 79, 81, 83, 97–118, 122, 124–5, 128–32, 134, 148–9, 156, 193, 198, 203–4, 208, 215–6, 223; Western culture / values 34–5, 57–8, 73; *see also* tradition
customary law 8, 70, 97, 161; *see also* adat

decentralization (law) 8, 11, 59–60, 98, 145–6
democratization, democratic (transformation), democracy 4, 7–8, 60, 84, 124, 176, 184, 193–5, 199, 208–9, 220, 223; *see also* history
Dewan Dakwah Islamiyah Indonesia (Indonesian Islamic Missionary Council) 219, 227
displacement 4, 17, 80, 138–54

Index 235

East Timor / Timor Leste 4, 6–8, 10, 13, 131, 156, 192, 194, 196, 209
education 4, 110, 112, 181, 184, 220; Competency-Based Curriculum (*Kurikulum Berbasis Kompetensi*, KBK) 184; Education Unit Level Curriculum (*Kurikulum Tingkat Satuan Pendidikan*, KTSP) 184–5; educational institutions / means 14–15, 77, 79–80 (theater) 184; history education *see* history; public education 15, 81, 177, 198, 203; women (Poso) 165, 167
El Salvador 196
enlightenment 34–5, 40
ethics 9, 34–5, 41, 48; Balinese 36; anthropocentric 43; *see also* ethos
ethnic: communities 78, 140; conflicts / violence / divisions 8, 12, 59, 80–1, 84, 90, 97, 101, 156–8, 167–8; discrimination 8; ethnicity (Poso, Sulawesi) 157; instrumentalization 8; marginalized ethnic groups 39, 45, 84; multi-ethnic peace tour 79; music 81; *putra daerah* (literally 'sons of the region') 8, 11
ethnographic 3, 16, 97, 102, 139
ethos: anthropocentric 35; Balinese 35–8, 43–5, 47–8; common / global / universal 5, 9, 34, 36; cosmocentric 35; enlightenment 40; world 41, 43, 47, 49
evil 9–10, 19, 36, 40–3, 47–8, 61, 182, 199, 227

Fiji 78
forgiveness 3, 7, 12, 43, 57, 71, 156, 163, 197, 199–200, 202, 208, 221–2
(religious) fundamentalism / radicalism 23, 36, 49, 102, 158

Galtung, Johan 12, 22–3, 98, 112
gandong 105–8, 111, 148
garap (collective oath-taking ordeal) 10, 13, 57–8, 60–72
gender 4–5, 12, 17–18, 138, 155–6, 158, 162–5, 168–9; *see also* women
genocide 6, 16, 196
Germany 6
Gerwani (*Gerakan Wanita Indonesia*) 83, 180, 188, 205–7
Ghazali, Abdul Moqsith (Ma'had Aly, Situbondo) 221–2
good and evil *see* evil
Guatemala 189

Habibie 8, 39, 196
harmony 92, 99–100 (*adat*) 104, 112, 123, 125, 130, 157; re-establishment / creation / restoration / achieving 9, 48, 156, 220, 228
Hasyim, Yusuf (NU) 217–9, 222, 224
Hatuhaha (traditional village / *adat* union, Moluccas) 102–13
Hindu(s) 9, 36–40, 44–5, 216; Hindu-chauvinism 39; (Balinese) Hinduism 37–41
history, historical background / setting, historically 3–8, 24, 47, 79–82, 112, 121, 129, 133–4, 144, 146, 155, 158, 193–4, 215, 227; Center for History and Political Ethics (*Pusat Sejarah dan Etika Politik*, PUSdEP) 82; curriculum 177, 184–5, 187, 219, 224; democratization 8, 184–7; epic history 84–90; historical memory 183; history education 6, 20, 81, 175–91; History Teacher Consultative Group 184, 186; history war 221; Indonesian Institute of Social History (ISSI) 177, 186–7; *Indonesian National History Textbook* (Sejarah Nasional Indonesia) 180–1; manipulation (history, memory) 20, 228; nationalism, nationalist 178; (re)negotiating / knowledge / perceptions / (re)interpretation / re-evaluation / rethinking / rewriting / revision 8, 20, 105–8, 176, 182, 188–9, 192, 198–9, 203, 207, 214, 218–19, 222; oral histories 100–2, 112
human rights 3, 5–8, 15–17, 22, 194–6; Asian values debate 10; collective / cultural / indigenous rights 10–11; and culture 10–12, 15; human rights court (HRC) 122–3, 195–6, 208; Indonesia 8, 23, 82, 110, 121–2, 124–8, 132–4, 175–7, 182–3, 185, 187, 192, 195–9, 203, 207–9, 219–20, 226–7; National Commission for Human Rights (*Komisi Nasional Hak Asasi Manusia*, Komnas HAM) 110, 134, 198–200, 208; universalism-relativism debate 10
humanity 9, 15–16, 20, 22, 35, 43, 48, 49, 77, 183, 202; crimes against humanity 196, 214
Hurgronje, Snouck 129–30

identity (not all listed): Balinese 36, 38–40, 45, 47–8; collective / common / community / group / shared 14–15, 59,

236 Index

identity (not all listed): Balinese (*cont*.): 80–3, 89, 91–2, 101–2, 108, 111–12; conflict 12, 19; identity construction (processes) 24, 101, 138; Islam 21, 215, 228, Moluccan 98, 105, 108–9, 146, 148; national 182, 188; politics 45, 100 (battles over identity); recategorization process 14, 19, 101–2, 108; religious 148, 159; religious minorities 17; transformation / change / widening / renegotiation 13–15, 20, 48, 84, 101–2, 108

impunity 5, 132–3, 162, 195

Independence Day 84, 90

India(n) 39, 78, 158, 222

inter-religious: (social) interaction 17, 139, 146–7; solidarity 147; (inter-)religious conflict / violence 8, 12, 34, 36–8, 47–9, 80–1, 84, *see also* Islamic–Christian violence / conflict

Internally Displaced Persons (IDPs) 139–40; *see also* refuge(es)

intimate theft 57–63, 71

invention of *adat* / culture / tradition *see* revival

islah (making peace) 10, 16, 126, 200; *see also* Islam

Islam: 1965–66 killings / Islam and communism 214–32; *fikih* (Islamic jurisprudence) 221–2; fundamentalist Islam / fundamentalism 36, 49; fundamentalist / radical Islamic groups *or* Muslims 23, 81, 147; Indonesian / national 21, 36–40; and *adat* (Moluccas) 106–10, 146; and violence 216–19; internal conflicts 104, 144, 214–32; 'Islam kiri' (leftist Islam) 21, 224; Java 192–232; Islamism 37, 46; Islamist(s) 21, 34–41, 43–4, 47–9; Islamization 37, 39; *kafir* (unbelievers) / *kafir harbi* (hostile infidels) / non-believers 216, 218, 222, 228; Qu'ran 199, 220–2, 228; *kyai* (Islamic scholars/preachers) 64–9, 198, 200, 202, 216–8, 222, 227; Lombok (Sasak) 60, 62, 64, 70; making peace (*islah*) / peace-building / peace / reconciliation 10, 16, 21, 126, 199–200, 215–6, 219–23, 228; orthodox 37, 39, 104 (Islam Syariah); *pesantren* (Islamic schools) 197–8, 200, 214–8, 220, 223; religious duty / 'just war' 216, 218; syncretistic / pluralistic 37, 39; *tabliq akhbar* (Islamic rally) 59; teachings 21, 129, 200, 221, 224; theological interpretations / justifications (of peace / war) 220–2, 228; traditional Islam *or* Islam Hatuhaha (Moluccas) 103–4, *see also* Hatuhaha; *see also* Muslim

Islamic–Christian violence / conflict 37–8, 45, 97–118, 138–72

Israel 77, 104

Jakarta 16, 81, 110, 127, 145, 175, 177, 184–6, 193, 196, 200, 203, 205, 207, 218, 227

Java, Javanese 5, 37, 39–40, 44, 46–7, 58, 82–4, 90, 92–3, 98, 146–7, 157, 192–3, 197, 216–17; Central Java 21, 81–2, 92, 181, 186, 192–213; East Java 81, 199, 215–18, 220, 224–7

Jemaah Islamiyah 44, 158

jihad 35, 38, 45, 48; Jihad forces / Laskar Jihad 98, 147; Jihadists 157

Jimbaran (Bali) 39, 48

justice (not all listed) 3, 6–8, 11–13; access to 13n18, 14, 17, 130, 132, 155–6; formal 13, 129–30, 132; hybridized / multidimensional 13, 17; informal 18, 129–32; performing 13, 57–76; restorative 13–15, 18, 22, 58, 61, 71–2; retributive 6–7, 7n9, 9, 12–13, 18–19, 22, 58, 60–1, 71–2, 156, 183, 228; transitional 6–7, 6n5, 7n8, 24, 58, 72–3, 122–3, 195; *see also* traditional justice

Kariu (Moluccas) 16, 102–13

ketoprak (Javanese popular melodrama) 82–3, 85, 87, 89–90, 92

Komisi Kebenaran dan Rekonsiliasi (KKR) *see* Truth and Reconciliation Commission (TRC)

Komnas Perempuan (National Commission for Women against Violence) 161, 186

Kuta (Bali) 35, 39, 44–48

land: access to 17, 138–9, 142–4, 146, 149–50; Basic Agrarian Law (BAL) 145; issues / disputes / conflicts / rights / management 4, 10, 17, 22, 35, 104, 107, 112, 133, 138–54, 158, 224; traditional / *adat* land 14, 104, 106–7, 111, 138, 142–6; (communist) land reforms / seizures (1964 and 1965) 214–15, 218, 224; culture 138

Latin America 6

Lederach, John Paul 12, 14, 16, 61, 101, 123, 125, 148, 156

legal pluralism 17, 22, 130, 143–4

lesung (rice-stamping trough) 85, 87–8
local context *see* culture
Lombok 5, 10, 13, 37–8, 44, 57–76

Madiun Affair (1948) 217–9, 228
Malino (Sulawesi, peace agreement) 98, 158, 161, 163–4
Maori 78
media 14, 20, 24, 46, 48, 127–8, 132, 155, 157, 160–1, 185, 203, 205; books 20–1, 176, 178, 198; documentary films 21, 184, 186, 198, 203–7 (*Kado Untuk Ibu*); films 20, 81, 183–4, 220–1; newspaper, journals, magazines 21, 37, 42, 46, 98, 123, 187, 198, 221–7; propaganda film (*The Betrayal of the 30 September Movement/Communist Party of Indonesia*) 180, 183; television / TV 38, 44, 46–7, 85, 180; (history) textbooks 180–1, 184–7, 219; websites 123, 224
Megawati 8, 39, 196
Melanesia 35
memory / memories 5–6, 20, 58–9, 66, 158, 194, 199; collective / social / cultural / shared 20, 22, 24, 48, 100–2, 104–5, 108, 111–12, 175–91, 208; divided 16, 19, 21–2, 97, 100–2, 111; historical 183; media 20; sites of 178, 181, 183; struggle over memory / memory war 5, 24, 216, 222; suppressed 72
migrants 98, 157; Muslim migrants 40, 44, 46, 142, 144, 147, 157
(Indonesian) military / army / security forces (TNI) 8, 16–17, 19, 21, 23, 59–60, 83–4, 86–7, 98, 108, 110, 112, 121–2, 125–8, 131–3, 157, 160–3, 175–81, 193, 195, 197, 200–3, 205–6, 214–16, 220; Dutch military / Dutch Colonial Armed Forces (*Koninklijk Nederlands Indisch Leger*, KNIL) 47–8, 142
modernity: modern 34–5, 38, 41, 44, 46, 49, 61, 73, 145; modern theater 82, 85, 90; (Western) modernity 11, 21, 36–40, 47, 49; modernization 16, 36, 49
Moluccan Protestant Church (*Gereja Protestan Maluku*, GPM) 142, 144
Moluccas / Maluku 4–5, 9, 15–17, 37–8, 44, 59, 81, 93, 97–118, 138–54, 156
monotheism / monotheist 36, 40–2
Mozambique 13, 19, 158
Muhammadiyah 217, 222, 224, 227; *Aisyiyah* (women's wing) 160, 167

Muslim (not all listed): Muslim organizations in Indonesia *see Nahdlatul Ulama*, *Muhammadiya* and *Syarikat*; Muslims (Bali) 36–51; *santri* (devout Muslims) 217–20, 225; Sasak Muslims (Lombok) 13, 57–76; traditionalist Muslims 62; *see also* Islam
Muslim–Christian: *adat* union (Moluccas) *see* Hatuhaha; alliances (Moluccas) *see pela*; relationship *see* Christian–Islamic relationship; violence *see* Islamic–Christian violence
Muzadi, Hasyim (current head of NU) 223

Nahdlatul Ulama (NU, Indonesian Islamic mass organization) 21, 82–4, 167, 197–203, 214–28; Ansor (youth wing) 21, 203, 214–18, 220, 222–4, 227–8; *AULA* magazine (provincial-level NU magazine in East Java) 224–7; Banser (*Barisan Serbaguna*, Multipurpose Ansor Brigade) 195, 198–9, 202, 215, 217, 220; *Fatayat NU* (women's wing) 167; Lakpesdam NU (*Lembaga Kajian dan Pengembangan Sumber Daya Manusia*, NU Institute for Research and Development of Human Resources) 220–8; *Tashwirul Afkar: Journal Refleksi Pemikiran Keagamaan dan Kebudayaan* (Journal of Reflection of Religious and Cultural Thinking, Lakpesdam) 221–3
New Order (*Orde Baru*) 18, 20–1, 39, 59–60, 65, 81–3, 85, 87, 131, 145–6, 155, 158, 176–8, 181–2, 197, 201, 203, 205–6, 209, 214, 218, 220, 228
New Zealand 78
niskala (invisible or spiritual) 42–6
non-governmental organization (NGO) 5–6, 8, 14, 21, 80–1, 106–7, 109, 111, 139, 141–2, 164, 167, 192–4, 196, 208, 214, 224, 227; *see also* Syarikat
Northern Ireland 77, 80, 208
Nugroho Notosusanto 178

oath(-taking) 13, 57, 61–72; *see also garap*
offenders *see* perpetrators
ordeal 13, 57, 60, 62–9, 70–2; *see also garap*
ownership (reconciliation processes) 5, 9, 110, 125, 148

Pakistan 158
pamswakarsa see security groups (civilian)

Pancasila 180, 201, 203; Sacred Pancasila Monument 178–180
Papua 4, 8, 81, 192
Passo (Moluccas) 148
Paya Bakong (Aceh) 126–8, 131–3
pela 98, 105, 108–9, 111, 148
performances 4, 15, 36, 204; restorative 5, 12–16, 55–118; *see also Calonarang, garap, ketoprak,* theater
perpetrators (not all listed): dehumanizing 9; (re)integration 9–10, 13, 20, 72; misusing cultural means 16, 121–37; perpetrator-oriented 19; sanctioning / punishing 6–7, 23, 61, 188, 195–7; women 160
perpetrators–victims *see* victims–perpetrators
personhood 11, 19
Peru 19, 196
PKI *see* Communist Party of Indonesia
Plantungan (prison, Central Java) 205–6
playback theater *see* theater
police 23, 59–60, 65, 98, 125–6, 131, 157–8, 161–4, 187
Poso 18, 155–72, 192
power (relations) / hierarchy 5, 16–17, 23, 42–3, 45, 48–9, 82–3, 103–4, 110, 112, 123, 129–31, 148–9, 156, 164, 195, 197
puputan 47–8

Rangda 42
reconciliation (not all listed): definition 6n7, 14–15, 15n25; multidimensional process / approaches 3, 6, 24; terminology (Indonesia) 9–10
Reformasi / Reformation (Indonesia) 4–5, 23, 58–61, 69, 146, 176
refuge(es) 5, 17, 78, 106–11, 139–42, 144, 156, 162, 164, 167
rehabilitation 18, 22, 57, 165, 168, 194, 196, 198–203, 205, 208, 217, 219–20
relationship-building / restoring relations(hips) (reconciliation as a process of) 9–10, 13–15, 18–19, 21–2, 57, 61, 71–2, 77, 101, 110–11, 123–4, 126, 149, 156, 163, 165, 194, 198–9, 203
religious conflict *see* inter-religious
reparations 7, 13, 22, 123, 128–9, 194, 208
resettle(ment) 139–42, 163
(individual) responsibility 34–6, 42–3, 46–9, 108, 111
restorative *see* justice, performances
retributive justice *see* justice
revival / revitalization / (re)invention / resurgence of (return to) *adat*, culture, tradition 8–9, 11–13, 15–17, 39, 45, 57, 60–1, 70, 90, 97–102, 104, 106–12, 123–4, 144–6, 163
rituals 5, 10, 13–17, 22, 39–40, 42, 44–8, 57–73, 79–80, 97, 101–3, 111, 125–6, 148, 163; *see also garap, peusijeuk, puputan*
Rwanda 6, 13, 131, 158, 189

sakti (spiritual power) 41–2, 201
Sambas 156
Sasak (Lombok) 13, 57–76
secessionist / separatist conflicts 5, 121
security groups (civilian) 13, 23, 57–60, 70–1
sekala (visible or material) 42–3
Sekitarkita Community (human rights organization) 177, 185–7
sexual attacks / abuse / exploitation / harassment / torture / violence / slavery 17, 83, 155, 158, 160–2, 164, 168, 206; *see also* women
social reconciliation 77–96, 156, 163, 168
Solo 15, 81, 90–1, 181
South Africa 6–8, 73, 84, 192, 196, 208–9
Southeast Asia 35, 138; economic crisis 60
Spain 6
Sri Lanka 78–9, 81
state 3, 5, 7, 9, 12–14, 16–17, 20, 23–4, 37–9, 59–60, 91, 110, 124, 128, 130–2, 142, 144–5, 148, 164, 176, 178, 180–1, 184, 188, 193–7, 222
Suharto 7, 8, 18, 20–2, 37, 39, 60, 81, 85–7, 145, 175–93, 196–9, 202–3, 205–7, 214, 217
Sukarno 18, 86–7, 176, 215, 217–19
Sulawesi 5, 10, 18, 37–8, 44, 80–1, 98, 155–72
Syarikat (*Masyarakat Santri untuk Advokasi Rakyat*, Muslim Community for People's Advocacy) 21, 82–3, 184, 193, 197–209, 220–8; Imam Aziz (current head of Syarikat) 199, 220–6; *see also* NGO
symbols, symbolism, symbolic 5, 14–15, 20, 22, 57, 63, 66, 68, 82–4, 90, 92, 98, 101–2, 104, 111, 138, 148–9, 160, 168, 178–9, 216

Tanjung Priok (Northern Jakarta) 16, 196, 207

terror, terrorist attacks, Islamist / religious terror 5, 34–42, 44, 47, 49, 163; Asian terrorist network (Jemaah Islamiyah) 158; global terrorism network 158; terrorism 34, 38, 227; war on terror 9, 23, 35–8, 43
theater 5, 15, 22, 36, 46, 77–96; playback theater 78–9; people's / community / folk (*teater rakyat*) 78, 80–1, 90
theodicy 40–1
theological notions of reconciliation 57, 156
tourism 36, 40, 44
(local) tradition 4, 11, 15–16, 22, 34–40, 42, 46, 48–9, 57, 60, 70, 79, 90, 93, 97–118, 122, 124, 128–32, 155, 158, 161, 169; exclusivity 8, 11, 108–10, 112; instrumentalization / politicization / mobilization 5, 59, 97–118, 132; oral 100–5; traditional arbitrators / mediators 14, 16, *see also* traditional village heads; traditional leaders(hip) / rulers 5, 8, 11, 16, 17, 22, 66, 142; *see also adat*, authenticity, culture, *gandong*, land, *pela*, performances, *peusijuek*, revival, rituals, symbols, traditional justice, traditional village heads
traditional conflict / dispute resolution, justice mechanism *see* traditional justice
traditional justice 4–5, 9–10, 13–14, 13n19, 16–19, 22, 57–76, 97, 121–37; reinforcement of inequalities 17–18; shortcomings / disadvantages / misuse 5, 15–17, 121–37, 138–54; *see also adat*, communal, performances, traditional mechanisms for restoring social relationships, traditional village heads
traditional mechanisms for restoring social relationships and reintegrating the community / reconciliation: *adat meulangga* (Sumatra) 129; *baku bae* (Moluccas) 9; *meka sareka* or *tapan holo* (Flores) 9; *motambu tana* (Sulawesi) 10, 163; *nahe biti* (East Timor) 10; *peusijuek* (Aceh) 9, 16–17, 125–9, 132, 134; *Rujuk Sintuwu Maroso* (Sulawesi) 163–4; *To Poso* (Sulawesi) 163
traditional village heads: *keuchik* (Aceh) 129–31; *klian* (Lombok) 64–70; *raja* (Moluccas) 98, 104, 106–9
truth 6–7, 9, 13, 20, 22, 41, 58, 72–3, 84, 89, 110–11, 123–5, 128, 162–4, 181–2, 187–8, 192–3, 195, 197, 199, 202–3, 207, 209, 220–1
Truth and Reconciliation Commission (TRC) 3, 6–8, 13, 18–20, 73, 122–4, 128, 148, 169, 176, 181–2, 192, 194–7, 207, 209, 219, 227
truth commission *see* Truth and Reconciliation Commission (TRC)
tuhan 38

Uganda 13
universal ethical values 34–6, 47, 49; *see also* ethos

victims (not all listed): agency 24, 34, 43, 61, 68; (re)integration 177, 221; involvement 7, 163; organizations / associations / forums / groups 186, 192, 198–203, 207, 214, 220–1; responsibility 34, 43; restoration / rehabilitation 13, 194, 196, 198–9, 202, 208; victim-oriented 7, 19; women 18, 82, 155–72, 198, 203–7, 220
victims–perpetrators 5–6, 13, 34, 43, 49, 70, 122, 125, 127, 129, 161–2; conceptualizations 6, 18–22, 173–232

Wahid, Abdurrahman 8, 21, 163, 196–7, 217, 219–20, 223–4
witch(craft) 41–2, 47, 61
women (peace, reconciliation, conflict) 5, 14, 17–18, 22, 81–3, 89, 155–72, 180, 188, 198, 203–7, 220, 227; culture / tradition 18, 155–72; violence against women 158, 160–2, 164, 168, 186

Yogyakarta 21, 80–2, 85, 92, 197, 199, 203, 205, 207, 220, 226

A World of Online Content!

Did you know that Taylor & Francis has over 20,000 books available electronically?

What's more, they are all available for browsing and individual purchase on the Taylor & Francis eBookstore.

www.ebookstore.tandf.co.uk

eBooks for libraries

Free trials available

Choose from annual subscription or outright purchase and select from a range of bespoke subject packages, or tailor make your own.

www.ebooksubscriptions.com

For more information, email
online.sales@tandf.co.uk

Taylor & Francis eBooks
Taylor & Francis Group

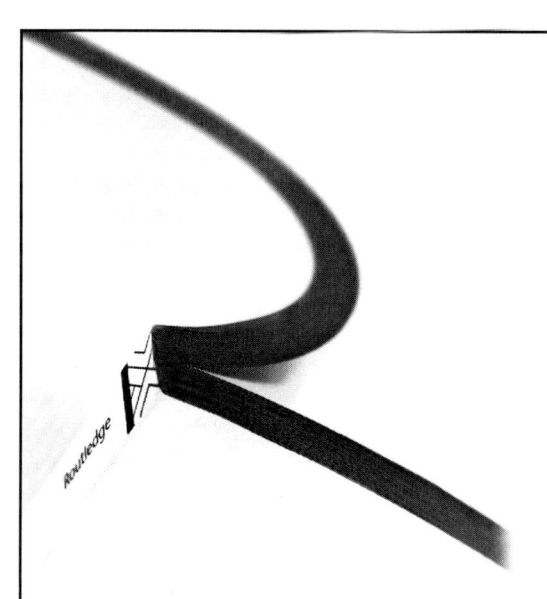

Routledge Paperbacks Direct

Bringing you the cream of our hardback publishing at paperback prices

This exciting new initiative makes the best of our hardback publishing available in paperback format for authors and individual customers.

Routledge Paperbacks Direct is an ever-evolving programme with new titles being added regularly.

To take a look at the titles available, visit our website.

www.routledgepaperbacksdirect.com

Routledge
Taylor & Francis Group